CONSTITUTIONAL LAW
FOURTH EDITION
2005 Supplement

Norman Redlich
*Dean Emeritus and Judge Edward Weinfeld Professor of Law
Emeritus
New York University School of Law*

John Attanasio
*Dean and William Hawley Atwell Professor of Constitutional Law
Dedman School of Law, Southern Methodist University*

Joel K. Goldstein
*Vincent C. Immel Professor of Law
Saint Louis University School of Law*

LexisNexis™

Editorial Offices
744 Broad Street, Newark, NJ 07102 (973) 820-2000
201 Mission St., San Francisco, CA 94105-1831 (415) 908-3200
701 East Water Street, Charlottesville, VA 22902-7587 (804) 972-7600
www.lexis.com

(Pub.170)

PREFACE

This 2005 Supplement focuses on significant decisions of the most recent Supreme Court terms. The events of September 11, 2001 put some venerable constitutional issues back on the nation's agenda, and accordingly we have included some materials, especially in Chapter 5, which relate to some of those topics.

In editing cases, we have at times deleted footnotes, case citations and statutory references without so indicating.

We would like to express our appreciation to several people whose efforts helped us prepare this 2005 Supplement. We would like to thank Kathleen Spartana for her administrative and editing work, research assistants Jennifer Allen, Jessica Benoit, Henry Childs, Kate Douglas, Anthony Gilbreth, Matthew Guyman, Meredith Head, Leslie Mattingly, Mandi Montgomery, Tina Potter, Lacey Searfoss, Paul Stohr, Kevin Sullivan, and Elise Voges for their contributions, and Tina Brosseau, Mary Dougherty, and Stephanie Haley for their help in typing the book. As always, we appreciate the institutional support of the Dedman School of Law at Southern Methodist University, Saint Louis University School of Law, and Wachtell, Lipton, Rosen & Katz.

Norman Redlich
John Attanasio
Joel K. Goldstein
July, 2005

PREFACE

TABLE OF CONTENTS

Page

Page

Chapter I

JUDICIAL REVIEW: ESTABLISHMENT AND OPERATION

§ 1.05   Non–Article III Courts

Page 40: [Insert the following after Note (1)]

(a) Does Congress violate the Compensation Clause of Art. III § 1 when it legislates to preclude from taking effect automatic annual cost-of-living adjustments in judicial pay which earlier laws provided? The Court denied certiorari in *Spencer Williams, Judge et al. v. United States*, 535 U.S. 911 (2002) in which a number of United States federal judges challenged as unconstitutional Congress so acting four times in the 1990s to block the annual adjustments in the Ethics Reform Act of 1989 from taking effect. Justice Breyer, joined by Justices Scalia and Kennedy, dissented from the denial of certiorari and published a dissent declaring the question "both difficult and important," Justice Breyer did not resolve the question although he opined that the "holding may well be wrong." *Id.* at 921. He did observe that "the Founders created a one-way compensation ratchet because they believed that permitting the legislature to diminish judicial compensation would allow the legislature to threaten judicial independence." *Id.* at 914. He thought the Court should have resolved the constitutional question "whether the Compensation Clause permits a later Congress to renege on . . . [a] commitment" of an earlier Congress to maintain salaries of judges when those of average workers and civil servants have been maintained. *Id.* at 921. The possible embarrassment of deciding an issue which would impact the justices' pocketbooks should not deter the Court from addressing that issue, he argued.

Page 41: [Insert the following after Note (4)]

(5) In the aftermath of the terrorist attacks on the United States of September 11, 2001, President Bush issued the "Military Order of November 13, 2001," which is set forth in Chapter 5. The Order calls for military commissions to try individuals not citizens of the United States who the President determines is or were members of Al Qaida or "engaged in, aided or abetted" acts of international terrorism injurious to the United States. The President's Order provides that individuals subject to the Order would "not be privileged to seek any remedy or maintain any proceeding, directly or indirectly, or to have any such remedy or proceeding sought on the individual's behalf, in any court of the United States, or any State thereof. . . ." Military tribunals have occasionally been used by the United States during wartime under some circumstances to prosecute alleged war

1

crimes or offenses in areas subject to military occupation or martial law. During World War II and its aftermath, the Court allowed military tribunals to try alleged Japanese war criminals, *Application of Yamashita*, 327 U.S. 1 (1946) and German spies arrested in the United States charged with violating laws of war, *Ex parte Quirin*, 317 U.S. 1 (1942), as well as civilians who allegedly committed crimes in post-war Germany while occupied by American troops, *Madsen v. Kinsella*, 343 U.S. 341 (1952).

(6) In *Hamdi v. Rumsfeld* 524 U.S. 507 (2004), the Court held that the Government could not detain an American citizen on American soil as an enemy combatant without affording some opportunity at least to challenge that classification. The Court left open, however, the possibility that such a determination could be made "by an appropriately authorized and properly constituted military tribunal."

§ 1.07   Standing

[4]—Rights of Others

Page 59: [Insert the following after note (3)]

(4) In *Elk Grove v. Newdow,* 542 U.S. 1 (2004), the Court invoked prudential standing doctrine to hold that a noncustodial parent lacked standing to challenge, on his daughter's behalf, a California law which required every public school to begin each day by reciting the Pledge of Allegiance. Newdow, an atheist, claimed that the law violated the First Amendment's guarantees under the Establishment and Free Exercise Clauses. Sandra Banning, the mother and legal custodian of Newdow's daughter, contended that her daughter believed in God, was not bothered by reciting "under God" in the Pledge, and would be harmed by inclusion in the lawsuit.

The Court noted that third party standing generally fell within "the prudential dimensions of the standing doctrine." *Id.* at 17. Consistent with the federal judiciary's general reluctance to intervene in cases which turn on domestic relations issues, the Court concluded that it was "improper" for federal courts "to entertain a claim by a plaintiff whose standing to sue is founded on family law rights that are in dispute when prosecution of the lawsuit may have an adverse effect on the person who is the source of the plaintiff's claimed standing." *Id.* at 26. Since California had deprived Newdow of the right to sue as next friend, he lacked prudential standing. *Id.*

(5) In *Kowalski v. Tesmer*, 125 S. Ct. 564 (2004), the Court held, 6-3, that attorneys who routinely received court appointments in criminal cases lacked third party standing to challenge, on behalf of hypothetical future clients, Michigan's new procedure for appointing appellate counsel for indigent criminal defendants who pled guilty. Although the Court had previously held that an existing attorney-client relationship satisfied the close relationship requirement for third party standing, *see, e.g., Caplan & Drysdale, Chartered v. United States*, 491 U.S. 617 (1989), the attorneys here had "no relationship" with hypothetical future clients. *Id.* at 568. The

Court raised a slippery slope argument, too; it would be a "short step" to allowing lawyers generally to assert third party standing on behalf of hypothetical future clients. *Id.* at 570. Moreover, the lack of an attorney was not a "hindrance" to an indigent criminal defendant challenging denial to him of counsel. Justice Ginsburg (joined by Justices Stevens and Souter) dissented. The attorney satisfied constitutional standing requirements since the Michigan procedure would cause them economic harm. They also satisfied the prudential "close relation" and "hindrance" criteria. *Id.* at 571-72. Previous cases had allowed litigants third party standing to assert rights of future customers. *Id.* at 572-73. The hindrance requirement was easily satisfied by "the incapacities under which these defendants labor and the complexity of the issues their cases may entail." *Id.* at 573.

§ 1.08   Ripeness; mootness

Page 60: [Insert at end of Note (2)]

Similarly, the Court held unripe a facial challenge to a National Park Service (NPS) regulation that provided that a NPS concession contract was not subject to the Contract Disputes Act which otherwise governed government contracts, *National Park Hospitality Association v. Department of the Interior*, 538 U.S. 803 (2003).

The Court raised the ripeness issue *sua sponte*, a judicial prerogative in cases involving ripeness issues based on either constitutional or prudential concerns. *Id.* at 808. The absence of a concrete factual context to define the scope of the controversy made the issues unfit for review. *Id.* at 812.Since the regulation did not affect "primary conduct" withholding review imposed no hardship. *Id.* at 810.

In dissent, Justice Breyer found the case ripe because the regulation created legal uncertainty which was likely to increase contract implementation costs. *Id.* at 818. Accordingly, the petitioners suffered "immediate and particularized" harm. *Id.* at 820. But the majority, speaking through Justice Thomas, rejected that logic. Under it, "courts would soon be overwhelmed with requests for what essentially would be advisory opinions because most business transactions could be priced more accurately if even a small portion of existing legal uncertainties were resolved." *Id.* at 811.

§ 1.09   Political Questions

Page 77: [Insert following Note (6)]

(a) In *Vieth v. Jubelirer,* 541 U.S. 267 (2004), the Court dismissed a challenge to Pennsylvania's congressional redistricting plan. In a plurality opinion, four members of the Court (Justice Scalia, Chief Justice Rehnquist, Justices O'Connor and Thomas) argued that political gerrymandering claims regarding drawing congressional districts were nonjusticiable and that accordingly *Davis v. Bandemer,* 478 U.S. 109 (1986) should be overruled. In the course of his opinion, Justice Scalia observed that the six *Baker v. Carr* tests [casebook, p. 69] "are probably listed in descending order of both importance and certainty." 541 U.S. at 278. *Vieth* turned, in the plurality's view, on the second test, an absence of judicially discernible and manageable standards. The *Bandemer* standard [casebook, p. 920] was "misguided when proposed" and had not improved during the intervening 18 years and accordingly should be abandoned. 541 U.S. at 283. Although Justice Kennedy agreed that the complaint should be dismissed, he was not prepared to foreclose all judicial review of gerrymandering claims "if some limited and precise rationale were found" to implement the Fourteenth Amendment. *Id.* at 327. Like Justice Kennedy, the four dissenters all thought the issue of partisan gerrymandering was justiciable. *See* 2005 Supplement, *infra* p. 185.

Chapter II

CONGRESSIONAL POWERS

§ 2.01   Enumerated and Implied Powers

Page 90: [Insert the following after Note (11)]

(12) In *Jinks v. Richland County, South Carolina*, 538 U.S. 456 (2003), the Court unanimously held Congress had power under the Necessary and Proper Clause to enact 28 U.S.C. § 1367(d) which required state statutes of limitation to be tolled while a claim was pending under a federal court's supplemental jurisdiction. The statute was necessary and proper to implement Congress' power to "constitute tribunals inferior to the Supreme Court" under Art. I § 8 cl. 9 and to assure that those courts efficiently exercise federal judicial power. 538 U.S. at 462. Justice Scalia, for the Court, followed Chief Justice Marshall's reasoning in *McCulloch* and found the provision within the Necessary and Proper Clause since it was " 'conducive to the due administration of justice' " in federal courts and was " 'plainly adapted' " to that end. *Id.*

Justice Scalia pointed out that Congress had not passed 1367(d) as a "pretext" for accomplishing objectives not entrusted to federal government nor was the connection between 1367(d) and Congress' authority regarding federal courts "so attenuated as to undermine the enumeration of powers set forth in Article I § 8." *Id.* at 464. Do these references suggest an effort to impose limits on Congress' power under the Necessary and Proper Clause by emphasizing doctrine from *McCulloch*, *Lopez* and *Morrison*?

§ 2.05   The Commerce Clause: A New Turning Point?

Page 154: [Insert the following after Note (11)]

(12) Notwithstanding *Lopez* and *Morrison*, the Rehnquist Court does not always rule that Congress has transcended its power under the Commerce Clause. In *Pierce County, Washington v. Guillen*, 537 U.S. 129 (2003), the Court unanimously held that Congress had power to protect from discovery or admission into evidence state reports identifying potential accident sites in connection with federal highway safety programs. Congress made certain federal funds available to states to improve highway safety provided the states surveyed public roads to identify those that were unsafe. *Id.* at 133. The program was impeded by the fear of some states that aggressive survey efforts might provide knowledge which would subject them to liability for accidents before improvements occurred. *Id.* at 133–34. Accordingly, Congress adopted 23 U.S.C. § 409 which protected such records from being

discovered or offered into evidence in civil actions for damages. The Court held that Congress could regulate the nation's highways and Congress "could reasonably believe that adopting [§ 409]" would ultimately promote highway safety. *Id.* at 147. Is it significant that the Court allowed Congress to act under the Commerce Clause even though the regulation had a very "indirect" effect on commerce?

ALBERTO R. GONZALES, ATTORNEY GENERAL, ET AL., v. ANGEL McCLARY RAICH ET AL.

125 S. Ct. 2195 (2005)

Justice STEVENS delivered the opinion of the Court.

California is one of at least nine States that authorize the use of marijuana for medicinal purposes. The question presented in this case is whether the power vested in Congress by Article I, § 8, of the Constitution "[t]o make all Laws which shall be necessary and proper for carrying into Execution" its authority to "regulate Commerce with foreign Nations, and among the several States" includes the power to prohibit the local cultivation and use of marijuana in compliance with California law.

I

. . . In 1996, California voters passed Proposition 215, now codified as the Compassionate Use Act of 1996. The proposition was designed to ensure that "seriously ill" residents of the State have access to marijuana for medical purposes, and to encourage Federal and State Governments to take steps towards ensuring the safe and affordable distribution of the drug to patients in need. The Act creates an exemption from criminal prosecution for physicians, as well as for patients and primary caregivers who possess or cultivate marijuana for medicinal purposes with the recommendation or approval of a physician. A "primary caregiver" is a person who has consistently assumed responsibility for the housing, health, or safety of the patient.

Respondents Angel Raich and Diane Monson are California residents who suffer from a variety of serious medical conditions and have sought to avail themselves of medical marijuana pursuant to the terms of the Compassionate Use Act. They are being treated by licensed, board-certified family practitioners, who have concluded, after prescribing a host of conventional medicines to treat respondents' conditions and to alleviate their associated symptoms, that marijuana is the only drug available that provides effective treatment. Both women have been using marijuana as a medication for several years pursuant to their doctors' recommendation, and both rely heavily on cannabis to function on a daily basis. Indeed, Raich's physician believes that forgoing cannabis treatments would certainly cause Raich excruciating pain and could very well prove fatal.

Respondent Monson cultivates her own marijuana, and ingests the drug in a variety of ways including smoking and using a vaporizer. Respondent Raich, by contrast, is unable to cultivate her own, and thus relies on two caregivers . . . to provide her with locally grown marijuana at no charge. . . .

[After federal drug agents seized and destroyed Monson's cannabis plants,] Respondents . . . brought this action against the Attorney General of the United States and the head of the DEA seeking injunctive and declaratory relief prohibiting the enforcement of the federal Controlled Substances Act (CSA), 84 Stat. 1242, 21 U.S.C. § 801 *et seq.*, to the extent it prevents them from possessing, obtaining, or manufacturing cannabis for their personal medical use. In their complaint and supporting affidavits, Raich and Monson described the severity of their afflictions, their repeatedly futile attempts to obtain relief with conventional medications, and the opinions of their doctors concerning their need to use marijuana. Respondents claimed that enforcing the CSA against them would violate the Commerce Clause, the Due Process Clause of the Fifth Amendment, the Ninth and Tenth Amendments of the Constitution, and the doctrine of medical necessity.

The District Court denied respondents' motion for a preliminary injunction. *Raich v. Ashcroft*, 248 F. Supp. 2d 918 (N.D.Cal.2003). Although the court found that the federal enforcement interests "wane[d]" when compared to the harm that California residents would suffer if denied access to medically necessary marijuana, it concluded that respondents could not demonstrate a likelihood of success on the merits of their legal claims. *Id.,* at 931.

A divided panel of the Court of Appeals for the Ninth Circuit reversed and ordered the District Court to enter a preliminary injunction. *Raich v. Ashcroft*, 352 F.3d 1222 (2003). The court found that respondents had "demonstrated a strong likelihood of success on their claim that, as applied to them, the CSA is an unconstitutional exercise of Congress' Commerce Clause authority." . . .

The obvious importance of the case prompted our grant of certiorari. 542 U.S. 936 (2004). The case is made difficult by respondents' strong arguments that they will suffer irreparable harm because, despite a congressional finding to the contrary, marijuana does have valid therapeutic purposes. The question before us, however, is not whether it is wise to enforce the statute in these circumstances; rather, it is whether Congress' power to regulate interstate markets for medicinal substances encompasses the portions of those markets that are supplied with drugs produced and consumed locally. Well-settled law controls our answer. The CSA is a valid exercise of federal power, even as applied to the troubling facts of this case. We accordingly vacate the judgment of the Court of Appeals.

II

[President Nixon's "war on drugs"] culminated in the passage of the Comprehensive Drug Abuse Prevention and Control Act of 1970 [including the

CSA]. The main objectives of the CSA were to conquer drug abuse and to control the legitimate and illegitimate traffic in controlled substances. Congress was particularly concerned with the need to prevent the diversion of drugs from legitimate to illicit channels. To effectuate these goals, Congress devised a closed regulatory system making it unlawful to manufacture, distribute, dispense, or possess any controlled substance except in a manner authorized by the CSA. . . .

III

Respondents in this case do not dispute that passage of the CSA, as part of the Comprehensive Drug Abuse Prevention and Control Act, was well within Congress' commerce power. . . . Nor do they contend that any provision or section of the CSA amounts to an unconstitutional exercise of congressional authority. Rather, respondents' challenge is actually quite limited; they argue that the CSA's categorical prohibition of the manufacture and possession of marijuana as applied to the intrastate manufacture and possession of marijuana for medical purposes pursuant to California law exceeds Congress' authority under the Commerce Clause.

In assessing the validity of congressional regulation, none of our Commerce Clause cases can be viewed in isolation. As charted in considerable detail in *United States v. Lopez*, our understanding of the reach of the Commerce Clause, as well as Congress' assertion of authority thereunder, has evolved over time. The Commerce Clause emerged as the Framers' response to the central problem giving rise to the Constitution itself: the absence of any federal commerce power under the Articles of Confederation. For the first century of our history, the primary use of the Clause was to preclude the kind of discriminatory state legislation that had once been permissible. Then, in response to rapid industrial development and an increasingly interdependent national economy, Congress "ushered in a new era of federal regulation under the commerce power," [in the late nineteenth century].

Cases decided during that "new era," which now spans more than a century, have identified three general categories of regulation in which Congress is authorized to engage under its commerce power. First, Congress can regulate the channels of interstate commerce. *Perez v. United States*, 402 U.S. 146, 150 (1971). Second, Congress has authority to regulate and protect the instrumentalities of interstate commerce, and persons or things in interstate commerce. *Ibid.* Third, Congress has the power to regulate activities that substantially affect interstate commerce. *Ibid.*; *NLRB v. Jones & Laughlin Steel Corp.*, 301 U.S. 1, 37 (1937). Only the third category is implicated in the case at hand.

Our case law firmly establishes Congress' power to regulate purely local activities that are part of an economic "class of activities" that have a substantial effect on interstate commerce. *See, e.g., Perez.* . . . *Wickard v. Filburn*, 317 U.S. 111, 128-129 (1942). As we stated in *Wickard*, "even if appellee's activity be local and though it may not be regarded as commerce, it may still, whatever its nature, be reached by Congress if it exerts a substantial economic effect on interstate commerce." *Id.*, at 125. We have never required Congress to legislate with scientific exactitude. When Congress decides that the "'total incidence'" of a practice poses a threat to a national market, it may regulate the entire class. *See Perez*, 402 U.S., at 154-155, . . . In this vein, we have reiterated that when "'a general regulatory statute bears a substantial relation to commerce, the *de minimis* character of individual instances arising under that statute is of no consequence.'" *E.g., Lopez*, 514 U.S., at 558 (emphasis deleted) (quoting *Maryland v. Wirtz*, 392 U.S. 183, 196, n. 27, (1968)).

Our decision in *Wickard*, 317 U.S. 111, is of particular relevance . . . *Wickard* . . . establishes that Congress can regulate purely intrastate activity that is not itself "commercial," in that it is not produced for sale, if it concludes that failure to regulate that class of activity would undercut the regulation of the interstate market in that commodity.

The similarities between this case and *Wickard* are striking. Like the farmer in *Wickard*, respondents are cultivating, for home consumption, a fungible commodity for which there is an established, albeit illegal, interstate market. Just as the Agricultural Adjustment Act was designed "to control the volume [of wheat] moving in interstate and foreign commerce in order to avoid surpluses . . ." and consequently control the market price . . . a primary purpose of the CSA is to control the supply and demand of controlled substances in interstate and foreign commercein order to avoid surpluses . . ." and consequently control the market price . . . a primary purpose of the CSA is to control the supply and demand of controlled substances in both lawful and unlawful drug markets. [. . .] In *Wickard*, we had no difficulty concluding that Congress had a rational basis for believing that, when viewed in the aggregate, leaving home-consumed wheat outside the regulatory scheme would have a substantial influence on price and market conditions. Here too, Congress had a rational basis for concluding that leaving home-consumed marijuana outside federal control would similarly affect price and market conditions.

More concretely, one concern prompting inclusion of wheat grown for home consumption in the 1938 Act was that rising market prices could draw such wheat into the interstate market, resulting in lower market prices. . . . The parallel concern making it appropriate to include marijuana grown for home consumption in the CSA is the likelihood that the high demand in the interstate market will draw such marijuana into that market. While the diversion of homegrown wheat tended to frustrate the federal interest in stabilizing prices by regulating the volume of commercial transactions in the interstate market, the diversion of homegrown marijuana tends to frustrate the federal interest in eliminating commercial transactions in the interstate market in their entirety. In both cases, the regulation is squarely within Congress' commerce power because production of the commodity meant for home consumption, be it wheat or marijuana, has a substantial effect on supply and demand in the national market for that commodity.

Nonetheless, respondents suggest that *Wickard* differs from this case in three respects: (1) the Agricultural Adjustment Act, unlike the CSA, exempted small farming operations; (2) *Wickard* involved a "quintessential economic activity" — a commercial farm — whereas respondents do not sell marijuana; and (3) the *Wickard* record made it clear that the aggregate production of wheat for use on farms had a significant impact on market prices. Those differences, though factually accurate, do not diminish the precedential force of this Court's reasoning.

The fact that Wickard's own impact on the market was "trivial by itself" was not a sufficient reason for removing him from the scope of federal regulation. . . . That the Secretary of Agriculture elected to exempt even smaller farms from regulation does not speak to his power to regulate all those whose aggregated production was significant, nor did that fact play any role in the Court's analysis. Moreover, even though Wickard was indeed a commercial farmer, the activity he was engaged in — the cultivation of wheat for home consumption — was not treated by the Court as part of his commercial farming operation. And while it is true that the record in the *Wickard* case itself established the causal connection between the production for local use and the national market, we have before us findings by Congress to the same effect.

. . . [M]arijuana has dimensions that are fully comparable to those defining the class of activities regulated by the Secretary pursuant to the 1938 statute. Respondents . . . insist that the CSA cannot be constitutionally applied to their activities because Congress did not make a specific finding that the intrastate cultivation and possession of marijuana for medical purposes based on the recommendation of a physician would substantially affect the larger interstate marijuana market. Be that as it may, we have never required Congress to make particularized findings in order to legislate, *see Lopez*, 514 U.S., at 562; *Perez*, 402 U.S., at 156, absent a special concern such as the protection of free speech . . . While congressional findings are certainly helpful in reviewing the substance of a congressional statutory scheme, particularly when the connection to commerce is not self-evident, and while we will consider congressional findings in our analysis when they are available, the absence of particularized findings does not call into question Congress' authority to legislate.

In assessing the scope of Congress' authority under the Commerce Clause, we stress that the task before us is a modest one. We need not determine whether respondents' activities, taken in the aggregate, substantially affect interstate commerce in fact, but only whether a "rational basis" exists for so concluding. *Lopez*, 514 U.S., at 557. . . . Given the enforcement difficulties that attend distinguishing between marijuana cultivated locally and marijuana grown elsewhere, . . ., and concerns about diversion into illicit channels, we have no difficulty concluding that Congress had a rational basis for believing that failure to regulate the intrastate manufacture and possession of marijuana would leave a gaping hole in the CSA. Thus, as in *Wickard*, when it enacted comprehensive legislation to regulate the interstate market in a fungible commodity, Congress was acting well within its authority to "make all Laws which shall be necessary and proper" to "regulate Commerce . . . among the several States." U.S. Const., Art. I, § 8. That the regulation ensnares some purely intrastate activity is of no moment. As we have done many times before, we refuse to excise individual components of that larger scheme.

IV

To support their contrary submission, respondents rely heavily on two of our more recent Commerce Clause cases. In their myopic focus, they overlook the larger context of modern-era Commerce Clause jurisprudence preserved by those cases. Moreover, even in the narrow prism of respondents' creation, they read those cases far too broadly.

Those two cases, of course, are *Lopez* . . . and [*United States v.*] *Morrison* . . . As an initial matter, the statutory challenges at issue in those cases were markedly different from the challenge respondents pursue in the case at hand. Here, respondents ask us to excise individual applications of a concededly valid statutory scheme. In contrast, in both *Lopez* and *Morrison,* the parties asserted that a particular statute or provision fell outside Congress' commerce power in its entirety. This distinction is pivotal for we have often reiterated that "[w]here the class of activities is regulated and that class is within the reach of federal power, the courts have no power 'to excise, as trivial, individual instances' of the class." *Perez*, 402 U.S., at 154 (emphasis deleted) (quoting *Wirtz,* 392 U.S., at 193); *see also Hodel*, 452 U.S., at 308.

At issue in *Lopez* . . . , was the validity of the Gun-Free School Zones Act of 1990, which was a brief, single-subject statute making it a crime for an individual to possess a gun in a school zone. . . . The Act did not regulate any economic activity and did not contain any requirement that the possession of a gun have any connection to past interstate activity or a predictable impact on future commercial activity. Distinguishing our earlier cases holding that comprehensive regulatory statutes may be validly applied to local conduct that does not, when viewed in isolation, have a significant impact on interstate commerce, we held the statute invalid. . . . The statutory scheme that the Government is defending in this litigation is at the opposite end of the regulatory spectrum. As explained above, the CSA, enacted in 1970 as part of the Comprehensive Drug Abuse Prevention and Control Act . . . , was a lengthy and detailed statute creating a comprehensive framework for regulating the production, distribution, and possession of five classes of "controlled substances." . . .

Nor does this Court's holding in *Morrison*, 529 U.S. 598 [cast doubt on CSA]. The Violence Against Women Act of 1994 . . . created a federal civil remedy for the victims of gender-motivated crimes of violence. The remedy was enforceable in both state and federal courts, and generally depended on proof of the violation of a state law. Despite congressional findings that such crimes had an adverse impact on interstate commerce, we held the statute unconstitutional because, like the statute in *Lopez*, it did not regulate economic activity. . . .

Unlike those at issue in *Lopez* and *Morrison*, the activities regulated by the CSA are quintessentially economic. "Economics" refers to "the production, distribution, and consumption of commodities." Webster's Third New International Dictionary 720 (1966). The CSA is a statute that regulates the production, distribution, and consumption of commodities for which there is an established, and lucrative, interstate market. Prohibiting the intrastate possession or manufacture of an article of commerce is a rational (and commonly utilized) means of regulating commerce in that product. . . . Because the CSA is a statute that directly regulates economic, commercial activity, our opinion in *Morrison* casts no doubt on its constitutionality.

The Court of Appeals was able to conclude otherwise only by isolating a "separate and distinct" class of activities that it held to be beyond the reach of federal power, defined as "the intrastate, noncommercial cultivation, possession and use of marijuana for personal medical purposes on the advice of a physician and in accordance with state law." 352 F.3d, at 1229. The court characterized this class as "different in kind from drug trafficking." *Id.*, at 1228. The differences between the members of a class so defined and the principal traffickers in Schedule I substances might be sufficient to justify a policy decision exempting the narrower class from the coverage of the CSA. The question, however, is whether Congress' contrary policy judgment, *i.e.*, its decision to include this narrower "class of activities" within the larger regulatory scheme, was constitutionally deficient. We have no difficulty concluding that Congress acted rationally in determining that none of the characteristics making up the purported class, whether viewed individually or in the aggregate, compelled an exemption from the CSA; rather, the subdivided class of activities defined by the Court of Appeals was an essential part of the larger regulatory scheme. . . .

[L]imiting the activity to marijuana possession and cultivation "in accordance with state law" cannot serve to place respondents' activities beyond congressional reach. The Supremacy Clause unambiguously provides that if there is any conflict between federal and state law, federal law shall prevail. It is beyond peradventure that federal power over commerce is " 'superior to that of the States to provide for the welfare or necessities of their inhabitants,' " however legitimate or dire those necessities may be. *Wirtz*, 392 U.S., at 196, (quoting *Sanitary Dist. of Chicago v. United States*, 266 U.S. 405, 426, (1925)). . . . Just as state acquiescence to federal regulation cannot expand the bounds of the Commerce Clause, . . . so too state action cannot circumscribe Congress' plenary commerce power. . . .

Respondents acknowledge this proposition, but nonetheless contend that their activities were not "an essential part of a larger regulatory scheme" because they had been "isolated by the State of California, and [are] policed by the State of California," and thus remain "entirely separated from the market." . . . The dissenters fall prey to similar reasoning. . . . The notion that California law has surgically excised a discrete activity that is hermetically sealed off from the larger interstate marijuana market is a dubious proposition, and, more importantly, one that Congress could have rationally rejected. . . .

So, from the "separate and distinct" class of activities identified by the Court of Appeals (and adopted by the dissenters), we are left with "the intrastate, noncommercial cultivation, possession and use of marijuana." . . . Thus the case for the exemption comes down to the claim that a locally cultivated product that is used domestically rather than sold on the open market is not subject to federal regulation. Given the findings in the CSA and the undisputed magnitude of the commercial market for marijuana, our decisions in *Wickard v. Filburn* and the later cases endorsing its reasoning foreclose that claim.

V

Respondents also raise a substantive due process claim and seek to avail themselves of the medical necessity defense. These theories of relief were set forth in their complaint but were not reached by the Court of Appeals. We therefore do not address the question whether judicial relief is available to respondents on these alternative bases. We do note, however, the presence of another avenue of relief. As the Solicitor General confirmed during oral argument, the statute authorizes procedures for the reclassification of Schedule I drugs. But perhaps even more important than these legal avenues is the democratic process, in which the voices of voters allied with these respondents may one day be heard in the halls of Congress. Under the present state of the law, however, the judgment of the Court of Appeals must be vacated. The case is remanded for further proceedings consistent with this opinion.

It is so ordered.

Justice SCALIA, concurring in the judgment.

I agree with the Court's holding that the Controlled Substances Act (CSA) may validly be applied to respondents' cultivation, distribution, and possession of marijuana for personal, medicinal use. I write separately because my understanding of the doctrinal foundation on which that holding rests is, if not inconsistent with that of the Court, at least more nuanced.

Since *Perez v. United States*, 402 U.S. 146 (1971), our cases have mechanically recited that the Commerce Clause permits congressional regulation of three categories: (1) the channels of interstate commerce; (2) the instrumentalities of interstate commerce, and persons or things in interstate commerce; and (3) activities that "substantially affect" interstate commerce. . . . The first two categories are self-evident, since they are the ingredients of interstate commerce itself. . . . The third category, however, is different in kind, and its recitation without explanation is misleading and incomplete.

It is *misleading* because, unlike the channels, instrumentalities, and agents of interstate commerce, activities that substantially affect interstate commerce are not themselves part of interstate commerce, and thus the power to regulate them cannot come from the Commerce Clause alone. Rather, as this Court has acknowledged since at least *United States v. Coombs,* 12 Pet. 72 (1838), Congress's regulatory authority over intrastate activities that are not themselves part of interstate commerce (including activities that have a substantial effect on interstate commerce) derives from the Necessary and Proper Clause. . . . And the category of "activities that substantially affect interstate commerce," *Lopez,* . . . is *incomplete* because the authority to enact laws necessary and proper for the regulation of interstate commerce is not limited to laws governing intrastate activities that substantially affect interstate commerce. Where necessary to make a regulation of interstate commerce effective, Congress may regulate even those intrastate activities that do not themselves substantially affect interstate commerce.

I

Our cases show that the regulation of intrastate activities may be necessary to and proper for the regulation of interstate commerce in two general circumstances. Most directly, the commerce power permits Congress not only to devise rules for the governance of commerce between States but also to facilitate interstate commerce by eliminating potential obstructions, and to restrict it by eliminating potential stimulants. *See NLRB v. Jones & Laughlin Steel Corp.*, 301 U.S. 1, 36-37 (1937). That is why the Court has repeatedly sustained congressional legislation on the ground that the regulated activities had a substantial effect on interstate commerce. . . . *Lopez* and *Morrison* recognized the expansive scope of Congress's authority in this regard: "[T]he pattern is clear. Where economic activity substantially affects interstate commerce, legislation regulating that activity will be sustained." . . .

This principle is not without limitation. In *Lopez* and *Morrison*, the Court — conscious of the potential of the "substantially affects" test to " 'obliterate the distinction between what is national and what is local,' " . . . rejected the argument that Congress may regulate *noneconomic* activity based solely on the effect that it may have on interstate commerce through a remote chain of inferences. . . . "[I]f we were to accept [such] arguments," the Court reasoned in *Lopez*, "we are hard pressed to posit any activity by an individual that Congress is without power to regulate." . . . Thus, although Congress's authority to regulate intrastate activity that substantially affects interstate commerce is broad, it does not permit the Court to "pile inference upon inference," *Lopez* . . . , in order to establish that noneconomic activity has a substantial effect on interstate commerce.

As we implicitly acknowledged in *Lopez*, however, Congress's authority to enact laws necessary and proper for the regulation of interstate commerce is not limited to laws directed against economic activities that have a substantial effect on interstate commerce. Though the conduct in *Lopez* was not economic, the Court nevertheless recognized that it could be regulated as "an essential part of a larger regulation of economic activity, in which the regulatory scheme could be undercut unless the intrastate activity were regulated." . . . This statement referred to those cases permitting the regulation of intrastate activities "which in a substantial way interfere with or obstruct the exercise of the granted power." *Wrightwood Dairy Co.*, 315 U.S., at 119. . . . As the Court put it in *Wrightwood Dairy,* where Congress has the authority to enact a regulation of interstate commerce, "it possesses every power needed to make that regulation effective." . . .

Although this power "to make . . . regulation effective" commonly overlaps with the authority to regulate economic activities that substantially affect interstate commerce, and may in some cases have been confused with that authority, the two are distinct. The regulation of an intrastate activity may be essential to a comprehensive regulation of interstate commerce even though the intrastate activity does not itself "substantially affect" interstate commerce. Moreover, as the passage from *Lopez* quoted above suggests, Congress may regulate even noneconomic local activity if that regulation is a necessary part of a more general regulation of interstate commerce. . . . The relevant question is simply whether the means chosen are "reasonably adapted" to the attainment of a legitimate end under the commerce power. *See Darby, supra*, at 121. . . .

II

Today's principal dissent objects that, by permitting Congress to regulate activities necessary to effective interstate regulation, the Court reduces *Lopez* and *Morrison* to "little more than a drafting guide." . . . I think that criticism unjustified. Unlike the power to regulate activities that have a substantial effect on interstate commerce, the power to enact laws enabling effective regulation of interstate commerce can only be exercised in conjunction with congressional regulation of an interstate market, and it extends only to those measures necessary to make the interstate regulation effective. As *Lopez* itself states, and the Court affirms today, Congress may regulate noneconomic intrastate activities only where the failure to do so "could . . . undercut" its regulation of interstate commerce. . . . This is not a power that threatens to obliterate the line between "what is truly national and what is truly local." . . .

Lopez and *Morrison* affirm that Congress may not regulate certain "purely local" activity within the States based solely on the attenuated effect that such activity may have in the interstate market. But those decisions do not declare noneconomic intrastate activities to be categorically beyond the reach of the Federal Government. Neither case involved the power of Congress to exert control over intrastate activities in connection with a more comprehensive scheme of regulation; *Lopez* expressly disclaimed that it was such a case, . . . and *Morrison* did not even discuss the possibility that it was. . . . To dismiss this distinction as "superficial and formalistic," . . . (O'CONNOR, J., dissenting), is to misunderstand the nature of the Necessary and Proper Clause, which empowers Congress to enact laws in effectuation of its enumerated powers that are not within its authority to enact in isolation. *See McCulloch v. Maryland,* 4 Wheat. 316, 421-422 (1819).

And there are other restraints upon the Necessary and Proper Clause authority. As Chief Justice Marshall wrote in *McCulloch v. Maryland,* even when the end is constitutional and legitimate, the means must be "appropriate" and "plainly adapted" to that end. . . . Moreover, they may not be otherwise "prohibited" and must be "consistent with the letter and spirit of the constitution." *Ibid.* These phrases are not merely hortatory. For example, cases such as *Printz v. United States,* 521 U.S. 898 (1997), and *New York v. United States,* 505 U.S. 144 (1992), affirm that a law is not " '*proper* for carrying into Execution the Commerce Clause' " "[w]hen [it] violates [a constitutional] principle of state sovereignty." . . .

III

The application of these principles to the case before us is straightforward. In the CSA, Congress has undertaken to extinguish the interstate market in Schedule I controlled substances, including marijuana. The Commerce Clause unquestionably permits this. The power to regulate interstate commerce "extends not only to those regulations which aid, foster and protect the commerce, but embraces those which prohibit it." . . . To effectuate its objective, Congress has prohibited almost all intrastate activities related to Schedule I substances — both economic activities (manufacture, distribution, possession with the intent to distribute) and noneconomic activities (simple possession). . . . That simple possession is a noneconomic activity is immaterial to whether it can be prohibited as a necessary part of a larger regulation. Rather, Congress's authority to enact all of these prohibitions of intrastate controlled-substance activities depends only upon whether they are appropriate means of achieving the legitimate end of eradicating Schedule I substances from interstate commerce.

By this measure, I think the regulation must be sustained. Not only is it impossible to distinguish "controlled substances manufactured and distributed intrastate" from "controlled substances manufactured and distributed interstate," but it hardly makes sense to speak in such terms. Drugs like marijuana are fungible commodities. As the Court explains, marijuana that is grown at home and possessed for personal use is never more than an instant from the interstate market — and this is so whether or not the possession is for medicinal use or lawful use under the laws of a particular State. . . .

I thus agree with the Court that, however the class of regulated activities is subdivided, Congress could reasonably conclude that its objective of prohibiting marijuana from the interstate market "could be undercut" if those activities were excepted from its general scheme of regulation. *See Lopez*, 514 U.S., at 561. That is sufficient to authorize the application of the CSA to respondents.

Justice O'CONNOR, with whom THE CHIEF JUSTICE and Justice THOMAS join as to all but Part III, dissenting.

We enforce the "outer limits" of Congress' Commerce Clause authority not for their own sake, but to protect historic spheres of state sovereignty from excessive federal encroachment and thereby to maintain the distribution of power fundamental to our federalist system of government. *United States v. Lopez*, 514 U.S. 549, 557 (1995); *NLRB v. Jones & Laughlin Steel Corp.*, 301 U.S. 1, 37 (1937). One of federalism's chief virtues, of course, is that it promotes innovation by allowing for the possibility that "a single courageous State may, if its citizens choose, serve as a laboratory; and try novel social and economic experiments without risk to the rest of the country." . . .

This case exemplifies the role of States as laboratories. The States' core police powers have always included authority to define criminal law and to protect the health, safety, and welfare of their citizens. . . . Exercising those powers, California . . . has come to its own conclusion about the difficult and sensitive question of whether marijuana should be available to relieve severe pain and suffering. Today the Court sanctions an application of the federal Controlled Substances Act that extinguishes that experiment, without any proof that the personal cultivation, possession, and use of marijuana for medicinal purposes, if economic activity in the first place, has a substantial effect on interstate commerce and is therefore an appropriate subject of federal regulation. In so doing, the Court announces a rule that gives Congress a perverse incentive to legislate broadly pursuant to the Commerce Clause — nestling questionable assertions of its authority into comprehensive regulatory schemes — rather than with precision. That rule and the result it produces in this case are irreconcilable with our decisions in *Lopez, supra*, and *United States v. Morrison*, 529 U.S. 598 (2000). Accordingly I dissent.

I

In *Lopez*, we . . . explained that "Congress' commerce authority includes the power to regulate those activities having a substantial relation to interstate commerce . . ., *i.e.*, those activities that substantially affect interstate commerce." 514 U.S., at 558-559 (citation omitted). This power derives from the conjunction of the Commerce Clause and the Necessary and Proper Clause. . . . We held in *Lopez* that the Gun-Free School Zones Act could not be sustained as an exercise of that power. [Summary of four *Lopez* factors omitted] In my view, the case before us is materially indistinguishable from *Lopez* and *Morrison* when the same considerations are taken into account.

II

A

What is the relevant conduct subject to Commerce Clause analysis in this case? The Court takes its cues from Congress, applying the above considerations to the activity regulated by the Controlled Substances Act (CSA) in general. The Court's decision rests on two facts about the CSA: (1) Congress chose to enact a single statute providing a comprehensive prohibition on the production, distribution, and possession of all controlled substances, and (2) Congress did not distinguish between various forms of intrastate noncommercial cultivation, possession, and use of marijuana. . . . Today's decision suggests that the federal regulation of local activity is immune to Commerce Clause challenge because Congress chose to act with an ambitious, all-encompassing statute, rather than piecemeal. In my view, allowing Congress to set the terms of the constitutional debate in this way, *i.e.*, by packaging regulation of local activity in broader schemes, is tantamount to removing meaningful limits on the Commerce Clause.

The Court's principal means of distinguishing *Lopez* from this case is to observe that the Gun-Free School Zones Act of 1990 was a "brief, single-subject statute," . . . whereas the CSA is "a lengthy and detailed statute creating a comprehensive framework for regulating the production, distribution, and possession of five classes of 'controlled substances' " . . . . Thus, according to the Court, it was possible in *Lopez* to evaluate in isolation the constitutionality of criminalizing local activity (there gun possession in school zones), whereas the local activity that the CSA targets (in this case cultivation and possession of marijuana for personal medicinal use) cannot be separated from the general drug control scheme of which it is a part.

Today's decision allows Congress to regulate intrastate activity without check, so long as there is some implication by legislative design that regulating intrastate activity is essential (and the Court appears to equate "essential" with "necessary") to the interstate regulatory scheme. Seizing upon our language in *Lopez* that the statute prohibiting gun possession in school zones was "not an essential part of a larger regulation of economic activity, in which the regulatory scheme could be undercut unless the intrastate activity were regulated," . . . the Court appears to reason that the placement of local activity in a comprehensive scheme confirms that it is essential to that scheme. If the Court is right, then *Lopez* stands for nothing more than a drafting guide: Congress should have described the relevant crime as "transfer or possession of a firearm anywhere in the nation" — thus including commercial and noncommercial activity, and clearly encompassing some activity with assuredly substantial effect on interstate commerce. Had it done so, the majority hints, we would have sustained its authority to regulate possession of firearms in school zones. Furthermore, today's decision suggests we would readily sustain a congressional decision to attach the regulation of intrastate activity to a pre-existing comprehensive (or even not-so-comprehensive) scheme. If so, the

Court invites increased federal regulation of local activity even if, as it suggests, Congress would not enact a *new* interstate scheme exclusively for the sake of reaching intrastate activity. . . .

I cannot agree that our decision in *Lopez* contemplated such evasive or overbroad legislative strategies with approval. Until today, such arguments have been made only in dissent. . . . *Lopez* and *Morrison* did not indicate that the constitutionality of federal regulation depends on superficial and formalistic distinctions. Likewise I did not understand our discussion of the role of courts in enforcing outer limits of the Commerce Clause for the sake of maintaining the federalist balance our Constitution requires, *see Lopez*, 514 U.S., at 557; *id.*, at 578 (KENNEDY, J., concurring), as a signal to Congress to enact legislation that is more extensive and more intrusive into the domain of state power. If the Court always defers to Congress as it does today, little may be left to the notion of enumerated powers.

The hard work for courts, then, is to identify objective markers for confining the analysis in Commerce Clause cases. Here, respondents challenge the constitutionality of the CSA as applied to them and those similarly situated. I agree with the Court that we must look beyond respondents' own activities. Otherwise, individual litigants could always exempt themselves from Commerce Clause regulation merely by pointing to the obvious — that their personal activities do not have a substantial effect on interstate commerce. . . . The task is to identify a mode of analysis that allows Congress to regulate more than nothing (by declining to reduce each case to its litigants) and less than everything (by declining to let Congress set the terms of analysis). The analysis may not be the same in every case, for it depends on the regulatory scheme at issue and the federalism concerns implicated.

A number of objective markers are available to confine the scope of constitutional review here. Both federal and state legislation — including the CSA itself, the California Compassionate Use Act, and other state medical marijuana legislation — recognize that medical and nonmedical (*i.e.*, recreational) uses of drugs are realistically distinct and can be segregated, and regulate them differently. . . . Moreover, because fundamental structural concerns about dual sovereignty animate our Commerce Clause cases, it is relevant that this case involves the interplay of federal and state regulation in areas of criminal law and social policy, where "States lay claim by right of history and expertise." *Lopez, supra*, at 583, . . .(KENNEDY, J., concurring). . . . California, like other States, has drawn on its reserved powers to distinguish the regulation of medicinal marijuana. To ascertain whether Congress' encroachment is constitutionally justified in this case, then, I would focus here on the personal cultivation, possession, and use of marijuana for medicinal purposes.

B

Having thus defined the relevant conduct, we must determine whether, under our precedents, the conduct is economic and, in the aggregate, substantially affects interstate commerce. Even if intrastate cultivation and possession of marijuana for one's own medicinal use can properly be characterized as economic, and I question whether it can, it has not been shown that such activity substantially affects interstate commerce. Similarly, it is neither self-evident nor demonstrated that regulating such activity is necessary to the interstate drug control scheme.

The Court's definition of economic activity is breathtaking. It defines as economic any activity involving the production, distribution, and consumption of commodities. And it appears to reason that when an interstate market for a commodity exists, regulating the intrastate manufacture or possession of that commodity is constitutional either because that intrastate activity is itself economic, or because regulating it is a rational part of regulating its market. Putting to one side the problem endemic to the Court's opinion — the shift in focus from the activity at issue in this case to the entirety of what the CSA regulates, . . . — the Court's definition of economic activity for purposes of Commerce Clause jurisprudence threatens to sweep all of productive human activity into federal regulatory reach.

The Court uses a dictionary definition of economics to skirt the real problem of drawing a meaningful line between "what is national and what is local," *Jones & Laughlin Steel*, 301 U.S., at 37. It will not do to say that Congress may regulate noncommercial activity simply because it may have an effect on the demand for commercial goods, or because the noncommercial endeavor can, in some sense, substitute for commercial activity. Most commercial goods or services have some sort of privately producible analogue. Home care substitutes for daycare. Charades games substitute for movie tickets. Backyard or windowsill gardening substitutes for going to the supermarket. To draw the line wherever private activity affects the demand for market goods is to draw no line at all, and to declare everything economic. We have already rejected the result that would follow — a federal police power. *Lopez, supra*, at 564.

In *Lopez* and *Morrison,* we suggested that economic activity usually relates directly to commercial activity. . . . The homegrown cultivation and personal possession and use of marijuana for medicinal purposes has no apparent commercial character. Everyone agrees that the marijuana at issue in this case was never in the stream of commerce, and neither were the supplies for growing it. . . . *Lopez* makes clear that possession is not itself commercial activity. *Ibid.* And respondents have not come into possession by means of any commercial transaction; they have simply grown, in their own homes, marijuana for their own use, without acquiring, buying, selling, or bartering a thing of value. . . .

The Court suggests that *Wickard,* which we have identified as "perhaps the most far reaching example of Commerce Clause authority over intrastate activity," *Lopez, supra*, at 560, established federal regulatory power over any home consumption of a commodity for which a national market exists. I disagree. *Wickard* involved a challenge to the Agricultural Adjustment Act of 1938(AAA), which directed the Secretary of Agriculture to set

national quotas on wheat production, and penalties for excess production. . . . The AAA itself confirmed that Congress made an explicit choice
not to reach — and thus the Court could not possibly have approved of
federal control over — small-scale, noncommercial wheat farming. In
contrast to the CSA's limitless assertion of power, Congress provided an
exemption within the AAA for small producers. When Filburn planted the
wheat at issue in *Wickard*, the statute exempted plantings less than 200
bushels (about six tons), and when he harvested his wheat it exempted
plantings less than six acres. . . . *Wickard*, then, did not extend Commerce
Clause authority to something as modest as the home cook's herb garden.
This is not to say that Congress may never regulate small quantities of
commodities possessed or produced for personal use, or to deny that it
sometimes needs to enact a zero tolerance regime for such commodities.
It is merely to say that *Wickard* did not hold or imply that small-scale
production of commodities is always economic, and automatically within
Congress' reach.

Even assuming that economic activity is at issue in this case, the
Government has made no showing in fact that the possession and use of
homegrown marijuana for medical purposes, in California or elsewhere, has
a substantial effect on interstate commerce. Similarly, the Government has
not shown that regulating such activity is necessary to an interstate regulatory scheme. Whatever the specific theory of "substantial effects" at issue
(*i.e.*, whether the activity substantially affects interstate commerce,
whether its regulation is necessary to an interstate regulatory scheme, or
both), a concern for dual sovereignty requires that Congress' excursion into
the traditional domain of States be justified.

That is why characterizing this as a case about the Necessary and Proper
Clause does not change the analysis significantly. Congress must exercise
its authority under the Necessary and Proper Clause in a manner consistent with basic constitutional principles. . . . As Justice SCALIA recognizes, . . . Congress cannot use its authority under the Clause to contravene the principle of state sovereignty embodied in the Tenth Amendment. . . . Likewise, that authority must be used in a manner consistent
with the notion of enumerated powers — a structural principle that is as
much part of the Constitution as the Tenth Amendment's explicit textual
command. Accordingly, something more than mere assertion is required
when Congress purports to have power over local activity whose connection
to an intrastate market is not self-evident. Otherwise, the Necessary and
Proper Clause will always be a back door for unconstitutional federal
regulation. Indeed, if it were enough in "substantial effects" cases for the
Court to supply conceivable justifications for intrastate regulation related
to an interstate market, then we could have surmised in *Lopez* that guns
in school zones are "never more than an instant from the interstate market"
in guns already subject to extensive federal regulation, . . . recast *Lopez*
as a Necessary and Proper Clause case, and thereby upheld the Gun-Free
School Zones Act of 1990. . . .

There is simply no evidence that homegrown medicinal marijuana users constitute, in the aggregate, a sizable enough class to have a discernable, let alone substantial, impact on the national illicit drug market — or otherwise to threaten the CSA regime. Explicit evidence is helpful when substantial effect is not "visible to the naked eye." . . . And here, in part because common sense suggests that medical marijuana users may be limited in number and that California's Compassionate Use Act and similar state legislation may well isolate activities relating to medicinal marijuana from the illicit market, the effect of those activities on interstate drug traffic is not self-evidently substantial.

In this regard, again, this case is readily distinguishable from *Wickard*. To decide whether the Secretary could regulate local wheat farming, the Court looked to "the actual effects of the activity in question upon interstate commerce." . . . The Court recognizes that "the record in the *Wickard* case itself established the causal connection between the production for local use and the national market" and argues that "we have before us findings by Congress *to the same effect*. . . .

[The legislative findings here] amount to nothing more than a legislative insistence that the regulation of controlled substances must be absolute. They are asserted without any supporting evidence — descriptive, statistical, or otherwise. . . . Indeed, if declarations like these suffice to justify federal regulation, and if the Court today is right about what passes rationality review before us, then our decision in *Morrison* should have come out the other way. In that case, Congress had supplied numerous findings regarding the impact gender-motivated violence had on the national economy. . . . If, as the Court claims, today's decision does not break with precedent, how can it be that voluminous findings, documenting extensive hearings about the specific topic of violence against women, did not pass constitutional muster in *Morrison*, while the CSA's abstract, unsubstantiated, generalized findings about controlled substances do?

In particular, the CSA's introductory declarations are too vague and un-specific to demonstrate that the federal statutory scheme will be under-mined if Congress cannot exert power over individuals like respondents. The declarations are not even specific to marijuana. (Facts about substantial effects may be developed in litigation to compensate for the inadequacy of Congress' findings; in part because this case comes to us from the grant of a preliminary injunction, there has been no such development.) . . .

The Government has not overcome empirical doubt that the number of Californians engaged in personal cultivation, possession, and use of medical marijuana, or the amount of marijuana they produce, is enough to threaten the federal regime. Nor has it shown that Compassionate Use Act mari-juana users have been or are realistically likely to be responsible for the drug's seeping into the market in a significant way. . . . The Court also offers some arguments about the effect of the Compassionate Use Act on the national market. . . . But, without substantiation, they add little to the CSA's conclusory statements about diversion, essentiality, and market effect. Piling assertion upon assertion does not, in my view, satisfy the substantiality test of *Lopez* and *Morrison*.

III

We would do well to recall how James Madison, the father of the Constitution, described our system of joint sovereignty to the people of New York: "The powers delegated by the proposed constitution to the federal government are few and defined. Those which are to remain in the State governments are numerous and indefinite . . . . The powers reserved to the several States will extend to all the objects which, in the ordinary course of affairs, concern the lives, liberties, and properties of the people, and the internal order, improvement, and prosperity of the State." The Federalist No. 45, pp. 292-293 (C. Rossiter ed.1961).

Relying on Congress' abstract assertions, the Court has endorsed making it a federal crime to grow small amounts of marijuana in one's own home for one's own medicinal use. This overreaching stifles an express choice by some States, concerned for the lives and liberties of their people, to regulate medical marijuana differently. If I were a California citizen, I would not have voted for the medical marijuana ballot initiative; if I were a California legislator I would not have supported the Compassionate Use Act. But whatever the wisdom of California's experiment with medical marijuana, the federalism principles that have driven our Commerce Clause cases require that room for experiment be protected in this case. For these reasons I dissent.

Justice THOMAS, dissenting.

Respondents Diane Monson and Angel Raich use marijuana that has never been bought or sold, that has never crossed state lines, and that has had no demonstrable effect on the national market for marijuana. If Congress can regulate this under the Commerce Clause, then it can regulate virtually anything — and the Federal Government is no longer one of limited and enumerated powers.

I

Respondents' local cultivation and consumption of marijuana is not "Commerce . . . among the several States." U.S. Const., Art. I, § 8, cl. 3. By holding that Congress may regulate activity that is neither interstate nor commerce under the Interstate Commerce Clause, the Court abandons any attempt to enforce the Constitution's limits on federal power. The majority supports this conclusion by invoking, without explanation, the Necessary and Proper Clause. Regulating respondents' conduct, however, is not "necessary and proper for carrying into Execution" Congress' restrictions on the interstate drug trade. Art. I, § 8, cl. 18. Thus, neither the Commerce Clause nor the Necessary and Proper Clause grants Congress the power to regulate respondents' conduct.

A

As I explained at length in *United States v. Lopez*, 514 U.S. 549 (1995), the Commerce Clause empowers Congress to regulate the buying and selling of goods and services trafficked across state lines. . . . The Clause's text, structure, and history all indicate that, at the time of the founding, the term " 'commerce' consisted of selling, buying, and bartering, as well as transporting for these purposes." . . . Commerce, or trade, stood in contrast to productive activities like manufacturing and agriculture. . . . Throughout founding-era dictionaries, Madison's notes from the Constitutional Convention, The Federalist Papers, and the ratification debates, the term "commerce" is consistently used to mean trade or exchange — not all economic or gainful activity that has some attenuated connection to trade or exchange. . . . The term "commerce" commonly meant trade or exchange (and shipping for these purposes) not simply to those involved in the drafting and ratification processes, but also to the general public. . . .

Even the majority does not argue that respondents' conduct is itself "Commerce among the several States." Art. I, § 8, cl. 3. . . . Certainly no evidence from the founding suggests that "commerce" included the mere possession of a good or some purely personal activity that did not involve trade or exchange for value. In the early days of the Republic, it would have been unthinkable that Congress could prohibit the local cultivation, possession, and consumption of marijuana.

On this traditional understanding of "commerce," the [CSA] . . . regulates a great deal of marijuana trafficking that is interstate and commercial in character. The CSA does not, however, criminalize only the interstate buying and selling of marijuana. Instead, it bans the entire market — intrastate or interstate, noncommercial or commercial — for marijuana. Respondents are correct that the CSA exceeds Congress' commerce power as applied to their conduct, which is purely intrastate and noncommercial.

B

More difficult, however, is whether the CSA is a valid exercise of Congress' power to enact laws that are "necessary and proper for carrying into Execution" its power to regulate interstate commerce. Art. I, § 8, cl. 18. The Necessary and Proper Clause is not a warrant to Congress to enact any law that bears some conceivable connection to the exercise of an enumerated power. Nor is it, however, a command to Congress to enact only laws that are absolutely indispensable to the exercise of an enumerated power.

In *McCulloch v. Maryland*, 4 Wheat. 316, this Court, speaking through Chief Justice Marshall, set forth a test for determining when an Act of Congress is permissible under the Necessary and Proper Clause:

> "Let the end be legitimate, let it be within the scope of the constitution, and all means which are appropriate, which are plainly

adapted to that end, which are not prohibited, but consist with the letter and spirit of the constitution, are constitutional." . . .

To act under the Necessary and Proper Clause, then, Congress must select a means that is "appropriate" and "plainly adapted" to executing an enumerated power; the means cannot be otherwise "prohibited" by the Constitution; and the means cannot be inconsistent with "the letter and spirit of the [C]onstitution." . . . The CSA, as applied to respondents' conduct, is not a valid exercise of Congress' power under the Necessary and Proper Clause.

1

Congress has exercised its power over interstate commerce to criminalize trafficking in marijuana across state lines. The Government contends that banning Monson and Raich's intrastate drug activity is "necessary and proper for carrying into Execution" its regulation of interstate drug trafficking. Art. I, § 8, cl. 18. *See* 21 U.S.C. § 801(6). However, in order to be "necessary," the intrastate ban must be more than "a reasonable means [of] effectuat[ing] the regulation of interstate commerce." . . . It must be "plainly adapted" to regulating interstate marijuana trafficking — in other words, there must be an "obvious, simple, and direct relation" between the intrastate ban and the regulation of interstate commerce. . . .

On its face, a ban on the intrastate cultivation, possession and distribution of marijuana may be plainly adapted to stopping the interstate flow of marijuana. Unregulated local growers and users could swell both the supply and the demand sides of the interstate marijuana market, making the market more difficult to regulate. . . . But respondents do not challenge the CSA on its face. Instead, they challenge it as applied to their conduct. The question is thus whether the intrastate ban is "necessary and proper" as applied to medical marijuana users like respondents.

Respondents are not regulable simply because they belong to a large class (local growers and users of marijuana) that Congress might need to reach, if they also belong to a distinct and separable subclass (local growers and users of state-authorized, medical marijuana) that does not undermine the CSA's interstate ban. . . . The Court of Appeals found that respondents' "limited use is distinct from the broader illicit drug market," because "th[eir] medicinal marijuana . . . is not intended for, nor does it enter, the stream of commerce." *Raich v. Ashcroft*, 352 F.3d 1222, 1228 (C.A.9 2003). If that is generally true of individuals who grow and use marijuana for medical purposes under state law, then even assuming Congress has "obvious" and "plain" reasons why regulating intrastate cultivation and possession is necessary to regulating the interstate drug trade, none of those reasons applies to medical marijuana patients like Monson and Raich. . . .

But even assuming that States' controls allow some seepage of medical marijuana into the illicit drug market, there is a multibillion-dollar interstate market for marijuana. . . . It is difficult to see how this vast market could be affected by diverted medical cannabis, let alone in a way that makes regulating intrastate medical marijuana obviously essential to controlling the interstate drug market. . . .

In sum, neither in enacting the CSA nor in defending its application to respondents has the Government offered any obvious reason why banning medical marijuana use is necessary to stem the tide of interstate drug trafficking. Congress' goal of curtailing the interstate drug trade would not plainly be thwarted if it could not apply the CSA to patients like Monson and Raich. That is, unless Congress' aim is really to exercise police power of the sort reserved to the States in order to eliminate even the intrastate possession and use of marijuana.

2

Even assuming the CSA's ban on locally cultivated and consumed marijuana is "necessary," that does not mean it is also "proper." The means selected by Congress to regulate interstate commerce cannot be "prohibited" by, or inconsistent with the "letter and spirit" of, the Constitution. *McCulloch*, 4 Wheat., at 421.

In *Lopez*, I argued that allowing Congress to regulate intrastate, noncommercial activity under the Commerce Clause would confer on Congress a general "police power" over the Nation. . . . This is no less the case if Congress ties its power to the Necessary and Proper Clause rather than the Commerce Clause. When agents from the Drug Enforcement Administration raided Monson's home, they seized six cannabis plants. If the Federal Government can regulate growing a half-dozen cannabis plants for personal consumption (not because it is interstate commerce, but because it is inextricably bound up with interstate commerce), then Congress' Article I powers — as expanded by the Necessary and Proper Clause — have no meaningful limits. . . .

Even if Congress may regulate purely intrastate activity when essential to exercising some enumerated power, . . . Congress may not use its incidental authority to subvert basic principles of federalism and dual sovereignty. . . . Here, Congress has encroached on States' traditional police powers to define the criminal law and to protect the health, safety, and welfare of their citizens. . . . Further, the Government's rationale — that it may regulate the production or possession of any commodity for which there is an interstate market — threatens to remove the remaining vestiges of States' traditional police powers. . . . This would convert the Necessary and Proper Clause into precisely what Chief Justice Marshall did not envision, a "pretext . . . for the accomplishment of objects not intrusted to the government." *McCulloch*. . . .

II

A

The majority's treatment of the substantial effects test is rootless, because it is not tethered to either the Commerce Clause or the Necessary and Proper Clause. Under the Commerce Clause, Congress may regulate interstate commerce, not activities that substantially affect interstate commerce — any more than Congress may regulate activities that do not fall within, but that affect, the subjects of its other Article I powers. Whatever additional latitude the Necessary and Proper Clause affords, . . . the question is whether Congress' legislation is essential to the regulation of interstate commerce itself — not whether the legislation extends only to economic activities that substantially affect interstate commerce. . . .

The substantial effects test is easily manipulated for another reason. This Court has never held that Congress can regulate noneconomic activity that substantially affects interstate commerce. . . .To evade even that modest restriction on federal power, the majority defines economic activity in the broadest possible terms as the " 'the production, distribution, and consumption of commodities.' " . . . This carves out a vast swath of activities that are subject to federal regulation. . . . If the majority is to be taken seriously, the Federal Government may now regulate quilting bees, clothes drives, and potluck suppers throughout the 50 States. This makes a mockery of Madison's assurance to the people of New York that the "powers delegated" to the Federal Government are "few and defined," while those of the States are "numerous and indefinite." The Federalist No. 45, at 313 (J. Madison).

Moreover, even a Court interested more in the modern than the original understanding of the Constitution ought to resolve cases based on the meaning of words that are actually in the document. Congress is authorized to regulate "Commerce," and respondents' conduct does not qualify under any definition of that term. The majority's opinion only illustrates the steady drift away from the text of the Commerce Clause. There is an inexorable expansion from " 'commerce,' " . . . to "commercial" and "economic" activity, . . . and finally to all "production, distribution, and consumption" of goods or services for which there is an "established . . . interstate market.". . . Federal power expands, but never contracts, with each new locution. The majority is not interpreting the Commerce Clause, but rewriting it.

The majority's rewriting of the Commerce Clause seems to be rooted in the belief that, unless the Commerce Clause covers the entire web of human activity, Congress will be left powerless to regulate the national economy effectively. . . . The interconnectedness of economic activity is not a modern phenomenon unfamiliar to the Framers. . . . Moreover, the Framers understood what the majority does not appear to fully appreciate: There is a danger to concentrating too much, as well as too little, power in the Federal Government. This Court has carefully avoided stripping Congress of its ability to regulate *inter*state commerce, but it has casually allowed the Federal Government to strip States of their ability to regulate *intra*state commerce — not to mention a host of local activities, like mere drug possession, that are not commercial.

One searches the Court's opinion in vain for any hint of what aspect of American life is reserved to the States. Yet this Court knows that " '[t]he

Constitution created a Federal Government of limited powers.' " . . . That is why today's decision will add no measure of stability to our Commerce Clause jurisprudence: This Court is willing neither to enforce limits on federal power, nor to declare the Tenth Amendment a dead letter. If stability is possible, it is only by discarding the stand-alone substantial effects test and revisiting our definition of "Commerce among the several States." Congress may regulate interstate commerce — not things that affect it, even when summed together, unless truly "necessary and proper" to regulating interstate commerce. . . .

NOTES

(1) *Gonzales v. Raich* represented the third significant Commerce Clause case the Supreme Court decided in a decade. In *United States v. Lopez*, 514 U.S. 549 (1995), and *United States v. Morrison*, 528 U.S. 598 (2000), the Court, in 5-4 decisions, had struck down legislation as beyond Congress' power under the Commerce Clause. In each case, Justices O'Connor, Scalia, Kennedy and Thomas joined the majority opinion which Chief Justice Rehnquist wrote. In *Raich*, Justices Scalia and Kennedy switched sides, with the latter joining the majority opinion and Justice Scalia agreeing with its result. Professor Thomas W. Merrill suggested in 2003 that Justice Scalia had never been as committed to the Rehnquist Court's federalism agenda as had some of his colleagues in the Rehnquist-O'Connor-Kennedy-Thomas bloc. Professor Merrill argued Justice Scalia had joined with them in *Lopez, Morrison* and other cases due to strategic considerations. *See* Thomas W. Merrill, *The Making of the Second Rehnquist Court: A Preliminary Analysis*, 47 SAINT LOUIS U. L.J. 569, 604-20 (2003).

(2) *Lopez* had characterized *Wickard* as "perhaps the most far reaching example of Commerce Clause authority over intrastate activity" (casebook, p. 139) but had reaffirmed it as a proper use of Congress' constitutional power. In *Raich*, the Court found *Wickard* "of particular relevance" and found the "similarities" to *Wickard* "striking."

(3) In *Lopez* the Court observed that the statute under consideration was "not an essential part of a larger regulation of economic activity" implying that if it had been it would have been within Congress' power. (Casebook, p. 140). In *Raich*, the Court relies upon that language.

(4) Note that the Court's decision in *Raich* rests on the Necessary and Proper Clauses as well as on the Commerce Clause. Justice Scalia, in his concurring opinion, provides a detailed exposition of the manner in which the Necessary and Proper Clause augments federal authority. In *Printz v. United States*, 521 U.S. 989, 923 (1993) ,Justice Scalia had called that Clause "the last, best hope of those who defend ultra vires congressional activity."

(5) In discussing *Wickard*, the majority opinion confuses the parties to the case. It writes: "The fact that Wickard's own impact on the market was 'trivial by itself' was not a sufficient reason for removing him from the scope

of federal regulation." It continues: "Moreover, even though Wickard was indeed a commercial farmer . . ." 125 S. Ct. at 2207, Wickard was not the farmer who planted too much wheat; Claude R. Wickard was the Secretary of Agriculture. Roscoe Filburn was the farmer held subject to the regulation. *See Wickard v. Filburn*, 317 U.S. 111 (1942) Justice O'Connor's dissent got the parties right (as did the majority earlier in its opinion).

(6) How does the level of scrutiny that the majority prescribes for Commerce Clause cases compare to that Justice O'Connor favors? Does the majority adopt the rational basis formula of Justice Breyer's *Lopez* dissent? (*See* casebook, p. 149).

§ 2.07 Spending Power

Page 167: [Insert after Note (9)]

(10) In *Barnes v. Gorman*, 536 U.S. 181 (2002), the Court analogized federal legislation under the Spending Clause to contract law. Justice Scalia wrote for the Court:

> We have repeatedly characterized. . . . Spending Clause legisla-
> tion as "much in the nature of a *contract:* in return for federal funds,
> the [recipients] agree to comply with federally imposed conditions."
> . . . Just as a valid contract requires offer and acceptance of its
> terms, "[t]he legitimacy of Congress' power to legislate under the
> spending power . . . rests on whether the [recipient] voluntarily and
> knowingly accepts the terms of the 'contract.' . . . Accordingly, if
> Congress intends to impose a condition on the grant of federal mon-
> eys, it must do so unambiguously." . . . Although we have been
> careful not to imply that *all* contract-law rules apply to Spending
> Clause legislation, . . . we have regularly applied the contract-law
> analogy in cases defining the scope of conduct for which funding
> recipients may be held liable for money damages. Thus, a recipient
> may be held liable to third-party beneficiaries for intentional
> conduct that violates the clear terms of the relevant statute, . . .
> but not for its failure to comply with vague language describing the
> objectives of the statute, . . . and, if the statute implies that only
> violations brought to the attention of an official with power to
> correct them are actionable, not for conduct unknown to any such
> official. . . . We have also applied the contract-law analogy in
> finding a damages remedy available in private suits under Spend-
> ing Clause legislation. . . .

Id. at 186–187.

Two of the six justices (Justices Souter and O'Connor) who joined the Court's opinion cautioned that the contract law analogy might not always be appropriate in Spending Clause cases. *Id.* at 190–191.

(11) In *Sabri v. United States,* 541 U.S. 600 (2004), the Court held that under Article I of the Constitution, Congress could criminalize bribery of

state and local officials of entities receiving federal funds even absent any connection between the forbidden conduct and the federal funds. Sabri was indicted for violating 18 U.S.C. § 666(a)(2) which proscribed attempting to bribe, with anything of at least $5,000 value, a state, local or tribal official with an entity that received more than $10,000 in federal benefits. Sabri challenged the law as facially invalid because it failed to require a connection between the bribe and federal funds. In a unanimous decision, the Court rejected Sabri's argument. Under the Spending Clause, Congress could appropriate money to promote the general welfare, and under the Necessary and Proper Clause, it could take action to make certain that federal funds were not diverted from the general welfare to corrupt applications. *Id.* at 605. Congress was not limited to legislating with respect to bribes traceable to federal programs since the federal interest encompassed having any untrustworthy officials in possession of federal funds. *Id.*

The Court distinguished *Sabri* from the statutes at issue in *United States v. Lopez,* 514 U.S. 549 (1995), and *United States v. Morrison,* 529 U.S. 598 (2000), which the Court held were beyond Congress' commerce power since the relationship between the legislation and commerce was too attenuated. "No piling [of inference upon inference] is needed here to show that Congress was within its prerogative to protect spending objects from the menace of local administrators on the take," wrote Justice Souter for eight justices. 541 U.S. at 608.

Justice Thomas concurred, concluding that section 666(a)(2) was within the Court's Commerce Clause precedents (some of which he questioned), although he criticized the majority for adopting a "rational means" test for the Necessary and Proper Clause which was more permissive than that articulated in *McCulloch v. Maryland,* 17 U.S. (4 Wheat.) 316 (1819). 541 U.S. at 611.

(12) In *Jackson v. Birmingham Board of Education,* 125 S. Ct. 1497 (2005), the Court held that the requirement that recipients of federal funds have adequate notice that they could be liable for certain conduct was satisfied. A former girls' basketball coach claimed that his dismissal as coach was in retaliation for his complaints that the Board of Education was discriminating against the girls' basketball team in violation of Title IX of the Education Amendments of 1972. The Board claimed that it could not be liable to a private damage action for retaliatory discharge since it had not received adequate notice that such potential liability was a condition of its receipt of federal funds. The Court held that prior Court decisions gave adequate notice of this species of liability even though Congress did not specifically state that liability for retaliation might ensue. Justice Thomas (joined by Chief Justice Rehnquist, and Justices Scalia and Kennedy) dissented. He argued that such liability pursuant to Spending Clause legislation could only arise if the statute's clear terms authorized retaliation claims. Such notice could not be supplied by Court precedent (he also argued that the precedents did not give the notice required).

Chapter III

LIMITS ON NATIONAL POWER OVER THE STATES

§ 3.04   Immunity from Suit

Page 228: [Insert the following after Note (15)]

(16) The Court indicated that *Ex Parte Young* retains vitality and adopted Justice O'Connor's test in *Verizon Maryland Inc. v. Public Service Commission of Maryland*, 535 U.S. 635, 645 (2002). The Maryland Commission claimed the Eleventh Amendment barred a federal court from adjudicating Verizon's claim (for declaratory and injunctive relief) against it and its commissioners in connection with an order adverse to Verizon. The Court, without dissent, rejected that argument. Citing Justice O'Connor's *Coeur d'Alene* concurrence, Justice Scalia, for the Court, wrote: "In determining whether the doctrine of *Ex Parte Young* avoids an Eleventh Amendment bar to suit, a court need only conduct a straightforward inquiry into whether [the] complaint alleges an ongoing violation of federal law and seeks relief properly characterized as prospective." *Id.*

The relief sought — an injunction against state officials from enforcing an order in violation of federal law — satisfied this test and was the sort of order the Court had allowed in the past. *Id.* The prayer for declaratory relief did address the past, as well as future, effectiveness of the order but did not expose the state or its commissioners to "past liability." *Id.* at 646. Nor was an *Ex Parte Young* action precluded based upon an inference that Congress intended no such action as the Court had held in *Seminole Tribe of Florida v. Florida*, 517 U.S. 44 (1996). There the statute's "intricate procedures" regarding relief against the state implicitly foreclosed an *Ex Parte Young* action; here, the statute cryptically provided for judicial review of commission determinations without specifying defendant or remedy. *Id.* at 647.

Page 232: [Insert the following at the end of Note (7)]

In 2001, the Court held in a 5–4 decision that Congress could not, under § 5 of the Fourteenth Amendment, subject states to suit by private individuals seeking damages under the Americans with Disabilities Act. *Board of Trustees of the University of Alabama v. Garrett*, 531 U.S. 356 (2001). The Court found insufficient evidence that States, as opposed to society generally, had discriminated against disabled Americans. *See Garrett*, casebook p. 437.

During the 2002 term, however, the Court held Congress did have power under § 5 to create a private right of action for monetary relief against states for violating the Family and Medical Leave Act of 1993. *Nevada Department of Human Resources v. Hibbs*, 538 U.S. 721 (2003). In his majority opinion, Chief Justice Rehnquist found the remedy congruent and proportional to the injury and concluded that Congress had ample evidence of state discrimination regarding family leave, often based on gender stereotypes. *See* 2005 Supplement *infra*, p. 113.

Similarly, during the October 2003 term, the Court, in a 5-4 decision in *Tennessee v. Lane*, 541 U.S. 509 (2004), held Congress properly exercised its power under section 5 of the Fourteenth Amendment to abrogate the States' Eleventh Amendment immunity under Title II of the Americans with Disabilities Act of 1990. The case arose from a complaint by two paraplegics that the Tennessee state courthouses denied them access to the state judicial system. Tennessee moved to dismiss based on the Eleventh Amendment. Congress had clearly expressed its intent to abrogate the State's immunity ("A State shall not be immune under the eleventh amendment to the Constitution of the United States from an action in Federal or State court of competent jurisdiction for a violation of this chapter." 42 U.S.C. § 12202.) and the Court had power under section 5 since the legislation in question satisfied the congruence and proportionality test.

Page 232: [Insert the following after Note (9)]

(10) In *Federal Maritime Commission v. South Carolina State Ports Authority*, 535 U.S. 743 (2002), the Court held that state sovereign immunity prohibits executive administrative agencies from adjudicating the claims of private parties against unconsenting states. After its requests to berth a ship were denied by South Carolina State Ports Authority (SCSPA), South Carolina Maritime Services, Inc. (Maritime Services) filed a complaint with the Federal Maritime Commission (FMC) seeking compensatory and injunctive relief. Justice Thomas, for a five justice majority, reaffirmed that "the sovereign immunity enjoyed by the States extends beyond the literal text of the Eleventh Amendment." *Id*. at 754. The Framers did not intend the States to be subject to proceedings which were " 'anomalous and unheard of when the Constitution was adopted.' " *Id*. at 755. Observing the "strong similarities between FMC proceedings and civil litigation," the Court concluded that "[t]he affront to a State's dignity does not lessen when an adjudication takes place in an administrative tribunal as opposed to an Article III court." *Id*. at 760.

Justice Breyer wrote a dissent which Justices Stevens, Souter and Ginsburg joined. Though reasserting that *Seminole Tribe* and *Alden* were wrongly decided the dissenters argued that the Court's decision could not even stand on those precedents. Administrative proceedings typically involve Executive Branch agencies exercising Executive Branch powers to determine whether a state agency violated federal law. Such a paradigm stands outside the language or concerns of the Eleventh and Tenth Amendments. The decision "threatens to deny the Executive and Legislative Branches of Government the structural flexibility that the Constitution permits and which modern government demands." *Id.* at 786. It "set loose an interpretative principle that restricts far too severely the authority of the Federal Government to regulate innumerable relationships between State and citizen." *Id.* at 788.

(11) *South Carolina State Ports Authority* was one of several Eleventh Amendment/sovereign immunity cases the Court addressed during the October 2001 term as it continued to define the circumstances in which states could be sued. The Court held that a state waived its Eleventh Amendment immunity when it removed a lawsuit against it from state court to federal court, at least where it had explicitly waived immunity with respect to state court suits. In *Lapides v. Board of Regents of the University System of Georgia*, 535 U.S. 613 (2002), a professor sued the state university and other defendants under federal and state law in state court. Defendants removed the action to federal court at which point, the state moved to dismiss based upon its Eleventh Amendment immunity. Georgia had acknowledged that state law waived sovereign immunity regarding state law claims in state court. In a unanimous decision, an unusual event in Eleventh Amendment litigation, the Court concluded that since the state "voluntarily agreed to remove the case to federal court" it had "voluntarily invoked the federal court's jurisdiction." *Id.* at 620. *Lapides* stands for the rule "that removal is a form of voluntary invocation of a federal court's jurisdiction sufficient to waive the State's otherwise valid objection to litigation of a matter (here of state law) in a federal forum. *Id.* at 624.

(12) In *Raygor v. Regents of the University of Minnesota*, 534 U.S. 533 (2002), the Court applied the clear statement rule to 28 U.S.C. § 1367 in an Eleventh Amendment context. Petitioners had invoked 28 U.S.C. § 1367 on supplemental jurisdiction to file in federal court state law claims allegedly related to certain federal claims. After a federal court dismissed petitioner's state law discrimination claim, petitioner refiled them in state court. The state court dismissed the state law claim as untimely filed. Petitioners relied on the tolling feature of 28 U.S.C. § 1367 which tolled a statute of limitations for the pendency of the federal suit plus 30 days. The Court held that Congress had not clearly stated its intent to apply § 1367(d) to suits against nonconsenting states whose claims were dismissed on Eleventh Amendment grounds. *Id.* at 546.

Chapter IV

FEDERALISM AND STATE REGULATORY POWER

§ 4.06   State Regulation of Commerce; The Dormant Commerce Clause

[4]—Facially Neutral Statutes

Page 281: [Insert the following after note (9)]

In *American Trucking Association v. Michigan Public Service Commission*, 125 S. Ct. 2419 (2005), the Court unanimously held that Michigan's flat $100 fee on trucks engaged in intrastate commercial hauling did not violate the dormant Commerce Clause. The statute did not facially discriminate against interstate or out-of-state activities or entrepreneurs but operated in an even-handed way. The fee was an "unobjectionable exercise" of Michigan's police power which did not unfairly discriminate against interstate truckers or burden interstate commerce. Justice Scalia applied the test he articulated in his concurrence in *West Lynn Creamery, Inc. v. Healy*, 512 U.S. 186, 210 (1994) (casebook, pp. 279-80), and concurred since the statute did not finally discriminate and was distinguishable from Court precedents. Justice Thomas concurred on the grounds that the dormant Commerce Clause lacked a textual basis in the Constitution, "makes little sense" and was "virtually unworkable."

[6]—Congressional Action

Page 293: [Insert after Note (8)]

GRANHOLM v. HEALD

125 S. Ct. 1885 (2005)

Justice KENNEDY delivered the opinion of the Court.

These consolidated cases present challenges to state laws regulating the sale of wine from out-of-state wineries to consumers in Michigan and New York. The details and mechanics of the two regulatory schemes differ, but the object and effect of the laws are the same: to allow in-state wineries to sell wine directly to consumers in that State but to prohibit out-of-state wineries from doing so, or, at the least, to make direct sales impractical from an economic standpoint. It is evident that the object and design of the Michigan and New York statutes is to grant in-state wineries a competitive advantage over wineries located beyond the States' borders.

We hold that the laws in both States discriminate against interstate commerce in violation of the Commerce Clause, Art. I, § 8, cl. 3, and that the discrimination is neither authorized nor permitted by the Twenty-first Amendment. Accordingly, we affirm the judgment of the Court of Appeals for the Sixth Circuit, which invalidated the Michigan laws; and we reverse the judgment of the Court of Appeals for the Second Circuit, which upheld the New York laws.

I

Like many other States, Michigan and New York regulate the sale and importation of alcoholic beverages, including wine, through a three-tier distribution system. Separate licenses are required for producers, wholesalers, and retailers. . . . The three-tier scheme is preserved by a complex set of overlapping state and federal regulations. For example, both state and federal laws limit vertical integration between tiers. . . . We have held previously that States can mandate a three-tier distribution scheme in the exercise of their authority under the Twenty-first Amendment. *North Dakota v. United States*, 495 U.S. 423, 432, (1990). . . . As relevant to today's cases, though, the three-tier system is, in broad terms and with refinements to be discussed, mandated by Michigan and New York only for sales from out-of-state wineries. In-state wineries, by contrast, can obtain a license for direct sales to consumers. The differential treatment between in-state and out-of-state wineries constitutes explicit discrimination against interstate commerce.

This discrimination substantially limits the direct sale of wine to consumers, an otherwise emerging and significant business. . . . From 1994 to 1999, consumer spending on direct wine shipments doubled, reaching $500 million per year, or three percent of all wine sales. . . . The increasing winery-to-wholesaler ratio means that many small wineries do not produce enough wine or have sufficient consumer demand for their wine to make it economical for wholesalers to carry their products. . . . This has led many small wineries to rely on direct shipping to reach new markets. Technological improvements, in particular the ability of wineries to sell wine over the Internet, have helped make direct shipments an attractive sales channel.

Approximately 26 States allow some direct shipping of wine, with various restrictions. Thirteen of these States have reciprocity laws, which allow direct shipment from wineries outside the State, provided the State of origin affords similar nondiscriminatory treatment. . . . In many parts of the country, however, state laws that prohibit or severely restrict direct shipments deprive consumers of access to the direct market. . . .

The wine producers in the cases before us are small wineries that rely on direct consumer sales as an important part of their businesses. Domaine Alfred, one of the plaintiffs in the Michigan suit, is a small winery located in San Luis Obispo, California. It produces 3,000 cases of wine per year. Domaine Alfred has received requests for its wine from Michigan consumers but cannot fill the orders because of the State's direct-shipment ban. Even if the winery could find a Michigan wholesaler to distribute its wine, the wholesaler's markup would render shipment through the three-tier system economically infeasible.

Similarly, Juanita Swedenburg and David Lucas, two of the plaintiffs in the New York suit, operate small wineries in Virginia (the Swedenburg Estate Vineyard) and California (the Lucas Winery). Some of their customers are tourists, from other States, who purchase wine while visiting the wineries. If these customers wish to obtain Swedenburg or Lucas wines after they return home, they will be unable to do so if they reside in a State with restrictive direct-shipment laws. For example, Swedenburg and Lucas are unable to fill orders from New York, the Nation's second-largest wine market, because of the limits that State imposes on direct wine shipments.

A

We first address the background of the suit challenging the Michigan direct-shipment law. Most alcoholic beverages in Michigan are distributed through the State's three-tier system. Producers or distillers of alcoholic beverages, whether located in state or out of state, generally may sell only to licensed in-state wholesalers. . . . Wholesalers, in turn, may sell only to in-state retailers. . . . Licensed retailers are the final link in the chain, selling alcoholic beverages to consumers at retail locations and, subject to certain restrictions, through home delivery. . . .

Under Michigan law, wine producers, as a general matter, must distribute their wine through wholesalers. There is, however, an exception for Michigan's approximately 40 in-state wineries, which are eligible for "wine maker" licenses that allow direct shipment to in-state consumers. . . . The cost of the license varies with the size of the winery. For a small winery, the license is $25. . . . Out-of-state wineries can apply for a $300 "outside seller of wine" license, but this license only allows them to sell to in-state wholesalers.

Some Michigan residents brought suit against various state officials in the United States District Court for the Eastern District of Michigan. Domaine Alfred, the San Luis Obispo winery, joined in the suit. The plaintiffs contended that Michigan's direct-shipment laws discriminated against interstate commerce in violation of the Commerce Clause. The trade association Michigan Beer & Wine Wholesalers intervened as a defendant. Both the State and the wholesalers argued that the ban on direct shipment from out-of-state wineries is a valid exercise of Michigan's power under § 2 of the Twenty-first Amendment.

On cross-motions for summary judgment the District Court sustained the Michigan scheme. The Court of Appeals for the Sixth Circuit reversed. *Heald v. Engler*, 342 F.3d 517 (2003). Relying on *Bacchus Imports, Ltd. v.*

Dias, 468 U.S. 263 (1984), the court rejected the argument that the Twenty-first Amendment immunizes all state liquor laws from the strictures of the Commerce Clause, . . . and held the Michigan scheme was unconstitutional because the defendants failed to demonstrate the State could not meet its proffered policy objectives through nondiscriminatory means. . . .

B

New York's licensing scheme is somewhat different. It channels most wine sales through the three-tier system, but it too makes exceptions for in-state wineries. As in Michigan, the result is to allow local wineries to make direct sales to consumers in New York on terms not available to out-of-state wineries. Wineries that produce wine only from New York grapes can apply for a license that allows direct shipment to in-state consumers. . . . These licensees are authorized to deliver the wines of other wineries as well . . . but only if the wine is made from grapes "at least seventy-five percent the volume of which were grown in New York state". . . . An out-of-state winery may ship directly to New York consumers only if it becomes a licensed New York winery, which requires the establishment of "a branch factory, office or storeroom within the state of New York." . . .

Juanita Swedenburg and David Lucas, joined by three of their New York customers, brought suit in the Southern District of New York against the officials responsible for administering New York's Alcoholic Beverage Control Law seeking, *inter alia*, a declaration that the State's limitations on the direct shipment of out-of-state wine violate the Commerce Clause. New York liquor wholesalers and representatives of New York liquor retailers intervened in support of the State.

The District Court granted summary judgment to the plaintiffs. 232 F. Supp. 2d 135 (2002). The court first determined that, under established Commerce Clause principles, the New York direct-shipment scheme discriminates against out-of-state wineries. . . . The court then rejected the State's Twenty-first Amendment argument, finding that the "[d]efendants have not shown that New York's ban on the direct shipment of out-of-state wine, and particularly the in-state exceptions to the ban, implicate the State's core concerns under the Twenty-first Amendment." . . .

The Court of Appeals for the Second Circuit reversed. 358 F.3d 223 (2004). The court "recognize[d] that the physical presence requirement could create substantial dormant Commerce Clause problems if this licensing scheme regulated a commodity other than alcohol." . . . The court nevertheless sustained the New York statutory scheme because, in the court's view, "New York's desire to ensure accountability through presence is aimed at the regulatory interests directly tied to the importation and transportation of alcohol for use in New York" . . . As such, the New York direct shipment laws were "within the ambit of the powers granted to states by the Twenty-first Amendment." . . .

C

We consolidated these cases and granted certiorari on the following question: " 'Does a State's regulatory scheme that permits in-state wineries directly to ship alcohol to consumers but restricts the ability of out-of-state wineries to do so violate the dormant Commerce Clause in light of § 2 of the Twenty-first Amendment?' " 541 U.S. 1062 (2004).

For ease of exposition, we refer to the respondents from the Michigan challenge . . . and the petitioners in the New York challenge . . . collectively as the wineries. We refer to their opposing parties — Michigan, New York, and the wholesalers and retailers — simply as the States.

II

A

Time and again this Court has held that, in all but the narrowest circumstances, state laws violate the Commerce Clause if they mandate "differential treatment of in-state and out-of-state economic interests that benefits the former and burdens the latter." *Oregon Waste Systems, Inc. v. Department of Environmental Quality of Ore.*, 511 U.S. 93, 99 (1994). . . . The mere fact of nonresidence should not foreclose a producer in one State from access to markets in other States. *H.P. Hood & Sons, Inc. v. Du Mond*, 336 U.S. 525, 539(1949). States may not enact laws that burden out-of-state producers or shippers simply to give a competitive advantage to in-state businesses. This mandate "reflect[s] a central concern of the Framers that was an immediate reason for calling the Constitutional Convention: the conviction that in order to succeed, the new Union would have to avoid the tendencies toward economic Balkanization that had plagued relations among the Colonies and later among the States under the Articles of Confederation." *Hughes v. Oklahoma*, 441 U.S. 322, 325-326 (1979).

The rule prohibiting state discrimination against interstate commerce follows also from the principle that States should not be compelled to negotiate with each other regarding favored or disfavored status for their own citizens. States do not need, and may not attempt, to negotiate with other States regarding their mutual economic interests. Cf. U.S. Const., Art. I, § 10, cl. 3. Rivalries among the States are thus kept to a minimum, and a proliferation of trade zones is prevented. *See C & A Carbone, Inc. v. Clarkstown*, 511 U.S. 383, 390 (1994) (citing The Federalist No. 22, pp. 143-145 (C. Rossiter ed. 1961) (A.Hamilton). . . .

Laws of the type at issue in the instant cases contradict these principles. They deprive citizens of their right to have access to the markets of other States on equal terms. The perceived necessity for reciprocal sale privileges risks generating the trade rivalries and animosities, the alliances and exclusivity, that the Constitution and, in particular, the Commerce Clause were designed to avoid. State laws that protect local wineries have led to the enactment of statutes under which some States condition the right of out-of-state wineries to make direct wine sales to in-state consumers on a reciprocal right in the shipping State. California, for example, passed a reciprocity law in 1986, retreating from the State's previous regime that allowed unfettered direct shipments from out-of-state wineries. . . . Prior to 1986, all but three States prohibited direct-shipments of wine. The obvious aim of the California statute was to open the interstate direct-shipping market for the State's many wineries. The current patchwork of laws — with some States banning direct shipments altogether, others doing so only for out-of-state wines, and still others requiring reciprocity — is essentially the product of an ongoing, low-level trade war. Allowing States to discriminate against out-of-state wine "invite [s] a multiplication of preferential trade areas destructive of the very purpose of the Commerce Clause." *Dean Milk Co. v. Madison,* 340 U.S. 349, 356 (1951). . . .

B

The discriminatory character of the Michigan system is obvious. Michigan allows in-state wineries to ship directly to consumers, subject only to a licensing requirement. Out-of-state wineries, whether licensed or not, face a complete ban on direct shipment. The differential treatment requires all out-of-state wine, but not all in-state wine, to pass through an in-state wholesaler and retailer before reaching consumers. These two extra layers of overhead increase the cost of out-of-state wines to Michigan consumers. The cost differential, and in some cases the inability to secure a wholesaler for small shipments, can effectively bar small wineries from the Michigan market.

The New York regulatory scheme differs from Michigan's in that it does not ban direct shipments altogether. Out-of-state wineries are instead required to establish a distribution operation in New York in order to gain the privilege of direct shipment. . . . This, though, is just an indirect way of subjecting out-of-state wineries, but not local ones, to the three-tier system. New York and those allied with its interests defend the scheme by arguing that an out-of-state winery has the same access to the State's consumers as in-state wineries: All wine must be sold through a licensee fully accountable to New York; it just so happens that in order to become a licensee, a winery must have a physical presence in the State. . . .

The New York scheme grants in-state wineries access to the State's consumers on preferential terms. The suggestion of a limited exception for direct shipment from out-of-state wineries does nothing to eliminate the discriminatory nature of New York's regulations. In-state producers, with the applicable licenses, can ship directly to consumers from their wineries. . . . Out-of-state wineries must open a branch office and warehouse in New York, additional steps that drive up the cost of their wine. . . . For most wineries, the expense of establishing a bricks-and-mortar distribution operation in 1 State, let alone all 50, is prohibitive. It comes as no surprise that not a single out-of-state winery has availed itself of New York's direct-shipping privilege. We have "viewed with particular suspicion state statutes requiring business operations to be performed in the home State that could more efficiently be performed elsewhere." *Pike v. Bruce Church, Inc.,* 397 U.S. 137, 145 (1970). New York's in-state presence requirement runs contrary to our admonition that States cannot require an out-of-state firm "to become a resident in order to compete on equal terms." *Halliburton Oil Well Cementing Co. v. Reily,* 373 U.S. 64, 72 (1963). . . .

In addition to its restrictive in-state presence requirement, New York discriminates against out-of-state wineries in other ways. Out-of-state wineries that establish the requisite branch office and warehouse in New York are still ineligible for a "farm winery" license, the license that provides the most direct means of shipping to New York consumers. . . . Out-of-state wineries may apply only for a commercial winery license. . . . Unlike farm wineries, however, commercial wineries must obtain a separate certificate from the state liquor authority authorizing direct shipments to consumers; and, of course, for out-of-state wineries there is the additional requirement of maintaining a distribution operation in New York. New York law also allows in-state wineries without direct-shipping licenses to distribute their wine through other wineries that have the applicable licenses. . . . This is another privilege not afforded out-of-state wineries.

We have no difficulty concluding that New York, like Michigan, discriminates against interstate commerce through its direct-shipping laws.

III

State laws that discriminate against interstate commerce face "a virtually *per se* rule of invalidity." *Philadelphia v. New Jersey,* 437 U.S. 617, 624 (1978). The Michigan and New York laws by their own terms violate this proscription. The two States, however, contend their statutes are saved by § 2 of the Twenty-first Amendment, which provides:

> The transportation or importation into any State, Territory, or possession of the United States for delivery or use therein of intoxicating liquors, in violation of the laws thereof, is hereby prohibited.

The States' position is inconsistent with our precedents and with the Twenty-first Amendment's history. Section 2 does not allow States to regulate the direct shipment of wine on terms that discriminate in favor of in-state producers.

A

Before 1919, the temperance movement fought to curb the sale of alcoholic beverages one State at a time. The movement made progress, and many States passed laws restricting or prohibiting the sale of alcohol. This Court upheld state laws banning the production and sale of alcoholic beverages, *Mugler v. Kansas,* 123 U.S. 623 (1887), but was less solicitous of laws aimed at imports. In a series of cases before ratification of the

Eighteenth Amendment the Court, relying on the Commerce Clause, invalidated a number of state liquor regulations.

These cases advanced two distinct principles. First, the Court held that the Commerce Clause prevented States from discriminating against imported liquor. *Scott v. Donald*, 165 U.S. 58 (1897); *Walling v. Michigan,* 116 U.S. 446 (1886). . . . In *Walling*, for example, the Court invalidated a Michigan tax that discriminated against liquor imports by exempting sales of local products. The Court held that States were not free to pass laws burdening only out-of-state products[.] . . .

Second, the Court held that the Commerce Clause prevented States from passing facially neutral laws that placed an impermissible burden on interstate commerce. . . . For example, in *Bowman v. Chicago & Northwestern R. Co.*, 125 U.S. 465 (1888), the Court struck down an Iowa statute that required all liquor importers to have a permit. *Bowman* and its progeny rested in part on the since-rejected original-package doctrine. Under this doctrine goods shipped in interstate commerce were immune from state regulation while in their original package. . . . *Bowman* reserved the question whether a State could ban the sale of imported liquor altogether. . . . Iowa responded to *Bowman* by doing just that but was thwarted once again. In *Leisy [v. Hardin*, 135 U.S. 100 (1890)], the Court held that Iowa could not ban the sale of imported liquor in its original package.

Leisy left the States in a bind. They could ban the production of domestic liquor, *Mugler, supra*, but these laws were ineffective because out-of-state liquor was immune from any state regulation as long as it remained in its original package. . . . To resolve the matter, Congress passed the Wilson Act (so named for Senator Wilson of Iowa), which empowered the States to regulate imported liquor on the same terms as domestic liquor[.] . . .

By its own terms, the Wilson Act did not allow States to discriminate against out-of-state liquor; rather, it allowed States to regulate imported liquor only "to the same extent and in the same manner" as domestic liquor. . . .

The Wilson Act reaffirmed, and the Webb-Kenyon Act did not displace, the Court's line of Commerce Clause cases striking down state laws that discriminated against liquor produced out of state. . . . States were required to regulate domestic and imported liquor on equal terms. . . .

B

The ratification of the Eighteenth Amendment in 1919 provided a brief respite from the legal battles over the validity of state liquor regulations. With the ratification of the Twenty-first Amendment 14 years later, however, nationwide Prohibition came to an end. Section 1 of the Twenty-first Amendment repealed the Eighteenth Amendment. Section 2 of the Twenty-first Amendment is at issue here.

Michigan and New York say the provision grants to the States the authority to discriminate against out-of-state goods. The history we have recited does not support this position. To the contrary, it provides strong support for the view that § 2 restored to the States the powers they had under the Wilson and Webb-Kenyon Acts. "The wording of § 2 of the Twenty-first Amendment closely follows the Webb-Kenyon and Wilson Acts, expressing the framers' clear intention of constitutionalizing the Commerce Clause framework established under those statutes." *Craig v. Boren*, 429 U.S. 190, 205-206 (1976).

The aim of the Twenty-first Amendment was to allow States to maintain an effective and uniform system for controlling liquor by regulating its transportation, importation, and use. The Amendment did not give States the authority to pass nonuniform laws in order to discriminate against out-of-state goods, a privilege they had not enjoyed at any earlier time. . . .

Our more recent cases, furthermore, confirm that the Twenty-first Amendment does not supersede other provisions of the Constitution and, in particular, does not displace the rule that States may not give a discriminatory preference to their own producers.

C

The modern § 2 cases fall into three categories.

First, the Court has held that state laws that violate other provisions of the Constitution are not saved by the Twenty-first Amendment. The Court has applied this rule in the context of the First Amendment, . . . the Establishment Clause, . . . the Equal Protection Clause, . . . the Due Process Clause, . . . and the Import-Export Clause. . . . Second, the Court has held that § 2 does not abrogate Congress' Commerce Clause powers with regard to liquor. . . . Finally, and most relevant to the issue at hand, the Court has held that state regulation of alcohol is limited by the nondiscrimination principle of the Commerce Clause. . . . "When a state statute directly regulates or discriminates against interstate commerce, or when its effect is to favor in-state economic interests over out-of-state interests, we have generally struck down the statute without further inquiry." *Brown-Forman Distillers Corp. v. New York State Liquor Authority*, 476 U.S. 573, 579 (1986).

Bacchus provides a particularly telling example of this proposition. At issue was an excise tax enacted by Hawaii that exempted certain alcoholic beverages produced in that State. The Court rejected the argument that Hawaii's discrimination against out-of-state liquor was authorized by the Twenty-first Amendment. . . . "The central purpose of the [Amendment] was not to empower States to favor local liquor industries by erecting barriers to competition.". . . Despite attempts to distinguish it in the instant cases, *Bacchus* forecloses any contention that § 2 of the Twenty-first Amendment immunizes discriminatory direct-shipment laws from Commerce Clause scrutiny. . . . Recognizing that *Bacchus* is fatal to their position, the States suggest it should be overruled or limited to its facts. As the foregoing analysis makes clear, we decline their invitation. . . .

The States argue that any decision invalidating their direct-shipment laws would call into question the constitutionality of the three-tier system. This does not follow from our holding. "The Twenty-first Amendment grants the States virtually complete control over whether to permit importation or sale of liquor and how to structure the liquor distribution system." . . . A State which chooses to ban the sale and consumption of alcohol altogether could bar its importation; and, as our history shows, it would have to do so to make its laws effective. States may also assume direct control of liquor distribution through state-run outlets or funnel sales through the three-tier system. We have previously recognized that the three-tier system itself is "unquestionably legitimate." . . . State policies are protected under the Twenty-first Amendment when they treat liquor produced out of state the same as its domestic equivalent. The instant cases, in contrast, involve straightforward attempts to discriminate in favor of local producers. The discrimination is contrary to the Commerce Clause and is not saved by the Twenty-first Amendment.

IV

Our determination that the Michigan and New York direct-shipment laws are not authorized by the Twenty-first Amendment does not end the inquiry. We still must consider whether either State regime "advances a legitimate local purpose that cannot be adequately served by reasonable nondiscriminatory alternatives." . . . The States offer two primary justifications for restricting direct shipments from out-of-state wineries: keeping alcohol out of the hands of minors and facilitating tax collection. We consider each in turn.

The States, . . . claim that allowing direct shipment from out-of-state wineries undermines their ability to police underage drinking. Minors, the States argue, have easy access to credit cards and the Internet and are likely to take advantage of direct wine shipments as a means of obtaining alcohol illegally.

The States provide little evidence that the purchase of wine over the Internet by minors is a problem. Indeed, there is some evidence to the contrary. . . . Without concrete evidence that direct shipping of wine is likely to increase alcohol consumption by minors, we are left with the States' unsupported assertions. Under our precedents, which require the "clearest showing" to justify discriminatory state regulation, *C & A Carbone, Inc.*, 511 U.S., at 393, this is not enough.

Even were we to credit the States' largely unsupported claim that direct shipping of wine increases the risk of underage drinking, this would not justify regulations limiting only out-of-state direct shipments. As the wineries point out, minors are just as likely to order wine from in-state producers as from out-of-state ones. Michigan, for example, already allows its licensed retailers (over 7,000 of them) to deliver alcohol directly to consumers. . . .

The States' tax-collection justification is also insufficient. Increased direct shipping, whether originating in state or out of state, brings with it the potential for tax evasion. With regard to Michigan, however, the tax-collection argument is a diversion. That is because Michigan, unlike many other States, does not rely on wholesalers to collect taxes on wines imported from out-of-state. Instead, Michigan collects taxes directly from out-of-state wineries on all wine shipped to in-state wholesalers. . . . If licensing and self-reporting provide adequate safeguards for wine distributed through the three-tier system, there is no reason to believe they will not suffice for direct shipments.

New York and its supporting parties also advance a tax-collection justification for the State's direct-shipment laws. While their concerns are not wholly illusory, their regulatory objectives can be achieved without discriminating against interstate commerce. In particular, New York could protect itself against lost tax revenue by requiring a permit as a condition of direct shipping. This is the approach taken by New York for in-state wineries. The State offers no reason to believe the system would prove ineffective for out-of-state wineries. Licensees could be required to submit regular sales reports and to remit taxes. Indeed, various States use this approach for taxing direct interstate wine shipments. . . . The States have not shown that tax evasion from out-of-state wineries poses such a unique threat that it justifies their discriminatory regimes.

. . . Finally, it should be noted that improvements in technology have eased the burden of monitoring out-of-state wineries. Background checks can be done electronically. Financial records and sales data can be mailed, faxed, or submitted via e-mail.

In summary, the States provide little concrete evidence for the sweeping assertion that they cannot police direct shipments by out-of-state wineries. Our Commerce Clause cases demand more than mere speculation to support discrimination against out-of-state goods. The "burden is on the State to show that 'the *discrimination* is demonstrably justified,'" *Chemical Waste Management, Inc. v. Hunt*, 504 U.S. 334, 344 (1992). The Court has upheld state regulations that discriminate against interstate commerce only after finding, based on concrete record evidence, that a State's nondiscriminatory alternatives will prove unworkable. *See, e.g., Maine v. Taylor*, 477 U.S. 131, 141-144 (1986). Michigan and New York have not satisfied this exacting standard.

V

States have broad power to regulate liquor under § 2 of the Twenty-first Amendment. This power, however, does not allow States to ban, or severely limit, the direct shipment of out-of-state wine while simultaneously authorizing direct shipment by in-state producers. If a State chooses to allow direct shipment of wine, it must do so on evenhanded terms. Without demonstrating the need for discrimination, New York and Michigan have enacted regulations that disadvantage out-of-state wine producers. Under our Commerce Clause jurisprudence, these regulations cannot stand.

We affirm the judgment of the Court of Appeals for the Sixth Circuit; and we reverse the judgment of the Court of Appeals for the Second Circuit and remand the case for further proceedings consistent with our opinion.

It is so ordered.

Justice STEVENS, with whom Justice O'CONNOR joins, dissenting.

Congress' power to regulate commerce among the States includes the power to authorize the States to place burdens on interstate commerce. *Prudential Ins. Co. v. Benjamin*, 328 U.S. 408 (1946). Absent such congressional approval, a state law may violate the unwritten rules described as the "dormant Commerce Clause" either by imposing an undue burden on both out-of-state and local producers engaged in interstate activities or by treating out-of-state producers less favorably than their local competitors. . . . A state law totally prohibiting the sale of an ordinary article of commerce might impose an even more serious burden on interstate commerce. If Congress may nevertheless authorize the States to enact such laws, surely the people may do so through the process of amending our Constitution.

The New York and Michigan laws challenged in these cases would be patently invalid under well settled dormant Commerce Clause principles if they regulated sales of an ordinary article of commerce rather than wine. But ever since the adoption of the Eighteenth Amendment and the Twenty-first Amendment, our Constitution has placed commerce in alcoholic beverages in a special category. Section 2 of the Twenty-first Amendment expressly provides that "[t]he transportation or importation into any State, Territory, or possession of the United States for delivery or use therein of intoxicating liquors, in violation of the laws thereof, is hereby prohibited." . . .

The views of judges who lived through the debates that led to the ratification of those Amendments are entitled to special deference. Foremost among them was Justice Brandeis, whose understanding of a State's right to discriminate in its regulation of out-of-state alcohol could not have been clearer:

> The plaintiffs ask us to limit [§ 2's] broad command. They request us to construe the Amendment as saying, in effect: The State may prohibit the importation of intoxicating liquors provided it prohibits the manufacture and sale within its borders; but if it permits such manufacture and sale, it must let imported liquors compete with the domestic on equal terms. To say that, would involve not a construction of the Amendment, but a rewriting of it . . . . Can it be doubted that a State might establish a state monopoly of the manufacture and sale of beer, and either prohibit all competing importations, or discourage importation by laying a heavy impost, or channelize desired importations by confining them to a single

consignee? *State Bd. of Equalization of Cal. v. Young's Market Co.*, 299 U.S. 59, 62-63 (1936).[2]

In the years following the ratification of the Twenty-first Amendment, States adopted manifold laws regulating commerce in alcohol, and many of these laws were discriminatory. So-called "dry states" entirely prohibited such commerce; others prohibited the sale of alcohol on Sundays; others permitted the sale of beer and wine but not hard liquor; most created either state monopolies or distribution systems that gave discriminatory preferences to local retailers and distributors. The notion that discriminatory state laws violated the unwritten prohibition against balkanizing the American economy — while persuasive in contemporary times when alcohol is viewed as an ordinary article of commerce — would have seemed strange indeed to the millions of Americans who condemned the use of the "demon rum" in the 1920's and 1930's. Indeed, they expressly authorized the "balkanization" that today's decision condemns. Today's decision may represent sound economic policy and may be consistent with the policy choices of the contemporaries of Adam Smith who drafted our original Constitution; it is not, however, consistent with the policy choices made by those who amended our Constitution in 1919 and 1933.

. . . Indeed, the fact that the Twenty-first Amendment was the only Amendment in our history to have been ratified by the people in state conventions, rather than by state legislatures, provides further reason to give its terms their ordinary meaning. Because the New York and Michigan laws regulate the "transportation or importation" of "intoxicating liquors" for "delivery or use therein," they are exempt from dormant Commerce Clause scrutiny.

As Justice THOMAS has demonstrated, the text of the Twenty-first Amendment is a far more reliable guide to its meaning than the unwritten rules that the majority enforces today. I therefore join his persuasive and comprehensive dissenting opinion.

Justice THOMAS, with whom THE CHIEF JUSTICE, Justice STEVENS, and Justice O'CONNOR join, dissenting.

A century ago, this Court repeatedly invalidated, as inconsistent with the negative Commerce Clause, state liquor legislation that prevented out-of-state businesses from shipping liquor directly to a State's residents. The Webb-Kenyon Act and the Twenty-first Amendment cut off this intrusive review, as their text and history make clear and as this Court's early cases on the Twenty-first Amendment recognized. The Court today seizes back this power, based primarily on a historical argument that this Court decisively rejected long ago in *State Bd. of Equalization of Cal. v. Young's Market Co.*, 299 U.S. 59, 64 (1936). Because I would follow *Young's Market* and the language of both the statute that Congress enacted and the

---

[2] According to Justice Black, who participated in the passage of the Twenty-first Amendment in the Senate, § 2 was intended to return " 'absolute control' of liquor traffic to the States, free of all restrictions which the Commerce Clause might before that time have imposed." *Hostetter v. Idlewild Bon Voyage Liquor Corp.*, 377 U.S. 324, 338 (1964) (dissenting opinion).

Amendment that the Nation ratified, rather than the Court's questionable reading of history and the "negative implications" of the Commerce Clause, I respectfully dissent.

I

The Court devotes much attention to the Twenty-first Amendment, yet little to the terms of the Webb-Kenyon Act. This is a mistake, because that Act's language displaces any negative Commerce Clause barrier to state regulation of liquor sales to in-state consumers.

A

The Webb-Kenyon Act immunizes from negative Commerce Clause review the state liquor laws that the Court holds are unconstitutional. The Act "prohibit[s]" any "shipment or transportation" of alcoholic beverages "into any State" when those beverages are "intended, by any person interested therein, to be received, possessed, sold, or in any manner used . . . in violation of any law of such State." State laws that regulate liquor imports in the manner described by the Act are exempt from judicial scrutiny under the negative Commerce Clause, as this Court has long held. . . .

The Michigan and New York direct-shipment laws are within the Webb-Kenyon Act's terms and therefore do not run afoul of the negative Commerce Clause. Those laws restrict out-of-state wineries from shipping and selling wine directly to Michigan and New York consumers. . . . Any winery that ships wine directly to a Michigan or New York consumer in violation of those state-law restrictions is a "person interested therein" "intend[ing]" to "s[ell]" wine "in violation of" Michigan and New York law, and thus comes within the terms of the Webb-Kenyon Act. . . .

II

There is no need to interpret the Twenty-first Amendment, because the Webb-Kenyon Act resolves these cases. However, the state laws the Court strikes down are lawful under the plain meaning of § 2 of the Twenty-first Amendment, as this Court's case law in the wake of the Amendment and the contemporaneous practice of the States reinforce.

A

Section 2 of the Twenty-first Amendment provides: "The transportation or importation into any State, Territory, or possession of the United States for delivery or use therein of intoxicating liquors, in violation of the laws thereof, is hereby prohibited." As the Court notes, . . . this language tracked the Webb-Kenyon Act by authorizing state regulation that would otherwise conflict with the negative Commerce Clause. To remove any doubt regarding its broad scope, the Amendment simplified the language of the Webb-Kenyon Act and made clear that States could regulate importation destined for in-state delivery free of negative Commerce Clause restraints. Though the Twenty-first Amendment mirrors the basic terminology of the Webb-Kenyon Act, its language is broader, authorizing States to regulate all "transportation or importation" that runs afoul of state law. The broader language even more naturally encompasses discriminatory state laws. Its terms suggest, for example, that a State may ban imports entirely while leaving in-state liquor unregulated, for they do not condition the State's ability to prohibit imports on the manner in which state law treats domestic products.

The state laws at issue in these cases fall within § 2's broad terms. They prohibit wine manufacturers from "transport[ing] or import[ing]" wine directly to consumers in New York and Michigan "for delivery or use therein." Michigan law does so by requiring all out-of-state wine manufacturers to distribute wine through licensed in-state wholesalers. . . . New York law does so by prohibiting out-of-state wineries from shipping wine directly to consumers unless they establish an in-state physical presence, something that in-state wineries naturally have. . . . The Twenty-first Amendment prohibits out-of-state wineries from shipping wine into Michigan and New York in violation of these laws. In holding that the Constitution prohibits Michigan's and New York's laws, the majority turns the Amendment's text on its head.

The majority's holding is also at odds with this Court's early Twenty-first Amendment case law. In *Young's Market Co.*, this Court considered the constitutionality of a California law that facially discriminated against beer importers and, by extension, out-of-state producers. The California law required wholesalers to pay a special $500 license fee to import beer, in addition to the $50 fee California charged for wholesalers to distribute beer generally. . . . California law thus discriminated against out-of-state beer by charging wholesalers of imported beer 11 times the fee charged to wholesalers of domestic beer.

Young's Market held that this explicit discrimination against out-of-state beer products came within the terms of the Twenty-first Amendment, and therefore did not run afoul of the negative Commerce Clause. The Court reasoned that the Twenty-first Amendment's words are "apt to confer upon the State the power to forbid all importations which do not comply with the conditions which it prescribes." . . . The Court rejected the argument that a State "must let imported liquors compete with the domestic on equal terms," declaring that "[t]o say that, would involve not a construction of the Amendment, but a rewriting of it." . . . It recognized that a State could adopt a "discriminatory" regulation of out-of-state manufacturers as an incident to a "lesser degree of regulation than total prohibition," for example, by imposing "a state monopoly of the manufacture and sale of beer," or by "channel[ing] desired importations by confining them to a single consignee." . . . And far from "not consider [ing]" the historical argument that forms the core of the majority's reasoning, . . . *Young's Market* expressly rejected its relevance . . .

The plaintiffs in *Young's Market* advanced virtually the same historical argument the Court today accepts. . . . *Young's Market* properly reasoned that the text of our Constitution is the best guide to its meaning. That logic requires sustaining the state laws that the Court invalidates.

Young's Market was no outlier. The next Term, the Court upheld a Minnesota law that prohibited the importation of 50-proof liquor, concluding that "discrimination against imported liquor is permissible." *Mahoney v. Joseph Triner Corp.*, 304 U.S. 401, 403 (1938). One Term after that, the Court upheld two state laws that prohibited the importation of liquor from States that discriminated against domestic liquor. *See Indianapolis Brewing Co. v. Liquor Control Comm'n*, 305 U.S. 391, 394 (1939) (noting that the Twenty-first Amendment permitted States to "discriminat[e] between domestic and imported intoxicating liquors"); *Joseph S. Finch & Co. v. McKittrick*, 305 U.S. 395, 398 (1939). In sum, the Court recognized from the start that "[t]he Twenty-first Amendment sanctions the right of a State to legislate concerning intoxicating liquors brought from without, unfettered by the Commerce Clause." *Ziffrin, Inc. v. Reeves*, 308 U.S. 132, 138 (1939). . . .

B

The widespread, unquestioned acceptance of the three-tier system of liquor regulation, . . . and the contemporaneous practice of the States following the ratification of the Twenty-first Amendment confirm that the Amendment freed the States from negative Commerce Clause restraints on discriminatory regulation. Like the Webb-Kenyon Act, the Twenty-first Amendment was designed to remove any doubt regarding whether state monopoly and licensing schemes violated the Commerce Clause, as the majority properly acknowledges. . . . Accordingly, in response to the end of Prohibition, States that made liquor legal imposed either state monopoly systems, or licensing schemes strictly circumscribing the ability of private interests to sell and distribute liquor within state borders. . . . These liquor regulation schemes discriminated against out-of-state economic interests, just as Michigan's and New York's direct-shipment laws do. . . .

III

Though the majority dismisses this Court's early Twenty-first Amendment case law, it relies on the reasoning, if not the holdings, of our more recent Twenty-first Amendment cases. . . . But the Court's later cases do not require the result the majority reaches. Moreover, I would resolve any conflict in this Court's precedents in favor of those cases most contemporaneous with the ratification of the Twenty-first Amendment.

A

The test set forth in this Court's more recent Twenty-first Amendment cases shows that Michigan's and New York's direct-shipment laws are constitutional. In *Bacchus Imports, Ltd.* . . , this Court established a standard for determining when a discriminatory state liquor regulation is permissible under the Twenty-first Amendment. At issue in *Bacchus* was a Hawaii statute that imposed a 20 percent excise tax on liquor, but exempted certain locally produced products from the tax. The Court held that the Twenty-first Amendment did not save the discriminatory tax. The Court reasoned that the Twenty-first Amendment did not permit state laws that constituted "mere economic protectionism," because the Twenty-first Amendment's "central purpose . . . was not to empower States to favor local liquor industries by erecting barriers to competition." . . . The Court noted that the State did "not seek to justify its tax on the ground that it was designed to promote temperance or to carry out any other purpose of the Twenty-first Amendment, but instead acknowledg[ed] that the purpose was 'to promote a local industry.' " . . . The Court therefore struck down the tax, "because [it] violate[d] a central tenet of the Commerce Clause but [was] not supported by any clear concern of the Twenty-first Amendment." . . .

Michigan's and New York's direct-shipment laws are constitutional under *Bacchus*. Allowing States to regulate the direct shipment of liquor was of "clear concern" to the framers of the Webb-Kenyon Act and the Twenty-first Amendment. . . .

Moreover, if the three-tier liquor regulation system falls within the "core concerns" of the Twenty-first Amendment, then so do Michigan's and New York's direct-shipment laws. The same justifications for requiring wholesalers and retailers to be in-state businesses equally apply to Michigan's and New York's direct-shipment laws. For example, States require liquor to be shipped through in-state wholesalers because it is easier to regulate in-state wholesalers and retailers. State officials can better enforce their regulations by inspecting the premises and attaching the property of in-state entities; "[p]resence ensures accountability." . . . It is therefore understandable that the framers of the Twenty-first Amendment and the Webb-Kenyon Act would have wanted to free States to discriminate between in-state and out-of-state wholesalers and retailers, especially in the absence of the modern technological improvements and federal enforcement mechanisms that the Court argues now make regulating liquor easier. . . . Michigan's and New York's laws simply allow some in-state wineries to act as their own wholesalers and retailers in limited circumstances. If allowing a State to require all wholesalers and retailers to be in-state companies is a core concern of the Twenty-first Amendment, so is allowing a State to select only in-state manufacturers to ship directly to consumers, and therefore act, in effect, as their own wholesalers and retailers.

B

The Court places much weight upon the authority of *Bacchus*. . . . This is odd, because the Court does not even mention, let alone apply, the "core concerns" test that *Bacchus* established. The Court instead *sub silentio* casts aside that test, employing otherwise-applicable negative Commerce

Clause scrutiny and giving no weight to the Twenty-first Amendment and the Webb-Kenyon Act. . . . The Court therefore at least implicitly acknowledges the unprincipled nature of the test *Bacchus* established and the grave departure *Bacchus* was from this Court's precedents. . . . *Bacchus* should be overruled, not fortified with a textually and historically unjustified "nondiscrimination against products" test.

Bacchus' reasoning is unpersuasive. It swept aside the weighty authority of this Court's early Twenty-first Amendment case law, . . . because the *Bacchus* Court thought it " 'an absurd oversimplification' " to conclude that " 'the Twenty-first Amendment has somehow operated to "repeal" the Commerce Clause' " . . . . The Twenty-first Amendment did not impliedly repeal the Commerce Clause, but that does not justify *Bacchus'* narrowing of the Twenty-first Amendment to its "core concerns."

The Twenty-first Amendment's text has more modest effect than *Bacchus* supposed. Though its terms are broader than the Webb-Kenyon Act, the Twenty-first Amendment also parallels the Act's structure. In particular, the Twenty-first Amendment provides that any importation into a State contrary to state law violates the Constitution, just as the Webb-Kenyon Act provides that any such importation contrary to state law violates federal law. Its use of those same terms of art shows that just as the Webb-Kenyon Act repealed liquor's negative Commerce Clause immunity, the Twenty-first Amendment likewise insulates state liquor laws from negative Commerce Clause scrutiny. Authorizing States to regulate liquor importation free from negative Commerce Clause restraints is a far cry from precluding Congress from regulating in that field at all. . . . Moreover, *Bacchus'* concern that the Twenty-first Amendment repealed the Commerce Clause is no excuse for ignoring the independent force of the Webb-Kenyon Act, which equally divested discriminatory state liquor laws of Commerce Clause immunity.

Stripped of *Bacchus*, the Court's holding is bereft of support in our cases. *Bacchus* is the only decision of this Court holding that the Twenty-first Amendment does not authorize the in-state regulation of imported liquor free of the negative Commerce Clause. Given the uniformity of our early case law supporting even discriminatory state laws regulating imports into States, then, Michigan's and New York's laws easily pass muster under this Court's cases. . . .

IV

The Court begins its opinion by detailing the evils of state laws that restrict the direct shipment of wine. . . . The Court's focus on these effects suggests that it believes that its decision serves this Nation well. I am sure that the judges who repeatedly invalidated state liquor legislation, even in the face of clear congressional direction to the contrary, thought the same. . . . The Twenty-first Amendment and the Webb-Kenyon Act took those policy choices away from judges and returned them to the States. Whatever the wisdom of that choice, the Court does this Nation no service by ignoring the textual commands of the Constitution and Acts of Congress. The Twenty-first Amendment and the Webb-Kenyon Act displaced the negative Commerce Clause as applied to regulation of liquor imports into a State. They require sustaining the constitutionality of Michigan's and New York's direct-shipment laws. I respectfully dissent.

§ 4.07   Privileges and Immunities

Page 299: [Insert the following after Note (4)]

In *Hillside Dairy Inc. v. Lyons*, 539 U.S. 59 (2003), the Court considered whether California's milk pricing laws violated the Privileges and Immunities Clause of Art. IV even though they did not discriminate on their face against out-of-state citizens. The Court of Appeals for the Ninth Circuit had rejected the claims of individual dairy farmers from Nevada and Arizona that the Privileges and Immunities Clause was violated by a 1997 California provision requiring payments to a pool on certain out-of-state milk purchases. (Instate purchases of raw milk resold as fluid milk were already subject to such a requirement). The farmers argued that the holding conflicted with *Chalker v. Birmingham & Northwestern R. Co.*, 249 U.S. 522 (1919) which held unconstitutional a Tennessee tax which did not discriminate on its face against noncitizens but set a higher tax on persons with principal offices out-of-state. The Court, in *Hillside Dairy,* reversed. For a unanimous court, Justice Stevens wrote:

> Whether *Chalker* should be interpreted as merely applying the Clause to classifications that are but proxies for differential treatment against out-of-state residents, or as prohibiting any classification with the practical effect of discriminating against such residents, is a matter we need not decide at this stage of the case. Under either interpretation, we agree with petitioners that the absence of an express statement in the California laws and regulations identifying out-of-state citizenship as a basis for disparate treatment is not a sufficient basis for rejecting this claim. In so holding, however, we express no opinion on the merits of petitioners' Privileges and Immunities Clause claim.

539 U.S. at 67.

Chapter V

THE PRESIDENCY AND SEPARATION OF POWERS

Introduction

The tragic events of September 11, 2001 pushed new constitutional issues to the forefront of public discussion. Some of these relate to separation of powers generally and presidential power specifically. We are including some additional materials in this Chapter to allow fuller consideration of some of these current issues. We have included these materials in § 5.04 Foreign Affairs, casebook p. 371, but they may inform a discussion especially in connection with *Youngstown Sheet & Tube Co. v. Sawyer*, casebook, p. 301, or in connection with the materials dealing with Emergency Powers, casebook, p. 319, both in § 5.01 Inherent Power, p. 301.

§ 5.04   Foreign Affairs

[2]—Executive Agreements

Page 371: [Insert the following after Note (11)]

(12) In *American Insurance Association v. Garamendi*, 539 U.S. 396 (2003), the Court held, in a 5–4 decision, that California's Holocaust Victim Insurance Relief Act of 1999 (HIVRA) interfered with the Executive Branch's conduct of foreign policy and, accordingly, was preempted. President Clinton had entered into an executive agreement with Germany whereby Germany would create a fund and apparatus to pay some compensation to Holocaust survivors for the atrocities of the Nazi period. As part of the executive agreement, President Clinton agreed to take steps to dissuade American courts from entertaining such suits against Germany and German companies. HIVRA, however, required insurance companies doing business in California to disclose information regarding life insurance policies sold in Europe between 1920 and 1945.

Relying on past practice and precedents, the Court reasoned that the Executive Branch had broad power to set foreign policy. Prior decisions upheld the President's power to enter into executive agreements which preempted inconsistent state law, Justice Souter wrote for the Court.

Justice Ginsburg dissented in an opinion Justices Stevens, Scalia and Thomas joined. They argued that the executive agreement should not preempt California's law absent a clear statement by the President in the agreement against state disclosure laws.

§ 5.06   Commander-in-Chief

Page 375: [Insert after Note (12)]

EX PARTE MILLIGAN

71 U.S. (4 Wall.) 2, 18 L. Ed. 281 (1867)

MR. JUSTICE DAVIS delivered the opinion of the court.

[Editor's Note: On May 10, 1865, Lambdin P. Milligan petitioned the United States Circuit Court for the District of Indiana, to be discharged from an alleged unlawful imprisonment. He claimed he was a United States citizen who had lived for twenty years in Indiana who had never been in the United States military. He was arrested on October 5, 1864 and confined by order of General Alvin P. Hovey, commanding the military district of Indiana. A few weeks later, he was tried before a military commission at Indianapolis on certain charges, found guilty, and sentenced to be hanged on May 19, 1865. In January, 1865 a grand jury was empanelled by the United States Circuit Court for Indiana but returned no indictment or presentment against Milligan. Milligan argued that the military commission lacked jurisdiction to try him because he was a citizen of the United States and of Indiana, and had not been a resident of a confederate state and that the right of trial by jury was guaranteed to him by the Constitution of the United States.

He invoked the act of Congress of March 3d, 1863 relating to *habeas corpus* and asked to be proceeded against by the proper civil tribunal according to law or discharged from custody. The Circuit Court certified these questions to the Supreme Court:

"1st. 'On the facts stated in said petition and exhibits, ought a writ of *habeas corpus* to be issued?'

"2d. 'On the facts stated in said petition and exhibits, ought the said Lambdin P. Milligan to be discharged from custody as in said petition prayed?'

"3d. 'Whether, upon the facts stated in said petition and exhibits, the military commission mentioned therein had jurisdiction legally to try and sentence said Milligan in manner and form as in said petition and exhibits is stated?' "]

The importance of the main question presented by this record cannot be overstated; for it involves the very framework of the government and the fundamental principles of American liberty.

During the late wicked Rebellion, the temper of the times did not allow that calmness in deliberation and discussion so necessary to a correct conclusion of a purely judicial question. *Then*, considerations of safety were mingled with the exercise of power; and feelings and interests prevailed which are happily terminated. *Now* that the public safety is assured, this question, as well as all others, can be discussed and decided without passion or the admixture of any element not required to form a legal judgment. We approach the investigation of this case, fully sensible of the magnitude of the inquiry and the necessity of full and cautious deliberation.

. . . Milligan claimed his discharge from custody by virtue of the act of Congress 'relating to *habeas corpus*, and regulating judicial proceedings in certain cases,' approved March 3d, 1863. Did that act confer jurisdiction on the Circuit Court of Indiana to hear this case?

In interpreting a law, the motives which must have operated with the legislature in passing it are proper to be considered. This law was passed in a time of great national peril, when our heritage of free government was in danger. . . . [T]he public safety required that the privilege of the writ of *habeas corpus* should be suspended. The President had practically suspended it, and detained suspected persons in custody without trial; but his authority to do this was questioned. It was claimed that Congress alone could exercise this power; and that the legislature, and not the President, should judge of the political considerations on which the right to suspend it rested. The privilege of this great writ had never before been withheld from the citizen; and as the exigence of the times demanded immediate action, it was of the highest importance that the lawfulness of the suspension should be fully established. It was under these circumstances, which were such as to arrest the attention of the country, that this law was passed. The President was authorized by it to suspend the privilege of the writ of *habeas corpus*, whenever, in his judgment, the public safety required; and he did, by proclamation, bearing date the 15th of September, 1863, reciting, among other things, the authority of this statute, suspend it. The suspension of the writ does not authorize the arrest of any one, but simply denies to one arrested the privilege of this writ in order to obtain his liberty.

It is proper, therefore, to inquire under what circumstances the courts could rightfully refuse to grant this writ, and when the citizen was at liberty to invoke its aid.

The second and third sections of the law are explicit on these points. The language used is plain and direct, and the meaning of the Congress cannot be mistaken. The public safety demanded, if the President thought proper to arrest a suspected person, that he should not be required to give the cause of his detention on return to a writ of *habeas corpus*. But it was not contemplated that such person should be detained in custody beyond a certain fixed period, unless certain judicial proceedings, known to the common law, were commenced against him. The Secretaries of State and War were directed to furnish to the judges of the courts of the United States, a list of the names of all parties, not prisoners of war, resident in their respective jurisdictions, who then were or afterwards should be held in custody by the authority of the President, and who were citizens of states in which the administration of the laws in the Federal tribunals was unimpaired. After the list was furnished, if a grand jury of the district convened and adjourned, and did not indict or present one of the persons thus named, he was entitled to his discharge; and it was the duty of the judge of the court to order him brought before him to be discharged, if he desired it. . . .

Milligan, in his application to be released from imprisonment, averred the existence of every fact necessary under the terms of this law to give the Circuit Court of Indiana jurisdiction. . . .

[I]t is said that this case is ended, as the presumption is, that Milligan was hanged in pursuance of the order of the President.

Although we have no judicial information on the subject, yet the inference is that he is alive; for otherwise learned counsel would not appear for him and urge this court to decide his case. It can never be in this country of written constitution and laws, with a judicial department to interpret them, that any chief magistrate would be so far forgetful of his duty, as to order the execution of a man who denied the jurisdiction that tried and convicted him; *after* his case was before Federal judges with power to decide it, who, being unable to agree on the grave questions involved, had, according to known law, sent it to the Supreme Court of the United States for decision. But even the suggestion is injurious to the Executive, and we dismiss it from further consideration. There is, therefore, nothing to hinder this court from an investigation of the merits of this controversy.

The controlling question in the case is . . . had the military commission . . . *jurisdiction*, legally, to try and sentence him? Milligan, not a resident of one of the rebellious states, or a prisoner of war, but a citizen of Indiana for twenty years past, and never in the military or naval service, is, while at his home, arrested by the military power of the United States, imprisoned, and, on certain criminal charges preferred against him, tried, convicted, and sentenced to be hanged by a military commission, organized under the direction of the military commander of the military district of Indiana. . . .

No graver question was ever considered by this court, nor one which more nearly concerns the rights of the whole people; for it is the birthright of every American citizen when charged with crime, to be tried and punished according to law. The power of punishment is, alone through the means which the laws have provided for that purpose, and if they are ineffectual, there is an immunity from punishment, no matter how great an offender the individual may be, or how much his crimes may have shocked the sense of justice of the country, or endangered its safety. By the protection of the law human rights are secured; withdraw that protection, and they are at the mercy of wicked rulers, or the clamor of an excited people. If there was law to justify this military trial, it is not our province to interfere; if there was not, it is our duty to declare the nullity of the whole proceedings. The decision of this question does not depend on argument or judicial precedents, numerous and highly illustrative as they are. These precedents inform us of the extent of the struggle to preserve liberty and to relieve those in civil life from military trials. The founders of our government were familiar with the history of that struggle; and secured in a written constitution every right which the people had wrested from power during a contest of ages. By that Constitution and the laws authorized by it this question must be determined. . . .

Have any of the rights guaranteed by the Constitution been violated in the case of Milligan? and if so, what are they?

Every trial involves the exercise of judicial power; and from what source did not military commission that tried him derive their authority? Certainly no part of judicial power of the country was conferred on them; because the Constitution expressly vests it 'in one supreme court and such inferior courts as the Congress may from time to time ordain and establish,' and it is not pretended that the commission was a court ordained and established by Congress. They cannot justify on the mandate of the President; because he is controlled by law, and has his appropriate sphere of duty, which is to execute, not to make, the laws; and there is 'no unwritten criminal code to which resort can be had as a source of jurisdiction.'

But it is said that the jurisdiction is complete under the 'laws and usages of war.'

It can serve no useful purpose to inquire what those laws and usages are, whence they originated, where found, and on whom they operate; they can never be applied to citizens in states which have upheld the authority of the government, and where the courts are open and their process unobstructed. This court has judicial knowledge that in Indiana the Federal authority was always unopposed, and its courts always open to hear criminal accusations and redress grievances; and no usage of war could sanction a military trial there for any offerce whatever of a citizen in civil life, in nowise connected with the military service. Congress could grant no such power; and to the honor of our national legislature be it said, it has never been provoked by the state of the country even to attempt its exercise. One of the plainest constitutional provisions was, therefore, infringed when Milligan was tried by a court not ordained and established by Congress, and not composed of judges appointed during good behavior.

Why was he not delivered to the Circuit Court of Indiana to be proceeded against according to law? No reason of necessity could be urged against it; because Congress had declared penalties against the offences charged, provided for their punishment, and directed that court to hear and determine them. And soon after this military tribunal was ended, the Circuit Court met, peacefully transacted its business, and adjourned. . . . The government had no right to conclude that Milligan, if guilty, would not receive in that court merited punishment; for its records disclose that it was constantly engaged in the trial of similar offences, and was never interrupted in its administration of criminal justice. . . .

Another guarantee of freedom was broken when Milligan was denied a trial by jury. The great minds of the country have differed on the correct interpretation to be given to various provisions of the Federal Constitution; and judicial decision has been often invoked to settle their true meaning; but until recently no one ever doubted that the right of trial by jury was fortified in the organic law against the power of attack. It is *now* assailed; but if ideas can be expressed in words, and language has any meaning, *this right* — one of the most valuable in a free country — is preserved to every one accused of crime who is not attached to the army, or navy, or militia in actual service. The sixth amendment affirms that 'in all criminal prosecutions the accused shall enjoy the right to a speedy and public trial by an impartial jury,' language broad enough to embrace all persons and cases; but the fifth, recognizing the necessity of an indictment, or presentment, before any one can be held to answer for high crimes, '*excepts* cases arising in the land or naval forces, or in the militia, when in actual service, in time of war or public danger;' and the framers of the Constitution, doubtless, meant to limit the right of trial by jury, in the sixth amendment, to those persons who were subject to indictment or presentment in the fifth.

The discipline necessary to the efficiency of the army and navy, required other and swifter modes of trial than are furnished by the common law courts; and, in pursuance of the power conferred by the Constitution, Congress has declared the kinds of trial, and the manner in which they shall be conducted, for offences committed while the party is in the military or naval service. Every one connected with these branches of the public service is amenable to the jurisdiction which Congress has created for their government, and, while thus serving, surrenders his right to be tried by the civil courts. *All other persons*, citizens of states where the courts are open, if charged with crime, are guaranteed the inestimable privilege of trial by jury. This privilege is a vital principle, underlying the whole administration of criminal justice; it is not held by sufferance, and cannot be frittered away on any plea of state or political necessity. When peace prevails, and the authority of the government is undisputed, there is no difficulty of preserving the safeguards of liberty; for the ordinary modes of trial are never neglected, and no one wishes it otherwise; but if society is disturbed by civil commotion — if the passions of men are aroused and the restraints of law weakened, if not disregarded — these safeguards need, and should receive, the watchful care of those intrusted with the guardianship of the Constitution and laws. In no other way can we transmit to posterity unimpaired the blessings of liberty, consecrated by the sacrifices of the Revolution.

It is claimed that martial law covers with its broad mantle the proceedings of this military commission. The proposition is this: that in a time of war the commander of an armed force (if in his opinion the exigencies of the country demand it, and of which he is to judge), has the power, within the lines of his military district, to suspend all civil rights and their remedies, and subject citizens as well as soldiers to the rule of *his will;* and in the exercise of his lawful authority cannot be restrained, except by his superior officer or the President of the United States.

If this position is sound to the extent claimed, then when war exists, foreign or domestic, and the country is subdivided into military departments for mere convenience, the commander of one of them can, if he chooses, within his limits, on the plea of necessity, with the approval of the Executive, substitute military force for and to the exclusion of the laws, and punish all persons, as he thinks right and proper, without fixed or certain rules.

The statement of this proposition shows its importance; for, if true, republican government is a failure, and there is an end of liberty regulated by law. Martial law, established on such a basis, destroys every guarantee of the Constitution, and effectually renders the 'military independent of and superior to the civil power' — the attempt to do which by the King of Great Britain was deemed by our fathers such an offence, that they assigned it to the world as one of the causes which impelled them to declare their independence. Civil liberty and this kind of martial law cannot endure together; the antagonism is irreconcilable; and, in the conflict, one or the other must perish.

This nation, as experience has proved, cannot always remain at peace, and has no right to expect that it will always have wise and humane rulers, sincerely attached to the principles of the Constitution. Wicked men, ambitious of power, with hatred of liberty and contempt of law, may fill the place once occupied by Washington and Lincoln; and if this right is conceded, and the calamities of war again befall us, the dangers to human liberty are frightful to contemplate. If our fathers had failed to provide for just such a contingency, they would have been false to the trust reposed in them. They knew — the history of the world told them — the nation they were founding, be its existence short or long, would be involved in war; how often or how long continued, human foresight could not tell; and that unlimited power, wherever lodged at such a time, was especially hazardous to freemen. For this, and other equally weighty reasons, they secured the inheritance they had fought to maintain, by incorporating in a written constitution the safeguards which *time* had proved were essential to its preservation. Not one of these safeguards can the President, or Congress, or the Judiciary disturb, except the one concerning the writ of *habeas corpus*.

It is essential to the safety of every government that, in a great crisis, like the one we have just passed through, there should be a power somewhere of suspending the writ of *habeas corpus*. In every war, there are men of previously good character, wicked enough to counsel their fellow-citizens to resist the measures deemed necessary by a good government to sustain its just authority and overthrow its enemies; and their influence may lead to dangerous combinations. In the emergency of the times, an immediate public investigation according to law may not be possible; and yet, the period to the country may be too imminent to suffer such persons to go at large. Unquestionably, there is then an exigency which demands that the government, if it should see fit in the exercise of a proper discretion to make arrests, should not be required to produce the persons arrested in answer to a writ of *habeas corpus*. The Constitution goes no further. It does not say after a writ of *habeas corpus* is denied a citizen, that he shall be tried otherwise than by the course of the common law; if it had intended this result, it was easy by the use of direct words to have accomplished it. The illustrious men who framed that instrument were guarding the foundations of civil liberty against the abuses of unlimited power; they were full of wisdom, and the lessons of history informed them that a trial by an established court, assisted by an impartial jury, was the only sure way of protecting the citizen against oppression and wrong. Knowing this, they limited the suspension to one great right, and left the rest to remain forever inviolable. But, it is insisted that the safety of the country in time of war demands that this broad claim for martial law shall be sustained. If this were true, it could be well said that a country, preserved at the sacrifice of all the cardinal principles of liberty, is not worth the cost of preservation. Happily, it is not so.

It will be borne in mind that this is not a question of the power to proclaim martial law, when war exists in a community and the courts and civil authorities are overthrown. Nor is it a question what rule a military commander, at the head of his army, can impose on states in rebellion to cripple their resources and quell the insurrection. The jurisdiction claimed is much more extensive. The necessities of the service, during the late Rebellion, required that the loyal states should be placed within the limits of certain military districts and commanders appointed in them; and, it is urged, that this, in a military sense, constituted them the theater of military operations; and, as in this case, Indiana had been and was again threatened with invasion by the enemy, the occasion was furnished to establish martial law. The conclusion does not follow from the premises. If armies were collected in Indiana, they were to be employed in another locality, where the laws were obstructed and the national authority disputed. On *her* soil there was no hostile foot; if once invaded, that invasion was at an end, and with it all pretext for martial law. Martial law cannot arise from a *threatened* invasion. The necessity must be actual and present; the invasion real, such as effectually closes the courts and deposes the civil administration.

It is difficult to see how the *safety* for the country required martial law in Indiana. If any of her citizens were plotting treason, the power of arrest could secure them, until the government was prepared for their trial, when the courts were open and ready to try them. It was as easy to protect witnesses before a civil as a military tribunal; and as there could be no wish to convict, except on sufficient legal evidence, surely an ordained and establish court was better able to judge of this than a military tribunal composed of gentlemen not trained to the profession of the law.

It follows, from what has been said on this subject, that there are occasions when martial rule can be properly applied. If, in foreign invasion or civil war, the courts are actually closed, and it is impossible to administer criminal justice according to law, *then*, on the theatre of active military operations, where war really prevails, there is a necessity to furnish a substitute for the civil authority, thus overthrown, to preserve the safety of the army and society; and as no power is left but the military, it is allowed to govern by martial rule until the laws can have their free course. As necessity creates the rule, so it limits its duration; for, if this government is continued *after* the courts are reinstated, it is a gross usurpation of power. Martial rule can never exist where the courts are open, and in the proper and unobstructed exercise of their jurisdiction. It is also confined to the locality of actual war. . . . And so in the case of a foreign invasion, martial rule may become a necessity in one state, when, in another, it would be 'mere lawless violence.'

We are not without precedents in English and American history illustrating our views of this question; but it is hardly necessary to make particular reference to them. . . .

To the third question, then, on which the judges below were opposed in opinion, an answer in the negative must be returned. . . .

The two remaining questions in this case must be answered in the affirmative. The suspension of the privilege of the writ of *habeas corpus* does not suspend the writ itself. The writ issues as a matter of course; and on the return made to it the court decides whether the party applying is denied the right of proceeding any further with it.

If the military trial of Milligan was contrary to law, then he was entitled, on the facts stated in his petition, to be discharged from custody by the terms of the act of Congress of March 3d, 1863. . . .

But it is insisted that Milligan was a prisoner of war, and, therefore, excluded from the privileges of the statute. It is not easy to see how he can be treated as a prisoner of war, when he lived in Indiana for the past twenty years, was arrested there, and had not been, during the late troubles, a resident of any of the states in rebellion. If in Indiana he conspired with bad men to assist the enemy, he is punishable for it in the courts of Indiana; but, when tried for the offence, he cannot plead the rights of war; for he was not engaged in legal acts of hostility against the government, and only such persons, when captured, are prisoners of war. If he cannot enjoy the immunities attaching to the character of a prisoner of war, how can he be subject to their pains and penalties?

This case, as well as the kindred cases of Bowles and Horsey, were disposed of at the last term, and the proper orders were entered of record. There is, therefore, no additional entry required.

The CHIEF JUSTICE delivered the following opinion.

Four members of the court, concurring with their brethren in the order heretofore made in this cause, but unable to concur in some important particulares with the opinion which has just been read, think it their duty to make a separate statement of their views of the whole case.

We do not doubt that the Circuit Court for the District of Indiana had jurisdiction of the petition of Milligan for the writ of *habeas corpus* . . . .
It is clear . . . that the Circuit Court was bound to hear Milligan's petition

for the writ of *habeas corpus*, called in the act an order to bring the prisoner before the judge or the court, and to issue the writ, or, in the language of the act, to make the order. The first question, therefore — Ought the writ to issue? — must be answered in the affirmative.

And it is equally clear that he was entitled to the discharge prayed for. It must be borne in mind that the prayer of the petition was not for an absolute discharge, but to be delivered from military custody and imprisonment, and if found probably guilty of any offence, to be turned over to the proper tribunal for inquiry and punishment; or, if not found thus probably guilty, to be discharged altogether. . . .

That the third question, namely: Had the military commission in Indiana, under the facts stated, jurisdiction to try and sentence Milligan? must be answered negatively is an unavoidable inference from affirmative answers to the other two. . . .

But the opinion . . . as we understand it, asserts not only that the military commission held in Indiana was not authorized by Congress, but that it was not in the power of Congress to authorize it; from which it may be thought to follow, that Congress has no power to indemnify the officers who composed the commission against liability in civil courts for acting as members of it. We cannot agree to this.

We agree in the proposition that no department of the government of the United States — neither President, nor Congress, nor the Courts — possesses any power not given by the Constitution.

We assent, fully, to all that is said, in the opinion, of the inestimable value of the trial by jury, and of the other constitutional safeguards of civil liberty. And we concur, also, in what is said of the writ of *habeas corpus*, and of its suspension, with two reservations: (1.) That, in our judgment, when the writ is suspended, the Executive is authorized to arrest as well as to detain; and (2.) that there are cases in which, the privilege of the writ being suspended, trial and punishment by military commission, in states where civil courts are open, may be authorized by Congress, as well as arrest and detention.

We think that Congress had power, though not exercised, to authorize the military commission which was held in Indiana. . . . The Constitution itself provides for military government as well as for civil government. And we do not understand it to be claimed that the civil safeguards of the Constitution have application in cases within the proper sphere of the former. . . .

Congress has power to raise and support armies; to provide and maintain a navy; to make rules for the government and regulation of the land and naval forces; and to provide for governing such part of the militia as may be in the service of the United States.

It is not denied that the power to make rules for the government of the army and navy is a power to provide for trial and punishment by military courts without a jury. It has been so understood and exercised from the adoption of the Constitution to the present time. . . .

We think . . . that the power of Congress, in the government of the land and naval forces and of the militia, is not at all affected by the fifth or any other amendment. . . .

Congress has the power not only to raise and support and govern armies but to declare war. It has, therefore, the power to provide by law for carrying on war. This power necessarily extends to all legislation essential to the prosecution of war with vigor and success, except such as interferes with the command of the forces and the conduct of campaigns. That power and duty belong to the President as commander-in-chief. Both these powers are derived from the Constitution, but neither is defined by that instrument. Their extent must be determined by their nature, and by the principles of our institutions.

The power to make the necessary laws is in Congress; the power to execute in the President. Both powers imply many subordinate and auxiliary powers. Each includes all authorities essential to its due exercise. But neither can the President, in war more than in peace, intrude upon the proper authority of Congress, nor Congress upon the proper authority of the President. Both are servants of the people, whose will is expressed in the fundamental law. Congress cannot direct the conduct of campaigns, nor can the President, or any commander under him, without the sanction of Congress, institute tribunals for the trial and punishment of offences, either of soldiers or civilians, unless in cases of a controlling necessity, which justifies what it compels, or at least insures acts of indemnity from the justice of the legislature.

We by no means assert that Congress can establish and apply the laws of war where no war has been declared or exists. Where peace exists the laws of peace must prevail. What we do maintain is, that when the nation is involved in war, and some portions of the country are invaded, and all are exposed to invasion, it is within the power of Congress to determine in what states or district such great and imminent public danger exists as justifies the authorization of military tribunals for the trial of crimes and offences against the discipline or security of the army or against the public safety. . . .

We have confined ourselves to the question of power. It was for Congress to determine the question of expediency. And Congress did determine it. That body did not see fit to authorize trials by military commission in Indiana, but by the strongest implication prohibited them. . . .

We have thus far said little of martial law, nor do we propose to say much. What we have already said sufficiently indicates our opinion that there is no law for the government of the citizens, the armies or the navy of the United States, within American jurisdiction, which is not contained in or derived from the Constitution. And wherever our army or navy may go beyond our territorial limits, neither can go beyond the authority of the President or the legislation of Congress.

There are under the Constitution three kinds of military jurisdiction: one to be exercised both in peace and war; another to be exercised in time of foreign war without the boundaries of the United States, or in time of rebellion and civil war within states or districts occupied by rebels treated as belligerents; and a third to be exercised in time of invasion or insurrection within the limits of the United States, or during rebellion within the limits of states maintaining adhesion to the National Government, when the public danger requires its exercise. The first of these may be called jurisdiction under MILITARY LAW, and is found in acts of Congress prescribing rules and articles of war, or otherwise providing for the government of the national forces; the second may be distinguished as MILITARY GOVERNMENT, superseding, as far as may be deemed expedient, the local law, and exercised by the military commander under the direction of the President, with the express or implied sanction of Congress; while the third may be denominated MARTIAL LAW PROPER, and is called into action by Congress, or temporarily, when the action of Congress cannot be invited, and in the case of justifying or excusing peril, by the President, in times of insurrection or invasion, or of civil or foreign war, within districts or localities where ordinary law no longer adequately secures public safety and private rights.

We think that the power of Congress, in such times and in such localities, to authorize trials for crimes against the security and safety of the national forces, may be derived from its constitutional authority to raise and support armies and to declare war, if not from its constitutional authority to provide for governing the national forces.

We have no apprehension that this power, under our American system of government, in which all official authority is derived from the people, and exercised under direct responsibility to the people, is more likely to be abused than the power to regulate commerce, or the power to borrow money. And we are unwilling to give our assent by silence to expressions of opinion which seem to us calculated, though not intended, to cripple the constitutional powers of the government, and to augment the public dangers in times of invasion and rebellion.

MR. JUSTICE WAYNE, MR. JUSTICE SWAYNE, and MR. JUSTICE MILLER concur with me in these views.

NOTES

(1) Can the President suspend the writ of habeas corpus? The Suspension Clause ("The Privilege of the court of habeas corpus shall not be suspended, unless when in cases of rebellion or invasion the public safety require it") appears in Article I (Art. I § 9 cl. 2) of the Constitution, not in Article II. In *Ex parte Merryman*, 17 F. Cas. 144 (1861), Chief Justice Taney emphatically held that the President lacked power to suspend the writ. The President "does not faithfully execute the laws, if he takes upon himself legislative power, by suspending the writ of habeas corpus, and the judicial power also, by arresting and imprisoning a person without due process."

Id. at 149. Proclaiming that he had "exercised all the power with the constitution and laws confer upon me, but that power has been resisted by a force too strong for me to overcome," Chief Justice Taney directed that his order be sent to President Lincoln for his consideration.

(2) Justice Davis suggested in dicta that where "the courts are actually closed" due to "foreign invasion or civil war" military tribunals might, of necessity, replace civil authority "until the laws can have their free course." Does this dicta suggest that the Constitution may be suspended due to emergency? The Constitution does not so provide in its text and Article III and various provisions of the Bill of Rights might support a contrary inference since they generally make no exception for emergency. How should this constitutional silence be construed? Professor David Currie criticizes Justice Davis' dicta for undermining the "earlier ringing statements" in his opinion. He suggests Justice Davis might have better avoided the question "whether the Framers meant to do away with traditional military powers to govern either military personnel or conquered territories" by observing that it was "unnecessary to the decision of the case at hand." DAVID P. CURRIE, THE CONSTITUTION IN THE SUPREME COURT: THE FIRST HUNDRED YEARS 1789–1888, 290 (1985).

(3) Justice Davis' opinion reasoned that Congress lacked power to pass a law providing for trial of defendants like Milligan before a military commission. Should the Court have addressed this issue? Chief Justice Rehnquist argued that since Congress had not enacted such a law, Justice Davis should not have reached the issue. Indeed, in addressing the issue, Chief Justice Rehnquist argued, the Court violated a cardinal principle of avoiding unnecessary constitutional pronouncements. The concurring justices argued in portions of their opinion not reproduced herein that the Habeas Corpus Act of 1863 required discharging Milligan since it allowed his detention only until a grand jury met to consider indicting him. Chief Justice Rehnquist argued that the majority could reasonably have interpreted the statute to apply only to those detained for trial in civil courts. Under that interpretation, the statute would not have reached *Milligan* leaving the Court with the issue of whether the President could unilaterally authorize wartime trial of civilians by military commissions. WILLIAM H. REHNQUIST, ALL THE LAWS BUT ONE: CIVIL LIBERTIES IN WARTIME 128–137 (1998).

Justice Davis does seem to create a bright line rule that military tribunals could not be used to try "citizens in states which have upheld the authority of the government, and where the courts are open and their process unobstructed."

(4) President Abraham Lincoln took extensive emergency action during the Civil War, blockading southern ports without Congress' authorization, raising the size of the military beyond statutory ceilings, spending funds for purposes not authorized and suspending the writ of habeas corpus. *See generally* DAVID HERBERT DONALD, LINCOLN 302–304 (1995). Lincoln's justification, in part, is suggested at Casebook, p. 319 note 17. "[A]re all

the laws, but one, to go unexecuted, and the government itself go to pieces, lest that one be violated?" he asked rhetorically. Congress was not in session when Lincoln took office on March 4, 1861. Does that put Lincoln's actions in a different light? In his *Special Session Message* of July 4, 1861, Lincoln justified these steps "whether strictly legal or not" due to "popular demand," "public necessity," his belief they were within Congress' power (Congress being out of session), and his belief Congress would ratify his actions. *See* Lincoln, *Special Session Message in* 7 MESSAGES AND PAPERS OF THE PRESIDENTS 3221,3225, 3226 (James Richardson ed., 1897).

(5) During the Civil War, the Court avoided the question *Ex parte Milligan* raised regarding the constitutionality of military trial of a civilian. *See Ex parte Vallandigham*, 68 U.S. (1 Wall.) 243 (1864) (no jurisdiction for direct review of military commission). *Ex parte Milligan* was decided after the conflict ended.

EX PARTE QUIRIN

317 U.S. 1, 63 S. Ct. 2, 87 L. Ed. 3 (1942)

MR. CHIEF JUSTICE STONE delivered the opinion of the Court.

These cases are brought here by petitioners' several applications for leave to file petitions for habeas corpus in this Court, and by their petitions for certiorari to review orders of the District Court for the District of Columbia, which denied their applications for leave to file petitions for habeas corpus in that court.

The question for decision is whether the detention of petitioners by respondent for trial by Military Commission, appointed by Order of the President of July 2, 1942, on charges preferred against them purporting to set out their violations of the law of war and of the Articles of War, is in conformity to the laws and Constitution of the United States. . . .

In view of the public importance of the questions raised by their petitions and of the duty which rests on the courts, in time of war as well as in time of peace, to preserve unimpaired the constitutional safeguards of civil liberty, and because in our opinion the public interest required that we consider and decide those questions without any avoidable delay, we directed that petitioners' applications be set down for full oral argument at a special term of this Court, convened on July 29, 1942. . . .

[All petitioners, except arguably one, were German citizens. All were trained in Germany in sabotage and had instructions to destroy war facilities in the United States. They travelled in two submarines from Germany to New York and Florida, landing under cover of darkness with explosives and related equipment. Upon landing they buried their uniforms and proceeded in civilian dress. They were arrested by federal officers.]

The President, as President and Commander in Chief of the Army and Navy, by Order of July 2, 1942, appointed a Military Commission and directed it to try petitioners for offenses against the law of war and the

Articles of War, and prescribed regulations for the procedure on the trial and for review of the record of the trial and of any judgment or sentence of the Commission. On the same day, by Proclamation, the President declared that "all persons who are subjects, citizens or residents of any nation at war with the United States or who give obedience to or act under the direction of any such nation, and who during time of war enter or attempt to enter the United States . . . through coastal or boundary defenses, and are charged with committing or attempting or preparing to commit sabotage, espionage, hostile or warlike acts, or violations of the law of war, shall be subject to the law of war and to the jurisdiction of military tribunals."

The Proclamation also stated in terms that all such persons were denied access to the courts. . . .

The Commission met on July 8, 1942, and proceeded with the trial, which continued in progress while the causes were pending in this Court. On July 27th, before petitioners' applications to the District Court, all the evidence for the prosecution and the defense had been taken by the Commission and the case had been closed except for arguments of counsel. It is conceded that ever since petitioners' arrest the state and federal courts in Florida, New York, and the District of Columbia, and in the states in which each of the petitioners was arrested or detained, have been open and functioning normally. . . .

Petitioners' main contention is that the President is without any statutory or constitutional authority to order the petitioners to be tried by military tribunal for offenses with which they are charged; that in consequence they are entitled to be tried in the civil courts with the safeguards, including trial by jury, which the Fifth and Sixth Amendments guarantee to all persons charged in such courts with criminal offenses. In any case it is urged that the President's Order, in prescribing the procedure of the Commission and the method for review of its findings and sentence, and the proceedings of the Commission under the Order, conflict with Articles of War adopted by Congress — articularly Articles 38, 43, 46, 50 ½ and 70 — and are illegal and void.

The Government challenges each of these propositions. But regardless of their merits, it also insists that petitioners must be denied access to the courts, both because they are enemy aliens or have entered our territory as enemy belligerents, and because the President's Proclamation undertakes in terms to deny such access to the class of persons defined by the Proclamation, which aptly describes the character and conduct of petitioners. It is urged that if they are enemy aliens or if the Proclamation has force, no court may afford the petitioners a hearing. But there is certainly nothing in the Proclamation to preclude access to the courts for determining its applicability to the particular case. And neither the Proclamation nor the fact that they are enemy aliens forecloses consideration by the courts of petitioners' contentions that the Constitution and laws of the United States constitutionally enacted forbid their trial by military commission. . . .

We are not here concerned with any question of the guilt or innocence of petitioners. Constitutional safeguards for the protection of all who are charged with offenses are not to be disregarded in order to inflict merited punishment on some who are guilty. But the detention and trial of petitioners — ordered by the President in the declared exercise of his powers as Commander in Chief of the Army in time of war and of grave public danger — are not to be set aside by the courts without the clear conviction that they are in conflict with the Constitution or laws of Congress constitutionally enacted.

Congress and the President, like the courts, possess no power not derived from the Constitution. But one of the objects of the Constitution, as declared by its preamble, is to "provide for the common defence." . . .

The Constitution . . . invests the President, as Commander in Chief, with the power to wage war which Congress has declared, and to carry into effect all laws passed by Congress for the conduct of war and for the government and regulation of the Armed Forces, and all laws defining and punishing offences against the law of nations, including those which pertain to the conduct of war.

By the Articles of War, 10 U.S.C. §§ 1471–1593 Congress has provided rules for the government of the Army. It has provided for the trial and punishment, by courts martial, of violations of the Articles by members of the armed forces and by specified classes of persons associated or serving with the Army. But the Articles also recognize the "military commission" appointed by military command as an appropriate tribunal for the trial and punishment of offenses against the law of war not ordinarily tried by court martial. Articles 38 and 46 authorize the President, with certain limitations, to prescribe the procedure for military commissions. Articles 81 and 82 authorize trial, either by court martial or military commission, of those charged with relieving, harboring or corresponding with the enemy and those charged with spying. And Article 15 declares that "the provisions of these articles conferring jurisdiction upon courts martial shall not be construed as depriving military commissions . . . or other military tribunals of concurrent jurisdiction in respect of offenders or offenses that by statute or by the law of war may be triable by such military commissions . . . or other military tribunals." Article 2 includes among those persons subject to military law the personnel of our own military establishment. But this, as Article 12 provides, does not exclude from that class "any other person who by the law of war is subject to trial by military tribunals" and who under Article 12 may be tried by court martial or under Article 15 by military commission. . . .

From the very beginning of its history this Court has recognized and applied the law of war as including that part of the law of nations which prescribes, for the conduct of war, the status, rights and duties of enemy nations as well as of enemy individuals. By the Articles of War, and especially Article 15, Congress has explicitly provided, so far as it may constitutionally do so, that military tribunals shall have jurisdiction to try offenders or offenses against the law of war in appropriate cases. Congress, in addition to making rules for the government of our Armed Forces, has thus exercised its authority to define and punish offenses against the law of nations by sanctioning, within constitutional limitations, the jurisdiction of military commissions to try persons for offenses which, according to the rules and precepts of the law of nations, and more particularly the law of war, are cognizable by such tribunals. And the President, as Commander in Chief, by his Proclamation in time of war has invoked that law. By his Order creating the present Commission he has undertaken to exercise the authority conferred upon him by Congress, and also such authority as the Constitution itself gives the Commander in Chief, to direct the performance of those functions which may constitutionally be performed by the military arm of the nation in time of war.

An important incident to the conduct of war is the adoption of measures by the military command not only to repel and defeat the enemy, but to seize and subject to disciplinary measures those enemies who in their attempt to thwart or impede our military effort have violated the law of war. It is unnecessary for present purposes to determine to what extent the President as Commander in Chief has constitutional power to create military commissions without the support of Congressional legislation. For here Congress has authorized trial of offenses against the law of war before such commissions. We are concerned only with the question whether it is within the constitutional power of the National Government to place petitioners upon trial before a military commission for the offenses with which they are charged. We must therefore first inquire whether any of the acts charged is an offense against the law of war cognizable before a military tribunal, and if so whether the Constitution prohibits the trial. . . .

By universal agreement and practice, the law of war draws a distinction between the armed forces and the peaceful populations of belligerent nations and also between those who are lawful and unlawful combatants. Lawful combatants are subject to capture and detention as prisoners of war by opposing military forces. Unlawful combatants are likewise subject to capture and detention, but in addition they are subject to trial and punishment by military tribunals for acts which render their belligerency unlawful. The spy who secretly and without uniform passes the military lines of a belligerent in time of war, seeking to gather military information and communicate it to the enemy, or an enemy combatant who without uniform comes secretly through the lines for the purpose of waging war by destruction of life or property, are familiar examples of belligerents who are generally deemed not to be entitled to the status of prisoners of war, but to be offenders against the law of war subject to trial and punishment by military tribunals. . . .

Our Government, by thus defining lawful belligerents entitled to be treated as prisoners of war, has recognized that there is a class of unlawful belligerents not entitled to that privilege, including those who, though combatants, do not wear "fixed and distinctive emblems." And by Article

15 of the Articles of War Congress has made provision for their trial and punishment by military commission, according to "the law of war."

By a long course of practical administrative construction by its military authorities, our Government has likewise recognized that those who during time of war pass surreptitiously from enemy territory into our own, discarding their uniforms upon entry, for the commission of hostile acts involving destruction of life or property, have the status of unlawful combatants punishable as such by military commission. This precept of the law of war has been so recognized in practice both here and abroad, and has so generally been accepted as valid by authorities on international law that we think it must be regarded as a rule or principle of the law of war recognized by this Government by its enactment of the Fifteenth Article of War.

Specification 1 of the first charge is sufficient to charge all the petitioners with the offense of unlawful belligerency, trial of which is within the jurisdiction of the Commission, and the admitted facts affirmatively show that the charge is not merely colorable or without foundation.

Specification 1 states that petitioners "being enemies of the United States and acting for . . . the German Reich, a belligerent enemy nation, secretly and covertly passed, in civilian dress, contrary to the law of war, through the military and naval lines and defenses of the United States . . . and went behind such lines, contrary to the law of war, in civilian dress . . . for the purpose of committing . . . hostile acts, and, in particular, to destroy certain war industries, war utilities and war materials within the United States."

This specification so plainly alleges violation of the law of war as to require but brief discussion of petitioners' contentions. As we have seen, entry upon our territory in time of war by enemy belligerents, including those acting under the direction of the armed forces of the enemy, for the purpose of destroying property used or useful in prosecuting the war, is a hostile and warlike act. It subjects those who participate in it without uniform to the punishment prescribed by the law of war for unlawful belligerents. . . . By passing our boundaries for such purposes without uniform or other emblem signifying their belligerent status, or by discarding that means of identification after entry, such enemies become unlawful belligerents subject to trial and punishment.

Citizenship in the United States of an enemy belligerent does not relieve him from the consequences of a belligerency which is unlawful because in violation of the law of war. Citizens who associate themselves with the military arm of the enemy government, and with its aid, guidance and direction enter this country bent on hostile acts, are enemy belligerents within the meaning of the Hague Convention and the law of war. . . .

But petitioners insist that, even if the offenses with which they are charged are offenses against the law of war, their trial is subject to the requirement of the Fifth Amendment that no person shall be held to answer for a capital or otherwise infamous crime unless on a presentment or indictment of a grand jury, and that such trials by Article III, § 2, and the Sixth Amendment must be by jury in a civil court. . . .

[Article III § 2 and the Fifth and Sixth Amendments preserved existing rights to jury trial without enlarging that right. They did not extend the jury right to trials by military commissions or confer a right to trial for offenses against the laws of war in civil courts.]

The fact that "cases arising in the land or naval forces" are excepted from the operation of the Amendments does not militate against this conclusion. Such cases are expressly excepted from the Fifth Amendment, and are deemed excepted by implication from the Sixth. *Ex parte Milligan, supra.* It is argued that the exception, which excludes from the Amendment cases arising in the armed forces, has also by implication extended its guaranty to all other cases; that since petitioners, not being members of the Armed Forces of the United States, are not within the exception, the Amendment operates to give to them the right to a jury trial. But we think this argument misconceives both the scope of the Amendment and the purpose of the exception.

We may assume, without deciding, that a trial prosecuted before a military commission created by military authority is not one "arising in the land . . . forces," when the accused is not a member of or associated with those forces. But even so, the exception cannot be taken to affect those trials before military commissions which are neither within the exception nor within the provisions of Article III, § 2, whose guaranty the Amendments did not enlarge. No exception is necessary to exclude from the operation of these provisions cases never deemed to be within their terms. An express exception from Article III, § 2, and from the Fifth and Sixth Amendments, of trials of petty offenses and of criminal contempts has not been found necessary in order to preserve the traditional practice of trying those offenses without a jury. It is no more so in order to continue the practice of trying, before military tribunals without a jury, offenses committed by enemy belligerents against the law of war.

Section 2 of the Act of Congress of April 10, 1806, 2 Stat. 371, derived from the Resolution of the Continental Congress of August 21, 1776, imposed the death penalty on alien spies "according to the law and usage of nations, by sentence of a general court martial." This enactment must be regarded as a contemporary construction of both Article III, § 2, and the Amendments as not foreclosing trial by military tribunals, without a jury, of offenses against the law of war committed by enemies not in or associated with our Armed Forces. It is a construction of the Constitution which has been followed since the founding of our Government, and is now continued in the 82nd Article of War. Such a construction is entitled to the greatest respect. It has not hitherto been challenged, and, so far as we are advised, it has never been suggested in the very extensive literature of the subject that an alien spy, in time of war, could not be tried by military tribunal without a jury.

The exception from the Amendments of "cases arising in the land or naval forces" was not aimed at trials by military tribunals, without a jury, of such offenses against the law of war. Its objective was quite different — to authorize the trial by court martial of the members of our Armed Forces for all that class of crimes which under the Fifth and Sixth Amendments might otherwise have been deemed triable in the civil courts. The cases mentioned in the exception are not restricted to those involving offenses against the law of war alone, but extend to trial of all offenses, including crimes which were of the class traditionally triable by jury at common law.

Since the Amendments, like § 2 of Article III, do not preclude all trials of offenses against the law of war by military commission without a jury when the offenders are aliens not members of our Armed Forces, it is plain that they present no greater obstacle to the trial in like manner of citizen enemies who have violated the law of war applicable to enemies. Under the original statute authorizing trial of alien spies by military tribunals, the offenders were outside the constitutional guaranty of trial by jury, not because they were aliens but only because they had violated the law of war by committing offenses constitutionally triable by military tribunal.

We cannot say that Congress in preparing the Fifth and Sixth Amendments intended to extend trial by jury to the cases of alien or citizen offenders against the law of war otherwise triable by military commission, while withholding it from members of our own armed forces charged with infractions of the Articles of War punishable by death. It is equally inadmissible to construe the Amendments — whose primary purpose was to continue unimpaired presentment by grand jury and trial by petit jury in all those cases in which they had been customary — as either abolishing all trials by military tribunals, save those of the personnel of our own armed forces, or, what in effect comes to the same thing, as imposing on all such tribunals the necessity of proceeding against unlawful enemy belligerents only on presentment and trial by jury. We conclude that the Fifth and Sixth Amendments did not restrict whatever authority was conferred by the Constitution to try offenses against the law of war by military commission, and that petitioners, charged with such an offense not required to be tried by jury at common law, were lawfully placed on trial by the Commission without a jury.

Petitioners, and especially petitioner Haupt, stress the pronouncement of this Court in the *Milligan* case, *supra*, that the law of war "can never be applied to citizens in states which have upheld the authority of the government, and where the courts are open and their process unobstructed." Elsewhere in its opinion, the Court was at pains to point out that Milligan, a citizen twenty years resident in Indiana, who had never been a resident of any of the states in rebellion, was not an enemy belligerent either entitled to the status of a prisoner of war or subject to the penalties imposed upon unlawful belligerents. We construe the Court's statement as to the inapplicability of the law of war to Milligan's case as having particular reference to the facts before it. From them the Court concluded that Milligan, not being a part of or associated with the armed forces of the enemy, was a non-belligerent, not subject to the law of war save as — in circumstances found not there to be present, and not involved here — martial law might be constitutionally established.

The Court's opinion is inapplicable to the case presented by the present record. We have no occasion now to define with meticulous care the ultimate boundaries of the jurisdiction of military tribunals to try persons according to the law of war. It is enough that petitioners here, upon the conceded facts, were plainly within those boundaries, and were held in good faith for trial by military commission, charged with being enemies who, with the purpose of destroying war materials and utilities, entered, or after entry remained in, our territory without uniform — an offense against the law of war. We hold only that those particular acts constitute an offense against the law of war which the Constitution authorizes to be tried by military commission. . . .

We need not inquire whether Congress may restrict the power of the Commander in Chief to deal with enemy belligerents. For the Court is unanimous in its conclusion that the Articles in question could not at any stage of the proceedings afford any basis for issuing the writ. . . .

Accordingly, we conclude that Charge I, on which petitioners were detained for trial by the Military Commission, alleged an offense which the President is authorized to order tried by military commission; that his Order convening the Commission was a lawful order and that the Commission was lawfully constituted; that the petitioners were held in lawful custody and did not show cause for their discharge. It follows that the orders of the District Court should be affirmed, and that leave to file petitions for habeas corpus in this Court should be denied.

MR. JUSTICE MURPHY took no part in the consideration or decision of these cases.

NOTES

(1) Justice Jackson circulated to his colleagues a memorandum in which he agreed that the prisoners were subject to trial by military commission but argued further that the prisoners, as spies and invaders, lacked standing to assert rights based on the Bill of Rights or laws of war. In response, Justice Frankfurter advised his colleagues to "[j]ust relax and don't be too engrossed in your own interest in verbalistic conflicts, because the inroads on energy and national unity that such conflict inevitably produces, is a pastime we had better postpone until peacetime." THE SU-PREME COURT IN CONFERENCE (1940–1985) 533–536 (Del Dickson ed. 2001).

(2) In *Ex parte Milligan*, the availability of civilian courts made Milligan's trial by a military tribunal unlawful. In *Ex parte Quirin*, civil courts were available but the Court rejected the claim that military trial was accordingly improper. Can *Ex parte Quirin* be distinguished from *Ex parte Milligan*? In *Quirin*, the Court construed the *Milligan* Court's "statement

as to the inapplicability of the law of war to Milligan's case as having particular reference to the facts before it." Milligan was a non-belligerent whereas Quirin was a belligerent.

(3) Does the President have power under the Commander-in-Chief clause to create military tribunals to try suspected war criminals? *Quirin*, at least, left that question open since Congress had authorized trial before military commissions of offenses against laws of war. What inferences might be drawn from the fact that the Constitution empowers Congress to "declare war" (Art. I § 8 cl. 11), to "define and punish offenses against the law of nations" (Art. I § 8 cl. 10), to "constitute tribunals inferior to the Supreme Court" (Art. I § 8 cl. 9).

(4) Two scholars have questioned Chief Justice Stone's implication that "even spies and prisoners of war had some rights under the Constitution." They write that this suggestion "had no legal basis at all, for nowhere in English or American legal history could one find evidence that military personnel had any of the rights belonging to citizens. Ever since the American Revolution, the United States had always tried enemy personnel in wartime by summary military procedures, a fact known to and accepted by the Framers of the Constitution." MELVIN I. UROFSKY & PAUL FINKELMAN, A MARCH OF LIBERTY: A CONSTITUTIONAL HISTORY OF THE UNITED STATES Vol II (2002) 727.

Authorization For Use of Military Force

S.J. Res. 23, 107th Cong. (2001) (enacted)

To authorize the use of United States Armed Forces against those responsible for the recent attacks launched against the United States.

Whereas, on September 11, 2001, acts of treacherous violence were committed against the United States and its citizens; and

Whereas, such acts render it both necessary and appropriate that the United States exercise its rights to self-defense and to protect United States citizens both at home and abroad; and

Whereas, in light of the threat to the national security and foreign policy of the United States posed by these grave acts of violence; and

Whereas, such acts continue to pose an unusual and extraordinary threat to the national security and foreign policy of the United States; and

Whereas, the President has authority under the Constitution to take action to deter and prevent acts of international terrorism against the United States: Now, therefore, be it

Resolved by the Senate and House of Representatives of the United States of America in Congress assembled,

[*1] SECTION 1. SHORT TITLE.

This joint resolution may be cited as the "Authorization for Use of Military Force".

[*2] SEC. 2. AUTHORIZATION FOR USE OF UNITED STATES ARMED FORCES.

(a) In General.—That the President is authorized to use all necessary and appropriate force against those nations, organizations, or persons he determines planned, authorized, committed, or aided the terrorist attacks that occurred on September 11, 2001, or harbored such organizations or persons, in order to prevent any future acts of international terrorism against the United States by such nations, organizations or persons.

(b) War Powers Resolution Requirements.—

(1) Specific statutory authorization.— Consistent with section 8(a)(1) of the War Powers Resolution, the Congress declares that this section is intended to constitute specific statutory authorization within the meaning of section 5(b) of the War Powers Resolution.

(2) Applicability of other requirements.— Nothing in this resolution supercedes any requirement of the War Powers Resolution.

Military Order of November 13, 2001

Detention, Treatment, and Trial of Certain Non–Citizens in the War Against Terrorism
66 Fed. Reg. 57833 (November 16, 2001)

By the authority vested in me as President and as Commander in Chief of the Armed Forces of the United States by the Constitution and the laws of the United States of America, including the Authorization for Use of Military Force Joint Resolution and sections 821 and 836 of title 10, United States Code, it is hereby ordered as follows:

Section 1. *Findings*.

(a) International terrorists, including members of al Qaida, have carried out attacks on United States diplomatic and military personnel and facilities abroad and on citizens and property within the United States on a scale that has created a state of armed conflict that requires the use of the United States Armed Forces. . . .

(c) The ability of the United States to protect the United States and its citizens, and to help its allies and other cooperating nations protect their nations and their citizens, from such further terrorist attacks depends in significant part upon using the United States Armed Forces to identify terrorists and those who support them, to disrupt their activities, and to eliminate their ability to conduct or support such attacks.

(d) To protect the United States and its citizens, and for the effective conduct of military operations and prevention of terrorist attacks, it is necessary for individuals subject to this order pursuant to section 2 hereof to be detained, and, when tried, to be tried for violations of the laws of war and other applicable laws by military tribunals.

(e) Given the danger to the safety of the United States and the nature of international terrorism, and to the extent provided by and under this order, I find consistent with section 836 of title 10, United States Code, that it is not practicable to apply in military commissions under this order the principles of law and the rules of evidence generally recognized in the trial of criminal cases in the United States district courts.

(f) Having fully considered the magnitude of the potential deaths, injuries, and property destruction that would result from potential acts of terrorism against the United States, and the probability that such acts will occur, I have determined that an extraordinary emergency exists for national defense purposes, that this emergency constitutes an urgent and compelling government interest, and that issuance of his order is necessary to meet the emergency.

Section 2. *Definition and Policy.*

(a) The term "individual subject to this order" hall mean any individual who is not a United States citizen with respect to whom I determine from time to time in writing that:

(1) there is reason to believe that such individual, at the relevant times,

(i) is or was a member of the organization known as al Qaida;

(ii) has engaged in, aided or abetted, or conspired to commit, acts of international terrorism, or acts in preparation therefor, that have caused, threaten to cause, or have as their aim to cause, injury to or adverse effects on the United States, its citizens, national security, foreign policy, or economy; or

(iii) has knowingly harbored one or more individuals described in subparagraphs (i) or (ii) of subsection 2(a)(1) of this order; and

(2) it is in the interest of the United States that such individual be subject to this order.

(b) It is the policy of the United States that the Secretary of Defense shall take all necessary measures to ensure that any individual subject to this order is detained in accordance with section 3, and, if the individual is to be tried, that such individual is tried only in accordance with section 4. . . .

Section 3. *Detention Authority of the Secretary of Defense. Any individual subject to this order shall be—*

(a) detained at an appropriate location designated by the Secretary of Defense outside or within the United States;

(b) treated humanely, without any adverse distinction based on race, color, religion, gender, birth, wealth, or any similar criteria;

(c) afforded adequate food, drinking water, shelter, clothing, and medical treatment;

(d) allowed the free exercise of religion consistent with the requirements of such detention; and

(e) detained in accordance with such other conditions as the Secretary of Defense may prescribe.

Section 4. *Authority of the Secretary of Defense Regarding Trials of Individuals Subject to this Order.*

(a) Any individual subject to this order shall, when tried, be tried by military commission for any and all offenses triable by military commission that such individual is alleged to have committed, and may be punished in accordance with the penalties provided under applicable law, including life imprisonment or death.

(b) As a military function and in light of the findings in section 1, including subsection (f) thereof, the Secretary of Defense shall issue such orders and regulations, including orders for the appointment of one or more military commissions, as may be necessary to carry out subsection (a) of this section.

(c) Orders and regulations issued under subsection (b) of this section shall include, but not be limited to, rules for the conduct of the proceedings of military commissions, including pretrial, trial, and post-trial procedures, modes of proof, issuance of process, and qualifications of attorneys, which shall at a minimum provide for —

(1) military commissions to sit at any time and any place, consistent with such guidance regarding time and place as the Secretary of Defense may provide;

(2) a full and fair trial, with the military commission sitting as the triers of both fact and law;

(3) admission of such evidence as would, in the opinion of the presiding officer of the military commission (or instead, if any other member of the commission so requests at the time the presiding officer renders that opinion, the opinion of the commission rendered at that time by a majority of the commission), have probative value to a reasonable person;

(4) in a manner consistent with the protection of information classified or classifiable under Executive Order 12958 of April 17, 1995, as amended, or any successor Executive Order, protected by statute or rule from unauthorized disclosure, or otherwise protected by law, (A) the handling of, admission into evidence of, and access to materials and information, and (B) the conduct, closure of, and access to proceedings;

(5) conduct of the prosecution by one or more attorneys designated by the Secretary of Defense and conduct of the defense by attorneys for the individual subject to this order;

(6) conviction only upon the concurrence of two-thirds of the members of the commission present at the time of the vote, a majority being present;

(7) sentencing only upon the concurrence of two-thirds of the members of the commission present at the time of the vote, a majority being present; and

(8) submission of the record of the trial, including any conviction or sentence, for review and final decision by me or by the Secretary of Defense if so designated by me for that purpose. . . .

Section 7. *Relationship to Other Law and Forums.*

(a) Nothing in this order shall be construed to —

(1) authorize the disclosure of state secrets to any person not otherwise authorized to have access to them;

(2) limit the authority of the President as Commander in Chief of the Armed Forces or the power of the President to grant reprieves and pardons; or

(3) limit the lawful authority of the Secretary of Defense, any military commander, or any other officer or agent of the United States or of any State to detain or try any person who is not an individual subject to this order.

(b) With respect to any individual subject to this order —

(1) military tribunals shall have exclusive jurisdiction with respect to offenses by the individual; and

(2) the individual shall not be privileged to seek any remedy or maintain any proceeding, directly or indirectly, or to have any such remedy or proceeding sought on the individual's behalf, in (i) any court of the United States, or any State thereof, (ii) any court of any foreign nation, or (iii) any international tribunal. . . .

NOTES

(1) Note that Congress has not declared war on Al Qaida but has authorized President Bush "to use all necessary and appropriate force against those nations, organizations, or persons he determines" were responsible for the September 11 attacks. "A state of declared war offers the clearest authority for the broadest use of war powers." American Bar Association Task Force on Terrorism and the Law, Report and Recommendations on Military Commissions (Jan. 4, 2002), p. 5. Does the Joint Resolution give implicit approval to use military tribunals in the same way that a formal declaration of war would? Note that Congress has rarely declared war, the last time being in World War II. The various military actions in Korea, Vietnam and Iraq rested in part on congressional resolutions short of formal declaration of war.

(2) Military tribunals or military commissions have existed throughout American history. Their validity is supported by considerable practice and by caselaw. In *Madsen v. Kinsella*, 343 U.S. 341, 346–47 (1952), the Court held that a military commission had jurisdiction to try an American citizen

for the alleged murder of her husband, an American serviceman, in Germany in 1950.

The Court has upheld the use of military tribunals to try enemies alleged to have committed war crimes. *Application of Yamashita*, 327 U.S. 1 (1946). That was true, the Court held, even after hostilities ended between the United States and Japan at least until peace was declared. Similarly, in *Ex parte Quirin*, the Court upheld the jurisdiction of a military tribunal to try eight German saboteurs captured in the United States during World War II.

(3) Does wartime make desirable "occasional presidential excesses and judicial restraint?" Chief Justice Rehnquist poses that as an "important philosophical question" although one which practice will answer affirmatively. He wrote:

> It is neither desirable nor is it remotely likely that civil liberty will occupy as favored a position in wartime as it does in peacetime. But it is both desirable and likely that more careful attention will be paid by the courts to the basis for the government's claims of necessity as a basis for curtailing civil liberty. The laws will thus not be silent in time of war, but they will speak with a somewhat different voice.

WILLIAM H. REHNQUIST, ALL THE LAWS BUT ONE, 224–25 (1998).

HAMDI v. RUMSFELD

542 U.S. 507 (2004)

Justice O'CONNOR announced the judgment of the Court and delivered an opinion, in which THE CHIEF JUSTICE, Justice KENNEDY, and Justice BREYER join.

At this difficult time in our Nation's history, we are called upon to consider the legality of the Government's detention of a United States citizen on United States soil as an "enemy combatant" and to address the process that is constitutionally owed to one who seeks to challenge his classification as such. The United States Court of Appeals for the Fourth Circuit held that petitioner's detention was legally authorized and that he was entitled to no further opportunity to challenge his enemy-combatant label. We now vacate and remand. We hold that although Congress authorized the detention of combatants in the narrow circumstances alleged here, due process demands that a citizen held in the United States as an enemy combatant be given a meaningful opportunity to contest the factual basis for that detention before a neutral decisionmaker.

I

On September 11, 2001, the al Qaeda terrorist network used hijacked commercial airliners to attack prominent targets in the United States.

Approximately 3,000 people were killed in those attacks. One week later, in response to these "acts of treacherous violence," Congress passed a resolution authorizing the President to "use all necessary and appropriate force against those nations, organizations, or persons he determines planned, authorized, committed, or aided the terrorist attacks" or "harbored such organizations or persons, in order to prevent any future acts of international terrorism against the United States by such nations, organizations or persons." Authorization for Use of Military Force ("the AUMF"), 115 Stat. 224. Soon thereafter, the President ordered United States Armed Forces to Afghanistan, with a mission to subdue al Qaeda and quell the Taliban regime that was known to support it.

This case arises out of the detention of a man whom the Government alleges took up arms with the Taliban during this conflict. His name is Yaser Esam Hamdi. Born an American citizen in Louisiana in 1980, Hamdi moved with his family to Saudi Arabia as a child. By 2001, the parties agree, he resided in Afghanistan. At some point that year, he was seized by members of the Northern Alliance, a coalition of military groups opposed to the Taliban government, and eventually was turned over to the United States military. The Government asserts that it initially detained and interrogated Hamdi in Afghanistan before transferring him to the United States Naval Base in Guantanamo Bay in January 2002. In April 2002, upon learning that Hamdi is an American citizen, authorities transferred him to a naval brig in Norfolk, Virginia, where he remained until a recent transfer to a brig in Charleston, South Carolina. The Government contends that Hamdi is an "enemy combatant," and that this status justifies holding him in the United States indefinitely — without formal charges or proceedings — unless and until it makes the determination that access to counsel or further process is warranted.

[Hamdi's father petitioned for a writ of habeas corpus under 28 U.S.C. § 2241 in the Eastern District of Virginia, naming as petitioners his son and himself as next friend. The elder Hamdi alleged that the Government had illegally held his son "without access to legal counsel or notice of any charges pending against him," and that his son's constitutional rights as an American citizen had been violated. He asked the court to appoint counsel for Hamdi, declare that he is being held in violation of the Fifth and Fourteenth Amendments, schedule an evidentiary hearing, and order him released from his "unlawful custody." Hamdi's father asserted that his son went to Afghanistan to do "relief work," and that he had been in that country less than two months before September 11, 2001, and could not have received military training.]

The District Court found that Hamdi's father was a proper next friend, appointed the federal public defender as counsel for the petitioners, and ordered that counsel be given access to Hamdi. The United States Court of Appeals for the Fourth Circuit reversed that order, holding that the District Court had failed to extend appropriate deference to the Government's security and intelligence interests. 296 F.3d 278, 279, 283 (2002).

It directed the District Court to consider "the most cautious procedures first," and to conduct a deferential inquiry into Hamdi's status. It opined that "if Hamdi is indeed an 'enemy combatant' who was captured during hostilities in Afghanistan, the government's present detention of him is a lawful one."

On remand, the Government filed a response and a motion to dismiss the petition. It attached to its response a declaration from one Michael Mobbs (hereinafter "Mobbs Declaration"), who identified himself as Special Advisor to the Under Secretary of Defense for Policy. . . . Mobbs [declared] that Hamdi "traveled to Afghanistan" in July or August 2001, and that he thereafter "affiliated with a Taliban military unit and received weapons training." . . . that Hamdi "remained with his Taliban unit following the attacks of September 11" and that, during the time when Northern Alliance forces were "engaged in battle with the Taliban," "Hamdi's Taliban unit surrendered" to those forces, after which he "surrender[ed] his Kalishnikov assault rifle" to them. The Mobbs Declaration also states that, because al Qaeda and the Taliban "were and are hostile forces engaged in armed conflict with the armed forces of the United States," "individuals associated with" those groups "were and continue to be enemy combatants."

After the Government submitted this declaration, the Fourth Circuit directed the District Court to proceed in accordance with its earlier ruling and, specifically, to " 'consider the sufficiency of the Mobbs Declaration as an independent matter before proceeding further.' " 316 F.3d at 450, 462 (C.A.4 2003). The District Court found that the Mobbs Declaration fell "far short" of supporting Hamdi's detention. . . . The Fourth Circuit reversed [stating] because it was "undisputed that Hamdi was captured in a zone of active combat in a foreign theater of conflict," no factual inquiry or evidentiary hearing allowing Hamdi to be heard or to rebut the Government's assertions was necessary or proper. Concluding that the factual averments in the Mobbs Declaration, "if accurate," provided a sufficient basis upon which to conclude that the President had constitutionally detained Hamdi pursuant to the President's war powers, it ordered the habeas petition dismissed. The Fourth Circuit emphasized that the "vital purposes" of the detention of uncharged enemy combatants — preventing those combatants from rejoining the enemy while relieving the military of the burden of litigating the circumstances of wartime captures halfway around the globe — were interests "directly derived from the war powers of Articles I and II." In that court's view, because "Article III contains nothing analogous to the specific powers of war so carefully enumerated in Articles I and II," separation of powers principles prohibited a federal court from "delv[ing] further into Hamdi's status and capture[.]" Accordingly, the District Court's more vigorous inquiry "went far beyond the acceptable scope of review." . . .

II

The threshold question before us is whether the Executive has the authority to detain citizens who qualify as "enemy combatants." There is some debate as to the proper scope of this term, and the Government has never provided any court with the full criteria that it uses in classifying individuals as such. It has made clear, however, that, for purposes of this case, the "enemy combatant" that it is seeking to detain is an individual who, it alleges, was " 'part of or supporting forces hostile to the United States or coalition partners' " in Afghanistan and who " 'engaged in an armed conflict against the United States' " there. We therefore answer only the narrow question before us: whether the detention of citizens falling within that definition is authorized.

The Government maintains that no explicit congressional authorization is required, because the Executive possesses plenary authority to detain pursuant to Article II of the Constitution. We do not reach the question whether Article II provides such authority, however, because we agree with the Government's alternative position, that Congress has in fact authorized Hamdi's detention, through the AUMF.

Our analysis on that point, set forth below, substantially overlaps with our analysis of Hamdi's principal argument for the illegality of his detention. He posits that his detention is forbidden by 18 U.S.C. § 4001(a) [which] states that "[n]o citizen shall be imprisoned or otherwise detained by the United States except pursuant to an Act of Congress." . . . [W]e conclude that the AUMF is explicit congressional authorization for the detention of individuals in the narrow category we describe (assuming, without deciding, that such authorization is required), and that the AUMF satisfied § 4001(a)'s requirement that a detention be "pursuant to an Act of Congress" (assuming, without deciding, that § 4001(a) applies to military detentions).

The AUMF authorizes the President to use "all necessary and appropriate force" against "nations, organizations, or persons" associated with the September 11, 2001, terrorist attacks. There can be no doubt that individuals who fought against the United States in Afghanistan as part of the Taliban, an organization known to have supported the al Qaeda terrorist network responsible for those attacks, are individuals Congress sought to target in passing the AUMF. We conclude that detention of individuals falling into the limited category we are considering, for the duration of the particular conflict in which they were captured, is so fundamental and accepted an incident to war as to be an exercise of the "necessary and appropriate force" Congress has authorized the President to use.

The capture and detention of lawful combatants and the capture, detention, and trial of unlawful combatants, by "universal agreement and practice," are "important incident[s] of war." *Ex parte Quirin,* 317 U.S. [1 (1942)]. The purpose of detention is to prevent captured individuals from returning to the field of battle and taking up arms once again.

There is no bar to this Nation's holding one of its own citizens as an enemy combatant. In *Quirin,* one of the detainees, Haupt, alleged that he was a naturalized United States citizen. We held that "[c]itizens who associate themselves with the military arm of the enemy government, and with its aid, guidance and direction enter this country bent on hostile acts, are enemy belligerents within the meaning of . . . the law of war." While Haupt was tried for violations of the law of war, nothing in *Quirin* suggests that his citizenship would have precluded his mere detention for the duration of the relevant hostilities. Nor can we see any reason for drawing such a line here. A citizen, no less than an alien, can be "part of or supporting forces hostile to the United States or coalition partners" and "engaged in an armed conflict against the United States," such a citizen, if released, would pose the same threat of returning to the front during the ongoing conflict.

In light of these principles, it is of no moment that the AUMF does not use specific language of detention. Because detention to prevent a combatant's return to the battlefield is a fundamental incident of waging war, in permitting the use of "necessary and appropriate force," Congress has clearly and unmistakably authorized detention in the narrow circumstances considered here.

Hamdi objects, nevertheless, that Congress has not authorized the *indefinite* detention to which he is now subject. The Government responds that "the detention of enemy combatants during World War II was just as 'indefinite' while that war was being fought." We take Hamdi's objection to be not to the lack of certainty regarding the date on which the conflict will end, but to the substantial prospect of perpetual detention. We recognize that the national security underpinnings of the "war on terror," although crucially important, are broad and malleable. As the Government concedes, "given its unconventional nature, the current conflict is unlikely to end with a formal cease-fire agreement." The prospect Hamdi raises is therefore not far-fetched. If the Government does not consider this unconventional war won for two generations, and if it maintains during that time that Hamdi might, if released, rejoin forces fighting against the United States, then the position it has taken throughout the litigation of this case suggests that Hamdi's detention could last for the rest of his life.

Hamdi contends that the AUMF does not authorize indefinite or perpetual detention. Certainly, we agree that indefinite detention for the purpose of interrogation is not authorized. Further, we understand Congress' grant of authority for the use of "necessary and appropriate force" to include the authority to detain for the duration of the relevant conflict, and our understanding is based on longstanding law-of-war principles. If the practical circumstances of a given conflict are entirely unlike those of the conflicts that informed the development of the law of war, that understanding may unravel. But that is not the situation we face as of this date. Active combat operations against Taliban fighters apparently are ongoing in Afghanistan. The United States may detain, for the duration of these hostilities, individuals legitimately determined to be Taliban combatants who "engaged in an armed conflict against the United States." . . .

Ex parte Milligan, [71 U.S.] (4 Wall. [)] 2, 125 (1866), does not undermine our holding about the Government's authority to seize enemy combatants, as we define that term today. In that case, the Court made repeated reference to the fact that its inquiry into whether the military tribunal had jurisdiction to try and punish Milligan turned in large part on the fact that Milligan was not a prisoner of war, but a resident of Indiana arrested while at home there. . . . Had Milligan been captured while he was assisting Confederate soldiers by carrying a rifle against Union troops on a Confederate battlefield, the holding of the Court might well have been different. . . . *Quirin* was a unanimous opinion. It both postdates and clarifies *Milligan,* providing us with the most apposite precedent that we have on the question of whether citizens may be detained in such circumstances. Brushing aside such precedent — particularly when doing so gives rise to a host of new questions never dealt with by this Court — is unjustified and unwise.

To the extent that Justice SCALIA accepts the precedential value of *Quirin,* he argues that it cannot guide our inquiry here because "[i]n *Quirin* it was uncontested that the petitioners were members of enemy forces," while Hamdi challenges his classification as an enemy combatant. But it is unclear why, in the paradigm outlined by Justice SCALIA, such a concession should have any relevance. . . . He does not explain . . . why a concession should carry any different effect than proof of enemy-combatant status in a proceeding that comports with due process. To be clear, our opinion only finds legislative authority to detain under the AUMF once it is sufficiently clear that the individual is, in fact, an enemy combatant; whether that is established by concession or by some other process that verifies this fact with sufficient certainty seems beside the point.

Further, Justice SCALIA largely ignores the context of this case: a United States citizen captured in a *foreign* combat zone. . . . Justice SCALIA can point to no case or other authority for the proposition that those captured on a foreign battlefield (whether detained there or in U.S. territory) cannot be detained outside the criminal process.

Moreover, Justice SCALIA presumably would come to a different result if Hamdi had been kept in Afghanistan or even Guantanamo Bay. This creates a perverse incentive. Military authorities faced with the stark choice of submitting to the full-blown criminal process or releasing a suspected enemy combatant captured on the battlefield will simply keep citizen-detainees abroad. Indeed, the Government transferred Hamdi from Guantanamo Bay to the United States naval brig only after it learned that he might be an American citizen. It is not at all clear why that should make a determinative constitutional difference.

III

Even in cases in which the detention of enemy combatants is legally authorized, there remains the question of what process is constitutionally due to a citizen who disputes his enemy-combatant status. . . . Though they reach radically different conclusions on the process that ought to attend the present proceeding, the parties begin on common ground. All agree that, absent suspension, the writ of habeas corpus remains available to every individual detained within the United States. U.S. Const., Art. I, § 9, cl. 2 ("The Privilege of the Writ of Habeas Corpus shall not be suspended, unless when in Cases of Rebellion or Invasion the public Safety may require it"). Only in the rarest of circumstances has Congress seen fit to suspend the writ. At all other times, it has remained a critical check on the Executive, ensuring that it does not detain individuals except in accordance with law. *See INS v. St. Cyr,* 533 U.S. 289, 301 (2001). All agree suspension of the writ has not occurred here. Thus, it is undisputed that Hamdi was properly before an Article III court to challenge his detention under 28 U.S.C. § 2241. Further, all agree that § 2241 and its companion provisions provide at least a skeletal outline of the procedures to be afforded a petitioner in federal habeas review. Most notably, § 2243 provides that "the person detained may, under oath, deny any of the facts set forth in the return or allege any other material facts," and § 2246 allows the taking of evidence in habeas proceedings by deposition, affidavit, or interrogatories.

The simple outline of § 2241 makes clear both that Congress envisioned that habeas petitioners would have some opportunity to present and rebut facts and that courts in cases like this retain some ability to vary the ways in which they do so as mandated by due process. The Government recognizes the basic procedural protections required by the habeas statute, but asks us to hold that, given both the flexibility of the habeas mechanism and the circumstances presented in this case, the presentation of the Mobbs Declaration to the habeas court completed the required factual development. It suggests two separate reasons for its position that no further process is due.

[The Court rejected the Government's argument that the habeas determination can be made as a matter of law, with no further hearing or factfinding necessary since Hamdi was seized in a combat zone; the Court found the facts were not undisputed].

The Government's second argument requires closer consideration. This is the argument that further factual exploration is unwarranted and inappropriate in light of the extraordinary constitutional interests at stake. Under the Government's most extreme rendition of this argument, "[r]espect for separation of powers and the limited institutional capabilities of courts in matters of military decision-making in connection with an ongoing conflict" ought to eliminate entirely any individual process, restricting the courts to investigating only whether legal authorization exists for the broader detention scheme. At most, the Government argues, courts should review its determination that a citizen is an enemy combatant under a very deferential "some evidence" standard. Under this review, a court would assume the accuracy of the Government's articulated basis for Hamdi's detention, as set forth in the Mobbs Declaration, and assess only whether that articulated basis was a legitimate one.

In response, Hamdi emphasizes that this Court consistently has recognized that an individual challenging his detention may not be held at the will of the Executive without recourse to some proceeding before a neutral tribunal to determine whether the Executive's asserted justifications for that detention have basis in fact and warrant in law. . . .

Both of these positions highlight legitimate concerns. And both emphasize the tension that often exists between the autonomy that the Government asserts is necessary in order to pursue effectively a particular goal and the process that a citizen contends he is due before he is deprived of a constitutional right. The ordinary mechanism that we use for balancing such serious competing interests, and for determining the procedures that are necessary to ensure that a citizen is not "deprived of life, liberty, or property, without due process of law," U.S. Const., Amdt. 5, is the test that we articulated in *Mathews v. Eldridge,* 424 U.S. 319 (1976). *Mathews* dictates that the process due in any given instance is determined by weighing "the private interest that will be affected by the official action" against the Government's asserted interest, "including the function involved" and the burdens the Government would face in providing greater process. The *Mathews* calculus then contemplates a judicious balancing of these concerns, through an analysis of "the risk of an erroneous deprivation" of the private interest if the process were reduced and the "probable value, if any, of additional or substitute safeguards." We take each of these steps in turn.

It is beyond question that substantial interests lie on both sides of the scale in this case. Hamdi's "private interest . . . affected by the official action," is the most elemental of liberty interests — the interest in being free from physical detention by one's own government. "In our society liberty is the norm," and detention without trial "is the carefully limited exception." . . .

Nor is the weight on this side of the *Mathews* scale offset by the circumstances of war or the accusation of treasonous behavior, for "[i]t is clear that commitment for *any* purpose constitutes a significant deprivation of liberty that requires due process protection." . . . Moreover, as critical as the Government's interest may be in detaining those who actually pose an immediate threat to the national security of the United States during ongoing international conflict, history and common sense teach us that an unchecked system of detention carries the potential to become a means for oppression and abuse of others who do not present that sort of threat. . . . We reaffirm today the fundamental nature of a citizen's right to be free from involuntary confinement by his own government without due process of law, and we weigh the opposing governmental interests against the curtailment of liberty that such confinement entails.

On the other side of the scale are the weighty and sensitive governmental interests in ensuring that those who have in fact fought with the enemy during a war do not return to battle against the United States. As discussed above, the law of war and the realities of combat may render such detentions both necessary and appropriate, and our due process analysis need not blink at those realities. Without doubt, our Constitution recognizes that core strategic matters of warmaking belong in the hands of those who are best positioned and most politically accountable for making them.

The Government also argues at some length that its interests in reducing the process available to alleged enemy combatants are heightened by the practical difficulties that would accompany a system of trial-like process. In its view, military officers who are engaged in the serious work of waging battle would be unnecessarily and dangerously distracted by litigation half a world away, and discovery into military operations would both intrude on the sensitive secrets of national defense and result in a futile search for evidence buried under the rubble of war. To the extent that these burdens are triggered by heightened procedures, they are properly taken into account in our due process analysis.

Striking the proper constitutional balance here is of great importance to the Nation during this period of ongoing combat. But it is equally vital that our calculus not give short shrift to the values that this country holds dear or to the privilege that is American citizenship. It is during our most challenging and uncertain moments that our Nation's commitment to due process is most severely tested; and it is in those times that we must preserve our commitment at home to the principles for which we fight abroad.

With due recognition of these competing concerns, we believe that neither the process proposed by the Government nor the process apparently envisioned by the District Court below strikes the proper constitutional balance when a United States citizen is detained in the United States as an enemy combatant. That is, "the risk of erroneous deprivation" of a detainee's liberty interest is unacceptably high under the Government's proposed rule, while some of the "additional or substitute procedural safeguards" suggested by the District Court are unwarranted in light of their limited "probable value" and the burdens they may impose on the military in such cases. *Mathews,* 424 U.S. at 335.

We therefore hold that a citizen-detainee seeking to challenge his classification as an enemy combatant must receive notice of the factual basis for his classification, and a fair opportunity to rebut the Government's factual assertions before a neutral decisionmaker. . . . These essential constitutional promises may not be eroded.

At the same time, the exigencies of the circumstances may demand that, aside from these core elements, enemy combatant proceedings may be tailored to alleviate their uncommon potential to burden the Executive at a time of ongoing military conflict. Hearsay, for example, may need to be accepted as the most reliable available evidence from the Government in such a proceeding. Likewise, the Constitution would not be offended by a presumption in favor of the Government's evidence, so long as that presumption remained a rebuttable one and fair opportunity for rebuttal were provided. Thus, once the Government puts forth credible evidence that the habeas petitioner meets the enemy-combatant criteria, the onus could shift to the petitioner to rebut that evidence with more persuasive evidence that he falls outside the criteria. . . .

We think it unlikely that this basic process will have the dire impact on the central functions of warmaking that the Government forecasts. The parties agree that initial captures on the battlefield need not receive the process we have discussed here; that process is due only when the determination is made to *continue* to hold those who have been seized. The Government has made clear in its briefing that documentation regarding battlefield detainees already is kept in the ordinary course of military affairs. Any factfinding imposition created by requiring a knowledgeable affiant to summarize these records to an independent tribunal is a minimal one. Likewise, arguments that military officers ought not have to wage war under the threat of litigation lose much of their steam when factual disputes at enemy-combatant hearings are limited to the alleged combatant's acts. This focus meddles little, if at all, in the strategy or conduct of war, inquiring only into the appropriateness of continuing to detain an individual claimed to have taken up arms against the United States. While we accord the greatest respect and consideration to the judgments of military authorities in matters relating to the actual prosecution of a war, and recognize that the scope of that discretion necessarily is wide, it does not infringe on the core role of the military for the courts to exercise their own time-honored and constitutionally mandated roles of reviewing and resolving claims like those presented here.

In sum, while the full protections that accompany challenges to detentions in other settings may prove unworkable and inappropriate in the enemy-combatant setting, the threats to military operations posed by a basic system of independent review are not so weighty as to trump a citizen's core rights to challenge meaningfully the Government's case and to be heard by an impartial adjudicator.

In so holding, we necessarily reject the Government's assertion that separation of powers principles mandate a heavily circumscribed role for the courts in such circumstances. Indeed, the position that the courts must forgo any examination of the individual case and focus exclusively on the legality of the broader detention scheme cannot be mandated by any reasonable view of separation of powers, as this approach serves only to *condense* power into a single branch of government. We have long since made clear that a state of war is not a blank check for the President when it comes to the rights of the Nation's citizens. *Youngstown Sheet & Tube,* 343 U.S. [579,] 587 [1952]. Whatever power the United States Constitution envisions for the Executive in its exchanges with other nations or with enemy organizations in times of conflict, it most assuredly envisions a role for all three branches when individual liberties are at stake. . . . Thus, while we do not question that our due process assessment must pay keen attention to the particular burdens faced by the Executive in the context of military action, it would turn our system of checks and balances on its head to suggest that a citizen could not make his way to court with a challenge to the factual basis for his detention by his government, simply because the Executive opposes making available such a challenge. Absent suspension of the writ by Congress, a citizen detained as an enemy combatant is entitled to this process.

Because we conclude that due process demands some system for a citizen detainee to refute his classification, the proposed "some evidence" standard is inadequate. Any process in which the Executive's factual assertions go wholly unchallenged or are simply presumed correct without any opportunity for the alleged combatant to demonstrate otherwise falls constitutionally short. As the Government itself has recognized, we have utilized the "some evidence" standard in the past as a standard of review, not as a standard of proof. That is, it primarily has been employed by courts in examining an administrative record developed after an adversarial proceeding — one with process at least of the sort that we today hold is constitutionally mandated in the citizen enemy-combatant setting. This standard therefore is ill suited to the situation in which a habeas petitioner has received no prior proceedings before any tribunal and had no prior opportunity to rebut the Executive's factual assertions before a neutral decisionmaker.

Today we are faced only with such a case. Aside from unspecified "screening" processes, and military interrogations in which the Government suggests Hamdi could have contested his classification, Hamdi has received no process. An interrogation by one's captor, however effective an intelligence-gathering tool, hardly constitutes a constitutionally adequate factfinding before a neutral decisionmaker. . . . Plainly, the "process" Hamdi has received is not that to which he is entitled under the Due Process Clause.

There remains the possibility that the standards we have articulated could be met by an appropriately authorized and properly constituted military tribunal. Indeed, it is notable that military regulations already provide for such process in related instances, dictating that tribunals be made available to determine the status of enemy detainees who assert prisoner-of-war status under the Geneva Convention. In the absence of such process, however, a court that receives a petition for a writ of habeas corpus from an alleged enemy combatant must itself ensure that the minimum requirements of due process are achieved. Both courts below recognized as much, focusing their energies on the question of whether Hamdi was due an opportunity to rebut the Government's case against him. The Government, too, proceeded on this assumption, presenting its affidavit and then seeking that it be evaluated under a deferential standard of review based on burdens that it alleged would accompany any greater process. As we have discussed, a habeas court in a case such as this may accept affidavit evidence like that contained in the Mobbs Declaration, so long as it also permits the alleged combatant to present his own factual case to rebut the Government's return. We anticipate that a District Court would proceed with the caution that we have indicated is necessary in this setting, engaging in a factfinding process that is both prudent and incremental. We have no reason to doubt that courts faced with these sensitive matters will pay proper heed both to the matters of national security that might arise in an individual case and to the constitutional limitations safeguarding essential liberties that remain vibrant even in times of security concerns. . . .

The judgment of the United States Court of Appeals for the Fourth Circuit is vacated, and the case is remanded for further proceedings.

It is so ordered.

Justice SOUTER, with whom Justice GINSBURG joins, concurring in part, dissenting in part, and concurring in the judgment.

. . . The plurality rejects any such limit on the exercise of habeas jurisdiction and so far I agree with its opinion. The plurality does, however, accept the Government's position that if Hamdi's designation as an enemy combatant is correct, his detention (at least as to some period) is authorized by [AUMF]. Here, I disagree and respectfully dissent. . . .

The threshold issue is how broadly or narrowly to read the Non-Detention Act, the tone of which is severe: "No citizen shall be imprisoned or otherwise detained by the United States except pursuant to an Act of Congress." Should the severity of the Act be relieved when the Government's stated factual justification for incommunicado detention is a war on terrorism, so that the Government may be said to act "pursuant" to congressional terms that fall short of explicit authority to imprison individuals? With one possible though important qualification, the answer has to be no. For a number of reasons, the prohibition within § 4001(a) has to be read broadly to accord the statute a long reach and to impose a burden of justification on the Government.

First, the circumstances in which the Act was adopted point the way to this interpretation. The provision superseded a cold-war statute . . . which had authorized the Attorney General, in time of emergency, to detain anyone reasonably thought likely to engage in espionage or sabotage. That statute was repealed in 1971 out of fear that it could authorize a repetition of the World War II internment of citizens of Japanese ancestry; Congress meant to preclude another episode like the one described in *Korematsu v. United States,* 323 U.S. 214 (1944). . . .

The fact that Congress intended to guard against a repetition of the World War II internments when it repealed the 1950 statute and gave us § 4001(a) provides a powerful reason to think that § 4001(a) was meant to require clear congressional authorization before any citizen can be placed in a cell. It is not merely that the legislative history shows that § 4001(a) was thought necessary in anticipation of times just like the present, in which the safety of the country is threatened. To appreciate what is most significant, one must only recall that the internments of the 1940s were accomplished by Executive action. . . . When, therefore, Congress repealed the 1950 Act and adopted § 4001(a) for the purpose of avoiding another *Korematsu,* it intended to preclude reliance on vague congressional authority (for example, providing "accommodations" for those subject to removal) as authority for detention or imprisonment at the discretion of the Executive (maintaining detention camps of American citizens, for example). In requiring that any Executive detention be "pursuant to an Act of Congress," then, Congress necessarily meant to require a congressional enactment that clearly authorized detention or imprisonment.

Finally, . . . [t]he defining character of American constitutional government is its constant tension between security and liberty, serving both by partial helpings of each. In a government of separated powers, deciding finally on what is a reasonable degree of guaranteed liberty whether in peace or war (or some condition in between) is not well entrusted to the Executive Branch of Government, whose particular responsibility is to maintain security. For reasons of inescapable human nature, the branch of the Government asked to counter a serious threat is not the branch on which to rest the Nation's entire reliance in striking the balance between the will to win and the cost in liberty on the way to victory; the responsibility for security will naturally amplify the claim that security legitimately raises. A reasonable balance is more likely to be reached on the judgment of a different branch, just as Madison said in remarking that "the constant aim is to divide and arrange the several offices in such a manner as that each may be a check on the other — that the private interest of every individual may be a sentinel over the public rights." The Federalist No. 51. Hence the need for an assessment by Congress before citizens are subject to lockup, and likewise the need for a clearly expressed congressional resolution of the competing claims.

Under this principle of reading § 4001(a) robustly to require a clear statement of authorization to detain, none of the Government's arguments suffices to justify Hamdi's detention. [Discussion omitted rejecting Government arguments based on statutory and international law grounds. — Eds.]

Since the Government has given no reason either to deflect the application of § 4001(a) or to hold it to be satisfied, I need to go no further; the Government hints of a constitutional challenge to the statute, but it presents none here. I will, however, stray across the line between statutory and constitutional territory just far enough to note the weakness of the Government's mixed claim of inherent, extrastatutory authority under a combination of Article II of the Constitution and the usages of war. It is in fact in this connection that the Government developed its argument that the exercise of war powers justifies the detention, and what I have just said about its inadequacy applies here as well. Beyond that, it is instructive to recall Justice Jackson's observation that the President is not Commander in Chief of the country, only of the military. *Youngstown Sheet & Tube Co. v. Sawyer*, 343 U.S. 579, 643-644 (1952) (concurring opinion); *see also, id.* at 637-638 (Presidential authority is "at its lowest ebb" where the President acts contrary to congressional will).

There may be room for one qualification to Justice Jackson's statement, however: in a moment of genuine emergency, when the Government must act with no time for deliberation, the Executive may be able to detain a citizen if there is reason to fear he is an imminent threat to the safety of the Nation and its people (though I doubt there is any want of statutory authority). This case, however, does not present that question, because an emergency power of necessity must at least be limited by the emergency; Hamdi has been locked up for over two years.

Whether insisting on the careful scrutiny of emergency claims or on a vigorous reading of § 4001(a), we are heirs to a tradition given voice 800 years ago by Magna Carta, which, on the barons' insistence, confined executive power by "the law of the land."

Because I find Hamdi's detention forbidden by § 4001(a) and unauthorized by the [AUMF], I would not reach any questions of what process he may be due in litigating disputed issues in a proceeding under the habeas statute or prior to the habeas enquiry itself. For me, it suffices that the Government has failed to justify holding him in the absence of a further Act of Congress, criminal charges, a showing that the detention conforms to the laws of war, or a demonstration that § 4001(a) is unconstitutional. I would therefore vacate the judgment of the Court of Appeals and remand for proceedings consistent with this view.

Since this disposition does not command a majority of the Court, however, the need to give practical effect to the conclusions of eight members of the Court rejecting the Government's position calls for me to join with the plurality in ordering remand on terms closest to those I would impose. Although I think litigation of Hamdi's status as an enemy combatant is unnecessary, the terms of the plurality's remand will allow Hamdi to offer evidence that he is not an enemy combatant, and he should at the least have the benefit of that opportunity.

It should go without saying that in joining with the plurality to produce a judgment, I do not adopt the plurality's resolution of constitutional issues that I would not reach. It is not that I could disagree with the plurality's determinations (given the plurality's view of the [AUMF]) that someone in Hamdi's position is entitled at a minimum to notice of the Government's claimed factual basis for holding him, and to a fair chance to rebut it before a neutral decision maker, nor, of course, could I disagree with the plurality's affirmation of Hamdi's right to counsel. On the other hand, I do not mean to imply agreement that the Government could claim an evidentiary presumption casting the burden of rebuttal on Hamdi, see ante, at 27, or that an opportunity to litigate before a military tribunal might obviate or truncate enquiry by a court on habeas.

Subject to these qualifications, I join with the plurality in a judgment of the Court vacating the Fourth Circuit's judgment and remanding the case.

Justice SCALIA, with whom Justice STEVENS joins, dissenting.

. . . This case brings into conflict the competing demands of national security and our citizens' constitutional right to personal liberty. Although I share the Court's evident unease as it seeks to reconcile the two, I do not agree with its resolution.

Where the Government accuses a citizen of waging war against it, our constitutional tradition has been to prosecute him in federal court for treason or some other crime. Where the exigencies of war prevent that, the Constitution's Suspension Clause, Art. I, § 9, cl. 2, allows Congress to relax the usual protections temporarily. Absent suspension, however, the Executive's assertion of military exigency has not been thought sufficient to permit detention without charge. No one contends that the congressional Authorization for Use of Military Force, on which the Government relies to justify its actions here, is an implementation of the Suspension Clause. Accordingly, I would reverse the decision below.

The very core of liberty secured by our Anglo-Saxon system of separated powers has been freedom from indefinite imprisonment at the will of the Executive. [Blackstone quote omitted.]

[Blackstone's] words were well known to the Founders. . . . The two ideas central to Blackstone's understanding — due process as the right secured, and habeas corpus as the instrument by which due process could be insisted upon by a citizen illegally imprisoned — found expression in the Constitution's Due Process and Suspension Clauses. *See* Amdt. 5; Art. I, § 9, cl. 2.

The gist of the Due Process Clause, as understood at the founding and since, was to force the Government to follow those common-law procedures traditionally deemed necessary before depriving a person of life, liberty, or property. When a citizen was deprived of liberty because of alleged criminal conduct, those procedures typically required committal by a magistrate followed by indictment and trial. . . . It is unthinkable that the Executive could render otherwise criminal grounds for detention noncriminal merely by disclaiming an intent to prosecute, or by asserting that it was incapacitating dangerous offenders rather than punishing wrongdoing. These due process rights have historically been vindicated by the writ of habeas corpus. [Historical discussion omitted]

The writ of habeas corpus was preserved in the Constitution — the only common-law writ to be explicitly mentioned. *See* Art. I, § 9, cl. 2. Hamilton lauded "the establishment of the writ of *habeas corpus*" in his Federalist defense as a means to protect against "the practice of arbitrary imprisonments . . . in all ages, [one of] the favourite and most formidable instruments of tyranny." The Federalist No. 84, *supra,* at 444. Indeed, availability of the writ under the new Constitution (along with the requirement of trial by jury in criminal cases, *see* Art. III, § 2, cl. 3) was his basis for arguing that additional, explicit procedural protections were unnecessary. *See* The Federalist No. 83, at 433.

The allegations here, of course, are no ordinary accusations of criminal activity. Yaser Esam Hamdi has been imprisoned because the Government believes he participated in the waging of war against the United States. The relevant question, then, is whether there is a different, special procedure for imprisonment of a citizen accused of wrongdoing *by aiding the enemy in wartime.*

Justice O'CONNOR, writing for a plurality of this Court, asserts that captured enemy combatants (other than those suspected of war crimes) have traditionally been detained until the cessation of hostilities and then released. That is probably an accurate description of wartime practice with respect to enemy *aliens*. The tradition with respect to American citizens, however, has been quite different. Citizens aiding the enemy have been treated as traitors subject to the criminal process. [Historical discussion omitted]

In more recent times, too, citizens have been charged and tried in Article III courts for acts of war against the United States, even when their noncitizen co-conspirators were not. For example, two American citizens alleged to have participated during World War I in a spying conspiracy on behalf of Germany were tried in federal court. A German member of the same conspiracy was subjected to military process. During World War II, the famous German saboteurs of *Ex parte Quirin,* 317 U.S. 1 (1942) received military process, but the citizens who associated with them (with the exception of one citizen-saboteur, discussed below) were punished under the criminal process.

There are times when military exigency renders resort to the traditional criminal process impracticable. English law accommodated such exigencies by allowing legislative suspension of the writ of habeas corpus for brief periods. . . . Where the Executive has not pursued the usual course of charge, committal, and conviction, it has historically secured the Legislature's explicit approval of a suspension. . . . Our Federal Constitution contains a provision explicitly permitting suspension, but limiting the situations in which it may be invoked: "The privilege of the Writ of Habeas Corpus shall not be suspended, unless when in Cases of Rebellion or Invasion the public Safety may require it." Art. I, § 9, cl. 2. Although this provision does not state that suspension must be effected by, or authorized by, a legislative act, it has been so understood, consistent with English practice and the Clause's placement in Article I. . . .

Of course the extensive historical evidence of criminal convictions and habeas suspensions does not *necessarily* refute the Government's position in this case. When the writ is suspended, the Government is entirely free from judicial oversight. It does not claim such total liberation here, but argues that it need only produce what it calls "some evidence" to satisfy a habeas court that a detained individual is an enemy combatant. Even if suspension of the writ on the one hand, and committal for criminal charges on the other hand, have been the only *traditional* means of dealing with citizens who levied war against their own country, it is theoretically possible that the Constitution does not *require* a choice between these alternatives.

I believe, however, that substantial evidence does refute that possibility. First, the text of the 1679 Habeas Corpus Act makes clear that indefinite imprisonment on reasonable suspicion is not an available option of treatment for those accused of aiding the enemy, absent a suspension of the writ.

In the United States, this Act was read as "enforc[ing] the common law," and shaped the early understanding of the scope of the writ. As noted above, the Act specifically addressed those committed for high treason, and provided a remedy if they were not *indicted and tried* by the second succeeding court term. That remedy was *not* a bobtailed judicial inquiry into whether there were reasonable grounds to believe the prisoner had taken up arms against the King. Rather, if the prisoner was not indicted and tried within the prescribed time, "he shall be discharged from his Imprisonment." 31 Car. 2, c. 2, § 7. The Act does not contain any exception for wartime. That omission is conspicuous, since § 7 explicitly addresses the offense of "High Treason," which often involved offenses of a military nature.

Writings from the founding generation also suggest that, without exception, the only constitutional alternatives are to charge the crime or suspend the writ. In 1788, Thomas Jefferson wrote to James Madison questioning the need for a Suspension Clause in cases of rebellion in the proposed Constitution. His letter illustrates the constraints under which the Founders understood themselves to operate:

> "Why suspend the Hab. corp. in insurrections and rebellions? The parties who may be arrested may be charged instantly with a well defined crime. Of course the judge will remand them. If the publick safety requires that the government should have a man imprisoned on less probable testimony in those than in other emergencies; let him be taken and tried, retaken and retried, while the necessity continues, only giving him redress against the government for damages." 13 Papers of Thomas Jefferson 442 (July 31, 1788) (J. Boyd ed.1956).

A similar view was reflected in the 1807 House debates over suspension during the armed uprising that came to be known as Burr's conspiracy:

> "With regard to those persons who may be implicated in the conspiracy, if the writ of habeas corpus be not suspended, what will be the consequence? When apprehended, they will be brought before a court of justice, who will decide whether there is any evidence that will justify their commitment for farther prosecution. From the communication of the Executive, it appeared there was sufficient evidence to authorize their commitment. Several months would elapse before their final trial, which would give time to collect evidence, and if this shall be sufficient, they will not fail to receive the punishment merited by their crimes, and inflicted by the laws of their country." 16 Annals of Congress, at 405 (remarks of Rep. Burwell).

The absence of military authority to imprison citizens indefinitely in wartime — whether or not a probability of treason had been established by means less than jury trial — was confirmed by three cases decided during and immediately after the War of 1812. . . .

President Lincoln, when he purported to suspend habeas corpus without congressional authorization during the Civil War, apparently did not doubt that suspension was required if the prisoner was to be held without criminal trial. In his famous message to Congress on July 4, 1861, he argued only that he could suspend the writ, not that even without suspension, his imprisonment of citizens without criminal trial was permitted. *See* Special Session Message, 6 Messages and Papers 20-31.

Further evidence comes from this Court's decision in *Ex parte Milligan, supra*. There, the Court issued the writ to an American citizen who had been tried by military commission for offenses that included conspiring to overthrow the Government, seize munitions, and liberate prisoners of war. *Id.* at 6–7. The Court rejected in no uncertain terms the Government's assertion that military jurisdiction was proper "under the 'laws and usages of war' " . . . .

Milligan responded to the argument, repeated by the Government in this case, that it is dangerous to leave suspected traitors at large in time of war:

> "If it was dangerous, in the distracted condition of affairs, to leave Milligan unrestrained of his liberty, because he 'conspired against the government, afforded aid and comfort to rebels, and incited the people to insurrection,' the *law* said arrest him, confine him closely, render him powerless to do further mischief; and then present his case to the grand jury of the district, with proofs of his guilt, and, if indicted, try him according to the course of the common law. If this had been done, the Constitution would have been vindicated, the law of 1863 enforced, and the securities for personal liberty preserved and defended." *Id.* at 122.

Thus, criminal process was viewed as the primary means — and the only means absent congressional action suspending the writ — not only to punish traitors, but to incapacitate them.

The proposition that the Executive lacks indefinite wartime detention authority over citizens is consistent with the Founders' general mistrust of military power permanently at the Executive's disposal. In the Founders' view, the "blessings of liberty" were threatened by "those military establishments which must gradually poison its very fountain." The Federalist No. 45, p. 238 (J. Madison). No fewer than 10 issues of the Federalist were devoted in whole or part to allaying fears of oppression from the proposed Constitution's authorization of standing armies in peacetime. Many safeguards in the Constitution reflect these concerns. . . . As Hamilton explained, the President's military authority would be "much inferior" to that of the British King. . . .

A view of the Constitution that gives the Executive authority to use military force rather than the force of law against citizens on American soil flies in the face of the mistrust that engendered these provisions.

The Government argues that our more recent jurisprudence ratifies its indefinite imprisonment of a citizen within the territorial jurisdiction of federal courts. It places primary reliance upon *Ex parte Quirin,* 317 U.S. 1 (1942), . . . The case was not this Court's finest hour. The Court upheld the commission and denied relief in a brief *per curiam* issued the day after oral argument concluded, a week later the Government carried out the commission's death sentence upon six saboteurs, including Haupt. The Court eventually explained its reasoning in a written opinion issued several months later.

Only three paragraphs of the Court's lengthy opinion dealt with the particular circumstances of Haupt's case. The Government argued that Haupt, like the other petitioners, could be tried by military commission under the laws of war. In agreeing with that contention, *Quirin* purported to interpret the language of *Milligan* quoted above (the law of war "can never be applied to citizens in states which have upheld the authority of the government, and where the courts are open and their process unobstructed"). . . .

In my view [*Quirin*] seeks to revise *Milligan* rather than describe it. *Milligan* had involved (among other issues) two separate questions: (1) whether the military trial of Milligan was justified by the laws of war, and if not (2) whether the President's suspension of the writ, pursuant to congressional authorization, prevented the issuance of habeas corpus. The Court's categorical language about the law of war's inapplicability to citizens where the courts are open (with no exception mentioned for citizens who were prisoners of war) was contained in its discussion of the first point. The factors pertaining to whether Milligan could reasonably be considered a belligerent and prisoner of war, while mentioned earlier in the opinion, were made relevant and brought to bear in the Court's later discussion, of whether Milligan came within the statutory provision that effectively made an exception to Congress's authorized suspension of the writ for (as the Court described it) "all parties, not prisoners of war, resident in their respective jurisdictions, . . . who were citizens of states in which the administration of the laws in the Federal tribunals was unimpaired." *Milligan* thus understood was in accord with the traditional law of habeas corpus I have described: Though treason often occurred in wartime, there was, absent provision for special treatment in a congressional suspension of the writ, no exception to the right to trial by jury for citizens who could be called "belligerents" or "prisoners of war."

But even if *Quirin* gave a correct description of *Milligan,* or made an irrevocable revision of it, *Quirin* would still not justify denial of the writ here. In *Quirin* it was uncontested that the petitioners were members of enemy forces. They were "*admitted* enemy invaders," and it was "undisputed" that they had landed in the United States in service of German forces. The specific holding of the Court was only that, "upon the *conceded* facts," the petitioners were "plainly within [the] boundaries" of military jurisdiction. But where those jurisdictional facts are *not* conceded — where the petitioner insists that he is *not* a belligerent — *Quirin* left the pre-existing law in place: Absent suspension of the writ, a citizen held where the courts are open is entitled either to criminal trial or to a judicial decree requiring his release.

It follows from what I have said that Hamdi is entitled to a habeas decree requiring his release unless (1) criminal proceedings are promptly brought, or (2) Congress has suspended the writ of habeas corpus. A suspension of the writ could, of course, lay down conditions for continued detention, similar to those that today's opinion prescribes under the Due Process Clause. But there is a world of difference between the people's representatives' determining the need for that suspension (and prescribing the conditions for it), and this Court's doing so.

The plurality finds justification for Hamdi's imprisonment in [AUMF]. . . . This is not remotely a congressional suspension of the writ, and no one claims that it is. Contrary to the plurality's view, I do not think this statute even authorizes detention of a citizen with the clarity necessary to satisfy the interpretive canon that statutes should be construed so as to avoid grave constitutional concerns, or with the clarity necessary to overcome the statutory prescription [in] 18 U.S.C. § 4001(a). But even if it did, I would not permit it to overcome Hamdi's entitlement to habeas corpus relief. The Suspension Clause of the Constitution, which carefully circumscribes the conditions under which the writ can be withheld, would be a sham if it could be evaded by congressional prescription of requirements *other than the common-law requirement of committal for criminal prosecution* that render the writ, though available, unavailing. If the Suspension Clause does not guarantee the citizen that he will either be tried or released, unless the conditions for suspending the writ exist and the grave action of suspending the writ has been taken; if it merely guarantees the citizen that he will not be detained unless Congress by ordinary legislation says he can be detained; it guarantees him very little indeed.

It should not be thought, however, that the plurality's evisceration of the Suspension Clause augments, principally, the power of Congress. As usual, the major effect of its constitutional improvisation is to increase the power of the Court. Having found a congressional authorization for detention of citizens where none clearly exists; and having discarded the categorical procedural protection of the Suspension Clause; the plurality then proceeds, under the guise of the Due Process Clause, to prescribe what procedural protections *it* thinks appropriate. It "weigh[s] the private interest . . . against the Government's asserted interest," and — just as though writing a new Constitution — comes up with an unheard-of system in which the citizen rather than the Government bears the burden of proof, testimony is by hearsay rather than live witnesses, and the presiding officer may well be a "neutral" military officer rather than judge and jury. It claims authority to engage in this sort of "judicious balancing" from *Mathews v. Eldridge,* a case involving . . . *the withdrawal of disability benefits!* Whatever the merits of this technique when newly recognized property rights are at issue (and even there they are questionable), it has no place where the Constitution and the common law already supply an answer.

Having distorted the Suspension Clause, the plurality finishes up by transmogrifying the Great Writ — disposing of the present habeas petition by remanding for the District Court to "engag[e] in a factfinding process that is both prudent and incremental." "In the absence of [the Executive's prior provision of procedures that satisfy due process], . . . a court that receives a petition for a writ of habeas corpus from an alleged enemy combatant must itself ensure that the minimum requirements of due process are achieved." This judicial remediation of executive default is unheard of. The role of habeas corpus is to determine the legality of executive detention, not to supply the omitted process necessary to make it legal. It is not the habeas court's function to make illegal detention legal by supplying a process that the Government could have provided, but chose not to. If Hamdi is being imprisoned in violation of the Constitution (because without due process of law), then his habeas petition should be granted; the Executive may then hand him over to the criminal authorities, whose detention for the purpose of prosecution will be lawful, or else must release him.

There is a certain harmony of approach in the plurality's making up for Congress's failure to invoke the Suspension Clause and its making up for the Executive's failure to apply what it says are needed procedures — an approach that reflects what might be called a Mr. Fix-it Mentality. The plurality seems to view it as its mission to Make Everything Come Out Right, rather than merely to decree the consequences, as far as individual rights are concerned, of the other two branches' actions and omissions. Has the Legislature failed to suspend the writ in the current dire emergency? Well, we will remedy that failure by prescribing the reasonable conditions that a suspension should have included. And has the Executive failed to live up to those reasonable conditions? Well, we will ourselves make that failure good, so that this dangerous fellow (if he is dangerous) need not be set free. The problem with this approach is not only that it steps out of the courts' modest and limited role in a democratic society; but that by repeatedly doing what it thinks the political branches ought to do it encourages their lassitude and saps the vitality of government by the people.

Several limitations give my views in this matter a relatively narrow compass. They apply only to citizens, accused of being enemy combatants, who are detained within the territorial jurisdiction of a federal court. This is not likely to be a numerous group; currently we know of only two, Hamdi and Jose Padilla. Where the citizen is captured outside and held outside the United States, the constitutional requirements may be different. Cf. *Johnson v. Eisentrager,* 339 U.S. 763, 769-771 (1950). Moreover, even within the United States, the accused citizen-enemy combatant may lawfully be detained once prosecution is in progress or in contemplation. The Government has been notably successful in securing conviction, and hence long-term custody or execution, of those who have waged war against the state.

I frankly do not know whether these tools are sufficient to meet the Government's security needs, including the need to obtain intelligence through interrogation. It is far beyond my competence, or the Court's competence, to determine that. But it is not beyond Congress's. If the situation demands it, the Executive can ask Congress to authorize suspension of the writ — which can be made subject to whatever conditions Congress deems appropriate, including even the procedural novelties invented by the plurality today. To be sure, suspension is limited by the Constitution to cases of rebellion or invasion. But whether the attacks of September 11, 2001, constitute an "invasion," and whether those attacks still justify suspension several years later, are questions for Congress rather than this Court. If civil rights are to be curtailed during wartime, it must be done openly and democratically, as the Constitution requires, rather than by silent erosion through an opinion of this Court.

The Founders well understood the difficult tradeoff between safety and freedom. . . . The Founders warned us about the risk, and equipped us with a Constitution designed to deal with it. Many think it not only inevitable but entirely proper that liberty give way to security in times of national crisis — that, at the extremes of military exigency, *inter arma silent leges*. Whatever the general merits of the view that war silences law or modulates its voice, that view has no place in the interpretation and application of a Constitution designed precisely to confront war and, in a manner that accords with democratic principles, to accommodate it. Because the Court has proceeded to meet the current emergency in a manner the Constitution does not envision, I respectfully dissent.

Justice THOMAS, dissenting.

The Executive Branch, acting pursuant to the powers vested in the President by the Constitution and with explicit congressional approval, has determined that Yaser Hamdi is an enemy combatant and should be detained. This detention falls squarely within the Federal Government's war powers, and we lack the expertise and capacity to second-guess that decision. As such, petitioners' habeas challenge should fail, and there is no reason to remand the case. The plurality reaches a contrary conclusion by failing adequately to consider basic principles of the constitutional structure as it relates to national security and foreign affairs and by using the balancing scheme of *Mathews v. Eldridge*. I do not think that the Federal Government's war powers can be balanced away by this Court. Arguably, Congress could provide for additional procedural protections, but until it does, we have no right to insist upon them. But even if I were to agree with the general approach the plurality takes, I could not accept the particulars. The plurality utterly fails to account for the Government's compelling interests and for our own institutional inability to weigh competing concerns correctly. I respectfully dissent.

"It is 'obvious and unarguable' that no governmental interest is more compelling than the security of the Nation." *Haig v. Agee,* 453 U.S. 280, 307 (1981) . . . But because the Founders understood that they could not foresee the myriad potential threats to national security that might later arise, they chose to create a Federal Government that necessarily possesses sufficient power to handle any threat to the security of the Nation. [Citations to the Federalist omitted. — Eds.]

The Founders intended that the President have primary responsibility — along with the necessary power — to protect the national security and to conduct the Nation's foreign relations. They did so principally because the structural advantages of a unitary Executive are essential in these domains. "Energy in the executive is a leading character in the definition of good government. It is essential to the protection of the community against foreign attacks." The Federalist No. 70, p. 471 (A. Hamilton). . . . These structural advantages are most important in the national-security and foreign-affairs contexts. . . . This Court has long recognized these features and has accordingly held that the President has *constitutional* authority to protect the national security and that this authority carries with it broad discretion. . . .

The Court has acknowledged that the President has the authority to "employ [the Nation's Armed Forces] in the manner he may deem most effectual to harass and conquer and subdue the enemy." With respect to foreign affairs as well, the Court has recognized the President's independent authority and need to be free from interference. *See, e.g., United States v. Curtiss-Wright Export Corp.*, 299 U.S. 304, 320 (1936).

Congress, to be sure, has a substantial and essential role in both foreign affairs and national security. But it is crucial to recognize that *judicial* interference in these domains destroys the purpose of vesting primary responsibility in a unitary Executive. I cannot improve on Justice Jackson's words, speaking for the Court:

"The President, both as Commander-in-Chief and as the Nation's organ for foreign affairs, has available intelligence services whose reports are not and ought not to be published to the world. It would be intolerable that courts, without the relevant information, should review and perhaps nullify actions of the Executive taken on information properly held secret. Nor can courts sit *in camera* in order to be taken into executive confidences. But even if courts could require full disclosure, the very nature of executive decisions as to foreign policy is political, not judicial. Such decisions are wholly confided by our Constitution to the political departments of the government, Executive and Legislative. They are delicate, complex, and involve large elements of prophecy. They are and should be undertaken only by those directly responsible to the people whose welfare they advance or imperil. They are decisions of a kind for which the Judiciary has neither aptitude, facilities nor responsibility and which has long been held to belong in the domain of political power not subject to judicial intrusion or inquiry." [*Chicago & Southern Air Lines, Inc. v. Waterman S.S. Corp.*, 333 U.S. 103, 111 (1948)]. . . .

For these institutional reasons and because "Congress cannot anticipate and legislate with regard to every possible action the President may find it necessary to take or every possible situation in which he might act," it should come as no surprise that "[s]uch failure of Congress . . . does not, 'especially . . . in the areas of foreign policy and national security,' imply 'congressional disapproval' of action taken by the Executive." *Dames & Moore v. Regan,* 453 U.S. 654, 678 (1981). Rather, in these domains, the fact that Congress has provided the President with broad authorities does not imply — and the Judicial Branch should not infer — that Congress intended to deprive him of particular powers not specifically enumerated. As far as the courts are concerned, "the enactment of legislation closely related to the question of the President's authority in a particular case which evinces legislative intent to accord the President broad discretion may be considered to 'invite' 'measures on independent presidential responsibility.' "

Finally, and again for the same reasons, where "the President acts pursuant to an express or implied authorization from Congress, he exercises not only his powers but also those delegated by Congress[, and i]n such a case the executive action 'would be supported by the strongest of presumptions and the widest latitude of judicial interpretation, and the burden of persuasion would rest heavily upon any who might attack it.' " That is why the Court has explained, in a case analogous to this one, that "the detention[,] ordered by the President in the declared exercise of his powers as Commander in Chief of the Army in time of war and of grave public danger[, is] not to be set aside by the courts without the clear conviction that [it is] in conflict with the Constitution or laws of Congress constitutionally enacted." *Ex parte Quirin,* 317 U.S. 1, 25, 63 (1942). This deference extends to the President's determination of all the factual predicates necessary to conclude that a given action is appropriate. To be sure, the Court has at times held, in specific circumstances, that the military acted beyond its warmaking authority. But these cases are distinguishable in important ways. [Distinctions omitted. — Eds.]

I acknowledge that the question whether Hamdi's executive detention is lawful is a question properly resolved by the Judicial Branch, though the question comes to the Court with the strongest presumptions in favor of the Government. The plurality agrees that Hamdi's detention is lawful if he is an enemy combatant. But the question whether Hamdi is actually an enemy combatant is "of a kind for which the Judiciary has neither aptitude, facilities nor responsibility and which has long been held to belong in the domain of political power not subject to judicial intrusion or inquiry." *Chicago & Southern Air Lines,* 333 U.S. at 111. That is, although it is appropriate for the Court to determine the judicial question whether the President has the asserted authority, we lack the information and expertise to question whether Hamdi is actually an enemy combatant, a question the resolution of which is committed to other branches. . . .

The decision whether someone is an enemy combatant is, no doubt, "delicate, complex, and involv[es] large elements of prophecy," *Chicago &*

Southern Air Lines, supra, at 111, 68 S. Ct. 431, which, incidentally might in part explain why "the Government has never provided any court with the full criteria that it uses in classifying individuals as such."

"The war power of the national government is 'the power to wage war successfully.'" *Lichter v. United States,* 334 U.S. 742, 767, n.9 (1948), It follows that this power "is not limited to victories in the field, but carries with it the inherent power to guard against the immediate renewal of the conflict," *In re Yamashita,* 327 U.S. 1, 12 (1946). . . .

Although the President very well may have inherent authority to detain those arrayed against our troops, I agree with the plurality that we need not decide that question because Congress has authorized the President to do so [in the AUMF]. . . .

The plurality, however, qualifies its recognition of the President's authority to detain enemy combatants in the war on terrorism in ways that are at odds with our precedent. Thus, the plurality relies primarily on Article 118 of the Geneva Convention (III) Relative to the Treatment of Prisoners of War, Aug. 12, 1949, [1955] 6 U.S.T. 3406, T.I.A.S. No. 3364, for the proposition that "[i]t is a clearly established principle of the law of war that detention may last no longer than active hostilities." It then appears to limit the President's authority to detain by requiring that the record establis[h] that United States troops are still involved in active combat in Afghanistan because, in that case, detention would be "part of the exercise of 'necessary and appropriate force.'" But I do not believe that we may diminish the Federal Government's war powers by reference to a treaty and certainly not to a treaty that does not apply. Further, we are bound by the political branches' determination that the United States is at war. And, in any case, the power to detain does not end with the cessation of formal hostilities.

Accordingly, the President's action here is "supported by the strongest of presumptions and the widest latitude of judicial interpretation." *Dames & Moore,* 453 U.S. at 668. The question becomes whether the Federal Government (rather than the President acting alone) has power to detain Hamdi as an enemy combatant. More precisely, we must determine whether the Government may detain Hamdi given the procedures that were used.

I agree with the plurality that the Federal Government has power to detain those that the Executive Branch determines to be enemy combatants. But I do not think that the plurality has adequately explained the breadth of the President's authority to detain enemy combatants, an authority that includes making virtually conclusive factual findings. In my view, the structural considerations discussed above, as recognized in our precedent, demonstrate that we lack the capacity and responsibility to second-guess this determination.

This makes complete sense once the process that is due Hamdi is made clear. As an initial matter, it is possible that the Due Process Clause requires only "that our Government must proceed according to the 'law of the land' — that is, according to written constitutional and statutory provisions." I need not go this far today because the Court has already explained the nature of due process in this context.

In a case strikingly similar to this one, the Court addressed a Governor's authority to detain for an extended period a person the executive believed to be responsible, in part, for a local insurrection. Justice Holmes wrote for a unanimous Court:

> "When it comes to a decision by the head of the State upon a matter involving its life, the ordinary rights of individuals must yield to what *he deems* the necessities of the moment. Public danger warrants the substitution of executive process for judicial process. This was admitted with regard to killing men in the actual clash of arms, and we think it obvious, although it was disputed, that the same is true of temporary detention to prevent apprehended harm." *Moyer [v. Peabody]*, 212 U.S., [78,] 85 [(1909)] (citation omitted; emphasis added).

The Court answered Moyer's claim that he had been denied due process by emphasizing that

> "it is familiar that what is due process of law depends on circumstances. It varies with the subject-matter and the necessities of the situation. Thus summary proceedings suffice for taxes, and executive decisions for exclusion from the country. . . . Such arrests are not necessarily for punishment, but are by way of precaution to prevent the exercise of hostile power." (citations omitted).

In this context, due process requires nothing more than a good-faith executive determination. To be clear: The Court has held that an executive, acting pursuant to statutory and constitutional authority may, consistent with the Due Process Clause, unilaterally decide to detain an individual if the executive deems this necessary for the public safety *even if he is mistaken.*

Moyer is not an exceptional case. In *Luther v. Borden,* 7 How. 1 (1849), the Court discussed the President's constitutional and statutory authority, in response to a request from a state legislature or executive, " 'to call forth such number of the militia of any other State or States, as may be applied for, as he may judge sufficient to suppress [an] insurrection.' " The Court explained that courts could not review the President's decision to recognize one of the competing legislatures or executives. If a court could second-guess this determination, "it would become the duty of the court (provided it came to the conclusion that the President had decided incorrectly) to discharge those who were arrested or detained by the troops in the service of the United States." . . . The Court clearly contemplated that the President had authority to detain as he deemed necessary, and such detentions evidently comported with the Due Process Clause as long as the President correctly decided to call forth the militia, a question the Court said it could not review.

The Court also addressed the natural concern that placing "this power in the President is dangerous to liberty, and may be abused." The Court noted that "[a]ll power may be abused if placed in unworthy hands," and explained that "it would be difficult . . . to point out any other hands in which this power would be more safe, and at the same time equally effectual." Putting that aside, the Court emphasized that this power "is conferred upon him by the Constitution and laws of the United States, and must therefore be respected and enforced in its judicial tribunals." Finally, the Court explained that if the President abused this power "it would be in the power of Congress to apply the proper remedy. But the courts must administer the law as they find it." . . .

The Government's asserted authority to detain an individual that the President has determined to be an enemy combatant, at least while hostilities continue, comports with the Due Process Clause. As these cases also show, the Executive's decision that a detention is necessary to protect the public need not and should not be subjected to judicial second-guessing. Indeed, at least in the context of enemy-combatant determinations, this would defeat the unity, secrecy, and dispatch that the Founders believed to be so important to the warmaking function.

I therefore cannot agree with Justice SCALIA's conclusion that the Government must choose between using standard criminal processes and suspending the writ. . . . I admit that *Milligan* supports his position. But because the Executive Branch there, unlike here, did not follow a specific statutory mechanism provided by Congress, the Court did not need to reach the broader question of Congress' power, and its discussion on this point was arguably dicta.

More importantly, the Court referred frequently and pervasively to the criminal nature of the proceedings instituted against Milligan. Although I do acknowledge that the reasoning of these cases might apply beyond criminal punishment, the punishment-nonpunishment distinction harmonizes all of the precedent. And, subsequent cases have at least implicitly distinguished *Milligan* in just this way. Finally, *Quirin* overruled *Milligan* to the extent that those cases are inconsistent. *See Quirin*, 317 U.S. at 45 (limiting *Milligan* to its facts). Because the Government does not detain Hamdi in order to punish him, as the plurality acknowledges, *Milligan* [does] not control.

Justice SCALIA also finds support in a letter Thomas Jefferson wrote to James Madison. I agree that this provides some evidence for his position. But I think this plainly insufficient to rebut the authorities upon which I have relied. In any event, I do not believe that Justice SCALIA's evidence leads to the necessary "clear conviction that [the detention is] in conflict with the Constitution or laws of Congress constitutionally enacted," *Quirin, supra,* at 25, to justify nullifying the President's wartime action.

Finally, Justice SCALIA's position raises an additional concern. Justice SCALIA apparently does not disagree that the Federal Government has all power necessary to protect the Nation. If criminal processes do not suffice, however, Justice SCALIA would require Congress to suspend the writ. But the fact that the writ may not be suspended "unless when in Cases of Rebellion or Invasion the public Safety may require it," Art. I, § 9, cl. 2, poses two related problems. First, this condition might not obtain here or during many other emergencies during which this detention authority might be necessary. Congress would then have to choose between acting unconstitutionally and depriving the President of the tools he needs to protect the Nation. Second, I do not see how suspension would make constitutional otherwise unconstitutional detentions ordered by the President. It simply removes a remedy. Justice SCALIA's position might therefore require one or both of the political branches to act unconstitutionally in order to protect the Nation. But the power to protect the Nation must be the power to do so lawfully.

Accordingly, I conclude that the Government's detention of Hamdi as an enemy combatant does not violate the Constitution. By detaining Hamdi, the President, in the prosecution of a war and authorized by Congress, has acted well within his authority. Hamdi thereby received all the process to which he was due under the circumstances. I therefore believe that this is no occasion to balance the competing interests, as the plurality unconvincingly attempts to do.

Although I do not agree with the plurality that the balancing approach of *Mathews v. Eldridge,* is the appropriate analytical tool with which to analyze this case, I cannot help but explain that the plurality misapplies its chosen framework, one that if applied correctly would probably lead to the result I have reached. . . . At issue here is the far more significant interest of the security of the Nation. The Government seeks to further that interest by detaining an enemy soldier not only to prevent him from rejoining the ongoing fight. Rather, as the Government explains, detention can serve to gather critical intelligence regarding the intentions and capabilities of our adversaries, a function that the Government avers has become all the more important in the war on terrorism. [In deleted material, Justice Thomas argued that the plurality also underestimated the costs of the procedures it would require. — Eds.]

Undeniably, Hamdi has been deprived of a serious interest, one actually protected by the Due Process Clause. Against this, however, is the Government's overriding interest in protecting the Nation. If a deprivation of liberty can be justified by the need to protect a town, the protection of the Nation, *a fortiori,* justifies it.

I acknowledge that under the plurality's approach, it might, at times, be appropriate to give detainees access to counsel and notice of the factual basis for the Government's determination. But properly accounting for the Government's interests also requires concluding that access to counsel and to the factual basis would not always be warranted. Though common sense suffices, the Government thoroughly explains that counsel would often destroy the intelligence gathering function. Equally obvious is the Government's interest in not fighting the war in its own courts, and protecting classified information.

For these reasons, I would affirm the judgment of the Court of Appeals.

NOTE

In *Rumsfeld v. Padilla,* 542 U.S. 426 (2004), a companion case to *Hamdi,* the Court did not reach the question of whether the President possessed authority to detain unilaterally Padilla, an American citizen arrested at O'Hare Airport in Chicago, since it concluded that Padilla had filed his habeas petition in the wrong court. Justice Stevens wrote for four dissenters:

> At stake in this case is nothing less than the essence of a free society. Even more important than the method of selecting the people's rulers and their successors is the character of the constraints imposed on the Executive by the rule of law. Unconstrained Executive detention for the purpose of investigating and preventing subversive activity is the hallmark of the Star Chamber. Access to counsel for the purpose of protecting the citizen from official mistakes and mistreatment is the hallmark of due process.

> Executive detention of subversive citizens, like detention of enemy soldiers to keep them off the battlefield, may sometimes be justified to prevent persons from launching or becoming missiles of destruction. It may not, however, be justified by the naked interest in using unlawful procedures to extract information. Incommunicado detention for months on end is such a procedure. Whether the information so procured is more or less reliable than that acquired by more extreme forms of torture is of no consequence. For if this Nation is to remain true to the ideals symbolized by its flag, it must not wield the tools of tyrants even to resist an assault by the forces of tyranny.

Id. at _____.

§ 5.07   Presidential Accountability

[1]—Privilege

Page 383: [Insert the following after Note (14)]

(15) In *Cheney v. United States District Court for the District of Columbia,* 542 U.S. 367 (2004), the Court concluded that executive privilege need not be asserted for the Government to object to production of certain sensitive documents in civil litigation based on separation of powers concerns.

The dispute arose when various public interest groups brought actions alleging that the National Energy Policy Development Group (NEPDG), which President George W. Bush created under the Chairmanship of Vice President Richard B. Cheney, violated the Federal Advisory Committee Act (FACA). More specifically, the litigants claimed that NEPDG regularly met with certain nongovernmental employees, including lobbyists, who accordingly were *de facto* members thereby subjecting the body to disclosure and open-meeting requirements of FACA. Litigants sued Vice President Cheney and other governmental and nongovernmental defendants and sought an injunction requiring them to produce materials subject to FACA. The United States District Court allowed plaintiffs to direct discovery to Vice President Cheney et al. regarding NEPDG's structure and membership. The Vice President filed an interlocutory appeal and sought a writ of mandamus from the Court of Appeals to vacate the lower court's discovery orders. The Court of Appeals dismissed the Vice President's appeal and declined to issue the writ, in part on the grounds that other remedies were available. In particular, under *United States v. Nixon,* 418 U.S. 683 (1974), the court said the government must assert executive privilege with particularity to protect the President's prerogatives.

The Court did not agree. The presence, as a party subject to discovery orders, of the Vice President and those "in closest operational proximity to the President" with respect to the process of advising the President removed the case from normal rules governing interlocutory appeals of discovery orders. The Executive should not have to claim executive privilege to respond to discovery but could avail itself of general separation of powers arguments. Executive privilege should be invoked in extraordinary circumstances, not as a matter of routine. Although the President was not above the law, other branches of government should recognize "the paramount necessity of protecting the Executive Branch from vexatious litigation that might distract it from the energetic performance of its constitutional duties." The appellate court's reliance on *United States v. Nixon* was misplaced. Whereas *United States v. Nixon* was a criminal case, this case was a civil proceeding in which information sought from the Executive had less weight. Whereas the criminal justice system afforded certain protections against prosecutorial overreaching, including the accountability of prosecutors, civil litigants were not subject to such restraints.

The Court remanded the case to the appellate court to consider the Government's mandamus petition, bearing in mind, among other factors (some of which pointed in different directions), "the burdens imposed on the Executive Branch in any future proceedings."

Justices Thomas and Scalia agreed that the appellate court's decision should have been reversed, but thought the remand should carry the instruction to issue the writ of mandamus the Vice President sought. Justices Ginsburg and Souter would have affirmed the appellate court.

Page 388: [Insert the following after Note (3)]

(4) In *Cheney v. United States District Court*, 542 U.S. 367 (2004), the Court sounded more deferential to the Executive than it had in *Clinton v. Jones*. The Court spoke of the need for the judiciary to "give recognition to the paramount necessity of protecting the Executive Branch from vexatious litigation that might distract it from the energetic performance of its constitutional duties." The Court left open the possibility, however, that the lower courts could shape appropriate discovery orders which would allow the case to proceed against the Vice President and other close presidential advisors without unduly impairing the Executive Branch's performance.

Chapter VI

CONGRESSIONAL PROTECTION OF CIVIL RIGHTS

§ 6.04   Congressional Enforcement Power: Fourteenth Amendment

Page 437: [Insert at end of Note (7), discussing *Board of Trustees of the University of Alabama v. Garrett*]

NEVADA DEPARTMENT OF HUMAN RESOURCES, ET AL., PETITIONERS v. WILLIAM HIBBS ET AL.

538 U.S. 721, 123 S. Ct. 1972 (2003), 155 L. Ed. 2d 953

Chief Justice REHNQUIST delivered the opinion of the Court.

The Family and Medical Leave Act of 1993 (FMLA or Act) entitles eligible employees to take up to 12 work weeks of unpaid leave annually for any of several reasons, including the onset of a "serious health condition" in an employee's spouse, child, or parent. . . . The Act creates a private right of action to seek both equitable relief and money damages "against any employer (including a public agency) in any Federal or State court of competent jurisdiction," . . . should that employer "interfere with, restrain, or deny the exercise of" FMLA rights. . . . We hold that employees of the State of Nevada may recover money damages in the event of the State's failure to comply with the family-care provision of the Act.

Petitioners include the Nevada Department of Human Resources (Department) and two of its officers. Respondent William Hibbs (hereinafter respondent) worked for the Department's Welfare Division. In April and May 1997, he sought leave under the FMLA to care for his ailing wife, who was recovering from a car accident and neck surgery. The Department granted his request for the full 12 weeks of FMLA leave and authorized him to use the leave intermittently as needed between May and December 1997. Respondent did so until August 5, 1997, after which he did not return to work. In October 1997, the Department informed respondent that he had exhausted his FMLA leave, that no further leave would be granted, and that he must report to work by November 12, 1997. Respondent failed to do so and was terminated.

Respondent sued petitioners in the United States District Court seeking damages and injunctive and declaratory relief for, *inter alia,* violations of [FMLA]. The District Court awarded petitioners summary judgment on the grounds that the FMLA claim was barred by the Eleventh Amendment and that respondent's Fourteenth Amendment rights had not been violated. Respondent appealed, and the United States intervened . . . to defend the validity of the FMLA's application to the States. The Ninth Circuit reversed. 273 F.3d 844 (2001).

We granted certiorari, 536 U.S. 938 (2002), to resolve a split among the Courts of Appeals on the question whether an individual may sue a State for money damages in federal court for violation of [FMLA]. . . .

For over a century now, we have made clear that the Constitution does not provide for federal jurisdiction over suits against nonconsenting States. . . . Congress may, however, abrogate such immunity in federal court if it makes its intention to abrogate unmistakably clear in the language of the statute and acts pursuant to a valid exercise of its power under § 5 of the Fourteenth Amendment. . . . This case turns, then, on whether Congress acted within its constitutional authority when it sought to abrogate the States' immunity for purposes of the FMLA's family-leave provision.

In enacting the FMLA, Congress relied on two of the powers vested in it by the Constitution: its Article I commerce power and its power under § 5 of the Fourteenth Amendment to enforce that Amendment's guarantees. Congress may not abrogate the States' sovereign immunity pursuant to its Article I power over commerce . . . Congress may, however, abrogate States' sovereign immunity through a valid exercise of its § 5 power, for "the Eleventh Amendment, and the principle of state sovereignty which it embodies, are necessarily limited by the enforcement provisions of § 5 of the Fourteenth Amendment." . . .

Two provisions of the Fourteenth Amendment are relevant here: Section 5 grants Congress the power "to enforce" the substantive guarantees of § 1 — among them, equal protection of the laws — by enacting "appropriate legislation." Congress may, in the exercise of its § 5 power, do more than simply proscribe conduct that we have held unconstitutional. " 'Congress' power "to enforce" the Amendment includes the authority both to remedy and to deter violation of rights guaranteed thereunder by prohibiting a somewhat broader swath of conduct, including that which is not itself forbidden by the Amendment's text.' " . . . In other words, Congress may enact so-called prophylactic legislation that proscribes facially constitutional conduct, in order to prevent and deter unconstitutional conduct.

City of Boerne also confirmed, however, that it falls to this Court, not Congress, to define the substance of constitutional guarantees. . . . "The ultimate interpretation and determination of the Fourteenth Amendment's substantive meaning remains the province of the Judicial Branch." . . . Section 5 legislation reaching beyond the scope of § 1's actual guarantees must be an appropriate remedy for identified constitutional violations, not "an attempt to substantively redefine the States' legal obligations." . . . We distinguish appropriate prophylactic legislation from "substantive redefinition of the Fourteenth Amendment right at issue," . . . by applying the test set forth in *City of Boerne:* Valid § 5 legislation must exhibit "congruence and proportionality between the injury to be prevented or remedied and the means adopted to that end." . . .

The FMLA aims to protect the right to be free from gender-based discrimination in the workplace. We have held that statutory classifications that distinguish between males and females are subject to heightened scrutiny. *See, e.g., Craig v. Boren,* 429 U.S. 190, 197–199, 97 S. Ct. 451, 50 L.Ed.2d 397 (1976). For a gender-based classification to withstand such scrutiny, it must "serv[e] important governmental objectives," and "the discriminatory means employed [must be] substantially related to the achievement of those objectives." . . . The State's justification for such a classification "must not rely on overbroad generalizations about the different talents, capacities, or preferences of males and females." . . . We now inquire whether Congress had evidence of a pattern of constitutional violations on the part of the States in this area.

The history of the many state laws limiting women's employment opportunities is chronicled in — and, until relatively recently, was sanctioned by — this Court's own opinions. . . . Congress responded to this history of discrimination by abrogating States' sovereign immunity in Title VII of the Civil Rights Act of 1964, 78 Stat. 255, 42 U.S.C. § 2000e2(a), and we sustained this abrogation in *Fitzpatrick, supra.* But state gender discrimination did not cease. . . . According to evidence that was before Congress when it enacted the FMLA, States continue to rely on invalid gender stereotypes in the employment context, specifically in the administration of leave benefits. . . . The long and extensive history of sex discrimination prompted us to hold that measures that differentiate on the basis of gender warrant heightened scrutiny; here, as in *Fitzpatrick,* the persistence of such unconstitutional discrimination by the States justifies Congress' passage of prophylactic § 5 legislation. . . . Congress also heard testimony that "[p]arental leave for fathers . . . is rare." . . . Finally, Congress had evidence that, even where state laws and policies were not facially discriminatory, they were applied in discriminatory ways. . . . In sum, the States' record of unconstitutional participation in, and fostering of, gender-based discrimination in the administration of leave benefits is weighty enough to justify the enactment of prophylactic § 5 legislation.

We reached the opposite conclusion in *Garrett* and *Kimel.* In those cases, the § 5 legislation under review responded to a purported tendency of state officials to make age- or disability-based distinctions. Under our equal protection case law, discrimination on the basis of such characteristics is not judged under a heightened review standard, and passes muster if there is "a rational basis for doing so at a class-based level, even if it 'is probably not true' that those reasons are valid in the majority of cases." . . . Thus, in order to impugn the constitutionality of state discrimination against the disabled or the elderly, Congress must identify, not just the existence of age-or disability-based state decisions, but a "widespread pattern" of irrational reliance on such criteria. . . . We found no such showing with respect to the ADEA and Title I of the Americans with Disabilities Act of 1990(ADA). . . .

Because the standard for demonstrating the constitutionality of a gender-based classification is more difficult to meet than our rational-basis test — it must "serv[e] important governmental objectives" and be "substantially related to the achievement of those objectives," . . . it was easier for Congress to show a pattern of state constitutional violations. . . .

The impact of the discrimination targeted by the FMLA is significant. Congress determined:

> "Historically, denial or curtailment of women's employment opportunities has been traceable directly to the pervasive presumption that women are mothers first, and workers second. This prevailing ideology about women's roles has in turn justified discrimination against women when they are mothers or mothers-to-be." Joint Hearing 100.

Stereotypes about women's domestic roles are reinforced by parallel stereotypes presuming a lack of domestic responsibilities for men. . . . These mutually reinforcing stereotypes created a self-fulfilling cycle of discrimination that forced women to continue to assume the role of primary family caregiver, and fostered employers' stereotypical views about women's commitment to work and their value as employees. Those perceptions, in turn, Congress reasoned, lead to subtle discrimination that may be difficult to detect on a case-by-case basis.

We believe that Congress' chosen remedy, the family-care leave provision of the FMLA, is "congruent and proportional to the targeted violation." . . . Here, as in *Katzenbach, supra,* Congress again confronted a "difficult and intractable proble[m]," . . . where previous legislative attempts had failed. Such problems may justify added prophylactic measures in response.

By creating an across-the-board, routine employment benefit for all eligible employees, Congress sought to ensure that family-care leave would no longer be stigmatized as an inordinate drain on the workplace caused by female employees, and that employers could not evade leave obligations simply by hiring men. By setting a minimum standard of family leave for *all* eligible employees, irrespective of gender, the FMLA attacks the formerly state-sanctioned stereotype that only women are responsible for family caregiving, thereby reducing employers' incentives to engage in discrimination by basing hiring and promotion decisions on stereotypes.

The dissent characterizes the FMLA as a "substantive entitlement program" rather than a remedial statute because it establishes a floor of 12 weeks' leave. *Post,* at 1992. In the dissent's view, in the face of evidence of gender-based discrimination by the States in the provision of leave benefits, Congress could do no more in exercising its § 5 power than simply proscribe such discrimination. But this position cannot be squared with our recognition that Congress "is not confined to the enactment of legislation that merely parrots the precise wording of the Fourteenth Amendment," but may prohibit "a somewhat broader swath of conduct, including that which is not itself forbidden by the Amendment's text." . . . For example, this Court has upheld certain prophylactic provisions of the Voting Rights Act as valid exercises of Congress' § 5 power, including the literacy test ban and preclearance requirements for changes in States' voting procedures. . . .

Unlike the statutes at issue in *City of Boerne, Kimel*, and *Garrett,* which applied broadly to every aspect of state employers' operations, the FMLA is narrowly targeted at the fault line between work and family — precisely where sex-based overgeneralization has been and remains strongest — and affects only one aspect of the employment relationship. . . .

We also find significant the many other limitations that Congress placed on the scope of this measure. . . . The FMLA requires only unpaid leave, . . . and applies only to employees who have worked for the employer for at least one year and provided 1,250 hours of service within the last 12 months. . . . Employees in high-ranking or sensitive positions are simply ineligible for FMLA leave; of particular importance to the States, the FMLA expressly excludes from coverage state elected officials, their staffs, and appointed policymakers. . . . Employees must give advance notice of foreseeable leave, . . . and employers may require certification by a health care provider of the need for leave. . . . In choosing 12 weeks as the appropriate leave floor, Congress chose "a middle ground, a period long enough to serve 'the needs of families' but not so long that it would upset 'the legitimate interests of employers.'". . . Moreover, the cause of action under the FMLA is a restricted one: The damages recoverable are strictly defined and measured by actual monetary losses, . . . and the accrual period for backpay is limited by the Act's 2-year statute of limitations. . . .

For the above reasons, we conclude that § 2612(a)(1)(C) is congruent and proportional to its remedial object, and can "be understood as responsive to, or designed to prevent, unconstitutional behavior." *City of Boerne, supra,* at 532, 117 S. Ct. 2157.

The judgment of the Court of Appeals is therefore

Affirmed.

[Justices Stevens, Souter, Ginsburg, and Breyer concurred but specifically reaffirmed views expressed previously regarding § 5 of the Fourteenth Amendment and/or the Eleventh Amendment and sovereign immunity.]

Justice SCALIA, dissenting.

I join Justice KENNEDY's dissent, and add one further observation: The constitutional violation that is a prerequisite to "prophylactic" congressional action to "enforce" the Fourteenth Amendment is a violation *by the State against which the enforcement action is taken.* There is no guilt by association, enabling the sovereignty of one State to be abridged under § 5 of the Fourteenth Amendment because of violations by another State, or by most other States, or even by 49 other States. Congress has sometimes displayed awareness of this self-evident limitation. That is presumably why the most sweeping provisions of the Voting Rights Act of 1965 — which we upheld in *City of Rome v. United States,* 446 U.S. 156, 100 S. Ct. 1548, 64 L. Ed.

2d 119 (1980), as a valid exercise of congressional power under § 2 of the Fifteenth Amendment — were restricted to States "with a demonstrable history of intentional racial discrimination in voting," *id.* at 177, 100 S. Ct. 1548.

Today's opinion for the Court does not even attempt to demonstrate that each one of the 50 States covered by [FMLA] was in violation of the Fourteenth Amendment. It treats "the States" as some sort of collective entity which is guilty or innocent as a body. "[T]he States' record of unconstitutional participation in, and fostering of, gender-based discrimination," it concludes, "is weighty enough to justify the enactment of prophylactic § 5 legislation." . . . This will not do. Prophylaxis in the sense of extending the remedy beyond the violation is one thing; prophylaxis in the sense of extending the remedy beyond the violator is something else. . . .

When a litigant claims that legislation has denied him individual rights secured by the Constitution, the court ordinarily asks first whether the legislation is constitutional *as applied to him.* . . . When, on the other hand, a federal statute is challenged as going beyond Congress's enumerated powers, under our precedents the court first asks whether the statute is unconstitutional *on its face.* . . . If the statute survives this challenge, however, it stands to reason that the court may, if asked, proceed to analyze whether the statute (constitutional on its face) can be validly applied to the litigant. In the context of § 5 prophylactic legislation applied against a State, this would entail examining whether the State has itself engaged in discrimination sufficient to support the exercise of Congress's prophylactic power.

It seems, therefore, that for purposes of defeating petitioner's challenge, it would have been enough for respondents to demonstrate that [FMLA] was *facially* valid — *i.e.,* that it could constitutionally be applied to *some* jurisdictions. . . . But when it comes to an as-applied challenge, I think Nevada will be entitled to assert that the mere facts that (1) it is a State, and (2) some States are bad actors, is not enough; it can demand that *it* be shown to have been acting in violation of the Fourteenth Amendment.

Justice KENNEDY, with whom Justice SCALIA and Justice THOMAS join, dissenting.

The Family and Medical Leave Act of 1993 makes explicit the congressional intent to invoke § 5 of the Fourteenth Amendment to abrogate state sovereign immunity and allow suits for money damages in federal courts. *Ante,* at 1976–1977, and n.1. The specific question is whether Congress may impose on the States this entitlement program of its own design, with mandated minimums for leave time, and then enforce it by permitting private suits for money damages against the States. This in turn must be answered by asking whether subjecting States and their treasuries to monetary liability at the insistence of private litigants is a congruent and proportional response to a demonstrated pattern of unconstitutional conduct by the States. . . . If we apply the teaching of [earlier] cases, the family leave provision . . . is invalid to the extent it allows for private suits against the unconsenting States.

Congress does not have authority to define the substantive content of the Equal Protection Clause; it may only shape the remedies warranted by the violations of that guarantee. . . . This requirement has special force in the context of the Eleventh Amendment, which protects a State's fiscal integrity from federal intrusion by vesting the States with immunity from private actions for damages pursuant to federal laws. The Commerce Clause likely would permit the National Government to enact an entitlement program such as this one; but when Congress couples the entitlement with the authorization to sue the States for monetary damages, it blurs the line of accountability the State has to its own citizens. . . .

The Court is unable to show that States have engaged in a pattern of unlawful conduct which warrants the remedy of opening state treasuries to private suits. The inability to adduce evidence of alleged discrimination, coupled with the inescapable fact that the federal scheme is not a remedy but a benefit program, demonstrate the lack of the requisite link between any problem Congress has identified and the program it mandated. . . .

The relevant question, as the Court seems to acknowledge, is whether, notwithstanding the passage of Title VII and similar state legislation, the States continued to engage in widespread discrimination on the basis of gender in the provision of family leave benefits. . . . If such a pattern were shown, the Eleventh Amendment would not bar Congress from devising a congruent and proportional remedy. The evidence to substantiate this charge must be far more specific, however, than a simple recitation of a general history of employment discrimination against women. When the federal statute seeks to abrogate state sovereign immunity, the Court should be more careful to insist on adherence to the analytic requirements set forth in its own precedents. Persisting overall effects of gender-based discrimination at the workplace must not be ignored; but simply noting the problem is not a substitute for evidence which identifies some real discrimination the family leave rules are designed to prevent. . . .

As the Court seems to recognize, the evidence considered by Congress concerned discriminatory practices of the private sector, not those of state employers. . . .

Considered in its entirety, the evidence fails to document a pattern of unconstitutional conduct sufficient to justify the abrogation of States' sovereign immunity. The few incidents identified by the Court "fall far short of even suggesting the pattern of unconstitutional discrimination on which § 5 legislation must be based." . . . Juxtaposed to this evidence is the States' record of addressing gender-based discrimination in the provision of leave benefits on their own volition. . . .

Our concern with gender discrimination, which is subjected to heightened scrutiny, as opposed to age-or disability-based distinctions, which are reviewed under rational standard, . . . does not alter this conclusion. The application of heightened scrutiny is designed to ensure gender-based classifications are not based on the entrenched and pervasive stereotypes which inhibit women's progress in the workplace. . . . This consideration does not divest respondents of their burden to show that "Congress identified a history and pattern of unconstitutional employment discrimination by the States." . . . The Court seems to reaffirm this requirement. *Ante,* at 1978 ("We now inquire whether Congress had evidence of a pattern of constitutional violations on the part of the States . . ."); *see also ante,* at 1981 ("[T]he States' record of unconstitutional participation in, and fostering of, gender-based discrimination in the administration of leave benefits is weighty enough to justify the enactment of prophylactic § 5 legislation"). In my submission, however, the Court does not follow it. Given the insufficiency of the evidence that States discriminated in the provision of family leave, the unfortunate fact that stereotypes about women continue to be a serious and pervasive social problem would not alone support the charge that a State has engaged in a practice designed to deny its citizens the equal protection of the laws. . . .

The paucity of evidence to support the case the Court tries to make demonstrates that Congress was not responding with a congruent and proportional remedy to a perceived course of unconstitutional conduct. Instead, it enacted a substantive entitlement program of its own. If Congress had been concerned about different treatment of men and women with respect to family leave, a congruent remedy would have sought to ensure the benefits of any leave program enacted by a State are available to men and women on an equal basis. Instead, the Act imposes, across the board, a requirement that States grant a minimum of 12 weeks of leave per year. . . . This requirement may represent Congress' considered judgment as to the optimal balance between the family obligations of workers and the interests of employers, and the States may decide to follow these guidelines in designing their own family leave benefits. It does not follow, however, that if the States choose to enact a different benefit scheme, they should be deemed to engage in unconstitutional conduct and forced to open their treasuries to private suits for damages.

Well before the federal enactment, Nevada not only provided its employees, on a gender-neutral basis, with an option of requesting up to one year of unpaid leave, . . . but also permitted, subject to approval and other conditions, leaves of absence in excess of one year. . . . Nevada state employees were also entitled to use up to 10 days of their accumulated paid sick leave to care for an ill relative. . . . Nevada, in addition, had a program of special "catastrophic leave." State employees could donate their accrued sick leave to a general fund to aid employees who needed additional leave to care for a relative with a serious illness. . . .

To be sure, the Nevada scheme did not track that devised by the Act in all respects. The provision of unpaid leave was discretionary and subject to a possible reporting requirement. . . . A congruent remedy to any discriminatory exercise of discretion, however, is the requirement that the grant of leave be administered on a gender-equal basis, not the displacement of the State's scheme by a federal one. The scheme enacted by the Act does not respect the States' autonomous power to design their own social benefits regime.

Were more proof needed to show that this is an entitlement program, not a remedial statute, it should suffice to note that the Act does not even purport to bar discrimination in some leave programs the States do enact and administer. Under the Act, a State is allowed to provide women with, say, 24 weeks of family leave per year but provide only 12 weeks of leave to men. As the counsel for the United States conceded during the argument, a law of this kind might run afoul of the Equal Protection Clause or Title VII, but it would not constitute a violation of the Act. . . . The Act on its face is not drawn as a remedy to gender-based discrimination in family leave.

It has been long acknowledged that federal legislation which "deters or remedies constitutional violations can fall within the sweep of Congress' enforcement power even if in the process it prohibits conduct which is not itself unconstitutional." . . . The Court has explained, however, that Congress may not "enforce a constitutional right by changing what the right is." . . . The dual requirement that Congress identify a pervasive pattern of unconstitutional state conduct and that its remedy be proportional and congruent to the violation is designed to separate permissible exercises of congressional power from instances where Congress seeks to enact a substantive entitlement under the guise of its § 5 authority. . . .

[T]he abrogation of state sovereign immunity pursuant to Title VII was a legitimate congressional response to a pattern of gender-based discrimination in employment. . . . The family leave benefit conferred by the Act is, by contrast, a substantive benefit Congress chose to confer upon state employees. . . .

It bears emphasis that, even were the Court to bar unconsented federal suits by private individuals for money damages from a State, individuals whose rights under the Act were violated would not be without recourse. The Act is likely a valid exercise of Congress' power under the Commerce Clause, Art. I, § 8, cl. 3, and so the standards it prescribes will be binding upon the States. The United States may enforce these standards in actions for money damages; and private individuals may bring actions against state officials for injunctive relief under Ex parte Young, 209 U.S. 123, 28 S. Ct. 441, 52 L.Ed. 714 (1908). What is at issue is only whether the States can be subjected, without consent, to suits brought by private persons seeking to collect moneys from the state treasury. Their immunity cannot be abrogated without documentation of a pattern of unconstitutional acts by the States, and only then by a congruent and proportional remedy. There has been a complete failure by respondents to carry their burden to establish each of these necessary propositions. I would hold that the Act is not a valid abrogation of state sovereign immunity and dissent with respect from the Court's conclusion to the contrary.

NOTE

The Court followed its decision in *Hibbs* the following term by holding in *Tennessee v. Lane,* 541 U.S. 509 (2004), that Congress had properly abrogated the States' Eleventh Amendment immunity under Title II of the Americans with Disabilities Act of 1990 (ADA), which precluded denying a "qualified individual with a disability" "benefits of the services, programs or activities of a public entity." 42 U.S.C. § 12132. The question resolved in *Lane* had been left open in *Board of Trustees of Univ. of Ala. v. Garrett,* 531 U.S. 356, 360 n.1 (2001), in which the Court had held that the Eleventh Amendment barred suits under Title I of the ADA. *Lane* arose when two paraplegics complained that they were effectively denied access to Tennessee's state courthouses.

Congress had clearly stated its intent to abrogate the States' immunity ("A State shall not be immune under the eleventh amendment to the Constitution of the United States from an action in Federal or State court of competent jurisdiction for a violation of this chapter." 42 U.S.C. § 12202). Writing for a five justice majority, Justice Stevens concluded that Title II was the sort of "prophylactic legislation" that was within the section 5 power because it proscribed practices which were "discriminatory in effect, if not in intent, to carry out the basic objectives of the Equal Protection Clause." 541 U.S. at 520. Title II sought to protect a range of basic constitutional rights including, but not limited to, those involving access to the courts which the Due Process Clause of the Fourteenth Amendment protected. Congressional proceedings had disclosed that many individuals were denied access to courts due to disabilities. The basic rights at issue called for "a standard of judicial review at least as searching, and in some cases more searching, than the standard that applies to sex-based classifications" at issue in *Hibbs*. *Id.* at 529. The Court need not consider whether Title II was "appropriately tailored to serve its objectives" in all of its potential applications (e.g., seating at state-owned hockey arenas), but need ask only whether it met the congruence and proportionality test with respect to the issue in question relating to access to the judicial system. *Id.* at 529–34. To that application, Title II "unquestionably is valid" section 5 legislation. *Id.* at 531. The "considerable evidence of the shortcomings of previous legislative responses" justified Congress in concluding that additional prophylactic legislation was needed and that when adopted, was a limited remedy appropriate in its scope. *Id.*

In dissent, Chief Justice Rehnquist (joined by Justices Kennedy and Thomas) argued that the Court had misapplied the congruence and proportionality test by considering evidence unrelated to access to courts issues and which involved "discrimination by nonstate governments." *Id.* at 542. Moreover, the dissent criticized the majority's "as applied" approach, arguing instead that the Court should have "measured the full breadth of the statute . . . that Congress enacted against the scope of the constitutional right it purported to enforce." *Id.* at 551–52.

Justice Scalia also dissented, but in doing so suggested a new doctrinal approach. He had joined the congruence and proportionality test in the past with misgivings. He now "yield[ed] to the lessons of experience" and concluded that it, "like all such flabby tests, is a standing invitation to judicial arbitrariness and policy-driven decisionmaking." *Id.* at 557–58. Moreover, the test made the Court Congress' "taskmaster" and required it to "regularly check Congress's homework." *Id.* at 558. The Court should not perform judicial review of congressional acts based only on a test "that has no demonstrable basis in the text of the Constitution and cannot objectively be shown to have been met or failed." *Id.* Justice Scalia would require that section 5 legislation "enforce, by appropriate legislation" the provisions of the Fourteenth Amendment; it should not serve as the basis for prophylactic measures "prohibiting primary conduct that is itself not forbidden by the Fourteenth Amendment." *Id.* at 560. Justice Scalia distinguished the cases authorizing a broader approach (except *Hibbs*) as involving racial discrimination which, he pointed out, was the Fourteenth Amendment's principal target. *Id.* at 561.

Chapter VII

LIBERTY AND PROPERTY RIGHTS IN THE DUE PROCESS, TAKING, AND CONTRACT CLAUSES

§ 7.03   Regulation of Business and Other Property Interests

[2]—Limiting Punitive Damages Under the Due Process Clause

Page 501: [Insert the following after the Note]

STATE FARM MUT. AUTO. INS. CO. v. CAMPBELL, 538 U.S. 408 (2003). In *State Farm*, the Court held that punitive damages which are 145 times the amount of compensatory damages violate due process. Campbell tried to pass 6 vans on a two-lane highway. Crossing into the lane of oncoming traffic, he caused an accident which killed one driver and left another permanently disabled. Campbell's insurance company, State Farm, declined settlement offers for the policy limit of $50,000 ($25,000 per claimant). State Farm took the case to trial and assured the Campbells that " 'their assets were safe, that they had no liability for the accident, that [State Farm] would represent their interests and that they did not need to procure separate counsel.' " The jury handed down a judgment for $185,849.

Originally, State Farm refused to cover the $135,849 in excess of the policy limit. Counsel for State Farm suggested to the Campbells that they might consider selling their house to cover the judgment. When State Farm would not appeal, Campbell contracted with the two original plaintiffs "not to seek satisfaction of their claims against the Campbells." The attorney for the plaintiffs would then represent Campbell in a bad faith action against State Farm. Both plaintiffs had to approve of any settlement reached with State Farm, and they would receive 90% of any award against State Farm.

Although State Farm eventually paid the entire judgment, the Campbells pursued their claims of bad faith, fraud, and intentional infliction of emotional distress. The jury awarded the Campbells $2.6 million in compensatory damages and $145 million in punitive damages. The trial court reduced this award to $1 million in compensatory damages and $25 million in punitive damages. The Utah Supreme Court, however, reinstated the $145 million in punitive damages.

Relying on *BMW of North America, Inc. v. Gore*, casebook p. 496, Justice Kennedy concluded that this case "is neither close nor difficult." *Gore* stated that " '[t]he most important indicium of the reasonableness of a punitive damages award is the degree of reprehensibility of the defendant's conduct.' "

In the instant case, punitive damages were used "as a platform to expose, and punish, the perceived deficiencies of State Farm's operations throughout the country." The Utah Supreme Court condemned State Farm for its "nationwide policies rather than for the conduct direct[ed] toward the Campbells." A state may not punish one for "conduct that may have been lawful where it occurred." Nor may a state punish "unlawful acts committed outside of the State's jurisdiction" with punitive damages. However, "[l]awful out-of-state conduct may be probative when it demonstrates the deliberateness and culpability of the defendant's action in the State where it is tortious, but that conduct must have a nexus to the specific harm suffered by the plaintiff." When so used, a jury must be instructed that "it may not use evidence of out-of-state conduct to punish a defendant for action that was lawful in the jurisdiction where it occurred." Central to the concept of federalism is the idea "that each State may make its own reasoned judgment about what conduct is permitted or proscribed within its borders, and each State alone can determine what measure of punishment, if any, to impose on a defendant who acts within its jurisdiction."

More fundamentally, the Utah courts attempted "to punish and deter conduct that bore no relation to the Campbells' harm." Punishment should be for "the conduct that harmed the plaintiff, not for being an unsavory individual or business."[1] The award cannot be based on classifying defendant as a "recidivist. Although 'our holdings that a recidivist may be punished more severely than a first offender recognize that repeat misconduct is more reprehensible than an individual instance of malfeasance,' in the context of civil actions courts must ensure the conduct in question replicates the prior transgressions." This "reprehensibility guidepost does not permit courts to expand the scope of the case so that a defendant may be punished for any malfeasance which in this case extended for a 20-year period."

Moving "to the second Gore guidepost," the Court has "been reluctant to identify concrete constitutional limits on the ratio between harm, or potential harm, to the plaintiff and the punitive damages award." Pac. Mut. Life Ins. Co. v. Haslip, casebook p. 494, concluded that an award of more than four times the amount of compensatory damages "might be close to the line of constitutional impropriety." The Court "cited that 4–to–1 ratio again in Gore." The Gore Court "further referenced a long legislative history, dating back over 700 years and going forward to today, providing for sanctions of double, treble, or quadruple damages to deter and punish. While these ratios are not binding, they are instructive. They demonstrate what should be obvious. Single-digit multipliers are more likely to comport

---

[1] Punishment based on reprehensibility "creates the possibility of multiple punitive damages awards for the same conduct; for in the usual case nonparties are not bound by the judgment some other plaintiff obtains."

with due process." While "there are no rigid benchmarks" for punitive damages, "ratios greater than those we have previously upheld may comport with due process where 'a particularly egregious act has resulted in only a small amount of economic damages.'" However, for substantial compensatory awards, "then a lesser ratio, perhaps only equal to compensatory damages" might be higher than due process would allow. The precise award in any case is, of course, dependent on "the facts and circumstances of the defendant's conduct and the harm to the plaintiff." Punitive awards must be "both reasonable and proportionate to the amount of harm to the plaintiff and to the general damages recovered."

In this case, the Court found a presumption against an award with a 145–to–1 ratio. "The compensatory award in this case was substantial; the Campbells were awarded $1 million for a year and a half of emotional distress. This was complete compensation." An unconstitutional punitive damages award cannot be justified simply because the defendant is wealthy.

"The third guidepost in *Gore* is the disparity between the punitive damages award and the 'civil penalties authorized or imposed in comparable cases.'" This Court has, in the past, looked "to criminal penalties that could be imposed." In Utah, the most relevant civil sanction appears to be a $10,000 fine for fraud.

Justice Kennedy concludes that the $145 million punitive damages award was "neither reasonable nor proportionate to the wrong committed, and it was an irrational and arbitrary deprivation of the property of the defendant."

Justices Scalia, Thomas, and Ginsburg each filed separate dissenting opinions. For Justice Scalia, the Due Process Clause does not provide substantive protection against "'excessive' or 'unreasonable' awards of punitive damages." Such scrutiny of punitive awards is "insusceptible of principled application." Consequently, *Gore* should not have stare decisis effect.

Justice Thomas also maintaned that the Constitution constrains the size of punitive damages.

In dissent, Justice Ginsburg maintains that "the Court 'works at this business [of checking state courts] alone,' unaided by the participation of federal district courts and courts of appeals." The majority account of the evidence is "abbreviated." For example, the claims-adjustment process "'has functioned, and continues to function, as an unlawful scheme . . . to deny benefits owed consumers by paying out less than fair value in order to meet preset, arbitrary payout targets designed to enhance corporate profits.'" Moreover, "State Farm made 'systematic' efforts to destroy internal company documents that might reveal its scheme."[2] Justice Ginsburg concludes that the "numerical controls" that this decision

---

[2] The majority acknowledges that evidence of out-of-state conduct "may be 'probative [even if the conduct is lawful in the state where it occurred] when it demonstrated the deliberateness and culpability of the defendant's action in the State where it is tortious."

establishes seem "boldly out of order." Gore's "flexible guides" are being transformed "into instructions that begin to resemble marching orders."

[4]—Government Takings of Property Requiring Just Compensation

Page 523: [Insert the following after Note (6)]

KELO v. CITY OF NEW LONDON, 125 S. Ct. 2655 (2005). In *Kelo v. City of New London*, a 5-4 Court held that a city's taking property for economic development did not violate the public use requirement of the Takings Clause. New London targeted for economic revitalization an area known as Fort Trumbull, and enlisted a non-profit group called New London Development Corporation (NLDC) to create "an integrated development plan focused on 90 acres of the Fort Trumbull area." Pfizer Inc. was planning to build a "$300 million research facility" near Fort Trumbull which the city hoped would further "the area's rejuvenation." The Fort Trumbull area encompasses "approximately 115 privately owned properties." Plaintiffs own property located in parcels 3 and 4A of the development plan. Parcel 3 "will contain at least 90,000 square feet of research and development office space" and 4A will support either the nearby state park or marina with visitor parking or retail.

Writing for the majority, Justice Stevens said "it has long been accepted that the sovereign may not take the property of A for the sole purpose of transferring it to another private party B, even though A is paid just compensation. On the other hand, it is equally clear that a State may transfer property from one private party to another if future 'use by the public' is the purpose of the taking."[3]

Justice Stevens rejected the argument that "using eminent domain for economic development impermissibly blurs the boundary between public and private takings." Instead, "the government's pursuit of a public purpose will often benefit individual private parties." The Court deferred to the legislature regarding the plan's effectiveness and the lands necessary to carry it out. Of course, "many States already impose 'public use' requirements that are stricter than the federal baseline."

Justice Kennedy concurred. *Hawaii Housing Authority v. Midkiff*, casebook, p. 516, permitted a taking "as long as it is "rationally related to a conceivable public purpose.'" Still, the public use requirement may forbid "transfers intended to confer benefits on particular, favored private entities, and with only incidental or pretextual public benefits." Moreover, private

---

[3] The record below establishes that the takings entailed "a 'carefully considered' development plan" that "was not intended to serve the interests of Pfizer, Inc., or any other private entity, but rather, to revitalize the local economy." Although a private developer will be involved, who will lease space to other private parties, "the identities of those private parties were not known when the plan was adopted." Consequently, it is "difficult to accuse the government of having taken A's property to benefit the private interests of B when the identity of B was unknown."

transfers may entail a "risk of undetected impermissible favoritism of private parties" so great as to create "a presumption (rebuttable or otherwise) of invalidity." However, this case does not "justify a more demanding standard" as the "taking occurred in the context of a comprehensive development plan meant to address a serious city-wide depression" and "the identity of most of the private beneficiaries were unknown at the time the city formulated its plans."

Justice O'Connor dissented, joined by Chief Justice Rehnquist, and Justices Scalia and Thomas. "To reason, as the Court does, that the incidental public benefits resulting from the subsequent ordinary use of private property render economic development takings 'for public use' is to wash out any distinction between private and public use of property — and thereby effectively to delete the words 'for public use' from the Takings Clause of the Fifth Amendment." Consequently, private property is "vulnerable to being taken and transferred to another private owner, so long as it might be upgraded."

There are "three categories of takings that comply with the public use requirement." One is "public ownership — such as for a road," another is "use-by-the-public," many times involving common carriers, and the third is designed "to meet certain exigencies" and allows certain takings "even if the property is destined for subsequent private use." Economic development takings are invalid for want of a valid public purpose. To satisfy this requirement, "the targeted property" must impose "affirmative harm on society" as was the case "in *Berman* [*v. Parker*, 348 U.S. 26 (1954),] through blight resulting from extreme poverty and in *Midkiff* through oligopoly." With the present case, the Court moves "away from our decisions sanctioning the condemnation of harmful property use" and "significantly expands the meaning of public use. It holds that the sovereign may take private property currently put to ordinary private use, and give it over for new, ordinary private use, so long as the new use is predicted to generate some secondary benefit for the public — such as increased tax revenue, more jobs, maybe even aesthetic pleasure." The rule adopted by the majority contains no mechanism to "prohibit property transfers generated with less care . . . whose only projected advantage is the incidence of higher taxes," or the transformation of "an already prosperous city into an even more prosperous one." The likely beneficiaries of this rule would be "citizens with disproportionate influence and power in the political process, including large corporations and development firms."

In a separate dissent, Justice Thomas argued that the originalist understanding of the Public Use Clause is "a meaningful limit on the government's eminent domain power." He would reconsider the "deferential conception of 'public use'" from *Hawaii Housing Authority v. Midkiff*. Upholding "'urban renewal' programs" and "extending the concept of public purpose to encompass any economically beneficial goal guarantees" a disproportionate impact on the poor, due to their lack of political influence and the fact that their land is likely not being used in the "highest and best social" manner. "Urban renewal projects have long been associated with the displacement of blacks." As Justice Thomas emphasized, "over 97 percent of the individuals forcibly removed from their homes by the 'slum-clearance' project upheld by this Court in *Berman* were black."

BROWN v. LEGAL FOUND. of WASHINGTON, 538 U.S. 216 (2003). In *Brown*, the Court held that a law requiring that funds that cannot earn interest for a client be deposited in an IOLTA account does not amount to a regulatory taking. However, a law that requires this interest to be transferred to another for a legitimate public use could be construed as a per se taking, which would require just compensation to the client. The state used interest on lawyers' trust accounts (IOLTA) to pay for legal services for the poor.

The aggregate value of contributions derived from IOLTA accounts exceeded $200 million. The funds that are subject to the IOLTA program are " 'only those funds that *cannot, under any circumstances*, earn *net* interest (after deducting transaction and administrative costs and bank fees) for the client.' "[4] The record suggests that legal services for the poor received some interest from the funds deposited by each of the private lawyer clients challenging the law. However, "without IOLTA those funds would not have produced any net interest for either" of these plaintiffs.

Writing for a 5–4 Court, Justice Stevens referred to *Phillips v. Washington Legal Foundation*, casebook p. 522, which held that interest generated by IOLTA accounts was the property of the clients who owned the principal. The Court did not address in *Phillips* "whether the income had been 'taken' by the State," nor did it address the amount of just compensation the respondents were due.

The Fifth Amendment requires that government takings of private property be for " 'public use' " and that government pay the owner of the property just compensation. The public use requirement is "unquestionably satisfied" in this case. "If the State had imposed a special tax, or perhaps a system of user fees, to generate the funds to finance the legal services supported by the Foundation, there would be no question as to the legitimacy of the use of the public's money."

The requirement that the funds be placed in an IOLTA account could be viewed as the "first step in a 'regulatory taking.' " In *Penn Central Transp. Co. v. New York City*, casebook p. 520, demonstrates that there was "no taking because the transaction had no adverse economic impact on petitioners and did not interfere with any investment-backed expectation."

Plaintiffs also characterize as a *per se* taking the requirement that the interest earned from their escrow funds that were placed in an IOLTA

---

[4] The Washington Supreme Court "rejected the argument that it had failed to consider the significance of advances in computer technology." The court stated that " 'as cost effective subaccounting services become available, making it possible to earn net interest for clients on increasingly smaller amounts held for increasingly shorter periods of time, more trust money will have to be invested for the clients' benefit under the new rule.' "

account be transferred to the Legal Foundation of Washington. The Court assumes that the clients "retained the beneficial ownership of at least a portion of their escrow deposits until the funds were disbursed at the closing, that those funds generated some interest in the IOLTA accounts, and that their interest was taken for a public use when it was ultimately turned over to the Foundation."

Nevertheless, the Court found that the state did not owe plaintiffs just compensation, which "is measured by the property owner's loss rather than the government's gain." If plaintiff's net loss was zero, the compensation that is due is also zero.[5]

Justice Stevens concludes with a summary of the Court's holding. "It is neither unethical nor illegal for lawyers to deposit their clients' funds in a single bank account." A state law that requires lawyers to deposit "client funds that could not otherwise generate net earnings for the client" into an IOLTA account is not a " 'regulatory taking.' A law that requires that the interest on those funds be transferred to a different owner for a legitimate public use, however, could be a *per se* taking requiring the payment of 'just compensation' to the client. Because that compensation is measured by the owner's pecuniary loss — which is zero whenever the Washington law is obeyed — there has been no violation of the *Just Compensation Clause of the Fifth Amendment* in this case."

Justices Scalia filed a dissenting opinion joined by the Chief Justice Rehnquist and Justices Kennedy and Thomas. Justice Scalia maintains that "the Court creates a novel exception to our oft-repeated rule that the just compensation owed to former owners of confiscated property is the fair market value of the property taken." Once the clients' funds earned interest in an IOLTA account, that interest became plaintiffs' property. The point that the State appropriates the interest generated from these accounts to fund the Legal Foundation is the point at which "just compensation for the taking must be assessed." Whether the clients could have earned interest without IOLTA's pooling is irrelevant. "[J]ust compensation is not to be measured by what would have happened in a hypothetical world in which the State's IOLTA program did not exist."

In a separate dissent, Justice Kennedy stated: "Had the State, with the help of Congress, not acted in violation of its constitutional responsibilities by taking for itself property which all concede to be that of the client, the free market might have created various and diverse funds for pooling small interest amounts. These funds would have allowed the true owners of the property the option to express views and policies of their own choosing."

---

[5] The dissenters considered hypothetical cases in which a lawyer mistakenly deposits "funds in an IOLTA account when those funds might have produced net earnings for the client." That lawyer violates the Washington Supreme Court rule which clearly requires lawyers to deposit such funds into a non-IOLTA account. "Any conceivable net loss to petitioners was the consequence of the LPOs' incorrect private decisions rather than any state action."

Page 527: [Insert the following before *Nollan v. California Coastal Commission*]

TAHOE–SIERRA PRESERVATION COUNCIL, INC. v. TAHOE REGIONAL PLANNING AGENCY, 535 U.S. 302 (2002). In *Tahoe–Sierra Preservation Council, Inc.*, the Court considered "whether a moratorium on development imposed during the process of devising a comprehensive land-use plan constitutes a *per se* taking of property requiring compensation."

In response to Lake Tahoe's "rapidly" deteriorating state, due in large part to "increased land development in the Lake Tahoe Basin," the California and Nevada legislatures created the Tahoe Regional Planning Agency (TRPA) "'to coordinate and regulate development in the Basin and to conserve its natural resources.'" While studying the "impact of development on Lake Tahoe and designing a strategy for environmentally sound growth," the TRPA ordered two moratoria, Ordinance 81–5 and Resolution 83–21, which, in combination, "effectively prohibited all construction on sensitive lands in California and on all SEZ lands [" 'Stream Environment Zones' "] in the entire Basin for 32 months, and on sensitive lands in Nevada (other than SEZ lands) for eight months."

Petitioners, who own land and represent landowners adversely affected by the moratoria, allege that a court need not "evaluate the landowners' investment-backed expectations, the actual impact of the regulation on any individual, the importance of the public interest served by the regulation, or the reasons for imposing the temporary restriction. For petitioners, it is enough, that a regulation imposes a temporary deprivation — no matter how brief — of all economically viable use to trigger a *per se* rule that a taking has occurred." Although another plan, the 1984 regional plan had been subjected to protracted litigation in the lower courts, the challenge to it was not before the Supreme Court "because both the District Court and the Court of Appeals held that it was the federal injunction against implementing that plan, rather than the plan itself, that caused the post-1984 injuries that petitioners allegedly suffered, and those rulings are not encompassed within our limited grant of certiorari." Thus, the Court limited its "discussion to the lower courts' disposition of the claims based on the 2-year moratorium (Ordinance 81–5) and the ensuing 8-month moratorium (Resolution 83–21)."

Writing for the majority, Justice Stevens concluded that no *per se* taking had occurred, and that "the circumstances in this case are best analyzed within the *Penn Central*, casebook, p. 520, framework." While the Court's "jurisprudence involving condemnations and physical takings . . . for the most part, involves the straightforward application of *per se* rules," Justice Stevens indicated that its regulatory takings jurisprudence, as in this case, "is characterized by 'essentially ad hoc, factual inquires,'" carefully weighing all the circumstances. "Land-use regulations are ubiquitous and most of them impact property values in some tangential way — often in completely unanticipated ways. Treating them all as *per se* takings would transform government regulation into a luxury few governments could afford." The *Penn Central* framework eschews set formulas. "In deciding whether a particular governmental action has effected a taking, this Court focuses both on the character of the action and on the nature and extent of the interference with rights in the parcel as a whole."

The Court stated that in *First English Evangelical Church of Glendale v. County of Los Angeles*, casebook, p. 523, the California Courts had decided that a taking had occurred, and that the Supreme Court only decided the question of remedy. Indeed, *First English* gave two reasons "why a regulation temporarily denying an owner all use of her property might not constitute a taking." First, "the county might avoid the conclusion that a compensable taking had occurred by establishing that the denial of all use was insulated as a part of the State's authority to enact safety regulations." Second, the *First English* Court recognized "the quite different questions that would arise in the case of normal delays in obtaining building permits, changes in zoning ordinances, variances, and the like which [were] not before us." Justice Stevens also maintained that *Lucas v. South Carolina Coastal Council*, casebook, p. 524, did not decide the question before the Court. The taking in *Lucas* "was unconditional and permanent." Consequently, the Court's holding "was limited to the 'extraordinary circumstance when *no* productive or economically beneficial use of land is permitted.'"

A court should begin by asking "whether there was a total taking of the entire parcel; if not, then *Penn Central* was the proper framework." To avoid that fact-driven inquiry, there must be "complete elimination of value," or a "total loss."

Nevertheless, Justice Stevens considered "whether the interest in protecting individual property owners from bearing public burdens 'which, in all fairness and justice, should be borne by the public as a whole,' justifies creating a new rule for these circumstances." Justice Stevens rejected petitioners' broad *per se* rule because it "would apply to numerous 'normal delays in obtaining building permits, changes in zoning ordinances, variances and the like,' as well as to orders temporarily prohibiting access to crime scenes, businesses that violate health codes, fire-damaged buildings," in addition to other traditional exercises of the police power. "[T]he extreme categorical rule that any deprivation of all economic use, no matter how brief, constitutes a compensable taking surely cannot be sustained." However, "we do not hold that the temporary nature of a land-use restriction precludes finding that it effects a taking; we simply recognize that it should not be given exclusive significance one way or the other." The Court would have created perverse incentives had it held "that landowners must wait for a taking claim to ripen so that planners can make well-reasoned decisions while, at the same time, holding that those planners must compensate landowners for the delay." A government's interest in well-reasoned decisions becomes "even stronger when an agency is developing a regional plan than when it is considering a permit for a single parcel." The two moratoria at issue in this case, for example, "enabled TRPA to obtain the benefit of comments and criticisms from interested parties, such as the petitioners, during its deliberations."

Moreover, "property values throughout the Basin can be expected to reflect the added assurance that Lake Tahoe will remain in its pristine state." The Court concluded "that the interest in 'fairness and justice' will be best served by relying on the familiar *Penn Central* approach when deciding cases like this, rather than by attempting to craft a new categorical rule."

Chief Justice Rehnquist dissented, joined by Justices Scalia and Thomas. "For over half a decade, petitioners were prohibited from building homes, or any other structures, on their land." And as such, the Takings Clause "requires the government to pay compensation." Specifically, "the District Court enjoined the 1984 Plan because the Plan did not comply with the environmental requirements of respondent's regulations and of the Compact itself." While the injunction remained in place, the planning agency was the " 'moving force' behind petitioners' inability to develop its land from April 1984 through the enactment of the 1987 plan."

The majority refused to apply *Lucas* "on the ground that the deprivation was 'temporary.' " However, "[t]he 'temporary' prohibition in this case that the Court finds is not a taking lasted almost six years," yet "[t]he 'permanent' prohibition that the Court held to be a taking in *Lucas* lasted less than two years," because the law changed "to allow the issuance of 'special permits' for the construction or reconstruction of habitable structures." From the owner's perspective, "what happened in this case is no different than if the government had taken a 6-year lease of their property." Consequently, the majority "allows the government to 'do by regulation what it cannot do through eminent domain.' "

Unlike the majority, Chief Justice Rehnquist did not read *Lucas* "as being fundamentally concerned with value," but with "the denial of 'all economically beneficial or productive use of land.' " He concluded that "the 'temporary' denial of all viable use of land for six years is a taking." Public and private nuisances can still be abated without effecting a taking. Similarly, "short-term delays attendant to zoning and permit regimes are a longstanding feature of state property law and part of a landowner's reasonable investment-backed expectations." Common "moratoria thus prohibit only certain categories of development, such as fast-food restaurants," rather than "deprive landowners of all economically beneficial use."

Justice Thomas dissented, joined by Justice Scalia. He maintained that *First English* "held that temporary and permanent takings 'are not different in kind' when a landowner is deprived of all beneficial use of his land." For Justice Thomas, "potential future value bears on the amount of compensation due and has nothing to do with the question whether there was a taking."

Page 532: [Insert the following after *Dolan v. City of Tigard*, before the Notes]

LINGLE v. CHEVRON U.S.A., INC., 125 S. Ct. 2074 (2005). In *Lingle*, a unanimous Court held that the "substantially advances" test of *Agins v.*

City of Tiburon, 447 U.S. 255 (1980), is not appropriate to apply in deciding whether a regulation constitutes a taking. Chevron controls a large percentage of Hawaii's gas market, particularly on the most populated island of Oahu. Chevron leases some of its gas stations in Hawaii to independent lessee-dealers, charging them rent based on the lessee-dealer's sales. The company makes profit through both rent and product sales. Hawaii enacted legislation that limits the amount Chevron can charge lessee-dealers for rent on its gas stations. Chevron challenged the rent cap provision as facially invalid under the Takings Clause.

Justice O'Connor noted that the Takings Clause bars "Government from forcing some people alone to bear public burdens which, in all fairness and justice, should be borne by the public as a whole." Until 1922, "it was generally thought that the Takings Clause reached only a 'direct appropriation' of property, or the functional equivalent of a 'practical ouster of [the owner's] possession.'" *Pennsylvania Coal Co. v. Mahon*, 260 U.S. 393 (1922), first recognized regulatory takings. As Justice Holmes noted, "while property may be regulated to a certain extent, if regulation goes too far it will be recognized as a taking." However, government regulation inherently "involves the adjustment of rights for the public good." Indeed, "Government hardly could go on if to some extent values incident to property could not be diminished without paying for every such change in the general law."

Justice O'Connor outlined several recognized categories of regulatory takings. "Our precedents stake out two categories of regulatory action that generally will be deemed *per se* takings for Fifth Amendment purposes. First, where government requires an owner to suffer a permanent physical invasion of her property — however minor — it must provide just compensation. A second categorical rule applies to regulations that completely deprive an owner of 'all economically beneficial use' of her property." *Penn Central Transportation Co. v. New York City*, casebook p. 520, identifies several factors that courts should consider in finding regulatory takings. "Primary among those factors are 'the economic impact of the regulation on the claimant and, particularly, the extent to which the regulation has interfered with distinct investment-backed expectations.' In addition, the 'character of the governmental action' — for instance whether it amounts to a physical invasion or instead merely affects property interests through 'some public program adjusting the benefits and burdens of economic life to promote the common good' — may be relevant in discerning whether a taking has occurred."

Courts have also used the "substantially advances" test of *Agins v. City of Tiburon* to determine whether a regulatory taking has occurred. However, this "formula was derived from due process, not takings, precedents." Such a means-ends test is inappropriate for takings analysis, as it does not help to determine whether property has been taken. "An inquiry of this nature has some logic in the context of a due process challenge, for a regulation that fails to serve any legitimate governmental objective may be so arbitrary or irrational that it runs afoul of the Due Process Clause.

But such a test is not a valid method of discerning whether private property has been 'taken' for purposes of the *Fifth Amendment*. The 'substantially advances' inquiry reveals nothing about the *magnitude or character of the burden* a particular regulation imposes upon private property rights. Nor does it provide any information about how any regulatory burden is *distributed* among property owners." The "substantially advances" test "is tethered neither to the text of the Takings Clause" nor to the basic rationale for regulatory takings. "A test that tells us nothing about the actual burden imposed on property rights, or how that burden is allocated cannot tell us when justice might require that the burden be spread among taxpayers through the payment of compensation. The owner of a property subject to a regulation that effectively serves a legitimate state interest may be just as singled out and just as burdened as the owner of a property subject to an ineffective regulation." Further, "if a government action is found to be impermissible — for instance because it fails to meet the 'public use' requirement or is so arbitrary as to violate due process — that is the end of the inquiry. No amount of compensation can authorize such action."

In the case at bar, Hawaii's legislation will cause Chevron to lose $207,000 in rental income per year. However, the parties stipulated that Chevron "expects to receive a return on its investment in these stations that satisfies any constitutional standard." Chevron could regain this lost income through increasing gas prices. Therefore, Hawaii's law will not cause Chevron to suffer any regulatory burden, and the Takings Clause should not apply.

Besides being doctrinally ineffective, the "substantially advances" test also creates serious practical problems in its application. "The *Agins* formula can be read to demand heightened means-ends review of virtually any regulation of private property. If so interpreted, it would require courts to scrutinize the efficacy of a vast array of state and federal regulations — a task for which courts are not well suited. Moreover, it would empower — and might often require — courts to substitute their predictive judgments for those of elected legislatures and expert agencies."

The Court was careful to state that its holding in *Lingle* does not "disturb any of our prior holdings," in particular *Nollan v. California Coastal Commission*, casebook p. 527, and *Dolan v. City of Tigard*, casebook p. 529. Although both of those opinions rely on *Agins*, "the rule those decisions established is entirely distinct from the 'substantially advances' test we address today. Whereas the 'substantially advances' inquiry before us now is unconcerned with the degree or type of burden a regulation places upon property, *Nollan* and *Dolan* both involved dedications of property so onerous that, outside the exactions context, they would be deemed *per se* physical takings. In neither case did the Court question whether the exaction would substantially advance some legitimate state interest. Rather, the issue was whether the exactions substantially advanced the same interests that land-use authorities asserted would allow them to deny the permit altogether."

In his brief concurring opinion, Justice Kennedy emphasized that "today's decision does not foreclose the possibility that a regulation might be so arbitrary or irrational as to violate due process."

§ 7.04   Liberty in Procreation and Other Personal Matters

[3]—Homosexuality

Page 617: [Insert the following after the Note]. This case reverses *Bowers v. Hardwick*; it should be read in lieu of *Bowers*.

LAWRENCE v. TEXAS

539 U.S. 558, 123 S. Ct. 2472, 156 L. Ed. 2d 508 (2003)

JUSTICE KENNEDY delivered the opinion of the Court.

Liberty protects the person from unwarranted government intrusions into a dwelling or other private places. In our tradition the State is not omnipresent in the home. And there are other spheres of our lives and existence, outside the home, where the State should not be a dominant presence. Freedom extends beyond spatial bounds. Liberty presumes an autonomy of self that includes freedom of thought, belief, expression, and certain intimate conduct. The instant case involves liberty of the person both in its spatial and more transcendent dimensions.

I

The question before the Court is the validity of a Texas statute making it a crime for two persons of the same sex to engage in certain intimate sexual conduct.

In Houston, Texas, officers of the Harris County Police Department were dispatched to a private residence in response to a reported weapons disturbance. They entered an apartment where one of the petitioners, John Geddes Lawrence, resided. The right of the police to enter does not seem to have been questioned. The officers observed Lawrence and another man, Tyron Garner, engaging in a sexual act. The two petitioners were arrested, held in custody over night, and charged and convicted before a Justice of the Peace.

The complaints described their crime as "deviate sexual intercourse, namely anal sex, with a member of the same sex (man)." . . . Tex. Penal Code Ann. § 21.06(a) (2003)provides: "A person commits an offense if he engages in deviate sexual intercourse with another individual of the same sex." The statute defines "deviate sexual intercourse" as follows:

"(A) any contact between any part of the genitals of one person and the mouth or anus of another person; or

(B) the penetration of the genitals or the anus of another person with an object." § 21.01(1).

. . . . The petitioners were each fined $ 200 and assessed court costs of $ 141.25. . . .

The petitioners were adults at the time of the alleged offense. Their conduct was in private and consensual.

II

We conclude the case should be resolved by determining whether the petitioners were free as adults to engage in the private conduct in the exercise of their liberty under the Due Process Clause of the Fourteenth Amendment to the Constitution. . . .

In *Griswold* [*v. Connecticut*, 381 U.S. 479, 14 L. Ed. 2d 510, 85 S. Ct. 1678 (1965)], the . . . Court described the protected interest as a right to privacy and placed emphasis on the marriage relation and the protected space of the marital bedroom.

. . . In *Eisenstadt v. Baird*, 405 U.S. 438, 31 L. Ed. 2d 349, 92 S. Ct. 1029 (1972), the Court invalidated a law prohibiting the distribution of contraceptives to unmarried persons. The case was decided under the Equal Protection Clause, *id.* at 454; but with respect to unmarried persons, the Court went on to state the fundamental proposition that the law impaired the exercise of their personal rights, *ibid.* . . .

. . . "If the right of privacy means anything, it is the right of the *individual*, married or single, to be free from unwarranted governmental intrusion into matters so fundamentally affecting a person as the decision whether to bear or beget a child." *Id.* at 453.

. . . *Roe* [*v. Wade*, 410 U.S. 113 (1973)] recognized the right of a woman to make certain fundamental decisions affecting her destiny. . . .

In *Carey v. Population Services Int'l*, 431 U.S. 678, 52 L. Ed. 2d 675, 97 S. Ct. 2010 (1977), the Court confronted a New York law forbidding sale or distribution of contraceptive devices to persons under 16 years of age. . . . Both *Eisenstadt* and *Carey*, as well as the holding and rationale in *Roe*, confirmed that the reasoning of *Griswold* could not be confined to the protection of rights of married adults. This was the state of the law with respect to some of the most relevant cases when the Court considered *Bowers v. Hardwick*.

The facts in *Bowers* had some similarities to the instant case. . . . One difference between the two cases is that the Georgia statute prohibited the conduct whether or not the participants were of the same sex, while the Texas statute, as we have seen, applies only to participants of the same sex. Hardwick was not prosecuted, but he brought an action in federal court to declare the state statute invalid. He alleged he was a practicing homosexual and that the criminal prohibition violated rights guaranteed to him by the Constitution. The Court, in an opinion by Justice White, sustained the Georgia law. . . .

The Court began its substantive discussion in *Bowers* as follows: "The issue presented is whether the Federal Constitution confers a fundamental right upon homosexuals to engage in sodomy and hence invalidates the laws of the many States that still make such conduct illegal and have done so for a very long time." *Id.* at 190. That statement, we now conclude, discloses the Court's own failure to appreciate the extent of the liberty at stake. To say that the issue in *Bowers* was simply the right to engage in certain sexual conduct demeans the claim the individual put forward, just as it would demean a married couple were it to be said marriage is simply about the right to have sexual intercourse. The laws involved in *Bowers* and here . . . [touch] upon the most private human conduct, sexual behavior, and in the most private of places, the home. The statutes do seek to control a personal relationship that, whether or not entitled to formal recognition in the law, is within the liberty of persons to choose without being punished as criminals.

This, as a general rule, should counsel against attempts by the State, or a court, to define the meaning of the relationship or to set its boundaries absent injury to a person or abuse of an institution the law protects. It suffices for us to acknowledge that adults may choose to enter upon this relationship in the confines of their homes and their own private lives and still retain their dignity as free persons. When sexuality finds overt expression in intimate conduct with another person, the conduct can be but one element in a personal bond that is more enduring. The liberty protected by the Constitution allows homosexual persons the right to make this choice.

Having misapprehended the claim of liberty there presented to it, and thus stating the claim to be whether there is a fundamental right to engage in consensual sodomy, the *Bowers* Court said: "Proscriptions against that conduct have ancient roots." *Id.* at 192. In academic writings, and in many of the scholarly *amicus* briefs filed to assist the Court in this case, there are fundamental criticisms of the historical premises relied upon by the majority and concurring opinions in *Bowers*. We need not enter this debate in the attempt to reach a definitive historical judgment, but the following considerations counsel against adopting the definitive conclusions upon which *Bowers* placed such reliance.

At the outset it should be noted that there is no longstanding history in this country of laws directed at homosexual conduct as a distinct matter. Beginning in colonial times there were prohibitions of sodomy derived from the English criminal laws passed in the first instance by the Reformation Parliament of 1533. The English prohibition was understood to include relations between men and women as well as relations between men and men. . . . Nineteenth-century commentators similarly read American sodomy, buggery, and crime-against-nature statutes as criminalizing certain relations between men and women and between men and men. The absence of legal prohibitions focusing on homosexual conduct may be explained in part by noting that according to some scholars the concept of the homosexual as a distinct category of person did not emerge until the late 19th century. . . . Thus early American sodomy laws were not directed at homosexuals as such but instead sought to prohibit nonprocreative sexual activity more generally. This does not suggest approval of homosexual conduct. It does tend to show that this particular form of conduct was not thought of as a separate category from like conduct between heterosexual persons.

Laws prohibiting sodomy do not seem to have been enforced against consenting adults acting in private. A substantial number of sodomy prosecutions and convictions for which there are surviving records were for predatory acts against those who could not or did not consent, as in the case of a minor or the victim of an assault. As to these, one purpose for the prohibitions was to ensure there would be no lack of coverage if a predator committed a sexual assault that did not constitute rape as defined by the criminal law. . . . Instead of targeting relations between consenting adults in private, 19th-century sodomy prosecutions typically involved relations between men and minor girls or minor boys, relations between adults involving force, relations between adults implicating disparity in status, or relations between men and animals.

To the extent that there were any prosecutions for the acts in question, 19th-century evidence rules imposed a burden that would make a conviction more difficult to obtain even taking into account the problems always inherent in prosecuting consensual acts committed in private. Under then-prevailing standards, a man could not be convicted of sodomy based upon testimony of a consenting partner, because the partner was considered an accomplice. A partner's testimony, however, was admissible if he or she had not consented to the act or was a minor, and therefore incapable of consent. The rule may explain in part the infrequency of these prosecutions. . . . The longstanding criminal prohibition of homosexual sodomy upon which the *Bowers* decision placed such reliance is as consistent with a general condemnation of nonprocreative sex as it is with an established tradition of prosecuting acts because of their homosexual character.

. . . American laws targeting same-sex couples did not develop until the last third of the 20th century. The reported decisions concerning the prosecution of consensual, homosexual sodomy between adults for the years 1880–1995 are not always clear in the details, but a significant number involved conduct in a public place.

It was not until the 1970's that any State singled out same-sex relations for criminal prosecution, and only nine States have done so. . . . Post-*Bowers* even some of these States did not adhere to the policy of suppressing homosexual conduct. Over the course of the last decades, States with same-sex prohibitions have moved toward abolishing them.

In summary, the historical grounds relied upon in *Bowers* . . . are not without doubt and, at the very least, are overstated.

It must be acknowledged, of course, that the Court in *Bowers* was making the broader point that for centuries there have been powerful voices to condemn homosexual conduct as immoral. . . . These considerations do not answer the question before us, however. . . . "Our obligation is to define the liberty of all, not to mandate our own moral code." *Planned Parenthood of Southeastern Pa. v. Casey*, 505 U.S. 833, 850, 120 L. Ed. 2d 674, 112 S. Ct. 2791 (1992).

Chief Justice Burger joined the opinion for the Court in *Bowers* and further explained his views as follows: "Decisions of individuals relating to homosexual conduct have been subject to state intervention throughout the history of Western civilization. Condemnation of those practices is firmly rooted in Judeo-Christian moral and ethical standards." 478 U.S. at 196. As with Justice White's assumptions about history, scholarship casts some doubt on the sweeping nature of the statement by Chief Justice Burger as it pertains to private homosexual conduct between consenting adults. *See, e.g.,* Eskridge, Hardwick and Historiography, 1999 U. Ill. L. Rev. 631, 656. In all events we think that our laws and traditions in the past half century are of most relevance here. These references show an emerging awareness that liberty gives substantial protection to adult persons in deciding how to conduct their private lives in matters pertaining to sex. "History and tradition are the starting point but not in all cases the ending point of the substantive due process inquiry." *County of Sacramento v. Lewis*, 523 U.S. 833, 857, 140 L. Ed. 2d 1043, 118 S. Ct. 1708 (1998) (Kennedy, J., concurring).

This emerging recognition should have been apparent when *Bowers* was decided. In 1955 the American Law Institute promulgated the Model Penal Code and made clear that it did not recommend or provide for "criminal penalties for consensual sexual relations conducted in private." ALI, Model Penal Code § 213.2, Comment 2, p. 372 (1980). . . . In *Bowers* the Court referred to the fact that before 1961 all 50 States had outlawed sodomy, and that at the time of the Court's decision 24 States and the District of Columbia had sodomy laws. Justice Powell pointed out that these prohibitions often were being ignored, however. Georgia, for instance, had not sought to enforce its law for decades. . . .

The sweeping references by Chief Justice Burger to the history of Western civilization and to Judeo-Christian moral and ethical standards did not take account of other authorities pointing in an opposite direction. A committee advising the British Parliament recommended in 1957 repeal of laws punishing homosexual conduct. The Wolfenden Report: Report of the Committee on Homosexual Offenses and Prostitution (1963). Parliament enacted the substance of those recommendations 10 years later. Sexual Offences Act 1967, § 1.

Of even more importance, almost five years before *Bowers* was decided the European Court of Human Rights considered a case with parallels to *Bowers* and to today's case. An adult male resident in Northern Ireland alleged he was a practicing homosexual who desired to engage in consensual homosexual conduct. . . . The court held that the laws proscribing the conduct were invalid under the European Convention on Human Rights.

Dudgeon v. United Kingdom, 45 Eur. Ct. H. R. (1981) P52. Authoritative in all countries that are members of the Council of Europe (21 nations then, 45 nations now), the decision is at odds with the premise in *Bowers* that the claim put forward was insubstantial in our Western civilization.

In our own constitutional system the deficiencies in *Bowers* became even more apparent in the years following its announcement. The 25 States with laws prohibiting the relevant conduct referenced in the *Bowers* decision are reduced now to 13, of which 4 enforce their laws only against homosexual conduct. In those States where sodomy is still proscribed, whether for same-sex or heterosexual conduct, there is a pattern of nonenforcement with respect to consenting adults acting in private. The State of Texas admitted in 1994 that as of that date it had not prosecuted anyone under those circumstances.

Two principal cases decided after *Bowers* cast its holding into even more doubt. . . . *Planned Parenthood of Southeastern Pa. v. Casey*, 505 U.S. 833, (1992), . . . again confirmed that our laws and tradition afford constitutional protection to personal decisions relating to marriage, procreation, contraception, family relationships, child rearing, and education. *Id.* at 851. . . .

"These matters, involving the most intimate and personal choices a person may make in a lifetime, . . . are central to the liberty protected by the Fourteenth Amendment. At the heart of liberty is the right to define one's own concept of existence, of meaning, of the universe, and of the mystery of human life. . . . *Ibid.* Persons in a homosexual relationship may seek autonomy for these purposes, just as heterosexual persons do. The decision in *Bowers* would deny them this right.

The second post-*Bowers* case of principal relevance is *Romer v. Evans*, 517 U.S. 620, (1996). . . .

As an alternative argument in this case, counsel for the petitioners and some *amici* contend that *Romer* provides the basis for declaring the Texas statute invalid under the Equal Protection Clause. That is a tenable argument, but we conclude the instant case requires us to address whether *Bowers* itself has continuing validity. Were we to hold the statute invalid under the Equal Protection Clause some might question whether a prohibition would be valid if drawn differently, say, to prohibit the conduct both between same-sex and different-sex participants.

. . . If protected conduct is made criminal and the law which does so remains unexamined for its substantive validity, its stigma might remain even if it were not enforceable as drawn for equal protection reasons. When homosexual conduct is made criminal by the law of the State, that declaration in and of itself is an invitation to subject homosexual persons to discrimination both in the public and in the private spheres. The central holding of *Bowers* . . . demeans the lives of homosexual persons.

The stigma this criminal statute imposes, moreover, is not trivial. The offense, to be sure, is but a class C misdemeanor. . . . Still, it remains a criminal offense with all that imports for the dignity of the persons charged. The petitioners will bear on their record the history of their criminal convictions. . . . We are advised that if Texas convicted an adult for private, consensual homosexual conduct under the statute here in question the convicted person would come within the registration laws of a least four States were he or she to be subject to their jurisdiction. . . . Furthermore, the Texas criminal conviction carries with it the other collateral consequences always following a conviction, such as notations on job application forms, to mention but one example.

The foundations of *Bowers* have sustained serious erosion from our recent decisions in *Casey* and *Romer*. When our precedent has been thus weakened, criticism from other sources is of greater significance. In the United States criticism of *Bowers* has been substantial and continuing, disapproving of its reasoning in all respects, not just as to its historical assumptions. *See, e.g.*, C. Fried, Order and Law: Arguing the Reagan Revolution — A Firsthand Account 81–84 (1991); R. Posner, Sex and Reason 341–350 (1992). The courts of five different States have declined to follow it in interpreting provisions in their own state constitutions parallel to the Due Process Clause of the Fourteenth Amendment.

To the extent *Bowers* relied on values we share with a wider civilization, it should be noted that the reasoning and holding in *Bowers* have been rejected elsewhere. The European Court of Human Rights has followed not *Bowers* but its own decision in *Dudgeon v. United Kingdom*. *See P. G. & J. H. v. United Kingdom*, App. No. 00044787/98, P56 (Eur. Ct. H. R., Sept. 25, 2001); *Modinos v. Cyprus*, 259 Eur. Ct. H. R. (1993); *Norris v. Ireland*, 142 Eur. Ct. H. R. (1988). Other nations, too, have taken action consistent with an affirmation of the protected right of homosexual adults to engage in intimate, consensual conduct. . . . There has been no showing that in this country the governmental interest in circumscribing personal choice is somehow more legitimate or urgent.

The doctrine of *stare decisis* is essential to the respect accorded to the judgments of the Court and to the stability of the law. It is not, however, an inexorable command. . . . In *Casey* we noted that when a Court is asked to overrule a precedent recognizing a constitutional liberty interest, individual or societal reliance on the existence of that liberty cautions with particular strength against reversing course. . . . [T]here has been no individual or societal reliance on *Bowers* of the sort that could counsel against overturning its holding once there are compelling reasons to do so. *Bowers* itself causes uncertainty, for the precedents before and after its issuance contradict its central holding. . . .

Bowers was not correct when it was decided, . . . and now is overruled.

The present case does not involve minors. It does not involve persons who might be injured or coerced or who are situated in relationships where consent might not easily be refused. It does not involve public conduct or prostitution. It does not involve whether the government must give formal recognition to any relationship that homosexual persons seek to enter. The case does involve two adults who, with full and mutual consent from each other, engaged in sexual practices common to a homosexual lifestyle. The petitioners are entitled to respect for their private lives. The State cannot demean their existence or control their destiny by making their private sexual conduct a crime. Their right to liberty under the Due Process Clause gives them the full right to engage in their conduct without intervention of the government. . . . The Texas statute furthers no legitimate state interest which can justify its intrusion into the personal and private life of the individual.

Had those who drew and ratified the Due Process Clauses of the Fifth Amendment or the Fourteenth Amendment known the components of liberty in its manifold possibilities, they might have been more specific. They did not presume to have this insight. They knew times can blind us to certain truths and later generations can see that laws once thought necessary and proper in fact serve only to oppress. . . .

JUSTICE O'CONNOR, concurring in the judgment.

The Court today overrules *Bowers v. Hardwick*, 478 U.S. 186, 92 L. Ed. 2d 140, 106 S. Ct. 2841 (1986). I joined *Bowers*, and do not join the Court in overruling it. Nevertheless, I agree with the Court that Texas' statute banning same-sex sodomy is unconstitutional. Rather than relying on the substantive component of the Fourteenth Amendment's Due Process Clause, as the Court does, I base my conclusion on the Fourteenth Amendment's Equal Protection Clause.

. . . Under our rational basis standard of review, "legislation is presumed to be valid and will be sustained if the classification drawn by the statute is rationally related to a legitimate state interest." *Cleburne v. Cleburne Living Center, supra,* at 440; *see also Department of Agriculture v. Moreno*, 413 U.S. 528, 534, 37 L. Ed. 2d 782, 93 S. Ct. 2821 (1973); *Romer v. Evans*, 517 U.S. 620, 632–633, 134 L. Ed. 2d 855, 116 S. Ct. 1620 (1996).

Laws such as economic or tax legislation that are scrutinized under rational basis review normally pass constitutional muster, since "the Constitution presumes that even improvident decisions will eventually be rectified by the democratic processes." *Cleburne v. Cleburne Living Center, supra*, at 440; *Williamson v. Lee Optical of Okla., Inc.*, 348 U.S. 483, 99 L. Ed. 563, 75 S. Ct. 461 (1955). We have consistently held, however, that some objectives, such as "a bare . . . desire to harm a politically unpopular group," are not legitimate state interests. *Department of Agriculture v. Moreno, supra*, at 534. *See also Cleburne v. Cleburne Living Center, supra*, at 446–447; *Romer v. Evans, supra*, at 632. When a law exhibits such a desire to harm a politically unpopular group, we have applied a more searching form of rational basis review to strike down such laws under the Equal Protection Clause.

We have been most likely to apply rational basis review to hold a law unconstitutional under the Equal Protection Clause where, as here, the challenged legislation inhibits personal relationships. In *Department of*

Agriculture v. Moreno, for example, we held that a law preventing those households containing an individual unrelated to any other member of the household from receiving food stamps violated equal protection because the purpose of the law was to " 'discriminate against hippies.' " 413 U.S. at 534. . . .

. . . Sodomy between opposite-sex partners . . . is not a crime in Texas. . . .

The Texas statute makes homosexuals unequal in the eyes of the law by making particular conduct — and only that conduct — subject to criminal sanction. . . . And while the penalty imposed on petitioners in this case was relatively minor, the consequences of conviction are not. As the Court notes, petitioners' convictions, if upheld, would disqualify them from or restrict their ability to engage in a variety of professions, including medicine, athletic training, and interior design. . . .

. . . Texas' sodomy law brands all homosexuals as criminals, thereby making it more difficult for homosexuals to be treated in the same manner as everyone else. Indeed, Texas itself has previously acknowledged the collateral effects of the law, stipulating in a prior challenge to this action that the law "legally sanctions discrimination against [homosexuals] in a variety of ways unrelated to the criminal law," including in the areas of "employment, family issues, and housing." *State v. Morales*, 826 S.W.2d 201, 203 (Tex. App. 1992).

. . . *Bowers* did not hold that moral disapproval of a group is a rational basis under the Equal Protection Clause to criminalize homosexual sodomy when heterosexual sodomy is not punished.

. . . Moral disapproval of this group, like a bare desire to harm the group, is an interest that is insufficient to satisfy rational basis review under the Equal Protection Clause. *See, e.g., Department of Agriculture v. Moreno, supra*, at 534; *Romer v. Evans*, 517 U.S. at 634–635. Indeed, we have never held that moral disapproval, without any other asserted state interest, is a sufficient rationale under the Equal Protection Clause to justify a law that discriminates among groups of persons.

. . . [B]ecause Texas so rarely enforces its sodomy law as applied to private, consensual acts, the law serves more as a statement of dislike and disapproval against homosexuals than as a tool to stop criminal behavior. . . .

Texas argues, however, that the sodomy law does not discriminate against homosexual persons. Instead, the State maintains that the law discriminates only against homosexual conduct. . . . Texas' sodomy law is . . . directed toward gay persons as a class. "After all, there can hardly be more palpable discrimination against a class than making the conduct that defines the class criminal." *Id.* at 641 (Scalia, J., dissenting). . . .

. . . In *Romer v. Evans*, we refused to sanction a law that singled out homosexuals "for disfavored legal status." 517 U.S. at 633. The same is true here. . . .

That this law as applied to private, consensual conduct is unconstitutional under the Equal Protection Clause does not mean that other laws distinguishing between heterosexuals and homosexuals would similarly fail under rational basis review. Texas cannot assert any legitimate state interest here, such as national security or preserving the traditional institution of marriage. Unlike the moral disapproval of same-sex relations — the asserted state interest in this case — other reasons exist to promote the institution of marriage beyond mere moral disapproval of an excluded group.

A law branding one class of persons as criminal solely based on the State's moral disapproval of that class and the conduct associated with that class runs contrary to the values of the Constitution and the Equal Protection Clause, under any standard of review. . . .

JUSTICE SCALIA, with whom THE CHIEF JUSTICE and JUSTICE THOMAS join, dissenting.

"Liberty finds no refuge in a jurisprudence of doubt." *Planned Parenthood of Southeastern Pa. v. Casey*, 505 U.S. 833, (1992). That was the Court's sententious response, barely more than a decade ago, to those seeking to overrule *Roe v. Wade*, 410 U.S. 113, (1973). The Court's response today, to those who have engaged in a 17-year crusade to overrule *Bowers v. Hardwick* is very different. The need for stability and certainty presents no barrier.

Most of the rest of today's opinion has no relevance to its actual holding — that the Texas statute "furthers no legitimate state interest which can justify" its application to petitioners under rational-basis review . . . *ibid.* nowhere does the Court's opinion declare that homosexual sodomy is a "fundamental right" under the Due Process Clause; nor does it subject the Texas law to the standard of review that would be appropriate (strict scrutiny) if homosexual sodomy *were* a "fundamental right." Thus, while overruling the *outcome* of *Bowers*, the Court leaves strangely untouched its central legal conclusion: "Respondent would have us announce . . . a fundamental right to engage in homosexual sodomy. This we are quite unwilling to do." 478 U.S. at 191. Instead the Court simply describes petitioners' conduct as "an exercise of their liberty" — which it undoubtedly is — and proceeds to apply an unheard-of form of rational-basis review that will have far-reaching implications beyond this case.

I

. . . I do not myself believe in rigid adherence to *stare decisis* in constitutional cases; . . . invoking the doctrine. Today's opinions in support of reversal do not bother to distinguish — or indeed, even bother to mention — the paean to *stare decisis* coauthored by three Members of today's majority in *Planned Parenthood v. Casey*. There, when *stare decisis* meant preservation of judicially invented abortion rights, the widespread criticism of *Roe* was strong reason to *reaffirm* it . . . .

Today, however, the widespread opposition to *Bowers*, a decision resolving an issue as "intensely divisive" as the issue in *Roe*, is offered as a reason in favor of *overruling* it. Gone, too, is any "enquiry" (of the sort conducted in *Casey*) into whether the decision sought to be overruled has "proven 'unworkable,'" *Casey, supra*, at 855.

Today's approach to *stare decisis* invites us to overrule an erroneously decided precedent (including an "intensely divisive" decision) *if*: (1) its foundations have been "eroded" by subsequent decisions; (2) it has been subject to "substantial and continuing" criticism; and (3) it has not induced "individual or societal reliance" that counsels against overturning. The problem is that *Roe* itself — which today's majority surely has no disposition to overrule — satisfies these conditions to at least the same degree as *Bowers*.

(1) A preliminary digressive observation with regard to the first factor: The Court's claim that *Planned Parenthood v. Casey, supra*, "casts some doubt" upon the holding in *Bowers* (or any other case, for that matter) does not withstand analysis. . . . *Casey* provided a *less* expansive right to abortion than did *Roe*, which was already on the books when Bowers was decided. And if the Court is referring . . . to the dictum of its famed sweet-mystery-of-life passage, *ante*, at 13 ("'At the heart of liberty is the right to define one's own concept of existence, of meaning, of the universe, and of the mystery of human life'"): That "casts some doubt" upon either the totality of our jurisprudence or else (presumably the right answer) nothing at all. . . . [I]f the passage calls into question the government's power to regulate *actions based on* one's self-defined "concept of existence, etc.," it is the passage that ate the rule of law.

I do not quarrel with the Court's claim that *Romer v. Evans*, 517 U.S. 620, (1996), "eroded" the "foundations" of *Bowers'* rational-basis holding. *See Romer, supra*, at 640–643 (Scalia, J., dissenting).) But *Roe* and *Casey* have been equally "eroded" by *Washington v. Glucksberg*, 521 U.S. 702, 721, (1997), which held that *only* fundamental rights which are "'deeply rooted in this Nation's history and tradition'" qualify for anything other than rational basis scrutiny under the doctrine of "substantive due process." . . .

(2) *Bowers*, the Court says, has been subject to "substantial and continuing [criticism], disapproving of its reasoning in all respects, not just as to its historical assumptions." . . .

(3) That leaves, to distinguish the rock-solid, unamendable disposition of *Roe* from the readily overrulable *Bowers*, only the third factor. "There has been," the Court says, "no individual or societal reliance on *Bowers* of the sort that could counsel against overturning its holding . . . ." It seems to me that the "societal reliance" on the principles confirmed in *Bowers* and discarded today has been overwhelming. Countless judicial decisions and legislative enactments have relied on the ancient proposition that a governing majority's belief that certain sexual behavior is "immoral and unacceptable" constitutes a rational basis for regulation. *See, e.g., Williams v. Pryor*,

240 F.3d 944, 949 (CA11 2001) (citing *Bowers* in upholding Alabama's prohibition on the sale of sex toys on the ground that "the crafting and safeguarding of public morality . . . indisputably is a legitimate government interest
under rational basis scrutiny"); *Milner v. Apfel*, 148 F.3d 812, 814 (CA7
1998) (citing *Bowers* for the proposition that "legislatures are permitted to
legislate with regard to morality . . . rather than confined to preventing
demonstrable harms"); *Holmes v. California Army National Guard*, 124
F.3d 1126, 1136 (CA9 1997) (relying on *Bowers* in upholding the federal
statute and regulations banning from military service those who engage
in homosexual conduct); *Owens v. State*, 352 Md. 663, 683, 724 A.2d 43,
53 (1999) (relying on *Bowers* in holding that "a person has no constitutional
right to engage in sexual intercourse, at least outside of marriage");
Sherman v. Henry, 928 S.W.2d 464, 469–473 (Tex. 1996) (relying on *Bowers*
in rejecting a claimed constitutional right to commit adultery). We ourselves
relied extensively on *Bowers* when we concluded, in *Barnes v. Glen Theatre,
Inc.*, 501 U.S. 560, 569, 115 L. Ed. 2d 504, 111 S. Ct. 2456 (1991), that
Indiana's public indecency statute furthered "a substantial government interest in protecting order and morality," *ibid.*, (plurality opinion); *see also
id.* at 575 (Scalia, J., concurring in judgment). State laws against bigamy,
same-sex marriage, adult incest, prostitution, masturbation, adultery,
fornication, bestiality, and obscenity are likewise sustainable only in light
of *Bowers'* validation of laws based on moral choices. Every single one of
these laws is called into question by today's decision . . . The impossibility
of distinguishing homosexuality from other traditional "morals" offenses is
precisely why *Bowers* rejected the rational-basis challenge. "The law," it
said, "is constantly based on notions of morality . . ." .

What a massive disruption of the current social order, therefore, the
overruling of *Bowers* entails. Not so the overruling of *Roe*, which would
simply have restored the regime that existed for centuries before 1973, in
which the permissibility of and restrictions upon abortion were determined
legislatively State-by-State. . . . Many States would unquestionably have
declined to prohibit abortion, and others would not have prohibited it within
six months (after which the most significant reliance interests would have
expired). Even for persons in States other than these, the choice would not
have been between abortion and childbirth, but between abortion nearby
and abortion in a neighboring State.

To tell the truth, it does not surprise me, and should surprise no one,
that the Court has chosen today to revise the standards of *stare decisis* set
forth in *Casey*. It has thereby exposed *Casey*'s extraordinary deference to
precedent for the result-oriented expedient that it is.

II

Having decided that it need not adhere to *stare decisis*, the Court still
must establish that *Bowers* was wrongly decided and that the Texas statute,
as applied to petitioners, is unconstitutional.

Texas Penal Code Ann. § 21.06(a) (2003) undoubtedly imposes constraints on liberty. So do laws prohibiting prostitution, recreational use of heroin, and, for that matter, working more than 60 hours per week in a bakery. But there is no right to "liberty" under the Due Process Clause . . . The Fourteenth Amendment *expressly allows* States to deprive their citizens of "liberty," *so long as "due process of law"* is provided.

. . . We have held repeatedly, in cases the Court today does not overrule, that *only* fundamental rights qualify for this socalled "heightened scrutiny" protection — *Washington v. Glucksberg*, 521 U.S. at 721. . . .[6]

. . . Noting that "proscriptions against that conduct have ancient roots," *id.* at 192, that "sodomy was a criminal offense at common law and was forbidden by the laws of the original 13 States when they ratified the Bill of Rights," *ibid.*, and that many States had retained their bans on sodomy, *id.* at 193, *Bowers* concluded that a right to engage in homosexual sodomy was not "'deeply rooted in this Nation's history and tradition,'" *id.* at 192.

. . . [T]he Court concludes that the application of Texas's statute to petitioners' conduct fails the rational-basis test, and overrules *Bowers'* holding to the contrary, *see id.* at 196. . . .

III

. . . [O]ur Nation has a longstanding history of laws prohibiting *sodomy in general* — regardless of whether it was performed by same-sex or opposite-sex couples:

> . . . "*Sodomy* was a criminal offense at common law and was forbidden by the laws of the original 13 States when they ratified the Bill of Rights. In 1868, when the Fourteenth Amendment was ratified, all but 5 of the 37 States in the Union had *criminal sodomy laws*. In fact, until 1961, all 50 States outlawed *sodomy*, and today, 24 States and the District of Columbia continue to provide criminal penalties for *sodomy* performed in private and between consenting adults. Against this background, to claim that a right to engage in such conduct is 'deeply rooted in this Nation's history and tradition' or 'implicit in the concept of ordered liberty' is, at best, facetious." 478 U.S. at 192–194 (citations and footnotes omitted; emphasis added).

> . . . Whether homosexual sodomy was prohibited by a law targeted at same-sex sexual relations or by a more general law prohibiting both homosexual and heterosexual sodomy, the only

---

6 [Court's footnote 3] . . . An asserted "fundamental liberty interest" must not only be "deeply rooted in this Nation's history and tradition," *Washington v. Glucksberg*, 521 U.S. 702, 721, 138 L. Ed. 2d 772, 117 S. Ct. 2258, 117 S. Ct. 2302 (1997), but it must *also* be "implicit in the concept of ordered liberty," so that "neither liberty nor justice would exist if [it] were sacrificed," *ibid.* Moreover, liberty interests unsupported by history and tradition, though not deserving of "heightened scrutiny," are *still* protected from state laws that are not rationally related to any legitimate state interest. *Id.* at 722. As I proceed to discuss, it is this latter principle that the Court applies in the present case.

relevant point is that it *was* criminalized — which suffices to establish that homosexual sodomy is not a right "deeply rooted in our Nation's history and tradition." . . .

Realizing that fact, the Court instead says: "We think that our laws and traditions in the past half century are of most relevance here. These references show *an emerging awareness* that liberty gives substantial protection to adult persons in deciding how to conduct their private lives *in matters pertaining to sex*." (emphasis added). Apart from the fact that such an "emerging awareness" does not establish a "fundamental right," the statement is factually false. States continue to prosecute all sorts of crimes by adults "in matters pertaining to sex": prostitution, adult incest, adultery, obscenity, and child pornography. Sodomy laws, too, have been enforced "in the past half century," in which there have been 134 reported cases involving prosecutions for consensual, adult, homosexual sodomy. [*See* W. Eslrodge, Gaylaw: Challenging the Apartheid of the Closet 375 (1999) (hereinafter Gaylaw)]. In relying, for evidence of an "emerging recognition," upon the American Law Institute's 1955 recommendation not to criminalize "'consensual sexual relations conducted in private,'" the Court ignores the fact that this recommendation was "a point of resistance in most of the states that considered adopting the Model Penal Code." Gaylaw 159.

In any event, an "emerging awareness" is by definition not "deeply rooted in this Nation's history and traditions," as we have said "fundamental right" status requires. Constitutional entitlements do not spring into existence because some States choose to lessen or eliminate criminal sanctions on certain behavior. . . .

IV

I turn now to the ground on which the Court squarely rests its holding: the contention that there is no rational basis for the law here under attack. This proposition is so out of accord with our jurisprudence — indeed, with the jurisprudence of *any* society we know — that it requires little discussion.

The Texas statute undeniably seeks to further the belief of its citizens that certain forms of sexual behavior are "immoral and unacceptable," *Bowers, supra,* at 196 — the same interest furthered by criminal laws against fornication, bigamy, adultery, adult incest, bestiality, and obscenity. . . . If, as the Court asserts, the promotion of majoritarian sexual morality is not even a *legitimate* state interest, none of the above-mentioned laws can survive rational-basis review.

V

Finally, I turn to petitioners' equal-protection challenge. . . .

. . . Even if the Texas law *does* deny equal protection to "homosexuals as a class," that denial *still* does not need to be justified by anything more than a rational basis, which our cases show is satisfied by the enforcement of traditional notions of sexual morality.

. . . [T]he Court has taken sides in the culture war, departing from its role of assuring, as neutral observer, that the democratic rules of engagement are observed. Many Americans do not want persons who openly engage in homosexual conduct as partners in their business, as scoutmasters for their children, as teachers in their children's schools, or as boarders in their home. They view this as protecting themselves and their families from a lifestyle that they believe to be immoral and destructive. The Court views it as "discrimination" which it is the function of our judgments to deter. So imbued is the Court with the law profession's anti-anti-homosexual culture, that it is seemingly unaware that the attitudes of that culture are not obviously "mainstream"; that in most States what the Court calls "discrimination" against those who engage in homosexual acts is perfectly legal; that proposals to ban such "discrimination" under Title VII have repeatedly been rejected by Congress, see Employment Non-Discrimination Act of 1994, S. 2238, 103d Cong., 2d Sess. (1994); Civil Rights Amendments, H. R. 5452, 94th Cong., 1st Sess. (1975); that in some cases such "discrimination" is *mandated* by federal statute, see 10 U.S.C. § 654(b)(1) (mandating discharge from the armed forces of any service member who engages in or intends to engage in homosexual acts); and that in some cases such "discrimination" is a constitutional right, see *Boy Scouts of America v. Dale*, 530 U.S. 640 (2000).

Let me be clear that I have nothing against homosexuals, or any other group, promoting their agenda through normal democratic means. Social perceptions of sexual and other morality change over time, and every group has the right to persuade its fellow citizens that its view of such matters is the best. That homosexuals have achieved some success in that enterprise is attested to by the fact that Texas is one of the few remaining States that criminalize private, consensual homosexual acts. . . . I would no more *require* a State to criminalize homosexual acts — or, for that matter, display *any* moral disapprobation of them — than I would *forbid* it to do so. . . .

JUSTICE THOMAS, dissenting.

I join Justice Scalia's dissenting opinion. I write separately to note that the law before the Court today "is . . . uncommonly silly." *Griswold v. Connecticut*, 381 U.S. 479, 527, 14 L. Ed. 2d 510, 85 S. Ct. 1678 (1965) (Stewart, J., dissenting). If I were a member of the Texas Legislature, I would vote to repeal it. Punishing someone for expressing his sexual preference through noncommercial consensual conduct with another adult does not appear to be a worthy way to expend valuable law enforcement resources.

. . . And, just like Justice Stewart, I "can find [neither in the Bill of Rights nor any other part of the Constitution a] general right of privacy," [*id.* at 530] or as the Court terms it today, the "liberty of the person both in its spatial and more transcendent dimensions."

§ 7.05   Personal Property Rights: New Forms of Protection for New Property Interests

Page 644: [Insert the following after Note (2)]

(3) *Sexual Offenders. Conn. Dep't of Pub. Safety v. Doe*, 538 U.S. 1 (2003) (registration requirement as a convicted sexual offender does not require a hearing of current dangerousness when the state explicitly disclaims that it is not holding out registrants as currently dangerous.)

Page 644: [Insert the following to end of paragraph before *Cleveland Board of Education v. Loudermill*]

; *City of Los Angeles v. David*, 538 U.S. 715 (2003) (a 30-day delay in a hearing regarding a $134.50 fine for a towed car is "no more than a routine delay substantially required by administrative needs").

Page 650: [Add (1) at the beginning of existing Note and insert the following as Note (2)]

(2) *Enforcement of restraining orders. In Town of Castle Rock, Colorado v. Gonzales*, 125 S. Ct. 2796 (2005), the Court held that lack of enforcement of a restraining order did not give rise to an action under the Due Process Clause. A father took his three children in violation of a restraining order and murdered them. The mother called the police about her husband having taken the children several times that evening, but the police failed to take action, telling her to wait a few hours in hopes that her husband would return the children. Writing for a 7-2 majority, Justice Scalia held that the Colorado statute did not specify a statutory entitlement as it did not make enforcement of the restraining order mandatory. "A well established tradition of police discretion has long coexisted with apparently mandatory arrest statutes." Under this case and *DeShaney v. Winnebago County Department of Social Services*, casebook p. 647, "the benefit that a third party may receive from having someone else arrested" seldom triggers either the procedural or substantive protection under the Due Process Clause. The Court has been reluctant "to treat the Fourteenth Amendment as 'a font of tort law.'" State law is the appropriate source of such a cause of action.

Justice Souter concurred, joined by Justice Breyer. Finding a statutory entitlement in this case "would federalize every mandatory state-law direction to executive officers." Justice Stevens dissented, joined by Justice Ginsburg. The majority did not sufficiently defer to the Court of Appeals' "eminently reasonable" conclusion that the Colorado legislature intended to remove police discretion in the enforcement of domestic restraining orders.

Chapter VIII

RACIAL EQUALITY

§ 8.02   Other Forms of Racial Discrimination

[1]—General Principles: Purposeful Discrimination and Suspect Classes

Page 710: [Insert the following to Note (8)]

(a) *Invalid Inmate Discrimination.* In *Johnson v. California*, 125 S. Ct. 1141 (2005), the Court in a 5-3 decision held that strict scrutiny is the proper standard of review to examine a challenge to California's racially segregated prison policy. According to an "unwritten policy" the California Department of Corrections (CDC) grouped prisoners who had just arrived at a facility by race when assigning them to "double cells," where they stayed for up to 60 days after their arrival, at which point they were then allowed to select their own cellmate. The CDC argued that their policy "neither benefits nor burdens one group or individual more than any other group or individual" and therefore strict scrutiny should not be applied. Writing for a 5-3 majority, Justice O'Connor stated that separate facilities cannot be equal. *See Brown v. Board of Education*, casebook, p. 658. Nearly all states and the federal government do not utilize racial segregation in managing their prisons. "The right not to be discriminated against based on one's race" need not "necessarily be compromised for the sake of proper prison administration."

Justice Ginsburg concurred, joined by Justices Souter and Breyer. Justice Stevens dissented. Rather than remand the case, he would invalidate the policy based on the record before the Court. Such "a blanket policy of even temporary segregation runs counter to the great weight of professional opinion on sound prison management." Moreover, the CDC had not even thought about "race-neutral methods of achieving its goals." Justice Thomas dissented, joined by Justice Scalia. As their names indicate, "the Aryan Brotherhood, the Black Guerrilla Family, the Mexican Mafia, the Nazi Low Riders, and La Nuestra Familia," are all race-based gangs. California has more inmates who are gang members than any other American prison system. Consequently, CDC policy "is reasonably related to legitimate penological interests." He would uphold the policy, in order to "accommodate the needs of prison administration." Chief Justice Rehnquist took no part in the decision of this case.

[3]—Housing and Zoning

Page 718: [Insert the following after Note (2)]

(3) *Discriminatory intent.* In *Cuyahoga Falls v. Buckeye Cmty. Hope Found.*, 538 U.S. 188 (2003), the Court held evidence of discriminatory intent was not enough for plaintiffs' equal protection action to survive summary judgment. Plaintiffs brought an action against city officials claiming that a referendum repealing a city affordable housing ordinance violated the Equal Protection Clause. The District Court granted plaintiffs' summary judgment motion. The Court of Appeals reversed, finding that genuine issues of material fact existed as to whether city officials having permitted a referendum against an affordable housing plan to go forward "gave effect to the racial bias reflected in the public's opposition to the project." A unanimous Supreme Court reversed. Defendants followed the "facially neutral petitioning procedure of the City Charter in submitting the referendum petition to the voters." During a "citizen-driven petition drive," a private individual can make statements that "while sometimes relevant to equal protection analysis, do not, in and of themselves, constitute state action for the purposes of the *Fourteenth Amendment.*" In contrast, "statements made by decisionmakers or referendum sponsors during deliberation over a referendum, may constitute relevant evidence of discriminatory intent." In the present case, the plaintiffs have not shown that "city officials exercised any power over voters' decisionmaking during the drive, much less the kind of 'coercive power' either 'overt or covert' that would render the voters' actions and statements, for all intents and purposes, state action." Justice Scalia filed a concurring opinion joined by Justice Thomas.

[5]—The Criminal Justice System

Page 757: [Insert the following to Note (2)]

(a) *Challenger's prima facie case.* In *Johnson v. California*, 125 S. Ct. 2410 (2005), the Court issued an 8-1 decision that invalidated California's application of the "more likely than not" standard to the first step of the defendant's prima facie case. In *Batson v. Kentucky*, casebook p. 754, the Court "did not intend the first step to be so onerous that a defendant would have to persuade the judge — on the basis of all the facts, some of which are impossible for the defendant to know with certainty — that the challenge was more likely than not the product of purposeful discrimination." At this early stage of the proceeding, a defendant need only produce "evidence sufficient to permit the trial judge to draw an inference that discrimination has occurred." While the defendant must ultimately persuade the court that the prosecutor discriminated in selecting jury members, the defendant bears this burden only after the prosecution has offered a reason for excluding the specific veniremen. A prosecutor's refusal to offer a reason supports the defendant's "inference of discrimination." In the case at bar, the prosecutor used peremptory challenges to remove all three black prospective jurors, prompting the trial judge and the California Supreme Court to note the possibility of discrimination. "Those inferences that discrimination may have occurred," not that discrimination "more likely than not" occurred, established the defendant's prima facie case.

Justice Breyer concurred. Justice Thomas dissented. *Batson* affords states broad discretion to construct their own method of implementing *Batson*'s prima facie case.

Page 760: [Insert the following before after Note (6)]

(7) *Voir dire questions and other techniques.* In *Miller-El v. Dretke*, 125 S. Ct. 2317 (2005), the Court reversed a Court of Appeals' determination that Miller-El was not entitled to habeas relief for discrimination in jury selection. The evidence established that the prosecutor had exercised peremptory challenges to remove black venire panel members based on their race. Of the 20 black persons on the original 108-person venire, the prosecution struck 9 for cause. The prosecution used its peremptory challenges to strike 10 of the 11 jurors who survived. The one surviving black venireman was the sole black person on the resulting 12-person jury. Writing for a 6-3 majority, Justice Souter stated that more compelling than statistical evidence is that a prosecutor dismisses a black panelist for a reason that also applies to "an otherwise-similar nonblack" panelist allowed to serve on the jury. While the prosecutor in the case at bar did accept a black member towards the end of jury selection, this action did not "neutralize the early-stage decision to challenge a comparable venireman." *Batson v. Kentucky*, casebook p. 754, permits "the prosecutor to give the reason for striking the juror and it requires the judge to assess the plausibility of that reason in light of all evidence with a bearing on it."

In addition to the above evidence, the trial court granted two of the three jury shuffles requested by the prosecution. Under Texas criminal procedure, these shuffles allowed a reordering of the questioning of jurors so that those toward the back are frequently never reached for questioning but simply excused. All three times the prosecution requested a shuffle, black jurors were among the first to be questioned on the panel. The evidence did not indicate the defense using jury shuffling in a similar race-based way. Second, the prosecution gave a graphic description of the death penalty to 86% of black veniremen, but only to 30% of nonblack veniremen who expressed any doubt about it. Similarly, prosecutors asked 100% of black veniremen but only 27% of nonblack veniremen who expressed such doubts the "trick question" of their views of the minimum sentence for murder even though a Texas statute required five years. Third, the Court noted evidence of an old policy at the District Attorney's office of excluding black jury members which had not been countermanded. Finally, the prosecution's "race-neutral reasons" for using peremptory strikes against black panel members "do not hold up and are so far at odds with the evidence that pretext is the fair conclusion."

Justice Breyer concurred, noting the practical difficulties in applying *Batson* and suggesting that the entire system of peremptory challenges should be reconsidered. Justice Thomas dissented, joined by Chief Justice Rehnquist and Justice Scalia. The majority findings violate the Antiterrorism and Effective Death Penalty Act of 1996 (AEDPA), which require that federal courts in habeas corpus matters consider only evidence that was presented in state court. Moreover, under *Batson*, a "strong presumption of validity attaches to a trial court's factual finding." This presumption is even stronger in habeas proceedings, as the AEDPA requires a defendant to prove discrimination by clear and convincing evidence. Finally, *Batson* will compare veniremen of different races only if they "are truly similar."

Chapter X

AFFIRMATIVE ACTION

§ 10.01   Education

Page 828: [Insert the following after Note (2)] This case may be read in lieu of *Regents of University of California v. Bakke.*

GRUTTER v. BOLLINGER

539 U.S. 306, 123 S. Ct. 2325, 156 L. Ed.2d 304 (2003)

JUSTICE O'CONNOR delivered the opinion of the Court.

This case requires us to decide whether the use of race as a factor in student admissions by the University of Michigan Law School (Law School) is unlawful.

I

A

The Law School ranks among the Nation's top law schools. It receives more than 3,500 applications each year for a class of around 350 students. Seeking to "admit a group of students who individually and collectively are among the most capable," the Law School looks for individuals with "substantial promise for success in law school" and "a strong likelihood of succeeding in the practice of law and contributing in diverse ways to the well-being of others." More broadly, the Law School seeks "a mix of students with varying backgrounds and experiences who will respect and learn from each other." In 1992, the dean of the Law School charged a faculty committee with crafting a written admissions policy to implement these goals. In particular, the Law School sought to ensure that its efforts to achieve student body diversity complied with this Court's most recent ruling on the use of race in university admissions. *See Regents of Univ. of Cal. v. Bakke*, 438 U.S. 265 (1978). Upon the unanimous adoption of the committee's report by the Law School faculty, it became the Law School's official admissions policy.

The hallmark of that policy is its focus on academic ability coupled with a flexible assessment of applicants' talents, experiences, and potential "to contribute to the learning of those around them." The policy requires admissions officials to evaluate each applicant based on all the information available in the file, including a personal statement, letters of recommendation, and an essay describing the ways in which the applicant will contribute to the life and diversity of the Law School. In reviewing an applicant's file, admissions officials must consider the applicant's undergraduate grade point average (GPA) and Law School Admissions Test (LSAT) score because they are important (if imperfect) predictors of academic success in law school. The policy stresses that "no applicant should be admitted unless we expect that applicant to do well enough to graduate with no serious academic problems."

The policy makes clear, however, that even the highest possible score does not guarantee admission to the Law School. Nor does a low score automatically disqualify an applicant. Rather, the policy requires admissions officials to look beyond grades and test scores to other criteria that are important to the Law School's educational objectives. So-called " 'soft' variables" such as "the enthusiasm of recommenders, the quality of the undergraduate institution, the quality of the applicant's essay, and the areas and difficulty of undergraduate course selection" are all brought to bear in assessing an "applicant's likely contributions to the intellectual and social life of the institution."

The policy aspires to "achieve that diversity which has the potential to enrich everyone's education and thus make a law school class stronger than the sum of its parts." The policy does not restrict the types of diversity contributions eligible for "substantial weight" in the admissions process, but instead recognizes "many possible bases for diversity admissions." The policy does, however, reaffirm the Law School's longstanding commitment to "one particular type of diversity," that is, "racial and ethnic diversity with special reference to the inclusion of students from groups which have been historically discriminated against, like African-Americans, Hispanics and Native Americans, who without this commitment might not be represented in our student body in meaningful numbers." By enrolling a " 'critical mass' of [underrepresented] minority students," the Law School seeks to "ensure their ability to make unique contributions to the character of the Law School."

The policy does not define diversity "solely in terms of racial and ethnic status." . . . Rather, the policy seeks to guide admissions officers in "producing classes both diverse and academically outstanding, classes made up of students who promise to continue the tradition of outstanding contribution by Michigan Graduates to the legal profession." *Ibid.*

B

Petitioner Barbara Grutter is a white Michigan resident who applied to the Law School in 1996 with a 3.8 grade point average and 161 LSAT score. The Law School initially placed petitioner on a waiting list, but subsequently rejected her application. In December 1997, petitioner filed suit in the United States District Court for the Eastern District of Michigan . . . .

. . . Dennis Shields, Director of Admissions when petitioner applied to the Law School, testified that he did not direct his staff to admit a particular percentage or number of minority students, but rather to consider an applicant's race along with all other factors. . . .

Erica Munzel, who succeeded Shields as Director of Admissions, testified that " 'critical mass' " means " 'meaningful numbers' " or " 'meaningful representation,' " which she understood to mean a number that encourages underrepresented minority students to participate in the classroom and not feel isolated. Munzel stated there is no number, percentage, or range of numbers or percentages that constitute critical mass. Munzel also asserted that she must consider the race of applicants because a critical mass of underrepresented minority students could not be enrolled if admissions decisions were based primarily on undergraduate GPAs and LSAT scores.

The current Dean of the Law School, Jeffrey Lehman, also testified. Like the other Law School witnesses, Lehman did not quantify critical mass in terms of numbers or percentages. He indicated that critical mass means numbers such that underrepresented minority students do not feel isolated or like spokespersons for their race. When asked about the extent to which race is considered in admissions, Lehman testified that it varies from one applicant to another. In some cases, according to Lehman's testimony, an applicant's race may play no role, while in others it may be a " 'determinative' " factor.

The District Court heard extensive testimony from Professor Richard Lempert, who chaired the faculty committee that drafted the 1992 policy. Lempert emphasized that the Law School seeks students with diverse interests and backgrounds to enhance classroom discussion and the educational experience both inside and outside the classroom. When asked about the policy's " 'commitment to racial and ethnic diversity with special reference to the inclusion of students from groups which have been historically discriminated against,' " Lempert explained that this language did not purport to remedy past discrimination, but rather to include students who may bring to the Law School a perspective different from that of members of groups which have not been the victims of such discrimination. Lempert acknowledged that other groups, such as Asians and Jews, have experienced discrimination, but explained they were not mentioned in the policy because individuals who are members of those groups were already being admitted to the Law School in significant numbers.

Kent Syverud was the final witness to testify about the Law School's use of race in admissions decisions. Syverud was a professor at the Law School when the 1992 admissions policy was adopted and is now Dean of Vanderbilt Law School. In addition to his testimony at trial, Syverud submitted several expert reports on the educational benefits of diversity. Syverud's testimony indicated that when a critical mass of underrepresented minority students is present, racial stereotypes lose their force because nonminority students learn there is no " 'minority viewpoint' " but rather a variety of viewpoints among minority students.

In an attempt to quantify the extent to which the Law School actually considers race in making admissions decisions, the parties introduced voluminous evidence at trial. Relying on data obtained from the Law School, petitioner's expert, Dr. Kinley Larntz, generated and analyzed "admissions grids" for the years in question (1995–2000). These grids show the number of applicants and the number of admittees for all combinations of GPAs and LSAT scores. . . . He concluded that membership in certain minority groups " 'is an extremely strong factor in the decision for acceptance,' " and that applicants from these minority groups " 'are given an extremely large allowance for admission' " as compared to applicants who are members of nonfavored groups. Dr. Larntz conceded, however, that race is not the predominant factor in the Law School's admissions calculus.

Dr. Stephen Raudenbush, the Law School's expert, focused on the predicted effect of eliminating race as a factor in the Law School's admission process. In Dr. Raudenbush's view, a race-blind admissions system would have a " 'very dramatic,' " negative effect on underrepresented minority admissions. He testified that in 2000, 35 percent of underrepresented minority applicants were admitted. Dr. Raudenbush predicted that if race were not considered, only 10 percent of those applicants would have been admitted. Under this scenario, underrepresented minority students would have comprised 4 percent of the entering class in 2000 instead of the actual figure of 14.5 percent.

In the end, the District Court concluded that the Law School's use of race as a factor in admissions decisions was unlawful. . . .

Sitting en banc, the Court of Appeals reversed the District Court's judgment . . .

We granted certiorari, 537 U.S. 1043 (2002), to resolve the disagreement among the Courts of Appeals on a question of national importance. . . .

II

A

. . . In the landmark *Bakke* case, we reviewed a racial set-aside program that reserved 16 out of 100 seats in a medical school class for members of certain minority groups. 438 U.S. 265 (1978). . . .

Since this Court's splintered decision in *Bakke*, Justice Powell's opinion announcing the judgment of the Court has served as the touchstone for constitutional analysis of race-conscious admissions policies. Public and private universities across the Nation have modeled their own admissions programs on Justice Powell's views on permissible race-conscious policies. . . . We therefore discuss Justice Powell's opinion in some detail.

Justice Powell began by stating that "the guarantee of equal protection cannot mean one thing when applied to one individual and something else when applied to a person of another color. . . . *Bakke*, 438 U.S. at 289–290. In Justice Powell's view, when governmental decisions "touch upon an individual's race or ethnic background, he is entitled to a judicial determination that the burden he is asked to bear on that basis is precisely tailored to serve a compelling governmental interest." *Id.* at 299. . . .

First, Justice Powell rejected an interest in " 'reducing the historic deficit of traditionally disfavored minorities in medical schools and in the medical profession' " as an unlawful interest in racial balancing. *Id.* at 306–307. Second, Justice Powell rejected an interest in remedying societal discrimination because such measures would risk placing unnecessary burdens on innocent third parties "who bear no responsibility for whatever harm the beneficiaries of the special admissions program are thought to have suffered." *Id.* at 310. Third, Justice Powell rejected an interest in "increasing the number of physicians who will practice in communities currently underserved," concluding that even if such an interest could be compelling in some circumstances the program under review was not "geared to promote that goal." *Id.* at 306, 310.

Justice Powell approved the university's use of race to further only one interest: "the attainment of a diverse student body." *Id.* at 311. With the important proviso that "constitutional limitations protecting individual rights may not be disregarded," Justice Powell grounded his analysis in the academic freedom that "long has been viewed as a special concern of the First Amendment." *Id.* at 312, 314. Justice Powell emphasized that nothing less than the " 'nation's future depends upon leaders trained through wide exposure' to the ideas and mores of students as diverse as this Nation of many peoples." *Id.* at 313 (quoting *Keyishian v. Board of Regents of Univ. of State of N. Y.*, 385 U.S. 589, 603 (1967)). In seeking the "right to select those students who will contribute the most to the 'robust exchange of ideas,' " a university seeks "to achieve a goal that is of paramount importance in the fulfillment of its mission." 438 U.S. at 313. . . .

Justice Powell was, however, careful to emphasize that . . . "the diversity that furthers a compelling state interest encompasses a far broader array of qualifications and characteristics of which racial or ethnic origin is but a single though important element." *Ibid.*

In the wake of our fractured decision in *Bakke*, courts have struggled to discern whether Justice Powell's diversity rationale, set forth in part of the opinion joined by no other Justice, is nonetheless binding precedent under *Marks.* In that case, we explained that "when a fragmented Court decides a case and no single rationale explaining the result enjoys the assent of five Justices, the holding of the Court may be viewed as that position taken by those Members who concurred in the judgments on the narrowest grounds." 430 U.S. at 193. . . .

We do not find it necessary to decide whether Justice Powell's opinion is binding under *Marks.* . . . [F]or the reasons set out below, today we endorse Justice Powell's view that student body diversity is a compelling state interest that can justify the use of race in university admissions.

B

. . . Because the Fourteenth Amendment "protects *persons*, not *groups*," all "governmental action based on race — a *group* classification long recognized as in most circumstances irrelevant and therefore prohibited — should be subjected to detailed judicial inquiry to ensure that the *personal* right to equal protection of the laws has not been infringed." *Adarand Constructors, Inc. v. Pena*, 515 U.S. 200, 227 (1995). . . . "[G]overnment may treat people differently because of their race only for the most compelling reasons." *Adarand Constructors, Inc. v. Pena*, 515 U.S. at 227.

We have held that all racial classifications imposed by government "must be analyzed by a reviewing court under strict scrutiny." *Ibid*. This means that such classifications are constitutional only if they are narrowly tailored to further compelling governmental interests. . . .

Strict scrutiny is not "strict in theory, but fatal in fact." *Adarand Constructors, Inc. v. Pena, supra*, at 237. . . . When race-based action is necessary to further a compelling governmental interest, such action does not violate the constitutional guarantee of equal protection so long as the narrow-tailoring requirement is also satisfied.

Context matters when reviewing race-based governmental action under the Equal Protection Clause. *See Gomillion v. Lightfoot*, 364 U.S. 339, 343–344 (1960). . . . [S]trict scrutiny is designed to provide a framework for carefully examining the importance and the sincerity of the reasons advanced by the governmental decisionmaker for the use of race in that particular context.

III

A

. . . [T]he Law School asks us to recognize, in the context of higher education, a compelling state interest in student body diversity.

. . . [W]e have never held that the only governmental use of race that can survive strict scrutiny is remedying past discrimination. Nor, since *Bakke*, have we directly addressed the use of race in the context of public higher education. Today, we hold that the Law School has a compelling interest in attaining a diverse student body.

. . . The Law School's assessment that diversity will, in fact, yield educational benefits is substantiated by respondents and their *amici*. Our scrutiny of the interest asserted by the Law School is no less strict for taking into account complex educational judgments in an area that lies primarily within the expertise of the university. Our holding today is in keeping with our tradition of giving a degree of deference to a university's academic decisions, within constitutionally prescribed limits.

We have long recognized that, given the important purpose of public education and the expansive freedoms of speech and thought associated with the university environment, universities occupy a special niche in our constitutional tradition. . . . "The freedom of a university to make its own judgments as to education includes the selection of its student body." *Bakke, supra*, at 312. . . . "[T]he right to select those students who will contribute the most to the 'robust exchange of ideas'" . . . is of paramount importance in the fulfillment of its mission." 438 U.S. at 313 (quoting *Keyishian v. Board of Regents of Univ. of State of N. Y., supra,* at 603). Our conclusion that the Law School has a compelling interest in a diverse student body is informed by our view that attaining a diverse student body is at the heart of the Law School's proper institutional mission, and that "good faith" on the part of a university is "presumed" absent "a showing to the contrary." 438 U.S. at 318–319.

. . . The Law School's interest is not simply "to assure within its student body some specified percentage of a particular group merely because of its race or ethnic origin." *Bakke,* 438 U.S. at 307 (opinion of Powell, J.). That would amount to outright racial balancing, which is patently unconstitutional. . . . Rather, the Law School's concept of critical mass is defined by reference to the educational benefits that diversity is designed to produce.

These benefits are substantial. As the District Court emphasized, the Law School's admissions policy promotes "cross-racial understanding," helps to break down racial stereotypes, and "enables [students] to better understand persons of different races." These benefits are "important and laudable," because "classroom discussion is livelier, more spirited, and simply more enlightening and interesting" when the students have "the greatest possible variety of backgrounds." *Id.* at 246a, 244a.

. . . [N]umerous studies show that student body diversity promotes learning outcomes, and "better prepares students for an increasingly diverse workforce and society, and better prepares them as professionals." Brief for American Educational Research Association et al. as *Amici Curiae* 3.

These benefits are not theoretical but real, as major American businesses have made clear that the skills needed in today's increasingly global marketplace can only be developed through exposure to widely diverse people, cultures, ideas, and viewpoints. Brief for 3M et al. as *Amici Curiae* 5; Brief for General Motors Corp. as *Amicus Curiae* 3–4. What is more, high-ranking retired officers and civilian leaders of the United States military assert that, "based on [their] decades of experience," a "highly qualified, racially diverse officer corps . . . is essential to the military's ability to fulfill its principle mission to provide national security." Brief for Julius W. Becton, Jr. et al. as *Amici Curiae* 27. The primary sources for the Nation's officer corps are the service academies and the Reserve Officers Training Corps (ROTC), the latter comprising students already admitted to participating colleges and universities. At present, "the military cannot achieve an officer corps that is *both* highly qualified *and* racially diverse unless the service academies and the ROTC used limited race-conscious recruiting and admissions policies." [*Id.* at 5]. . . . We agree that "it requires only a small step from this analysis to conclude that our country's other most selective institutions must remain both diverse and selective." *Ibid.*

We have repeatedly acknowledged the overriding importance of preparing students for work and citizenship, describing education as pivotal to "sustaining our political and cultural heritage" with a fundamental role in maintaining the fabric of society. *Plyler v. Doe*, 457 U.S. 202, 221 (1982). This Court has long recognized that "education . . . is the very foundation of good citizenship." *Brown v. Board of Education*, 347 U.S. 483, 493 (1954). For this reason, the diffusion of knowledge and opportunity through public institutions of higher education must be accessible to all individuals regardless of race or ethnicity. . . .

Moreover, universities, and in particular, law schools, represent the training ground for a large number of our Nation's leaders. *Sweatt v. Painter*, 339 U.S. 629, 634 (1950). . . . Individuals with law degrees occupy roughly half the state governorships, more than half the seats in the United States Senate, and more than a third of the seats in the United States House of Representatives. The pattern is even more striking when it comes to highly selective law schools. A handful of these schools accounts for 25 of the 100 United States Senators, 74 United States Courts of Appeals judges, and nearly 200 of the more than 600 United States District Court judges.

In order to cultivate a set of leaders with legitimacy in the eyes of the citizenry, it is necessary that the path to leadership be visibly open to talented and qualified individuals of every race and ethnicity. All members of our heterogeneous society must have confidence in the openness and integrity of the educational institutions that provide this training. . . . Access to legal education (and thus the legal profession) must be inclusive of talented and qualified individuals of every race and ethnicity, so that all members of our heterogeneous society may participate in the educational institutions that provide the training and education necessary to succeed in America.

The Law School does not premise its need for critical mass on "any belief that minority students always (or even consistently) express some characteristic minority viewpoint on any issue." To the contrary, diminishing the force of such stereotypes is both a crucial part of the Law School's mission, and one that it cannot accomplish with only token numbers of minority students. Just as growing up in a particular region or having particular professional experiences is likely to affect an individual's views, so too is one's own, unique experience of being a racial minority in a society, like our own, in which race unfortunately still matters. The Law School has determined, based on its experience and expertise, that a "critical mass" of underrepresented minorities is necessary to further its compelling interest in securing the educational benefits of a diverse student body.

B

. . . The means chosen to accomplish the [government's] asserted purpose must be specifically and narrowly framed to accomplish that purpose." . . .

To be narrowly tailored, a race-conscious admissions program cannot use a quota system. . . .

We find that the Law School's admissions program bears the hallmarks of a narrowly tailored plan. As Justice Powell made clear in *Bakke*, truly individualized consideration demands that race be used in a flexible, nonmechanical way. It follows from this mandate that universities cannot establish quotas for members of certain racial groups or put members of those groups on separate admissions tracks. [*See Bakke, supra*, at 315–316.] Nor can universities insulate applicants who belong to certain racial or ethnic groups from the competition for admission. Universities can, however, consider race or ethnicity more flexibly as a "plus" factor in the context of individualized consideration of each and every applicant. [*Id.* at 315–316.]

We are satisfied that the Law School's admissions program, like the Harvard plan described by Justice Powell, does not operate as a quota. Properly understood, a "quota" is a program in which a certain fixed number or proportion of opportunities are "reserved exclusively for certain minority groups." *Richmond v. J. A. Croson Co.,supra*, at 496 (plurality opinion). Quotas " 'impose a fixed number or percentage which must be attained, or which cannot be exceeded,' " *Sheet Metal Workers v. EEOC*, 478 U.S. 421, 495 (1986) (O'Connor, J., concurring in part and dissenting in part), and "insulate the individual from comparison with all other candidates for the available seats." *Bakke, supra*, at 317 (opinion of Powell, J.). In contrast, "a permissible goal . . . requires only a good-faith effort . . . to come within a range demarcated by the goal itself," *Sheet Metal Workers v. EEOC, supra*, at 495, and permits consideration of race as a "plus" factor in any given case while still ensuring that each candidate "competes with all other qualified applicants," *Johnson v. Transportation Agency, Santa Clara Cty.*, 480 U.S. 616, 638 (1987). Justice Powell's distinction between the medical school's rigid 16-seat quota and Harvard's flexible use of race as a "plus" factor is instructive. Harvard certainly had minimum *goals* for minority enrollment, even if it had no specific number firmly in mind. . . .

The Law School's goal of attaining a critical mass of underrepresented minority students does not transform its program into a quota. As the Harvard plan described by Justice Powell recognized, there is of course "some relationship between numbers and achieving the benefits to be derived from a diverse student body, and between numbers and providing a reasonable environment for those students admitted." [438 U.S. at] 323. . . . Nor, as Justice Kennedy posits, does the Law School's consultation of the "daily reports," which keep track of the racial and ethnic composition of the class (as well as of residency and gender), "suggest[ ] there was no further attempt at individual review save for race itself" during the final stages of the admissions process. To the contrary, the Law School's admissions officers testified without contradiction that they never gave race any more or less weight based on the information contained in these reports. Moreover, as Justice Kennedy concedes, between 1993 and 2000, the number of African-American, Latino, and Native-American students in each class at the Law School varied from 13.5 to 20.1 percent, a range inconsistent with a quota.

The Chief Justice believes that the Law School's policy conceals an attempt to achieve racial balancing, and cites admissions data to contend that the Law School discriminates among different groups within the critical mass. But, as The Chief Justice concedes, the number of underrepresented minority students who ultimately enroll in the Law School differs substantially from their representation in the applicant pool and varies considerably for each group from year to year.

That a race-conscious admissions program does not operate as a quota does not, by itself, satisfy the requirement of individualized consideration. When using race as a "plus" factor in university admissions, a university's admissions program must remain flexible enough to ensure that each applicant is evaluated as an individual and not in a way that makes an applicant's race or ethnicity the defining feature of his or her application. The importance of this individualized consideration in the context of a race-conscious admissions program is paramount. . . .

Here, the Law School engages in a highly individualized, holistic review of each applicant's file, giving serious consideration to all the ways an applicant might contribute to a diverse educational environment. The Law School affords this individualized consideration to applicants of all races. There is no policy, either *de jure* or *de facto*, of automatic acceptance or rejection based on any single "soft" variable. Unlike the program at issue in *Gratz v. Bollinger*, the Law School awards no mechanical, predetermined diversity "bonuses" based on race or ethnicity. . . . Like the Harvard plan, the Law School's admissions policy "is flexible enough to consider all pertinent elements of diversity in light of the particular qualifications of each applicant, and to place them on the same footing for consideration, although not necessarily according them the same weight." *Bakke, supra*, at 317 (opinion of Powell, J.).

We also find that, like the Harvard plan Justice Powell referenced in *Bakke*, the Law School's race-conscious admissions program adequately ensures that all factors that may contribute to student body diversity are meaningfully considered alongside race in admissions decisions. With respect to the use of race itself, all underrepresented minority students admitted by the Law School have been deemed qualified. By virtue of our Nation's struggle with racial inequality, such students are both likely to have experiences of particular importance to the Law School's mission, and less likely to be admitted in meaningful numbers on criteria that ignore those experiences.

. . . [T]he 1992 policy makes clear "there are many possible bases for diversity admissions," and provides examples of admittees who have lived or traveled widely abroad, are fluent in several languages, have overcome personal adversity and family hardship, have exceptional records of extensive community service, and have had successful careers in other fields. The Law School seriously considers each "applicant's promise of making a notable contribution to the class by way of a particular strength, attainment, or characteristic — *e.g.*, an unusual intellectual achievement, employment experience, nonacademic performance, or personal background." All applicants have the opportunity to highlight their own potential diversity contributions through the submission of a personal statement, letters of recommendation, and an essay describing the ways in which the applicant will contribute to the life and diversity of the Law School.

What is more, the Law School actually gives substantial weight to diversity factors besides race. The Law School frequently accepts nonminority applicants with grades and test scores lower than underrepresented minority applicants (and other nonminority applicants) who are rejected. This shows that the Law School seriously weighs many other diversity factors besides race that can make a real and dispositive difference for nonminority applicants as well. . . . Justice Kennedy speculates that "race is likely outcome determinative for many members of minority groups" who do not fall within the upper range of LSAT scores and grades. But the same could be said of the Harvard plan discussed approvingly by Justice Powell in *Bakke*, and indeed of any plan that uses race as one of many factors. . . .

. . . Narrow tailoring does not require exhaustion of every conceivable race-neutral alternative. Nor does it require a university to choose between maintaining a reputation for excellence or fulfilling a commitment to provide educational opportunities to members of all racial groups. *See Wygant v. Jackson Bd. of Ed.*, 476 U.S. 267, 280, n.6 (1986) (alternatives must serve the interest " 'about as well' "). . . . Narrow tailoring does, however, require serious, good faith consideration of workable race-neutral alternatives that will achieve the diversity the university seeks. . . .

. . . The District Court took the Law School to task for failing to consider race-neutral alternatives such as "using a lottery system" or "decreasing the emphasis for all applicants on undergraduate GPA and LSAT scores." But these alternatives would require a dramatic sacrifice of diversity, the academic quality of all admitted students, or both.

. . . Because a lottery would make that kind of nuanced judgment impossible, it would effectively sacrifice all other educational values, not to mention every other kind of diversity. So too with the suggestion that the Law School simply lower admissions standards for all students, a drastic remedy that would require the Law School to become a much different institution and sacrifice a vital component of its educational mission. The United States advocates "percentage plans," recently adopted by public undergraduate institutions in Texas, Florida, and California to guarantee admission to all students above a certain class-rank threshold in every high school in the State. The United States does not, however, explain how such plans could work for graduate and professional schools. Moreover, even assuming such plans are race-neutral, they may preclude the university from conducting the individualized assessments necessary to assemble a student body that is not just racially diverse, but diverse along all the qualities valued by the university. We are satisfied that the Law School adequately considered race-neutral alternatives currently capable of producing a critical mass without forcing the Law School to abandon the academic selectivity that is the cornerstone of its educational mission.

We acknowledge that "there are serious problems of justice connected with the idea of preference itself." *Bakke,* 438 U.S. at 298 (opinion of Powell, J.). . . . Even remedial race-based governmental action generally "remains subject to continuing oversight to assure that it will work the least harm possible to other innocent persons competing for the benefit." *Id.* at 308. To be narrowly tailored, a race-conscious admissions program must not "unduly burden individuals who are not members of the favored racial and ethnic groups." *Metro Broadcasting, Inc. v. FCC*, 497 U.S. 547, 630 (1990) (O'Connor, J., dissenting).

We are satisfied that the Law School's admissions program does not. Because the Law School considers "all pertinent elements of diversity," it can (and does) select nonminority applicants who have greater potential to enhance student body diversity over underrepresented minority applicants. *See Bakke, supra,* at 317 (opinion of Powell, J.). . . .

We are mindful, however, that "[a] core purpose of the Fourteenth Amendment was to do away with all governmentally imposed discrimination based on race." *Palmore v. Sidoti*, 466 U.S. 429, 432 (1984). Accordingly, race-conscious admissions policies must be limited in time. This requirement reflects that racial classifications, however compelling their goals, are potentially so dangerous that they may be employed no more broadly than the interest demands. Enshrining a permanent justification for racial preferences would offend this fundamental equal protection principle. . . .

In the context of higher education, the durational requirement can be met by sunset provisions in race-conscious admissions policies and periodic reviews to determine whether racial preferences are still necessary to achieve student body diversity. Universities in California, Florida, and Washington State, where racial preferences in admissions are prohibited by state law, are currently engaged in experimenting with a wide variety of alternative approaches. Universities in other States can and should draw on the most promising aspects of these race-neutral alternatives as they develop. . . .

The requirement that all race-conscious admissions programs have a termination point "assures all citizens that the deviation from the norm of equal treatment of all racial and ethnic groups is a temporary matter, a measure taken in the service of the goal of equality itself." *Richmond v. J. A. Croson Co.*, 488 U.S. at 510 (plurality opinion). . . .

We take the Law School at its word that it would "like nothing better than to find a race-neutral admissions formula" and will terminate its race-conscious admissions program as soon as practicable. . . . It has been 25 years since Justice Powell first approved the use of race to further an interest in student body diversity in the context of public higher education. Since that time, the number of minority applicants with high grades and test scores has indeed increased. We expect that 25 years from now, the use of racial preferences will no longer be necessary to further the interest approved today.

IV

In summary, the Equal Protection Clause does not prohibit the Law School's narrowly tailored use of race in admissions decisions to further a compelling interest in obtaining the educational benefits that flow from a diverse student body. Consequently, petitioner's statutory claims based on Title VI and 42 U.S.C. § 1981 also fail. *See Bakke, supra*, at 287 (opinion of Powell, J.) ("Title VI . . . proscribes only those racial classifications that would violate the Equal Protection Clause or the Fifth Amendment"); *General Building Contractors Assn., Inc. v. Pennsylvania*, 458 U.S. 375, 389–391 (1982) (the prohibition against discrimination in § 1981 is co-extensive with the Equal Protection Clause). . . .

JUSTICE GINSBURG, with whom JUSTICE BREYER joins, concurring.

The Court's observation that race-conscious programs "must have a logical end point," accords with the international understanding of the office of affirmative action. The International Convention on the Elimination of All Forms of Racial Discrimination, ratified by the United States in 1994, *see* State Dept., Treaties in Force 422–423 (June 1996), endorses "special and concrete measures to ensure the adequate development and protection of certain racial groups or individuals belonging to them, for the purpose of guaranteeing them the full and equal enjoyment of human rights and fundamental freedoms." Annex to G. A. Res. 2106, 20 U. N. GAOR Res. Supp. (No. 14) 47, U. N. Doc. A/6014, Art. 2(2) (1965). But such measures, the Convention instructs, "shall in no case entail as a consequence the maintenance of unequal or separate rights for different racial groups after the objectives for which they were taken have been achieved." *Ibid*; *see also* Art. 1(4) (similarly providing for temporally limited affirmative action); Convention on the Elimination of All Forms of Discrimination against Women, Annex to G. A. Res. 34/180, 34 U. N. GAOR Res. Supp. (No. 46) 194, U. N. Doc. A/34/46, Art. 4(1) (1979) (authorizing "temporary special measures aimed at accelerating *de facto* equality" that "shall be discontinued when the objectives of equality of opportunity and treatment have been achieved").

The Court further observes that "it has been 25 years since Justice Powell [in *Regents of Univ. of Cal. v. Bakke*, 438 U.S. 265 (1978),] first approved the use of race to further an interest in student body diversity in the context of public higher education." For at least part of that time, however, the law could not fairly be described as "settled," and in some regions of the Nation, overtly race-conscious admissions policies have been proscribed. *See Hopwood v. Texas*, 78 F.3d 932 (CA5 1996); *cf. Wessmann v. Gittens*, 160 F.3d 790 (CA1 1998); *Tuttle v. Arlington Cty. School Bd.*, 195 F.3d 698 (CA4 1999); *Johnson v. Board of Regents of Univ. of Ga.*, 263 F.3d 1234 (CA11 2001). Moreover, it was only 25 years before *Bakke* that this Court declared public school segregation unconstitutional, a declaration that, after prolonged resistance, yielded an end to a law-enforced racial caste system, itself the legacy of centuries of slavery.

It is well documented that conscious and unconscious race bias, even rank discrimination based on race, remain alive in our land, impeding realization of our highest values and ideals. As to public education, data for the years 2000–2001 show that 71.6% of African-American children and 76.3% of Hispanic children attended a school in which minorities made up a majority of the student body. . . .

However strong the public's desire for improved education systems may be, . . . it remains the current reality that many minority students encounter markedly inadequate and unequal educational opportunities. Despite these inequalities, some minority students are able to meet the high threshold requirements set for admission to the country's finest undergraduate and graduate educational institutions. As lower school education in minority communities improves, an increase in the number of such students may be anticipated. From today's vantage point, one may hope, but not firmly forecast, that over the next generation's span, progress toward nondiscrimination and genuinely equal opportunity will make it safe to sunset affirmative action.

CHIEF JUSTICE REHNQUIST, with whom JUSTICE SCALIA, JUSTICE KENNEDY, and JUSTICE THOMAS join, dissenting.

. . . I do not believe . . . that the University of Michigan Law School's (Law School) means are narrowly tailored to the interest it asserts. . . . Stripped of its "critical mass" veil, the Law School's program is revealed as a naked effort to achieve racial balancing.

. . . Our cases establish that, in order to withstand this demanding inquiry, respondents must demonstrate that their methods of using race " 'fit' " a compelling state interest "with greater precision than any alternative means." [*Wygant* v. *Jackson Bd. of Ed.*, 476 U.S. 267 at 280, n.6 (1986)] *Regents of Univ. of Cal.* v. *Bakke*, 438 U.S. 265, 299 (1978) (opinion of Powell, J.). . . .

Before the Court's decision today, we consistently applied the same strict scrutiny analysis regardless of the government's purported reason for using race and regardless of the setting in which race was being used. . . . [E]ven in the specific context of higher education, we emphasized that "constitutional limitations protecting individual rights may not be disregarded." *Bakke, supra*, at 314.

Although the Court recites the language of our strict scrutiny analysis, its application of that review is unprecedented in its deference. . . .

In practice, the Law School's program bears little or no relation to its asserted goal of achieving "critical mass." . . .

. . . In order for this pattern of admission to be consistent with the Law School's explanation of "critical mass," one would have to believe that the objectives of "critical mass" offered by respondents are achieved with only half the number of Hispanics and one-sixth the number of Native Americans as compared to African-Americans. . . .

. . . [T]he Law School states that "sixty-nine minority applicants were rejected between 1995 and 2000 with at least a 3.5 [Grade Point Average (GPA)] and a [score of] 159 or higher on the [Law School Admissions Test (LSAT)]" while a number of Caucasian and Asian-American applicants with similar or lower scores were admitted.

Review of the record reveals only 67 such individuals. Of these 67 individuals, 56 were Hispanic, while only 6 were African-American, and only 5 were Native American. This discrepancy reflects a consistent practice. For example, in 2000, 12 Hispanics who scored between a 159–160 on the LSAT and earned a GPA of 3.00 or higher applied for admission and only 2 were admitted. Meanwhile, 12 African-Americans in the same range of qualifications applied for admission and all 12 were admitted. Likewise, that same year, 16 Hispanics who scored between a 151–153 on the LSAT and earned a 3.00 or higher applied for admission and only 1 of those applicants was admitted. Twenty-three similarly qualified African-Americans applied for admission and 14 were admitted.

. . . [T]he Law School's disparate admissions practices with respect to these minority groups demonstrate that its alleged goal of "critical mass" is simply a sham. . . .

. . . [F]rom 1995 through 2000 the percentage of admitted applicants who were members of these minority groups closely tracked the percentage of individuals in the school's applicant pool who were from the same groups.

For example, in 1995, when 9.7% of the applicant pool was African-American, 9.4% of the admitted class was African-American. By 2000, only 7.5% of the applicant pool was African-American, and 7.3% of the admitted class was African-American. . . .

Not only do respondents fail to explain this phenomenon, they attempt to obscure it. *See id.* at 32, n.50 ("The Law School's minority enrollment percentages . . . diverged from the percentages in the applicant pool by as much as 17.7% from 1995–2000"). . . . Indeed, the ostensibly flexible nature of the Law School's admissions program that the Court finds appealing appears to be, in practice, a carefully managed program designed to ensure proportionate representation of applicants from selected minority groups.

. . . [T]his is precisely the type of racial balancing that the Court itself calls "patently unconstitutional."

Finally, I believe that the Law School's program fails strict scrutiny because it is devoid of any reasonably precise time limit on the Law School's use of race in admissions. . . .

. . . Our previous cases have required some limit on the duration of programs such as this because discrimination on the basis of race is invidious.

The Court suggests a possible 25-year limitation on the Law School's current program. Respondents, on the other hand, remain more ambiguous, explaining that "the Law School of course recognizes that race-conscious programs must have reasonable durational limits. . . . These discussions of a time limit are the vaguest of assurances. In truth, they permit the Law School's use of racial preferences on a seemingly permanent basis. . . .

[T]he flaw . . . is not merely a question of "fit" between ends and means. Here the means actually used are forbidden by the Equal Protection Clause of the Constitution.

JUSTICE KENNEDY, dissenting.

The separate opinion by Justice Powell in *Regents of Univ. of Cal.* v. *Bakke* is based on the principle that a university admissions program may take account of race as one, nonpredominant factor in a system designed to consider each applicant as an individual, provided the program can meet the test of strict scrutiny by the judiciary. 438 U.S. 265, 289–291, 315–318 (1978). . . . The opinion by Justice Powell, in my view, states the correct rule for resolving this case. . . .

Justice Powell's approval of the use of race in university admissions reflected a tradition, grounded in the First Amendment, of acknowledging a university's conception of its educational mission. . . .

. . . Preferment by race, when resorted to by the State, can be the most divisive of all policies, containing within it the potential to destroy confidence in the Constitution and in the idea of equality. The majority today refuses to be faithful to the settled principle of strict review designed to reflect these concerns.

. . . The dissenting opinion by The Chief Justice, which I join in full, demonstrates beyond question why the concept of critical mass is a delusion used by the Law School to mask its attempt to make race an automatic factor in most instances and to achieve numerical goals indistinguishable from quotas. . . .

About 80 to 85 percent of the places in the entering class are given to applicants in the upper range of Law School Admissions Test scores and grades. An applicant with these credentials likely will be admitted without consideration of race or ethnicity. With respect to the remaining 15 to 20 percent of the seats, race is likely outcome determinative for many members of minority groups. . . .

. . . There was little deviation among admitted minority students during the years from 1995 to 1998. The percentage of enrolled minorities fluctuated only by 0.3%, from 13.5% to 13.8%. The number of minority students to whom offers were extended varied by just a slightly greater magnitude of 2.2%, from the high of 15.6% in 1995 to the low of 13.4% in 1998.

. . . Admittedly, there were greater fluctuations among enrolled minorities in the preceding years, 1987–1994, by as much as 5 or 6%. . . . The data would be consistent with an inference that the Law School modified its target only twice, in 1991 (from 13% to 19%), and then again in 1995 (back from 20% to 13%). . . .

. . . Whether the objective of critical mass "is described as a quota or a goal, it is a line drawn on the basis of race and ethnic status," and so risks compromising individual assessment. *Bakke*, 438 U.S. at 289 (opinion of Powell, J.). In this respect the Law School program compares unfavorably with the experience of Little Ivy League colleges. *Amicus* Amherst College, for example, informs us that the offers it extended to students of African-American background during the period from 1993 to 2002 ranged between 81 and 125 out of 950 offers total, resulting in a fluctuation from 24 to 49 matriculated students in a class of about 425. The Law School insisted upon a much smaller fluctuation, both in the offers extended and in the students who eventually enrolled, despite having a comparable class size. . . .

The obvious tension between the pursuit of critical mass and the requirement of individual review increased by the end of the admissions season. Most of the decisions where race may decide the outcome are made during this period. . . .

The consultation of daily reports during the last stages in the admissions process suggests there was no further attempt at individual review save for race itself. The admissions officers could use the reports to recalibrate the plus factor given to race depending on how close they were to achieving the Law School's goal of critical mass. The bonus factor of race would then become divorced from individual review; it would be premised instead on the numerical objective set by the Law School.

. . . The Little Ivy League colleges . . . do not keep ongoing tallies of racial or ethnic composition of their entering students. *See* Brief for Amherst College et al. as *Amici Curiae* 10.

To be constitutional, a university's compelling interest in a diverse student body must be achieved by a system where individual assessment is safeguarded through the entire process. There is no constitutional objection to the goal of considering race as one modest factor among many others to achieve diversity, but an educational institution must ensure, through sufficient procedures, that each applicant receives individual consideration and that race does not become a predominant factor in the admissions decisionmaking. . . .

. . . Deference is antithetical to strict scrutiny, not consistent with it.

. . . Were the courts to apply a searching standard to race-based admissions schemes, that would force educational institutions to seriously explore race-neutral alternatives. The Court, by contrast, is willing to be satisfied by the Law School's profession of its own good faith.

For these reasons, though I reiterate my approval of giving appropriate consideration to race in this one context, I must dissent in the present case.

JUSTICE SCALIA, with whom JUSTICE THOMAS joins, concurring in part and dissenting in part. . . .[1]

Unlike a clear constitutional holding that racial preferences in state educational institutions are impermissible, or even a clear anticonstitu-

---

[1] [Court's footnote *] Part VII of Justice Thomas's opinion describes those portions of the Court's opinion in which I concur. *See post*, at 27–31.

tional holding that racial preferences in state educational institutions are OK, today's *Grutter–Gratz* split double header seems perversely designed to prolong the controversy and the litigation. Some future lawsuits will presumably focus on whether the discriminatory scheme in question contains enough evaluation of the applicant "as an individual," and sufficiently avoids "separate admissions tracks" to fall under *Grutter* rather than *Gratz*. Some will focus on whether a university has gone beyond the bounds of a " 'good faith effort' " and has so zealously pursued its "critical mass" as to make it an unconstitutional *de facto* quota system, rather than merely " 'a permissible goal.' " Other lawsuits may focus on whether, in the particular setting at issue, any educational benefits flow from racial diversity. (That issue was not contested in *Grutter*; and while the opinion accords "a degree of deference to a university's academic decisions," "deference does not imply abandonment or abdication of judicial review," *Miller–El* v. *Cockrell*, 537 U.S. 322, 340 (2003).) Still other suits may challenge the bona fides of the institution's expressed commitment to the educational benefits of diversity that immunize the discriminatory scheme in *Grutter*. (Tempting targets, one would suppose, will be those universities that talk the talk of multiculturalism and racial diversity in the courts but walk the walk of tribalism and racial segregation on their campuses — through minority-only student organizations, separate minority housing opportunities, separate minority student centers, even separate minority-only graduation ceremonies.) And still other suits may claim that the institution's racial preferences have gone below or above the mystical *Grutter*-approved "critical mass." Finally, litigation can be expected on behalf of minority groups intentionally short changed in the institution's composition of its generic minority "critical mass." . . .

JUSTICE THOMAS, with whom JUSTICE SCALIA joins as to Parts I– VII, concurring in part and dissenting in part.

Frederick Douglass, speaking to a group of abolitionists almost 140 years ago, delivered a message lost on today's majority:

"In regard to the colored people, there is always more that is benevolent, I perceive, than just, manifested towards us. What I ask for the negro is not benevolence, not pity, not sympathy, but simply *justice*. The American people have always been anxious to know what they shall do with us . . . . I have had but one answer from the beginning. Do nothing with us! Your doing with us has already played the mischief with us. Do nothing with us! If the apples will not remain on the tree of their own strength, if they are worm-eaten at the core, if they are early ripe and disposed to fall, let them fall! . . . And if the negro cannot stand on his own legs, let him fall also. All I ask is, give him a chance to stand on his own legs! Let him alone! . . . Your interference is doing him positive injury." What the Black Man Wants: An Address Delivered in Boston, Massachusetts, on 26 January 1865, reprinted in 4 The Frederick Douglass Papers 59, 68 (J. Blassingame & J. McKivigan eds. 1991) (emphasis in original).

Like Douglass, I believe blacks can achieve in every avenue of American life without the meddling of university administrators. . . .

No one would argue that a university could set up a lower general admission standard and then impose heightened requirements only on black applicants. . . . Racial discrimination is not a permissible solution to the self-inflicted wounds of this elitist admissions policy.

The majority upholds the Law School's racial discrimination not by interpreting the people's Constitution, but by responding to a faddish slogan of the cognoscenti. Nevertheless, I concur in part in the Court's opinion. First, I agree with the Court insofar as its decision, which approves of only one racial classification, confirms that further use of race in admissions remains unlawful. Second, I agree with the Court's holding that racial discrimination in higher education admissions will be illegal in 25 years. . . .

II

. . . Attaining "diversity," whatever it means,[2] is the mechanism by which the Law School obtains educational benefits, not an end of itself. The Law School, however, apparently believes that only a racially mixed student body can lead to the educational benefits it seeks. How, then, is the Law School's interest in these allegedly unique educational "benefits" *not* simply the forbidden interest in "racial balancing," that the majority expressly rejects?

I also use the term "aesthetic" because I believe it underlines the ineffectiveness of racially discriminatory admissions in actually helping those who are truly underprivileged. . . . It must be remembered that the Law School's racial discrimination does nothing for those too poor or uneducated to participate in elite higher education and therefore presents only an illusory solution to the challenges facing our Nation.

A distinction between these two ideas (unique educational benefits based on racial aesthetics and race for its own sake) is purely sophistic — so much so that the majority uses them interchangeably. . . . It is the *educational benefits* that are the end, or allegedly compelling state interest, not "diversity." . . .

The proffered interest that the majority vindicates today . . . is not simply "diversity." Instead the Court upholds the use of racial discrimination as a tool to advance the Law School's interest in offering a marginally superior education while maintaining an elite institution. Unless each constituent part of this state interest is of pressing public necessity, the Law School's use of race is unconstitutional. I find each of them to fall far short of this standard.

---

[2] [Court's footnote 3] . . . I refer to the Law School's interest as an "aesthetic." That is, the Law School wants to have a certain appearance, from the shape of the desks and tables in its classrooms to the color of the students sitting at them.

III

B

Under the proper standard, there is no pressing public necessity in maintaining a public law school at all and, it follows, certainly not an elite law school. Likewise, marginal improvements in legal education do not qualify as a compelling state interest. . . .

2

. . . Michigan has no compelling interest in having a law school at all, much less an *elite* one. Still, even assuming that a State may, under appropriate circumstances, demonstrate a cognizable interest in having an elite law school, Michigan has failed to do so here.

. . . The only interests that can satisfy the Equal Protection Clause's demands are those found within a State's jurisdiction.

The only cognizable state interests vindicated by operating a public law school are, therefore, the education of that State's citizens and the training of that State's lawyers. . . . Less than 16% of the Law School's graduating class elects to stay in Michigan after law school. Thus, while a mere 27% of the Law School's 2002 entering class are from Michigan, only half of these, it appears, will stay in Michigan.

. . . The Law School's decision to be an elite institution does little to advance the welfare of the people of Michigan or any cognizable interest of the State of Michigan.

[T]he fact that few States choose to maintain elite law schools raises a strong inference that there is nothing compelling about elite status. . . .

IV

. . . [T]he Law School should be forced to choose between its classroom aesthetic and its exclusionary admissions system — it cannot have it both ways.

With the adoption of different admissions methods, such as accepting all students who meet minimum qualifications, the Law School could achieve its vision of the racially aesthetic student body without the use of racial discrimination. The Law School concedes this . . . First, under strict scrutiny, the Law School's assessment of the benefits of racial discrimination and devotion to the admissions status quo are not entitled to any sort of deference, grounded in the First Amendment or anywhere else. Second, even if its "academic selectivity" must be maintained at all costs along with racial discrimination, the Court ignores the fact that other top law schools have succeeded in meeting their aesthetic demands without racial discrimination.

A

. . . The only source for the Court's conclusion that public universities are entitled to deference even within the confines of strict scrutiny is Justice Powell's opinion in *Bakke*. . . .

B

1

. . . The Court relies heavily on social science evidence to justify its deference. *[B]ut see also* Rothman, Lipset, & Nevitte, Racial Diversity Reconsidered, 151 Public Interest 25 (2003) (finding that the racial mix of a student body produced by racial discrimination of the type practiced by the Law School in fact hinders students' perception of academic quality). The Court never acknowledges, however, the growing evidence that racial (and other sorts) of heterogeneity actually impairs learning among black students. *See, e.g.*, Flowers & Pascarella, Cognitive Effects of College Racial Composition on African American Students After 3 Years of College, 40 J. of College Student Development 669, 674 (1999) (concluding that black students experience superior cognitive development at Historically Black Colleges (HBCs) and that, even among blacks, "a substantial diversity moderates the cognitive effects of attending an HBC"); Allen, The Color of Success: African-American College Student Outcomes at Predominantly White and Historically Black Public Colleges and Universities, 62 Harv. Educ. Rev. 26, 35 (1992) (finding that black students attending HBCs report higher academic achievement than those attending predominantly white colleges). . . .

The majority grants deference to the Law School's "assessment that diversity will, in fact, yield educational benefits." It follows, therefore, that an HBC's assessment that racial homogeneity will yield educational benefits would similarly be given deference. An HBC's rejection of white applicants in order to maintain racial homogeneity seems permissible, therefore, under the majority's view of the Equal Protection Clause. *But see United States* v. Fordice, 505 U.S. 717, 748 (1992) (Thomas, J., concurring) ("Obviously, a State cannot maintain . . . traditions by closing particular institutions, historically white or historically black, to particular racial groups"). Contained within today's majority opinion is the seed of a new constitutional justification for a concept I thought long and rightly rejected — racial segregation.

2

[I]n *United States* v. *Virginia*, 518 U.S. 515 (1996), . . . a majority of the Court, without a word about academic freedom, accepted the all-male Virginia Military Institute's (VMI) representation that some changes in its "adversative" method of education would be required with the admission of women, *id.* at 540, but did not defer to VMI's judgment that these changes would be too great. . . . Apparently where the status quo being defended is that of the elite establishment — here the Law School — rather than a less fashionable Southern military institution, the Court will defer without serious inquiry and without regard to the applicable legal standard.

C

. . . The sky has not fallen at Boalt Hall at the University of California, Berkeley, for example. Prior to Proposition 209's adoption of Cal. Const., Art. 1, § 31(a), which bars the State from "granting preferential treatment . . . on the basis of race . . . in the operation of . . . public education," Boalt Hall enrolled 20 blacks and 28 Hispanics in its first-year class for 1996. In 2002, without deploying express racial discrimination in admissions, Boalt's entering class enrolled 14 blacks and 36 Hispanics. University of California. . . . Total underrepresented minority student enrollment at Boalt Hall now exceeds 1996 levels. . . .

V

. . . Since its inception, selective admissions have been the vehicle for racial, ethnic, and religious tinkering and experimentation by university administrators. . . .

. . . Columbia employed intelligence tests precisely because Jewish applicants, who were predominantly immigrants, scored worse on such tests. . . .

Similarly no modern law school can claim ignorance of the poor performance of blacks, relatively speaking, on the Law School Admissions Test (LSAT). Nevertheless, law schools continue to use the test and then attempt to "correct" for black underperformance by using racial discrimination in admissions so as to obtain their aesthetic student body. The Law School's continued adherence to measures it knows produce racially skewed results is not entitled to deference by this Court. The Law School itself admits that the test is imperfect, as it must, given that it regularly admits students who score at or below 150 (the national median) on the test. *See* App. 156–203 (showing that, between 1995 and 2000, the Law School admitted 37 students — 27 of whom were black; 31 of whom were "underrepresented minorities" — with LSAT scores of 150 or lower). And the Law School's *amici* cannot seem to agree on the fundamental question whether the test itself is useful. Compare Brief for Law School Admission Council as *Amicus Curiae* 12 ("LSAT scores . . . are an effective predictor of students' performance in law school") with Brief for Harvard Black Law Students Association et al. as *Amici Curiae* 27 ("Whether [the LSAT] measures objective merit . . . is certainly questionable").

Having decided to use the LSAT, the Law School must accept the constitutional burdens that come with this decision. . . .

VI

. . . [N]owhere in any of the filings in this Court is any evidence that the purported "beneficiaries" of this racial discrimination prove themselves by performing at (or even near) the same level as those students who receive no preferences. Cf. Thernstrom & Thernstrom, Reflections on the Shape of the River, 46 UCLA L. Rev. 1583, 1605–1608 (1999) (discussing the failure of defenders of racial discrimination in admissions to consider the fact that its "beneficiaries" are underperforming in the classroom). . . .

The Law School tantalizes unprepared students with the promise of a University of Michigan degree and all of the opportunities that it offers. These overmatched students take the bait, only to find that they cannot succeed in the cauldron of competition. And this mismatch crisis is not restricted to elite institutions. See T. Sowell, Race and Culture 176–177 (1994) ("Even if most minority students are able to meet the normal standards at the 'average' range of colleges and universities, the systematic mismatching of minority students begun at the top can mean that such students are generally overmatched throughout all levels of higher education"). Indeed, to cover the tracks of the aestheticists, this cruel farce of racial discrimination must continue — in selection for the Michigan Law Review, see University of Michigan Law School Student Handbook 2002–2003, pp. 39–40 (noting the presence of a "diversity plan" for admission to the review), and in hiring at law firms and for judicial clerkships — until the "beneficiaries" are no longer tolerated. While these students may graduate with law degrees, there is no evidence that they have received a qualitatively better legal education (or become better lawyers) than if they had gone to a less "elite" law school for which they were better prepared. And the aestheticists will never address the real problems facing "underrepresented minorities," instead continuing their social experiments on other people's children. . . .

It is uncontested that each year, the Law School admits a handful of blacks who would be admitted in the absence of racial discrimination. Who can differentiate between those who belong and those who do not? The majority of blacks are admitted to the Law School because of discrimination, and because of this policy all are tarred as undeserving. . . . When blacks take positions in the highest places of government, industry, or academia, it is an open question today whether their skin color played a part in their advancement. The question itself is the stigma. . . .

Finally, the Court's disturbing reference to the importance of the country's law schools as training grounds meant to cultivate "a set of leaders with legitimacy in the eyes of the citizenry," ibid., through the use of racial discrimination deserves discussion. As noted earlier, the Court has soundly rejected the remedying of societal discrimination as a justification for governmental use of race. . . .

VII

As the foregoing makes clear, I believe the Court's opinion to be, in most respects, erroneous. I do, however, find two points on which I agree.

A

First, I note that the issue of unconstitutional racial discrimination among the groups the Law School prefers is not presented in this case, because petitioner has never argued that the Law School engages in such a practice, and the Law School maintains that it does not. I join the Court's opinion insofar as it confirms that this type of racial discrimination remains unlawful. Under today's decision, it is still the case that racial discrimination that does not help a university to enroll an unspecified number, or "critical mass," of underrepresented minority students is unconstitutional. Thus, the Law School may not discriminate in admissions between similarly situated blacks and Hispanics, or between whites and Asians. This is so because preferring black to Hispanic applicants, for instance, does nothing to further the interest recognized by the majority today. Indeed, the majority describes such racial balancing as "patently unconstitutional." Like the Court, I express no opinion as to whether the Law School's current admissions program runs afoul of this prohibition.

B

. . . While I agree that in 25 years the practices of the Law School will be illegal, they are, for the reasons I have given, illegal now. The majority does not and cannot rest its time limitation on any evidence that the gap in credentials between black and white students is shrinking or will be gone in that timeframe. In recent years there has been virtually no change, for example, in the proportion of law school applicants with LSAT scores of 165 and higher who are black.[3] In 1993 blacks constituted 1.1% of law school applicants in that score range, though they represented 11.1% of all applicants. Law School Admission Council, National Statistical Report (1994) (hereinafter LSAC Statistical Report). In 2000 the comparable numbers were 1.0% and 11.3%. LSAC Statistical Report (2001). No one can seriously contend, and the Court does not, that the racial gap in academic credentials will disappear in 25 years. Nor is the Court's holding that racial discrimination will be unconstitutional in 25 years made contingent on the gap closing in that time.[4]

Indeed, the very existence of racial discrimination of the type practiced by the Law School may impede the narrowing of the LSAT testing gap. An applicant's LSAT score can improve dramatically with preparation, but such preparation is a cost, and there must be sufficient benefits attached to an improved score to justify additional study. Whites scoring between 163 and 167 on the LSAT are routinely rejected by the Law School, and thus whites aspiring to admission at the Law School have every incentive

---

[3] [Court's footnote 14] I use a score of 165 as the benchmark here because the Law School feels it is the relevant score range for applicant consideration (absent race discrimination). . . .

[4] [Court's footnote 15] The majority's non sequitur observation that since 1978 the number of blacks that have scored in these upper ranges on the LSAT has grown, *ante*, at 30, says nothing about current trends. . . . In 1992, 63 black applicants to law school had LSAT scores above 165. In 2000, that number was 65. *See* LSAC Statistical Reports (1992 and 2000).

to improve their score to levels above that range. *See* App. 199 (showing that in 2000, 209 out of 422 white applicants were rejected in this scoring range). Blacks, on the other hand, are nearly guaranteed admission if they score above 155. *Id.* at 198 (showing that 63 out of 77 black applicants are accepted with LSAT scores above 155). As admission prospects approach certainty, there is no incentive for the black applicant to continue to prepare for the LSAT once he is reasonably assured of achieving the requisite score. . . .[5] [T]he possibility remains that this racial discrimination will help fulfill the bigot's prophecy about black underperformance — just as it confirms the conspiracy theorist's belief that "institutional racism" is at fault for every racial disparity in our society. . . .

GRATZ v. BOLLINGER, 539 U.S. 244 (2003). In *Gratz*, Chief Justice Rehnquist, writing for a 6–3 Court, invalidated the University of Michigan's policy that allocates one-fifth of the required points for admission to a student based solely on her race. Petitioners Gratz and Hamacher are Caucasian applicants that were both rejected from the University's College of Literature, Science, and the Arts even though the College determined that Gratz was "well qualified," and that Hamacher's "academic credentials [were] in the qualified range." They claimed that the University's admission policy violated the Equal Protection Clause, Title VI, and 42 U.S.C. § 1981.

The Court rejected a standing argument based on Hamacher's never having applied for admittance as a transfer student. The Chief Justice held that not only had he been denied admission as an undergraduate but he stood ready to transfer.

Respondents argue that their admission program closely follows both the guidelines that Justice Powell outlined in *Regents of Univ. of Cal. v. Bakke*, casebook p. 808, and the Harvard College program that Justice Powell endorsed. Disagreeing, the Court subjected all racial classifications to strict scrutiny, regardless of "the race of those burdened or benefited by a particular classification." Based on the University's undergraduate admission policy, an applicant must receive 100 points in order to be guaranteed admission. An applicant that falls into the category of an " 'underrepresented minority' " will automatically receive 20 points based solely on his/ her race. A policy that grants one-fifth of the points needed to be guaranteed admission to an applicant based entirely on the applicant's race "is not narrowly tailored to achieve the interest in educational diversity." Justice Powell's opinion in *Bakke* stresses that a university should consider "each particular applicant as an individual, assessing all of the qualities that individual possesses, and in turn, evaluating that individual's ability to contribute to the unique setting of higher education." Justice Powell required that each characteristic of an applicant be considered based on his entire application. By distributing 20 points to an applicant based on his race, Michigan has made race a decisive factor "for virtually every minimally qualified underrepresented minority applicant."

---

[5] [Court's footnote 16] I use the LSAT as an example, but the same incentive structure is in place for any admissions criteria, including undergraduate grades, on which minorities are consistently admitted at thresholds significantly lower than whites.

Even if an applicant's " 'extraordinary artistic talent' rivaled that of Monet or Picasso, the applicant would receive, at most, five points," for artistic talent whereas an underrepresented minority applicant "would automatically receive 20 points for submitting an application." The University notes that its undergraduate admissions program allows an applicant's file to be "flagged for individualized consideration." Although a review committee can look at a flagged applicant individually and dismiss the point system, this does not satisfy strict scrutiny. While it is not clear how often applicants are flagged, flagging was "the exception and not the rule" in the University's policy. Such "individualized review is only provided *after* admissions counselors automatically distribute the University's version of a 'plus' that makes race a decisive factor for virtually every minimally qualified underrepresented minority applicant." The University maintains that using its Law School's admission policy that the Court upheld in *Grutter v. Bollinger*, p. 157 of this Supplement, is impractical due to " 'the volume of applications and the presentation of applicant information[.]' "

The University's undergraduate admissions policy was not narrowly tailored and thus violates the Equal Protection Clause of the Fourteenth Amendment. Violations of the Clause "committed by an institution that accepts federal funds also constitutes a violation of Title VI. Likewise, with respect to § 1981," the Court states that "the provision was 'meant, by its broad terms, to proscribe discrimination in the making or enforcement of contracts against, or in favor of, any race.' " A contract that applies to "educational services is a 'contract' for purposes of § 1981." Moreover, purposeful discrimination under the Equal Protection Clause also violates § 1981.

Justice O'Connor's concurring opinion distinguishes the University's undergraduate admissions policy from Michigan Law School's policy upheld in *Grutter* by stating that the College's policy does "not provide for a meaningful individualized review of applicants." The undergraduate program uses a Selection Index Worksheet to distribute points to calculate an individual's score. Once an applicant receives 100 points on a 150 point scale, he is automatically admitted. Candidates in the 95–99 range are classified as " 'admit or postpone,' " while 90–94 points will put an applicant into the " 'postponed or admitted' " category. If an applicant scores between 75 and 89 points, he is " 'delayed or postponed.' " Finally, candidates with 74 points or less are " 'delayed or rejected.' " An undergraduate admissions counselor awards points for various factors to calculate each applicant's selection index score. "Up to 110 points can be assigned for academic performance, and up to 40 points can be assigned for the other, nonacademic factors. Michigan residents, for example, receive 10 points, and children of alumni receive 4. Counselors may assign an outstanding essay up to 3 points and may award up to 5 points for an applicant's personal achievement, leadership, or public service. Most importantly for this case, an applicant automatically receives a 20 point bonus if he or she possesses any one of the following 'miscellaneous' factors: membership in an underrepresented minority group; attendance at a predominantly minority or disadvantaged high school; or recruitment for athletics." The counselor may flag an application if he/she "is academically prepared, has a selection index score of at least 75 (for non-Michigan residents) or 80 (for Michigan residents), and possesses one of several qualities valued by the University. These qualities include 'high class rank, unique life experiences, challenges, circumstances, interests or talents, socioeconomic disadvantage, and under-represented race, ethnicity, or geography.' " Although the program does assign 20 points to some " 'soft' variables other than race, the points available for other diversity contributions, such as leadership and service, personal achievement, and geographic diversity, are capped at much lower levels." For example, an impressive high school leader cannot receive more than five points for her achievements.

The record offers little information about how individualized review occurs. The information offered depicts the review committee as an "after-thought." The record does not indicate whether the committee reviews a meaningful percentage of candidates. In sum, the University's undergradu-ate admissions program is a "nonindividualized, mechanical one."

Concurring, Justice Thomas says that "a State's use of racial discrimina-tion in higher education admissions is categorically prohibited by the Equal Protection Clause." Justice Breyer concurred in the judgment. He joined Justice O'Connor's concurring opinion except the part that joins the Court's opinion. Justice Breyer also joins Part I of Justice Ginsburg's dissent agreeing with her that "in implementing the Constitution's equality instruc-tion, government decisionmakers may properly distinguish between policies of inclusion and exclusion[.]" Policies of inclusion are "more likely to prove consistent with the basic constitutional obligation that the law respect each individual equally."

Justice Stevens files a dissenting opinion, which Justice Souter joins. Justice Stevens states that because neither petitioner was reapplying to the University at the time the suit was filed nor has done so since, neither has standing. The transfer policy is not at issue in this case and was not addressed by the District Court. Justice Souter dissented, joined by Justice Ginsburg. "Nonminority students may receive 20 points for athletic ability, socioeconomic disadvantage, attendance at a socioeconomically disadvan-taged or predominantly minority high school, or at the Provost's discretion; they may also receive 10 points for being residents of Michigan, 6 for resi-dence in an underrepresented Michigan county, 5 for leadership and service, and so on." The admission of " 'virtually every qualified under-represented minority applicant,' may reflect nothing more than the likeli-hood that very few qualified minority applicants apply, as well as the possi-bility that self-selection results in a strong minority applicant pool." Justice Souter would not require the University to adopt a percentage system simi-lar to those used at public universities in California, Florida, and Texas that would guarantee admission to a "fixed percentage of the top students from each high school in Michigan." This system is just as race conscious as Michigan's approach, but in a less open way.

Justice Ginsburg dissents, joined by Justice Souter and by Justice Breyer in Part I of her opinion. There are large disparities between the races in this country. "Unemployment, poverty, and access to health care vary disproportionately by race. Neighborhoods and schools remain racially divided. African-American and Hispanic children are all too often educated in poverty-stricken and underperforming institutions. Adult African-Americans and Hispanics generally earn less than whites with equivalent levels of education. Equally credentialed job applicants receive different receptions depending on their race. Irrational prejudice is still encountered in real estate markets and consumer transactions." Justice Ginsburg continues: "Actions designed to burden groups long denied full citizenship stature are not sensibly ranked with measures taken to hasten the day when entrenched discrimination and its after effects have been extirpated."[6]

She distinguishes between race-conscious laws that aim to increase inequality and those that aim to eliminate it. She says, "Contemporary human rights documents draw just this line; they distinguish between policies of oppression and measures designed to accelerate *de facto* equality." She cites United Nations-initiated Conventions that seek to eliminate racial and gender discrimination.

As non-minority applicants greatly outnumber minority applicants, even substantial race-based preferences will not significantly diminish admissions opportunities for applicants who do not receive them.[7] If universities are not permitted to use race in the admissions process, they will strive to "maintain their minority enrollment," using means other than open affirmative action plans. Instead, they may "resort to camouflage" in a quest to achieve "similar numbers through winks, nods, and disguises."

---

[6] Quoting Professor Stephen Carter, " 'To say that two centuries of struggle for the most basic of civil rights have been mostly about freedom from racial categorization rather than freedom from racial oppression is to trivialize the lives and deaths of those who have suffered under racism." To equate *Bakke* and *Brown v. Board of Education*, casebook p. 658, " 'is to pretend that history never happened and that the present doesn't exist.' " *See Carter, When Victims Happen to Be Black*, 97 YALE L.J. 420, 433–34 (1988).

[7] Admitting the top high school students based on high school grades will yield "significant minority enrollment in universities only if the majority-minority high school population is large enough to guarantee that, in many schools, most of the students in the top 10 or 20% are minorities. However, these plans create "perverse incentives" for parents to enroll their children in "low-performing segregated schools."

Chapter XI

EQUAL PROTECTION FOR OTHER GROUPS AND INTERESTS

§ 11.03 Equality in the Political Process

[2]—Other Barriers to Political Participation: Apportionment, Ballot Access for Minority Parties, Gerrymandering

Page 923: [Add (1) at the beginning of existing Note and insert the following as Note (2)]

VIETH v. JUBELIRER, 541 U.S. 267 (2004). In *Vieth v. Jubelirer*, petitioner Vieth challenged a Pennsylvania redistricting scheme on the grounds that "the districting constitutes an unconstitutional political gerrymander." Five Justices, for different reasons, held the issue of political gerrymandering non-justiciable. Writing for the four-justice plurality, Justice Scalia found political gerrymanders non-justiciable due to a lack of any discoverable or manageable standard of review. "Political gerrymanders are not new to the American scene"; however, "the Framers provided a remedy for such practices in the *Constitution. Article I, § 4,* while leaving in state legislatures the initial power to draw districts for federal elections, permitted Congress to 'make or alter' those districts if it wished." Congress has exercised this power "to regulate elections, and in particular to restrain the practice of political gerrymandering." The plurality refused to base a remedy in this case on *Davis v. Bandemer,* casebook p. 920. After reviewing the eighteen years of case law since *Bandemer,* Justice Scalia observed that *Bandemer* and its progeny have failed to provide "judicially discernible and manageable standards for adjudicating political gerrymandering claims." Consequently, *Bandemer* was wrongly decided.

Bandemer and the comparatively few lower court cases decided under it compare unfavorably with the racial gerrymandering cases. "The Constitution clearly contemplates districting by political entities." In "contrast, the purpose of segregating voters on the basis of race" is unlawful. In drawing this separation, one of the determining factors for the Court is "the fact that partisan districting is a lawful and common practice means that there is almost *always* room for an election-impeding lawsuit contending that partisan advantage was the predominant motivation; not so for claims of racial gerrymandering." While "courts might be justified in accepting a modest degree of unmanageability to enforce a constitutional command which (like the *Fourteenth Amendment* obligation to refrain from racial discrimination) is clear," no such obligation exists to enforce a standard "which is both dubious and severely unmanageable."

Ultimately, the *Bandemer* "standard rests upon the principle that groups (or at least political-action groups) have a right to proportional representation. But the Constitution contains no such principle. It guarantees equal protection of the law to persons, not equal representation in government to equivalently sized groups. It nowhere says that farmers or urban dwellers, Christian fundamentalists or Jews, Republicans or Democrats, must be accorded political strength proportionate to their numbers." The one-person, one-vote principle flowing out of *Reynolds v. Sims,* casebook p. 898, requires that each individual, not each group, has equal say in electing representatives. Moreover, that standard is easy to administer by simply making the number of representatives proportional to the population.

The three potential standards proposed in the dissenting opinions further illustrate that there is no single "constitutionally discernible standard." In addressing Justice Stevens' concerns that political gerrymanders are undemocratic, Justice Scalia commented that "the issue we have discussed is not whether severe partisan gerrymanders violate the Constitution, but whether it is for the courts to say when a violation has occurred, and to design a remedy." Although Justice Scalia noted that Justice Kennedy's concurrence left open the possibility that *Bandemer* claims may someday be justiciable, for the present his is "a reluctant fifth vote against justiciability at district and statewide levels." For the plurality, "[e]ighteen years of essentially pointless litigation have persuaded us that *Bandemer* is incapable of principled application."

Concurring in the judgment, Justice Kennedy agreed that "[a] decision ordering the correction of all election district lines drawn for partisan reasons would commit federal and state courts to unprecedented intervention in the American political process." Justice Kennedy also agreed with the plurality's position that there are currently no judicially manageable standards for political gerrymandering cases. However, he would not shut the door on such challenges forever, pointing out that "new technologies may produce new methods of analysis that make more evident the precise nature of the burdens gerrymanders impose on the representational rights of voters and parties." He continued by noting that "[w]here it is alleged that a gerrymander had the purpose and effect of imposing burdens on a disfavored party and its voters, the *First Amendment* may offer a sounder and more prudential basis for intervention than does the *Equal Protection Clause.*" Ultimately, Justice Kennedy agreed with the plurality that "[t]he failings of the many proposed standards for measuring the burden a gerrymander imposes on representational rights make our intervention improper. If workable standards do emerge to measure these burdens, however, courts should be prepared to order relief."

In dissent, Justice Stevens began by observing that five members of the Court felt that the plurality's holding that political gerrymandering claims were non justiciable was "erroneous," regardless of whether they believed the plaintiffs in this case should prevail. Justice Stevens agreed "with the Court's refusal to undertake [the] ambitious project" of crafting rules to review all political gerrymandering on a statewide basis; however, the District Court failed to follow precedent in dismissing plaintiffs' claim of district-based, political gerrymandering. Relying on gerrymandering cases, Justice Stevens "thought the question of justiciability in such cases as this — where a set of plaintiffs argues that a single motivation resulted in a districting scheme with discriminatory effects — to be well settled." For him, "the critical issue in both racial and political gerrymandering cases is the same: whether a single, non-neutral criterion controlled the districting process to such an extent that the Constitution was offended." Relying on the racial gerrymandering cases of *Shaw v. Reno,* casebook p. 727, and *Shaw v. Hunt,* casebook p. 747, Justice Stevens would "ask whether the legislature allowed partisan considerations to dominate and control the lines drawn, forsaking all neutral principals." When "the only possible explanation for a district's bizarre shape is a naked desire to increase partisan strength, then no rational basis exists to save the district from an equal protection challenge."

In a dissent joined by Justice Ginsburg, Justice Souter "would therefore preserve *Davis's* holding that political gerrymandering is a justiciable issue, but otherwise start anew. I would adopt a political gerrymandering test analogous to the summary judgment standard . . . [requiring] a plaintiff to satisfy elements of a prima facie cause of action, at which point the State would have the opportunity not only to rebut the evidence supporting the plaintiff's case, but to offer an affirmative justification for the districting choices." Agreeing with Justice Stevens, Justice Souter would focus "as much as possible on suspect characteristics of individual districts instead of state-wide patterns." In his dissent, Justice Breyer argued that "gerrymandering that leads to entrenchment amounts to an abuse that violates the *Constitution's Equal Protection Clause,*" and that the Court should be able to separate out the harm caused by "one important gerrymandering evil, the unjustified entrenching in power of a political party that voters have rejected" and "design a remedy for extreme cases."

Chapter XII

POLITICAL SPEECH AND ASSOCIATION

§ 12.01　Advocacy of Unlawful Objectives

Page 972: [Add (1) at the beginning of existing Note text and insert the following as Note (2)]

REPUBLICAN PARTY OF MINNESOTA v. WHITE, 536 U.S. 765 (2002). In *White,* the Court considered "whether the First Amendment permits the Minnesota Supreme Court to prohibit candidates for judicial election in that State from announcing their views on disputed legal and political issues."

Minnesota has always selected all of its judges through popular election, which, since 1912, have been nonpartisan. Such elections have subsequently been subject to a legal restriction based largely on "Canon 7(B) of the 1972 American Bar Association (ABA) Model Code of Judicial Conduct," which states "that a 'candidate for a judicial office, including an incumbent judge,' shall not 'announce his or her views on disputed legal or political issues.'" Judges who violate this "announce clause" risk "discipline, including removal, censure, civil penalties, and suspension without pay." Lawyers who are candidates "for judicial office must also comply with the announce clause," or be "subject to, *inter alia,* disbarment, suspension, and probation."

While campaigning for associate justice of the Minnesota Supreme Court, one of the petitioners "distributed literature criticizing several Minnesota Supreme Court decisions on issues such as crime, welfare, and abortion." Plaintiffs, including the Minnesota Republican Party, sought a declaratory judgment and an injunction against the announce clause.

Writing for the majority, Justice Scalia concluded that the "canon of judicial conduct prohibiting candidates for judicial election from announcing their views on disputed legal and political issues violates the First Amendment." Justice Scalia maintained that the announce clause covered "much more than *promising* to decide an issue a particular way," extending "to the candidate's mere statement of his current position, even if he does not bind himself to maintain that position after election." This is so, because the Minnesota Code also "contains a so-called 'pledges or promises' clause, which *separately* prohibits judicial candidates from making 'pledges or promises of conduct in office other than the faithful and impartial performance of the duties of the office.'" The scope of the announce clause is limited in some respects, such as excluding criticism of past decisions, reaching "only disputed issues that are likely to come before the candidate if he is elected judge," and allowing "general discussions of case law and judicial philosophy."

Despite these limitations, Justice Scalia stated that "the announce clause prohibits a judicial candidate from stating his views on any specific nonfanciful legal question within the province of the court for which he is running, except in the context of discussing past decisions — and in the latter context as well, if he expresses the view that he is not bound by *stare decisis*." Nor did the limiting constructions narrow the scope of the announce clause to the ABA's 1990 canon, which "prohibits a judicial candidate from making 'statements that commit or appear to commit the candidate with respect to cases, controversies or issues that are likely to come before the court.' " Unlike other jurisdictions, Minnesota did not adopt the new ABA canon. The Court limited its decision to the announce clause (as interpreted by state authorities) rather than the 1990 ABA canon.

Respondents also claimed that the announce clause did allow discussion of "a candidate's 'character,' 'education,' 'work habits,' and 'how [he] would handle administrative duties if elected.' " Moreover, "the Judicial Board has printed a list of preapproved questions which judicial candidates are allowed to answer." Such questions include "how the candidate feels about cameras in the courtroom, how he would go about reducing the caseload, how the costs of judicial administration can be reduced, and how he proposes to ensure that minorities and women are treated more fairly by the court system."

Justice Scalia subjected the announce clause to strict scrutiny, maintaining that the respondents had the "burden to prove that the announce clause is (1) narrowly tailored, to serve (2) a compelling state interest." As such, "they must demonstrate that it does not 'unnecessarily circumscrib[e] protected expression.' " Respondents set forth two interests alleged to justify the announce clause: "preserving the impartiality of the state judiciary and preserving the appearance of the impartiality of the state judiciary."

Justice Scalia, however, found the respondents' concept of impartiality vague. " '[I]mpartiality' in the judicial context — and of course its root meaning — is the lack of bias for or against either *party* to the proceeding." In this sense, the announce clause "is barely tailored to serve that interest *at all*, inasmuch as it does not restrict speech for or against particular *parties*, but rather speech for or against particular *issues*. To be sure, when a case arises that turns on a legal issue on which the judge (as a candidate) had taken a particular stand, the party taking the opposite stand is likely to lose. But not because of any bias against that party, or favoritism toward the other party. *Any* party taking that position is just as likely to lose. The judge is applying the law (as he sees it) evenhandedly."

Impartiality could also "mean lack of preconception in favor of or against a particular *legal view*." Such impartiality "would be concerned, not with guaranteeing litigants equal application of the law, but rather with guaranteeing them an equal chance to persuade the court on the legal points in their case." This type of impartiality does not comprise a compelling state interest. "For one thing, it is virtually impossible to find a judge who does not have preconceptions about the law." Even assuming the possibility of selecting "judges who did not have preconceived views on legal issues, it would hardly be desirable to do so." As "avoiding judicial preconceptions on legal issues is neither possible nor desirable, pretending otherwise by attempting to preserve the 'appearance' of that type of impartiality can hardly be a compelling state interest either."

The "third possible meaning of 'impartiality' " is "openmindedness," which "seeks to guarantee each litigant, not an *equal* chance to win the legal points in the case, but at least *some* chance of doing so." Respondents argue that the announce clause "relieves a judge from pressure to rule a certain way in order to maintain consistency with statements the judge has previously made." However, Justice Scalia doubted "that a mere statement of position enunciated during the pendency of an election will be regarded by a judge as more binding — or as more likely to subject him to popular disfavor if reconsidered — than a carefully considered holding that the judge set forth in an earlier opinion denying some individual's claim to justice."

Arguing "that the special context of electioneering justifies an *abridgement* of the right to speak out on disputed issues sets our First Amendment jurisprudence on its head. '[D]ebate on the qualifications of candidates' is 'at the core of our electoral process and of the First Amendment freedoms.' " The Court has "never allowed the government to prohibit candidates from communicating relevant information to voters during an election."

The Court neither asserted nor implied "that the First Amendment requires campaigns for judicial office to sound the same as those for legislative office." Rather, "the announce clause still fails strict scrutiny because it is woefully underinclusive, prohibiting announcements by judges (and would-be judges) only at certain times and in certain forms."

Justice Scalia maintained that Justice Ginsburg's dissent "greatly exaggerates the difference between judicial and legislative elections." Such "complete separation of the judiciary from the enterprise of 'representative government' might have some truth in those countries where judges neither make law themselves nor set aside the laws enacted by the legislature. It is not a true picture of the American system. Not only do state-court judges possess the power to 'make' common law, but they have the immense power to shape the States' constitutions as well."

While "a 'universal and long-established' tradition of prohibiting certain conduct creates 'a strong presumption' that the prohibition is constitutional," "prohibiting speech by judicial candidates on disputed issues . . . is neither long nor universal." By the "Civil War, the great majority of States elected their judges." Moreover, the Court knew of "no restrictions upon statements that could be made by judicial candidates (including judges) throughout the 19th and the first quarter of the 20th century." In fact, "judicial elections were generally partisan during this period." "[T]he movement toward nonpartisan judicial elections" did not even begin "until the 1870's." Justice Scalia concluded: "There is an obvious tension between the article of Minnesota's popularly approved Constitution which provides that judges shall be elected, and the Minnesota Supreme Court's announce clause which places most subjects of interest to the voters off limits."

Justice O'Connor's concurrence expressed "concerns about judicial elections generally," in particular, that "the very practice of electing judges undermines" the State's "compelling governmental interes[t] in an actual and perceived . . . impartial judiciary." Obviously, "contested elections generally entail campaigning," which generally "requires judicial candidates to engage in fundraising. Yet relying on campaign donations may leave judges feeling indebted to certain parties or interest groups." Even assuming that "judges were able to refrain from favoring donors, the mere possibility that judges' decisions may be motivated by the desire to repay campaign contributors is likely to undermine the public's confidence in the judiciary." "Despite these significant problems, 39 States currently employ some form of judicial elections for their appellate courts, general jurisdiction trial courts, or both." Others have adopted the Missouri Plan, in which "judges are appointed by a high elected official, generally from a list of nominees put together by a nonpartisan nominating commission, and then subsequently stand for unopposed retention elections in which voters are asked whether the judges should be recalled." This approach "reduces threats to judicial impartiality, even if it does not eliminate all popular pressure on judges." Nevertheless, "Minnesota has chosen to select its judges through contested popular elections instead of through an appointment system or a combined appointment and retention election system along the lines of the Missouri Plan. Any problem with judicial impartiality is largely one the State brought upon itself by continuing the practice of popularly electing judges."

Justice Kennedy concurred. For him, "content-based speech restrictions that do not fall within any traditional exception should be invalidated without inquiry into narrow tailoring or compelling government interests." Political speech by candidates "does not come within any of the exceptions to the First Amendment recognized by the Court."

Justice Stevens dissented, joined by Justices Souter, Ginsburg, and Breyer. "There is a critical difference between the work of the judge and the work of other public officials. In a democracy, issues of policy are properly decided by majority vote; it is the business of legislators and executives to be popular. But in litigation, issues of law or fact should not be determined by popular vote; it is the business of judges to be indifferent to unpopularity." Moreover, statements made regarding one's views "when one is running for an intermediate or trial court" office "mislead the voters by giving them the false impression that a candidate for the trial court will be able to and should decide cases based on his personal views rather than precedent." Justice Stevens continued: "By recognizing a conflict between the demands of electoral politics and the distinct characteristics of the judiciary, we do not have to put States to an all or nothing choice of abandoning judicial elections or having elections in which anything goes." In conclusion, "the judicial reputation for impartiality and openmindedness is compromised by electioneering that emphasizes the candidate's personal predilections rather than his qualifications for judicial office."

Justice Ginsburg dissented, joined by Justices Stevens, Souter, and Breyer. "Legislative and executive officials act on behalf of the voters who placed them in office; 'judge[s] represen[t] the Law.'" Those who framed "the Federal Constitution sought to advance the judicial function through the structural protections of Article III, which provide for the selection of judges by the President on the advice and consent of the Senate, generally for lifetime terms." This case examines "whether the First Amendment stops Minnesota from furthering its interest in judicial integrity through this precisely targeted speech restriction." Justice Ginsburg "would differentiate elections for political offices, in which the First Amendment holds full sway, from elections designed to select those whose office it is to administer justice without respect to persons." Those who stand for political office, "in keeping with their representative role, must be left free to inform the electorate of their positions on specific issues." In contrast, judges "are not political actors. They do not sit as representatives of particular persons, communities, or parties; they serve no faction or constituency." Instead, they "act only in the context of individual cases, the outcome of which cannot depend on the will of the public." Therefore, "the rationale underlying unconstrained speech in elections for political office — that representative government depends on the public's ability to chose agents who will act at its behest — does not carry over to campaigns for the bench."

For Justice Ginsburg, "the Court ignores a crucial limiting construction placed on the Announce Clause by the courts below. The provision does not bar a candidate from generally 'stating [her] views' on legal questions; it prevents her from 'publicly making known how [she] would *decide*' disputed issues." Moreover, the Announce Clause "does not prohibit candidates from discussing appellate court decisions." Thus, the Clause is "more tightly bounded, and campaigns conducted under that provision more robust, than the Court acknowledges."

Moreover, the type of impartiality guaranteed by due process advances a core principle: "[N]o man is permitted to try cases where he has an interest in the outcome." "[A] litigant is deprived of due process where the judge who hears his case has a 'direct, personal, substantial, and pecuniary' interest in ruling against him." That interest could affect maintenance of judicial office. Finally, "due process does not require a showing that the judge is actually biased as a result of his self-interest. Rather, our cases have 'always endeavored to prevent even the probability of unfairness.'"

Beyond the compelling state interests in safeguarding due process, "the pledges or promises clause advances another compelling state interest: preserving the public's confidence in the integrity and impartiality of its judiciary." By focusing on "statements that do not technically constitute pledges or promises but nevertheless 'publicly mak[e] known how [the candidate] would decide' legal issues, the Announce Clause prevents this end run around the letter and spirit of its companion provision." At bottom, "the Announce Clause is an indispensable part of Minnesota's effort to maintain the health of its judiciary."

Page 976: [Insert the following after Note (8)]

ILLINOIS EX REL. MADIGAN v. TELEMARKETING ASSOC., 538 U.S. 600 (2003). In *Madigan*, the Court concluded that the First Amendment does not protect for-profit organizations from fraudulent misrepresentations that they make concerning the percentage of proceeds that will go to charity. VietNow is a nonprofit organization working to "advance the welfare of Vietnam veterans." VietNow contracted a professional fundraiser, "Telemarketers," to collect donations. As a part of the contract, Telemarketers would retain 85 percent of the proceeds, with 15 percent going to VietNow. The Attorney General of Illinois filed a complaint in state court for fraud and breach of fiduciary duty, alleging that Telemarketers misrepresented the amount of funds collected that would go to VietNow. The trial court dismissed the complaint on First Amendment grounds.

Writing for a unanimous Court, Justice Ginsburg reversed. While a mere failure to disclose to potential donors the percentage of proceeds that will go directly to the charity does not establish fraud, "when nondisclosure is accompanied by intentionally misleading statements designed to deceive the listener, the *First Amendment* leaves room for a fraud claim." In response to a question concerning the percentage of contributions that would be used for fundraising expenses, one affiant " 'was told 90% or more goes to the vets.' Another affiant stated she was told her donation would not be used for 'labor expenses' because 'all members were volunteers.' " While the First Amendment protects charitable solicitation, this protection does not extend to fraud. An " 'intentional lie' is 'no essential part of any exposition of ideas.' " Similar to "other forms of public deception, fraudulent charitable solicitation is unprotected speech."

Schaumburg v. Citizens for a Better Environment, 444 U.S. 620 (1980), invalidated on overbreadth grounds an ordinance requiring charitable organizations to use at least 75 percent of contributions directly for the " 'charitable purpose of the organization.' " *Secretary of State of Md. v. Joseph H. Munson Co.*, 467 U.S. 947 (1984), invalidated a law with the same 25 percent limit except " 'where [it] would effectively prevent the charitable organization from raising contributions.' "[1] *Riley v. National Federation of Blind of N.C.*, Inc., 487 U.S. 781 (1988), struck down a law establishing a rebuttable presumption of unreasonableness if charities paid fundraising fees greater than 35 percent of the donations.[2] The law at issue in *Riley* also required the fundraisers to inform potential donors the percentage of donations that they had actually turned over to charity during the previous

---

[1] "The statute provided no shelter for a charity that incurred high solicitation costs because it chose to disseminate information as part of its fundraising. Nor did it shield a charity whose high solicitation costs stemmed from the unpopularity of its cause."

[2] " '[A] showing that the solicitation involved . . . advocacy or [the] dissemination of information [did] not alone establish that the total fee was reasonable.' "

year. This " 'unduly burdensome' prophylactic rule," incorrectly assumed that charities derived no benefit from the information disseminated through the solicitation process itself.[3]

In the present case, the complaint and affidavits relate not only what Telemarketers failed to disclose, but what they " 'misleadingly represented.' " Interpreting all evidence in favor of the Attorney General, the First Amendment does not protect such misrepresentations.[4] To prove fraud, Illinois requires the plaintiff to show by clear and convincing evidence that the defendant "made a false representation of a material fact knowing that the representation was false," and that the defendant "made the representation with the intent to mislead the listener, and succeeded in doing so." As a further protection "responsive to *First Amendment* concerns, an appellate court could independently review the trial court's findings."

Justice Scalia wrote a concurring opinion joined by Justice Thomas. *Riley* and *Munson* teach that the large differences in legitimate charitable fundraising expenses render impossible establishing "a maximum percentage that is reasonable" for those expenses. The judgment in this case, however, "rests upon a 'solid core' of misrepresentations that go well beyond" the issue of the percentage of funds committed to charitable purposes.

§ 12.04   Associational Rights in Other Contexts

Page 989: [Insert the following after Note (6)]

(7) *Semi-closed primaries.* In *Clingman v. Beaver*, 125 S. Ct. 2029 (2005), the Court upheld an Oklahoma semi-closed primary election system that allows voters registered to a particular political party to vote only in that party's primary election. The Libertarian Party of Oklahoma (LPO) wanted to open its primary to all registered voters. While the state opened the LPO's primary to independents, it would not allow voters who were registered with other parties to vote in the LPO's primary. Writing for the majority, Justice Thomas stated that "the Constitution grants States 'broad power to prescribe the "Time, Places and Manner of holding Elections for Senators and Representatives." ' " In this case, voters can easily switch their party registration to the LPO or change to independent status by filling out a form at the county election board. However, the individuals who brought this lawsuit have not taken this simple step, indicating that they "do not want to associate with the LPO" formally. "When a state electoral provision places no heavy burden on associational rights, 'a State's important regulatory interests will usually be enough to justify reasonable, nondiscriminatory restrictions.' " Here, Oklahoma's primary system ensures that primary elections reflect the views of party members; helps

---

[3] The statute at issue, like the one in *Riley*, requires professional fundraisers to disclose this status which could provoke donors to inquire about their amount retained.

[4] "Although fundraiser retention of 85 percent of donations is significantly higher than the 35 percent limit in *Riley*, this Court has not yet accepted any percentage-based measure as dispositive."

parties' "electioneering and party-building efforts"; and prevents individuals and other parties from manipulating the outcome of the parties' primaries by, for example, switching blocs of voters in an organized way.

Justice O'Connor, joined in part by Justice Breyer, concurred in part and concurred in the judgment. Had the issue been timely raised, the Court should consider the "*cumulative* burdens" of a state's election laws. A State's justifications for its regulations would receive greater scrutiny if that State's laws "imposed a weighty or discriminatory restriction on voters' ability to participate in" a party's primary. Justice Stevens dissented, joined by Justice Ginsburg and in part by Justice Souter. Justice Stevens argued that Oklahoma "denies a party the right to invite willing voters to participate in its primary elections." The case implicates not only the right of voters to associate, but also their right to vote. With the Democrats and Republicans increasingly gerrymandering "safe districts," primary elections are replacing general elections "as the most common method of actually determining the composition of our legislative bodies."

§ 12.05   Free Speech Problems of Government Employees

[2]—Restraints on Political Activity

Page 1019: [Insert the following after Note (9)]

(10) *Private roads.* In *Virginia v. Hicks*, 539 U.S. 113 (2003), Justice Scalia, writing for a unanimous Court, rejected an overbreadth challenge to the trespass policy imposed by Richmond Redevelopment and Housing Authority (RRHA). The city of Richmond conveyed public streets to RRHA, which were "closed to public use and travel." RRHA's trespass policy prohibited anyone other than a resident or employee from entering the streets without "*a legitimate business or social purpose* for being on the premises." Any such person found on the premises would be notified that she was barred and subject to arrest if she came back. The respondent was convicted of trespassing and challenged the policy on overbreadth grounds.

To be overbroad, a law must apply a substantial amount of protected speech "not only in an absolute sense, but also relative to the scope of the law's plainly legitimate applications." Whether or not the Virginia courts should have allowed the overbreadth challenge to be presented is a state law issue as the Case or Controversy clause of the United States Constitution only limits federal courts. The rules at issue extend to all persons seeking to enter these private streets regardless of whether they "seek to engage in expression." Overbreadth challenges rarely "succeed against a law or regulation that is not specifically addressed to speech or to conduct necessarily associated with speech (such as picketing or demonstrating.)" Alleged First Amendment violations caused by this law can be addressed through as-applied challenges. Justice Souter filed a concurring opinion, joined by Justice Breyer.

[3]—Employee's Right to Criticize Government

Page 1025: [Insert the following to Note (1)]

(a) *Speech unrelated to a matter of public concern.* In *City of San Diego, California v. Roe*, 125 S. Ct. 521 (2004), the Court, in a unanimous per curiam opinion, held that a police officer's sexually explicit videos were not protected government employee speech. In a video that he sold on eBay, the officer, wearing a police uniform, issued a ticket but revoked it after masturbating. The San Diego Police Department ordered the officer to stop distributing sexually explicit material, and after he failed to remove the description and price of the videos from his eBay profile, the Department terminated the officer.

The First Amendment protects the right of government employees to "speak on matters of public concern, typically matters concerning government policies that are of interest to the public at large." Moreover, under *United States v. Treasury Employees*, 513 U.S. 454 (1995), they may "speak or write on their own time on topics unrelated to their employment" unless the government has a "justification 'far stronger than mere speculation' in regulating it." Neither of these theories protect the police officer's speech in this case.

As the speech at issue was not a matter of public concern under *Connick v. Meyers*, casebook p. 1019, the *Pickering v. Board of Education* balancing test does not even apply to this case. Connick "directs courts to examine the 'content, form and context of a given statement, as revealed by the whole record' in assessing whether an employee's speech addresses a matter of public concern." This standard is the same as that for an invasion of privacy action at common law. Matters of public concern include subjects "of legitimate news interest." They can also include "certain private remarks, such as negative comments about the President." However, "this is not a close case," as the police officer's activities neither involved political news nor public information about the police department's functioning. Instead, the officer's speech was "designed to exploit his employer's image" and harmed its "mission and functions."

Chapter XIII

GOVERNMENT AND THE MEDIA: PRINT AND ELECTRONIC

§ 13.01   The Doctrine Against Prior Restraints

Page 1046: [Insert the following after Note (6)]

(7) *Plaintiff's death and mootness.* In *Tory v. Cochran*, 125 S. Ct. 2108 (2005), the Court in a 7-2 decision declined to address "whether a permanent injunction as a remedy in a defamation action, preventing all future speech about an admitted public figure, violates the *First Amendment*," but instead invalidated it as an overly broad prior restraint. The lower court had found that the defendant engaged in a continuos pattern of defamatory activity, including picketing, aimed at forcing plaintiff to pay him to stop. The injunction prohibited the defendant "from 'picketing,' from 'displaying signs, placards or other written or printed material,' and from 'orally uttering statements' " about plaintiff or his law firm "in any public forum."

Writing for a 7-2 majority, Justice Breyer held that despite plaintiff Johnnie Cochran's death, the case was not moot. Plaintiffs could point to nothing in California law suggesting that plaintiff's death nullified the injunction. However, because plaintiff had died, the picketing and other speech prohibited by the injunction could no longer move plaintiff to pay "tribute" to stop it. Consequently, the reason for the injunction was "much diminished" or had "disappeared" entirely. As a result, the injunction was "an overly broad prior restraint upon speech," without "plausible justification." The Court left open the possibility that another appropriate party might still request injunctive relief.

Justice Thomas dissented, joined by Justice Scalia, stating that he "would dismiss the writ of certiorari as improvidently granted."

ELDRED v. ASHCROFT, 537 U.S. 186 (2003). In *Eldred*, the Court held that Congress does not violate either the Copyright Clause of the Constitution or the First Amendment when they extend the length of protection for a copyright. Prior to the Copyright Term Extension Act (CTEA) in 1998, Congress increased copyright protection from 50 to 70 years following the death of the author. This protection applies to all material copyrighted after January 1, 1978.[1] Plaintiffs dealt with products or services that "build on

---

[1] For materials that copyrighted prior to January 1, 1978 that still retained a valid copyright at the time of the CTEA, the protection was extended to a term of 95 years from the date of publication. The CTEA granted anonymous works, pseudonymous works, and works made for hire a copyright with a term of 95 years from publication or 120 years from creation, whichever came first.

copyrighted works that have gone into the public domain." They objected to Congress' "enlarging the term for published works with existing copyrights."

In a 7–2 decision, Justice Ginsburg first rejected the argument that the " 'limited Times' " language in the Copyright Clause prohibits Congress from increasing the period of protection for existing copyrights. In 1993, the European Union (EU) passed a "directive instructing EU members to establish a copyright term of life plus 70 years." The EU directive denied this longer protection to the works of any non-member nation that did not afford the same protection. The CTEA secured for American authors the same copyright protection in Europe that their European counterparts would receive. Justice Ginsburg found the CTEA "rational." Moreover, its extension treating existing and future copyrights the same followed "unbroken congressional practice."

The Court also rejected the argument that the CTEA should receive heightened scrutiny under the First Amendment. As the Copyright Clause and the First Amendment were adopted close in time, it appears that the Framers viewed "copyright's limited monopolies" as "compatible with free speech principles. Indeed, copyright's purpose is to *promote* the creation and publication of free expression." Copyright laws accommodate First Amendment interests. They distinguish between ideas and expressions, and they allow only for the protection of the latter. As such, the ideas, theories, and facts that appear in a copyrighted work are not protected. They are "instantly available for public exploitation at the moment of publication." Even the expression of facts and ideas contained in a copyrighted work are available for " 'fair use.' " Under certain circumstances, " '[t]he fair use of a copyrighted work, including such use by reproduction in copies . . . for purposes such as criticism, comment, news reporting, teaching (including multiple copies for classroom use), scholarship, or research, is not an infringement of copyright.' "[2] The Court would not second guess Congress' judgment on copyright policy.

Justices Stevens and Breyer each filed a dissent. For Justice Stevens, the policy concerns underlying the Constitution's prohibition of ex post facto laws and laws impairing the obligation of contracts invalidate the CTEA's retroactive changes. Retroactively extending a copyright or patent changes "the public's bargain" with that author or inventor and amounts to a taking requiring just compensation. Persons intending to use an invention or copyrighted work when it enters the public domain should be protected against such "retroactive modification."

---

[2] The CTEA itself incorporated certain First Amendment safeguards. It allows "libraries, archives, and similar institutions to 'reproduce' and 'distribute, display, or perform in facsimile or digital form' copies of certain published works 'during the last 20 years of any term of copyright . . . for purposes of preservation, scholarship, or research' if the work is not already being exploited commercially and further copies are unavailable at a reasonable price." The CTEA also allows "small businesses, restaurants, and like entities" to play music from a "licensed radio, television, and similar facilities" without having to pay performance royalties.

In dissent, Justice Breyer stated that the Copyright Clause and the First Amendment each encourages the "creation and dissemination of information." When a statute exceeds the proper bounds of the Copyright Clause, however, it "may set Clause and Amendment at cross-purposes, thereby depriving the public of the speech-related benefits that the Founders, through both, have promised." He "would review plausible claims that a copyright statute seriously, and unjustifiably, restricts the dissemination of speech somewhat more carefully than reference to this Court's traditional Commerce Clause jurisprudence might suggest" — although he refused to characterize this review as " 'intermediate scrutiny.' "

Justice Breyer would find that such a copyright statute "lacks the constitutionally necessary rational support (1) if the significant benefits that it bestows are private, not public; (2) if it threatens seriously to undermine the expressive values that the Copyright Clause embodies; and (3) if it cannot find justification in any significant Clause-related objective."

Justice Breyer also said that the costs of this extension on education, learning, and research will multiply as "children become ever more dependent for the content of their knowledge upon computer-accessible databases." The costs of this extension outweigh the benefits as the extension will not act as "an economic spur encouraging authors to create new works."[3] The benefits will be a small amount of money incurring to "distant heirs, or shareholders in a successor corporation."

§ 13.07   Electronic Media

[3]—The Internet

Page 1129: [Insert the following as Notes (5)–(8)]

(5) *Community or national standard for Internet pornography?* In *Ashcroft v. The Free Speech Coalition*, a deeply divided court rejected a facial challenge to a statute imposing a community standard on Internet pornography viewed by minors. A majority of Justices appear to suggest that a national standard may eventually be necessary. For additional discussion of this case, see 2005 Supplement p. 253.

(6) *Morphed child pornography.* In *Ashcroft v. ACLU*, the Court extended First Amendment protection to computer-generated images of child pornography. The standards for pornography using actual children did not apply, as no real children were used. For further discussion of this case, see 2005 Supplement p. 202.

(7) *Library Pornography.* In *United States v. Am. Library Ass'n*, the Court upheld the Children's Internet Protection Act (CIPA) which required a library to install Internet filtering software in order to receive federal funding. Adults could request the librarian to disable the filter or unblock a specific site. This case appears at p. 250 of this supplement.

---

[3] "What potential Shakespeare, Wharton, or Hemingway would be moved by such a sum?"

(8) In *Ashcroft v. ACLU,* 542 U.S. 656 (2004), the Court in a 6-3 decision upheld an injunction enjoining enforcement of the Child Online Protection Act (COPA). Writing for the majority, Justice Kennedy focused the Court's inquiry to "whether to grant a preliminary injunction stage," noting that "[a]s the Government bears the burden of proof on the ultimate question of COPA's constitutionality, respondents must be deemed likely to prevail unless the Government has shown that respondents' proposed less restrictive alternatives are less effective than COPA. . . . That conclusion was not an abuse of discretion, because on this record there are a number of plausible, less restrictive alternatives to the statute."

The Court then turned to the less restrictive methods offered as an alternative to COPA, pointing out, "[f]ilters may well be more effective than COPA." The Court also questioned the potential of COPA to combat offensive materials, noting "that 40% of harmful-to-minors content comes from overseas," and "[i]n addition, the District Court found that verification systems may be subject to evasion and circumvention, for example by minors who have their own credit cards. . . . Finally, filters . . . can be applied. . . . to email, not just communication available via the World Wide Web." In their consideration of less restrictive alternatives, the Court referenced *United States v. American Library Association,* 2005 Supplement p. 250, where they upheld a law tying the use of filters in public libraries to the receipt of federal funds. Ultimately, the Court opined that since "the Government has failed to show" that the less restrictive alternatives proposed would be less effective, they did not meet their burden.

Several "practical reasons" also influenced the Court's decision. Principal among their concerns was that "the potential harms from reversing the injunction outweigh those of leaving it in place by mistake." The Court also noted that "the factual record does not reflect current technological reality. . . . Yet the factfindings of the District Court were entered in February 1999, over five years ago." The Court expressed hope that preserving the injunction would allow both parties to update the factual record prior to trial on the merits. The Court did not foreclose a later holding by the District Court that COPA is constitutional, holding only that the injunction should remain in place until trial on the merits. In his concurrence, joined by Justice Ginsburg, Justice Stevens emphasizes the restrictiveness of COPA, pointing out that violations carry a potential fine of "as much as $50,000 and a term of imprisonment as long as six months, for each offense"; moreover, "intentional" violators may be subject to "a fine of up to $50,000 for each day of the violation."

In dissent, Justice Scalia stated that the Court "err[ed], however, in subjecting COPA to strict scrutiny," arguing that the material targeted by COPA is not subject to protection. Justice Scalia noted that the Court previously held that businesses involved in " 'pandering' by 'deliberately emphasizing the sexually provocative aspects of [their nonobscene products] in order to catch the salaciously disposed' engage in constitutionally unprotected behavior.' " Joined in his dissent by Justices Rehnquist and

O'Connor, Justice Breyer emphasized that "the parties agreed that a Web site could store card numbers or passwords at between 15 and 20 cents per number," a nominal financial burden; "the Act most imposes a modest additional burden on adult access to legally obscene material, perhaps imposing a similar burden on access to some protected borderline obscene material as well." With regards to less restrictive alternatives, filters in particular, Justice Breyer pointed out that because filter " 'software relies on key words or phrases to block undesirable sites, it does not have the capacity to exclude a precisely defined category of images.' . . . [I]n the absence of words, the software alone cannot distinguish between the most obscene pictorial images and the Venus de Milo." Thus, "blocking lacks precision. . . [in] that it blocks a great deal of material that is valuable."

Chapter XIV

SPEECH IN PUBLIC PLACES

§ 14.01   Offensive Speech in Public Places

[1]—Defamation: General Principles

Page 1182: [Insert the following after *R.A.V. v. St. Paul*]

VIRGINIA v. BLACK, 538 U.S. 343 (2003). In *Black*, the Court invalidated a statute that defines cross burning as prima facie evidence of intent to intimidate. Writing for a 5–4 Court, Justice O'Connor held that a state may ban "cross burning carried out with the intent to intimidate;" however, Virginia has violated the First Amendment by passing a statute that allows the act of cross burning itself to be evidence of the intent to intimidate.

In 1998, defendant Black led a Ku Klux Klan rally which 25 to 30 people attended. This rally occurred on private property with the permission of the owner. When Black burned a cross at the rally, the sheriff arrested him for violating the cross burning statute at issue.

"The *First Amendment* permits 'restrictions upon the content of speech in a few limited areas, which are "of such slight social value as a step to truth that any benefit that may be derived from them is clearly outweighed by the social interest in order and morality."'" One such permissible restriction is upon "fighting words — 'those are personally abusive epithets which, when addressed to the ordinary citizen, are, as a matter of common knowledge, inherently likely to provoke violent reaction.'" The First Amendment also allows a State to restrict a "'true threat.'" This type of threat consists of statements where the speaker aims to "communicate a serious expression of an intent to commit an act of unlawful violence to a particular individual or group of individuals." For a true threat to exist, a speaker need not intend to carry out the threat. Rather a prohibition on true threats "'protects individuals from the fear of violence' and 'from the disruption that fear engenders.'" One type of true threat is constitutionally proscribable intimidation, "where a speaker directs a threat to a person or group of persons with the intent of placing the victim in fear of bodily harm or death." After reviewing the extensive history of cross burning, Justice O'Connor concluded that "the history of cross burning in this country shows that cross burning is often intimidating, intended to create a pervasive fear in victims that they are a target of violence."

In *R.A.V. v. City of St. Paul*, casebook p. 1178, this Court held that "it would be constitutional to ban only a particular type of threat." Consistent with this ruling, "Virginia's statute does not run afoul of the *First Amendment* insofar as it bans cross burning with intent to intimidate. Unlike the statute at issue in *R.A.V.*, the Virginia statute does not single out for opprobrium only that speech directed toward 'one of the specified disfavored topics.' It does not matter whether an individual burns a cross with intent to intimidate because of the victim's race, gender, or religion, or because of the victim's 'political affiliation, union membership, or homosexuality.' " Virginia may regulate only a "subset of intimidating messages in light of cross burning's long and pernicious history as a signal of impending violence. Thus, just as a State may regulate only that obscenity which is the most obscene due to its prurient content, so too may a State choose to prohibit only those forms of intimidation that are most likely to inspire fear of bodily harm."

The Supreme Court of Virginia has not yet interpreted the prima facie evidence part of the statute. This provision, "as interpreted by the jury instruction, renders the statute unconstitutional." The Virginia Supreme Court failed to "expressly disavow the jury instruction," which was the Model Jury Instruction. "The prima facie evidence provision permits a jury to convict in every cross burning case in which defendants exercise their constitutional right not to put on a defense. And even where a defendant like Black presents a defense, the prima facie evidence provision makes it more likely that the jury will find an intent to intimidate regardless of the particular facts of the case. The provision permits the Commonwealth to arrest, prosecute, and convict a person based solely on the fact of cross burning itself." So interpreted, this provision creates " 'an unacceptable risk of the suppression of ideas.' " This provision conflates situations in which an intent to intimidate exists with situations in which it does not. A burning of a cross at a political rally would " 'almost certainly be protected expression.' " For example, cross burnings that have appeared in movies such as Mississippi Burning are performed without an intent to intimidate.

"Unlike Justice Scalia, we refuse to speculate on whether *any* interpretation of the prima facie evidence provision would satisfy the *First Amendment*. Rather, all we hold is that because of the interpretation of the prima facie evidence provision given by the jury instruction, the provision makes the statute facially invalid at this point. We also recognize the theoretical possibility that the court, on remand, could interpret the provision in a manner different from that so far set forth in order to avoid the constitutional objections we have described. We leave open that possibility. We also leave open the possibility that the provision is severable."

Justice Stevens filed a concurring opinion. Dissenting, Justice Thomas noted that "[i]n our culture, cross burning has almost invariably meant lawlessness and understandably instills in its victims well-grounded fear of physical violence." "[T]his statute prohibits only conduct, not expression. And, just as one cannot burn down someone's house to make a political point and then seek refuge in the *First Amendment*, those who hate cannot terrorize and intimidate to make their point." Relying on Wigmore, Justice Thomas states that "*an inference, sometimes loosely referred to as a presumption of fact, does not compel a specific conclusion. An inference merely applies to the rational potency or probative value of an evidentiary fact to which the fact finder may attach whatever force or weight it deems best."* [1] In light of "the horrific effect cross burning has on its victims, it is also reasonable to presume intent to intimidate from the act itself." Justice Thomas found ironic that the Court had permitted restrictions on advice not wanted by persons seeking to obtain an abortion but not restrictions on cross burning because "one day an individual might wish to burn a cross" lacking "an intent to intimidate anyone."

Justice Scalia filed an opinion concurring in part, concurring in the judgment in part, and dissenting in part. Justice Thomas joined all parts of Justice Scalia's opinion discussed here. Justice Scalia said that cross burning intended not to intimidate but to convey ideological or artistic messages could be challenged on a case-by-case basis. In holding the prima facie evidence provision facially invalid, the plurality appears to rely on "some species of overbreadth doctrine." The class of persons who could impermissibly be convicted under this provision include individuals who: "(1) burn a cross in public view, (2) do not intend to intimidate, (3) are nonetheless charged and prosecuted, and (4) refuse to present a defense." This set of cases is not large enough "to render the statute *substantially* overbroad." [2] Although the plurality declares the statute "unconstitutional *on its face*," it still "holds out the possibility that the Virginia Supreme Court will offer some saving construction."

Justice Souter, joined by Justices Kennedy and Ginsburg, concurs in the judgment in part and dissents in part. Even when cross burning is intended to terrify, it "may carry a further, ideological message of white Protestant supremacy." He agrees with the majority that "the burning cross can broadcast threat and ideology together, ideology alone, or threat alone." The question in this case "is not the permissible scope of an arguably overbroad statute, but the claim of a clearly content-based statute to an exception from the general prohibition of content-based proscriptions." The prima facie case provision brings "within the statute's prohibition some expression that is doubtfully threatening though certainly distasteful." A content-based regulation "can only survive if narrowly tailored to serve a compelling state interest, a stringent test the statute cannot pass; a content-neutral statute banning intimidation would achieve the same object without singling out particular content."

[2]—Sexually Offensive Speech

Page 1195: [Insert the following to Note (3)]

(a) *Separating "adult establishments."* In *City of Los Angeles v. Alameda Books, Inc.*, 535 U.S. 425 (2002), the Court upheld a Los Angeles ordinance

---

[1] *An inference does not involve the "procedural consequence of shifting the burden of production."*

[2] Realizing that the statute is not substantially overbroad, "the plurality is driven to the truly startling assertion that a statute which is not invalid in all of its applications may nevertheless be facially invalidated even if it is not overbroad."

that prohibited "more than one adult entertainment business" occupying the same building. The ordinance defines adult establishments as "an adult arcade, bookstore, cabaret, motel, theater, or massage parlor or a place for sexual encounters." Respondents, operators of two adult establishments that rent and sell sexually oriented products "in the same commercial space" in which video booths are located, alleged that the provision was unconstitutional on its face. The case came up on summary judgment for the businesses, and the Supreme Court reversed.

Writing for a plurality of four, Justice O'Connor concluded that "it is rational for the city to infer that reducing the concentration of adult operations in a neighborhood, whether within separate establishments or in one large establishment," will advance the City's interest in reducing crime. *Renton v. Playtime Theatres, Inc.*, casebook, p. 1195, allows a municipality to rely "on any evidence that is 'reasonably believed to be relevant' for demonstrating a connection between speech and a substantial, independent government interest," in this case, reducing crime. The evidence need only "fairly support" that connection. A Los Angeles study found that concentrations of adult establishments helped to increase prostitution, robbery, assaults, and thefts. This study was sufficient to overcome the summary judgment against the city. Justice O'Connor left the question of the content neutrality of the ordinance to the lower courts.

Justice Scalia filed a concurring opinion. Justice Kennedy concurred in the judgment. He required that the purpose of the ordinance must be to split adult businesses, rather than forcing their closure in a way that would not substantially diminish the amount of speech.

Justice Souter dissented, joined by Justices Stevens, Ginsburg, and Breyer. By forcing adult businesses to divide into two or more separate units, the regulations will double overheads. Accordingly, the City's purpose may well be to drive adult establishments out of business.

§ 14.02 Speech in Traditional Public Forums: Streets, Sidewalks, Parks

Page 1203: [Insert the following to Note (2)]

(a) *Park Permits.* In *Thomas v. Chicago Park District*, 534 U.S. 316 (2002), the Court unanimously decided that a permit system to use public parks did not have to incorporate the procedural safeguards of *Freedman v. Maryland,* casebook, p. 1428. The Chicago ordinance "requires a person to obtain a permit in order to 'conduct a public assembly, parade, picnic, or other event involving more than fifty individuals,' or engage in any activity such as 'creating or emitting any Amplified Sound.' " Applications must be decided within 14 days, and can only be denied in writing based on 13 grounds, which limit administrative discretion. Applicants may appeal denials to the General Superintendent of Parks, and then to a judicial court.

Finding *Freedman* inapplicable, Justice Scalia neither required the Park District to "initiate litigation every time it denies a permit," nor specify a deadline for prompt judicial review of challenges. Unlike the censorship of films at issue in *Freedman*, the ordinance in this case is a content-neutral time, place, and manner restriction. Moreover, it contains "adequate standards to guide the official's decision and render it subject to effective judicial review." Such grounds include the filing of an incomplete or materially false application, unpaid damage to a park, a prior applicant for the same time and place, unreasonable health or safety dangers, and violation of a prior permit. The Court did not reach the question of whether the *Freedman* "requirement of prompt judicial review means a prompt judicial determination or the prompt commencement of judicial proceedings."

(b) *Home solicitation permits.* In *Watchtower Bible and Tract Society of New York, Inc. v. Village of Stratton,* 536 U.S. 150 (2002), the Court invalidated a municipal ordinance prohibiting " 'canvassers' from going on private property for the purpose of explaining or promoting any 'cause' unless they receive a permit and the residents visited have not opted for a 'no solicitation' sign." Petitioners are Jehovah's Witnesses who offer free religious literature. While they do not solicit contributions, they do accept donations. As this was a facial challenge, the Court considered "the door-to-door canvassing regulation not only as it applies to religious proselytizing, but also to anonymous political speech and the distribution of handbills."

The Village has never denied an application for a permit, nor has it ever revoked a permit. Another section of the ordinance permits residents to file a "No Solicitation Registration Form" that lists a series of 19 exceptions, including Scouting Organizations, Camp Fire Girls, Jehovah's Witnesses, and Christmas Carolers, that residents can prohibit "from canvassing unless expressly exempted."

Writing for the Court, Justice Stevens stated that several themes emerge from the Court's precedents on invalidating restrictions on "door-to-door canvassing and pamphleteering." First, freedom of speech and of the press protects the "hand distribution of religious tracts." Second, these activities are important to disseminating ideas, and must proceed *free and unhampered* by censorship. Third, the state has some interest in regulating these activities, particularly when soliciting money is involved. Fourth, door-to-door canvassing and leafleting is "essential to the poorly financed causes of little people."

The ordinance requires a permit to go on private property to explain or promote "any 'cause.' " "Had this provision been construed to apply only to commercial activities and the solicitation of funds, arguably the ordinance would have been tailored to the Village's interest in protecting the privacy of its residents and preventing fraud." However, it applies to " 'soliciting the votes of neighbors,' or ringing doorbells to enlist support for employing a more efficient garbage collector."

In addition to its sweeping effect, Justice Stevens identified three other concerns resulting from a permit requirement. First, the permit requirement undermines anonymous speech. While prohibiting anonymity may sometimes be justified — for example, to protect "the integrity of a ballot-initiative process," or to prevent fraudulent transactions, the Village ordinance goes well beyond such interests. Second, obtaining a permit may rail against a person's political or religious views. Third, the requirement curtails spontaneous speech.

The "breadth and unprecedented nature" rendered it invalid, as did its not being tailored to the Village's stated interests. The Village's interests in privacy and crime prevention were not asserted below. In any event, with respect to privacy, the ordinance allows posting "No Solicitation" signs, and residents can refuse to speak with visitors. With respect to the latter, permit requirements are unlikely to deter criminals from knocking.

Justice Breyer concurred, joined by Justices Souter and Ginsburg. Justice Scalia, joined by Justice Thomas, concurred in the judgment. Chief Justice Rehnquist dissented, indicating that he was unclear as to what test the majority applied, but that intermediate scrutiny allows a discretionless permit requirement.

§ 14.04　　The Modern Approach: Limiting Speech According to the Character of the Property

[1]—Public Property

Page 1269: [Add (1) at the beginning of existing Note and insert the following as Note (2)]

(2) In *Scheidler v. Nat'l Org. for Women, Inc.*, 537 U.S. 393 (2003), the Court held that shutting down an abortion clinic is not considered "obtaining" property as required for extortion by the Hobbs Act. The District Court had issued a nationwide injunction against § 1964(c) of the Racketeer Influenced and Corrupt Organizations Act (RICO). As the Court reversed the extortion conviction, RICO was not violated without this predicate offense. Regardless of where the outer boundaries of the crime of extortion lie, the characterization of the protestors' actions as the " 'obtaining of property' " falls beyond that line. The Field Code, used by Congress in formulating the Hobbs Act, defines extortion as a property crime that involved " 'the criminal acquisition of . . . property.' " If defendants' actions constitute extortion, the Court would replace the requirement "that property must be obtained from another" "with the notion that merely interfering with or depriving someone of property is sufficient to constitute extortion." Because all of the predicate acts that are necessary to find a RICO violation are reversed, Chief Justice Rehnquist reversed the RICO conviction.

Justice Ginsburg filed a concurring opinion which Justice Breyer joined. The Freedom of Access to Clinic Entrances Act of 1994 focuses on "criminal activity at health care facilities." The Solicitor General agreed in response to a question during oral argument about whether RICO " 'would have been applicable to the civil rights sit-ins' " that it would have been if " 'illegal force or threats were used to prevent a business from operating.' " For Justice Ginsburg, RICO has already " 'evolved into something quite different from the original conception of its enactors.' "

Justice Stevens' dissent states that extortion extended to infringing on someone's right to control her own property. The principal beneficiaries of the Court's retreat from their traditional position will be the "class of professional criminals whose conduct persuaded Congress that the public needed federal protection from extortion."

Chapter XV

SPECIAL DOCTRINES IN THE SYSTEM OF FREEDOM OF EXPRESSION

§ 15.02   Expenditures of Money in the Political Arena

Page 1345: [Insert the following after *Austin v. Michigan Chamber of Commerce*]

Contributions by advocacy corporations. In *Fed. Election Comm'n v. Beaumont*, 539 U.S. 146 (2003), Justice Souter, upheld (7-2) a 1907 federal law that prohibits nonprofit advocacy corporations from "contributing directly to candidates for federal office." The statute allows corporations to form and control PACs which can solicit contributions from corporate employees and shareholders. These PACs may in turn contribute to candidates for federal office.

Buckley v. Valeo, casebook p. 1315, afforded campaign contributions less deference than campaign expenditures. "*Within the realm of contributions generally, corporate contributions are furthest from the core of political expression, since corporations' First Amendment speech and association interests are derived largely from those of their members.*" Individual members of North Carolina Right to Life, Inc. could still make their own independent contributions. *Federal Election Comm'n v. Nat'l Right to Work Comm.*, 459 U.S. 197 (1982), approved limiting even advocacy corporations to making campaign contributions "only through its PAC and subject to a PAC's administrative burdens."

Justice Kennedy, concurring in the judgment, states that he might have joined Justice Thomas in dissent had the Court been comprehensively reviewing the different scrutiny for campaign contributions and expenditures. Justice Thomas, joined by Justice Scalia, dissents. He states that he continues to believe that strict scrutiny is the appropriate standard of review for all campaign finance laws.

Page 1346: [Insert after Note]

McCONNELL v. FEDERAL ELECTION COMMISSION

540 U.S. 93, 124 S. Ct. 619, 157 L. Ed. 2d 491 (2003)

Justice STEVENS and Justice O'CONNOR delivered the opinion of the Court with respect to BCRA Titles I and II.[1]

The Bipartisan Campaign Reform Act of 2002 (BCRA), contains a series of amendments to the Federal Election Campaign Act of 1971 (FECA), 2 U.S.C.A. § 431, et seq., the Communications Act of 1934, 48 Stat. 1088, as amended, 47 U.S.C.A. § 315, and other portions of the United States Code, 18 U.S.C.A. § 607, 36 U.S.C.A. §§ 510-511, that are challenged in these cases.[2] In this opinion we discuss Titles I and II of BCRA. The opinion of the Court delivered by The Chief Justice, discusses Titles III and IV, and the opinion of the Court delivered by Justice Breyer, discusses Title V.

I

More than a century ago the "sober-minded Elihu Root" advocated legislation that would prohibit political contributions by corporations in order to prevent " 'the great aggregations of wealth, from using their corporate funds, directly or indirectly,' " to elect legislators who would " 'vote for their protection and the advancement of their interests as against those of the public.' " *United States v. Automobile Workers,* 352 U.S. 567, 571 (1957) (quoting E. Root, Addresses on Government and Citizenship 143 (R. Bacon & J. Scott eds.1916)). In Root's opinion, such legislation would " 'strik[e] at a constantly growing evil which has done more to shake the confidence of the plain people of small means of this country in our political institutions than any other practice which has ever obtained since the foundation of our Government.' " 352 U.S. at 571. The Congress of the United States has repeatedly enacted legislation endorsing Root's judgment.

BCRA is the most recent federal enactment designed "to purge national politics of what was conceived to be the pernicious influence of 'big money' campaign contributions." *Id.* at 572. As Justice Frankfurter explained in his opinion for the Court in *Automobile Workers* . . . President Roosevelt stated that " 'directors should not be permitted to use stockholders' money' " for political purposes, and he recommended that " 'a prohibition' " on corporate political contributions " 'would be, as far as it went, an effective method of stopping the evils aimed at in corrupt practices acts.' " 352 U.S.

---

[1] [Court's footnote *] Justice SOUTER, Justice GINSBURG, and Justice BREYER join this opinion in its entirety.

[2] [Court's footnote 1] . . . [W]e refer to the parties who challenged the law in the District Court as the "plaintiffs," referring to specific plaintiffs by name where necessary. We refer to the parties who intervened in defense of the law as the "intervenor-defendants."

at 352. The resulting 1907 statute completely banned corporate contributions of "money . . . in connection with" any federal election. Congress soon amended the statute to require the public disclosure of certain contributions and expenditures and to place "maximum limits on the amounts that congressional candidates could spend in seeking nomination and election." *Automobile Workers, supra,* at 575–576.

In 1925 Congress extended the prohibition of "contributions" "to include 'anything of value,' and made acceptance of a corporate contribution as well as the giving of such a contribution a crime." *Federal Election Comm'n v. National Right to Work Comm.,* 459 U.S. 197, 209 (1982) (citing Federal Corrupt Practices Act). . . . We upheld the amended statute against a constitutional challenge, observing that "[t]he power of Congress to protect the election of President and Vice President from corruption being clear, the choice of means to that end presents a question primarily addressed to the judgment of Congress." *Burroughs v. United States,* 290 U.S. 534, 547 (1934).

. . . During and shortly after World War II, Congress. . . . first restricted union contributions in the Hatch Act, 18 U.S.C. § 610,[3] and it later prohibited "union contributions in connection with federal elections . . . altogether." *National Right to Work, supra,* at 209 (citing War Labor Disputes Act). . . . Congress' "careful legislative adjustment of the federal election laws, in a 'cautious advance, step by step,' to account for the particular legal and economic attributes of corporations and labor organizations warrants considerable deference." *National Right to Work,* 459 U.S. at 209.

In early 1972 the FECA also prohibited contributions made in the name of another person, and by Government contractors. The law ratified the earlier prohibition on the use of corporate and union general treasury funds for political contributions and expenditures, but it expressly permitted corporations and unions to establish and administer separate segregated funds (commonly known as political action committees, or PACs) for election-related contributions and expenditures.[4]

As the 1972 presidential elections made clear, however, FECA's passage did not deter unseemly fundraising and campaign practices. Evidence of those practices persuaded Congress to enact the Federal Election Campaign Act Amendments of 1974. . . . [T]he Court of Appeals for the District of Columbia Circuit described them as "by far the most comprehensive . . . reform legislation [ever] passed by Congress concerning the election of the President, Vice-President and members of Congress." *Buckley v. Valeo,* 519 F.2d 821, 831 (C.A.D.C.1975) (en banc) (*per curiam*).

The 1974 amendments closed the loophole that had allowed candidates to use an unlimited number of political committees for fundraising purposes

---

[3] [Court's footnote 2] The Hatch Act also limited both the amount political committees could expend and the amount they could receive in contributions. . . .

[4] [Court's footnote 3] As a general rule, FECA permits corporations and unions to solicit contributions to their PACs from their shareholders or members, but not from outsiders.

and thereby to circumvent the limits on individual committees' receipts and disbursements. They also limited individual political contributions to any single candidate to $1,000 per election, with an overall annual limitation of $25,000 by any contributor; imposed ceilings on spending by candidates and political parties for national conventions; required reporting and public disclosure of contributions and expenditures exceeding certain limits; and established the Federal Election Commission (FEC) to administer and enforce the legislation.

The Court of Appeals upheld the 1974 amendments almost in their entirety. . . . The court's opinion relied heavily on findings that large contributions facilitated access to public officials[5] and described methods of evading the contribution limits that had enabled contributors of massive sums to avoid disclosure.[6]

The Court of Appeals upheld the provisions establishing contribution and expenditure limitations on the theory that they should be viewed as regulations of conduct rather than speech. *Id.* at 840-841 (citing *United States v. O'Brien,* 391 U.S. 367 (1968)). This Court, however, concluded that each set of limitations raised serious — though different — concerns under the First Amendment. *Buckley v. Valeo,* 424 U.S. 1 (1976) (*per curiam*). We treated the limitations on candidate and individual expenditures as direct restraints on speech, but we observed that the contribution limitations, in contrast, imposed only "a marginal restriction upon the contributor's ability to engage in free communication." *Id.* at 20-21. . . . In the end, the Act's primary purpose — "to limit the actuality and appearance of corruption resulting from large individual financial contributions" — provided "a constitutionally sufficient justification for the $1,000 contribution limitation." *Id.* at 26.

We prefaced our analysis of the $1,000 limitation on expenditures by observing that it broadly encompassed every expenditure " 'relative to a clearly identified candidate.' " *Id.* at 39. To avoid vagueness concerns we construed that phrase to apply only to "communications that in express terms advocate the election or defeat of a clearly identified candidate for federal office." 424 U.S. at 42–44. We concluded, however, that as so narrowed, the provision would not provide effective protection against the dangers of *quid pro quo* arrangements, because persons and groups could eschew expenditures that expressly advocated the election or defeat of a clearly identified candidate while remaining "free to spend as much as they want to promote the candidate and his views." *Id.* at 45. . . .

We upheld all of the disclosure and reporting requirements in the Act that were challenged on appeal to this Court after finding that they vindicated three important interests: providing the electorate with relevant

---

[5] [Court's footnote 5] ". . .The record before Congress was replete with specific examples of improper attempts to obtain governmental favor in return for large campaign contributions. *See* Findings I, ¶¶ 159-64." . . . [*Buckley v. Valeo,* 519 F.2d 821], 839, n.37 [(C.A.D.C. 1075)].

[6] [Court's footnote 6] . . .The milk producers contributed large sums to the Nixon campaign "in order to gain a meeting with White House officials on price supports." *Id.* at 839, n.36.

information about the candidates and their supporters; deterring actual corruption and discouraging the use of money for improper purposes; and facilitating enforcement of the prohibitions in the Act. In order to avoid an overbreadth problem, however . . . we construed the reporting requirement for persons making expenditures of more than $100 in a year "to reach only funds used for communications that expressly advocate the election or defeat of a clearly identified candidate." *Id.* at 80.

Our opinion in *Buckley* addressed issues that primarily related to contributions and expenditures by individuals, since none of the parties challenged the prohibition on contributions by corporations and labor unions. . . .

Three important developments in the years after our decision in Buckley persuaded Congress that further legislation was necessary to regulate the role that corporations, unions, and wealthy contributors play in the electoral process. . . .

Soft Money

. . . [P]rior to the enactment of BCRA, federal law permitted corporations and unions, as well as individuals who had already made the maximum permissible contributions to federal candidates, to contribute "nonfederal money" — also known as "soft money" — to political parties for activities intended to influence state or local elections.

Shortly after *Buckley* was decided, questions arose concerning the treatment of contributions intended to influence both federal and state elections. Although a literal reading of FECA's definition of "contribution" would have required such activities to be funded with hard money, the FEC ruled that political parties could fund mixed-purpose activities — including get-out-the-vote drives and generic party advertising — in part with soft money. In 1995 the FEC concluded that the parties could also use soft money to defray the costs of "legislative advocacy media advertisements," even if the ads mentioned the name of a federal candidate, so long as they did not expressly advocate the candidate's election or defeat. FEC Advisory Op. 1995–25.

As the permissible uses of soft money expanded, the amount of soft money raised and spent by the national political parties increased exponentially. Of the two major parties' total spending, soft money accounted for 5% ($21.6 million) in 1984, 11% ($45 million) in 1988, 16% ($80 million) in 1992, 30% ($272 million) in 1996, and 42% ($498 million) in 2000. The national parties transferred large amounts of their soft money to the state parties, which were allowed to use a larger percentage of soft money to finance mixed-purpose activities under FEC rules. In the year 2000, for example, the national parties diverted $280 million — more than half of their soft money — to state parties.

Many contributions of soft money were dramatically larger than the contributions of hard money permitted by FECA. . . . In the most recent election cycle the political parties raised almost $300 million — 60% of their total soft-money fundraising — from just 800 donors, each of which contributed a minimum of $120,000. . . .

Not only were such soft-money contributions often designed to gain access to federal candidates, but they were in many cases solicited by the candidates themselves. . . .[7]

Issue Advertising

In *Buckley* we construed FECA's disclosure and reporting requirements, as well as its expenditure limitations, "to reach only funds used for communications that expressly advocate the election or defeat of a clearly identified candidate." 424 U.S. at 80 (footnote omitted). As a result of that strict reading of the statute, the use or omission of "magic words" such as "Elect John Smith" or "Vote Against Jane Doe" marked a bright statutory line separating "express advocacy" from "issue advocacy." *See id.* at 44, n.52. . . . So-called issue ads, on the other hand, not only could be financed with soft money, but could be aired without disclosing the identity of, or any other information about, their sponsors. . . .

. . . Corporations and unions spent hundreds of millions of dollars of their general funds to pay for these ads,[8] and those expenditures, like soft-money donations to the political parties, were unregulated under FECA. . . .

Senate Committee Investigation

In 1998 the Senate Committee on Governmental Affairs issued a six volume report summarizing the results of an extensive investigation into the campaign practices in the 1996 federal elections. . . .

The report . . . concluded that both parties promised and provided special access to candidates and senior Government officials in exchange for large soft-money contributions. . . .

In 1996 both parties began to use large amounts of soft money to pay for issue advertising designed to influence federal elections. The Committee found such ads highly problematic for two reasons. Since they accomplished the same purposes as express advocacy (which could lawfully be funded only

---

[7] [Court's footnote 15] . . . One former party official explained to the District Court: " 'Once you've helped a federal candidate by contributing hard money to his or her campaign, you are sometimes asked to do more for the candidate by making donations of hard and/or soft money to the national party committees, the relevant state party (assuming it can accept corporate contributions), or an outside group that is planning on doing an independent expenditure or issue advertisement to help the candidate's campaign.' " 251 F. Supp. 2d at 479 (Kollar-Kotelly, J.).

[8] [Court's footnote 20] . . . In the 1996 election cycle, $135 to $150 million was spent on multiple broadcasts of about 100 ads. In the next cycle (1997-1998), 77 organizations aired 423 ads at a total cost between $270 and $340 million. By the 2000 election, 130 groups spent over an estimated $500 million on more than 1,100 different ads. Two out of every three dollars spent on issue ads in the 2000 cycle were attributable to the two major parties and six major interest groups.

with hard money), the ads enabled unions, corporations, and wealthy contributors to circumvent protections that FECA was intended to provide. Moreover, though ostensibly independent of the candidates, the ads were often actually coordinated with, and controlled by, the campaigns. The ads thus provided a means for evading FECA's candidate contribution limits.

The report also emphasized the role of state and local parties. While the FEC's allocation regime permitted national parties to use soft money to pay for up to 40% of the costs of both generic voter activities and issue advertising, they allowed state and local parties to use larger percentages of soft money for those purposes. For that reason, national parties often made substantial transfers of soft money to "state and local political parties for 'generic voter activities' that in fact ultimately benefit[ed] federal candidates because the funds for all practical purposes remain[ed] under the control of the national committees." . . .

II

In BCRA, Congress enacted many of the committee's proposed reforms. BCRA's central provisions are designed to address Congress' concerns about the increasing use of soft money and issue advertising to influence federal elections. Title I regulates the use of soft money by political parties, office-holders, and candidates. Title II primarily prohibits corporations and labor unions from using general treasury funds for communications that are intended to, or have the effect of, influencing the outcome of federal elections.

Section 403 of BCRA provides special rules for actions challenging the constitutionality of any of the Act's provisions. . . . As required by § 403, those actions were filed in the District Court for the District of Columbia and heard by a three-judge court. . . . The three judges reached unanimity on certain issues but differed on many. Their judgment, entered on May 1, 2003, held some parts of BCRA unconstitutional and upheld others. 251 F. Supp. 2d 948.

As authorized by § 403, all of the losing parties filed direct appeals to this Court within 10 days. . . .

III

Title I is Congress' effort to plug the soft-money loophole. The cornerstone of Title I is new FECA § 323(a), which prohibits national party committees and their agents from soliciting, receiving, directing, or spending any soft money. In short, § 323(a) takes national parties out of the soft-money business.

The remaining provisions of new FECA § 323 largely reinforce the restrictions in § 323(a). New FECA § 323(b) prevents the wholesale shift of soft-money influence from national to state party committees by prohibiting state and local party committees from using such funds for activities that affect federal elections. . . . New FECA § 323(d) reinforces these soft-money restrictions by prohibiting political parties from soliciting and donating funds to tax-exempt organizations that engage in electioneering activities. New FECA § 323(e) restricts federal candidates and officeholders from receiving, spending, or soliciting soft money in connection with federal elections and limits their ability to do so in connection with state and local elections. Finally, new FECA § 323(f) prevents circumvention of the restrictions on national, state, and local party committees by prohibiting state and local candidates from raising and spending soft money to fund advertisements and other public communications that promote or attack federal candidates.

Plaintiffs mount a facial First Amendment challenge to new FECA § 323, as well as challenges based on the Elections Clause, U.S. Const., Art. I, § 4, principles of federalism, and the equal protection component of the Due Process Clause. We address these challenges in turn.

A

In *Buckley* and subsequent cases, we have subjected restrictions on campaign expenditures to closer scrutiny than limits on campaign contributions. In these cases we have recognized that contribution limits, unlike limits on expenditures, "entai[l] only a marginal restriction upon the contributor's ability to engage in free communication." *Buckley*, 424 U.S. at 20; In *Buckley* we said that:

> A contribution serves as a general expression of support for the candidate and his views, but does not communicate the underlying basis for the support. The quantity of communication by the contributor does not increase perceptibly with the size of the contribution, since the expression rests solely on the undifferentiated, symbolic act of contributing. . . . 424 U.S. at 21.

Because the communicative value of large contributions inheres mainly in their ability to facilitate the speech of their recipients, we have said that contribution limits impose serious burdens on free speech only if they are so low as to "preven[t] candidates and political committees from amassing the resources necessary for effective advocacy." *Ibid.*

We have recognized that contribution limits may bear "more heavily on the associational right than on freedom to speak," *Shrink Missouri, supra,* at 388, since contributions serve "to affiliate a person with a candidate" and "enabl[e] like-minded persons to pool their resources," *Buckley*, 424 U.S. at 22. Unlike expenditure limits, however, which "preclud[e] most associations from effectively amplifying the voice of their adherents," contribution limits both "leave the contributor free to become a member of any political association and to assist personally in the association's efforts on behalf of candidates," and allow associations "to aggregate large sums of money to promote effective advocacy." *Ibid.* The "overall effect" of dollar limits on contributions is "merely to require candidates and political committees to raise funds from a greater number of persons." *Id.* at 21–22. Thus, a contribution limit involving even " 'significant interference' " with associational rights is nevertheless valid if it satisfies the "lesser demand" of being " 'closely drawn' " to match a " 'sufficiently important interest.' " *Beaumont,* 539 U.S. 146, at 162 (quoting *Shrink Missouri, supra,* at 387–388).

Our treatment of contribution restrictions. . . . also reflects the importance of the interests that underlie contribution limits — interests in preventing "both the actual corruption threatened by large financial contributions and the eroding of public confidence in the electoral process through the appearance of corruption." *National Right to Work,* 459 U.S. at 208. . . . Because the electoral process is the very "means through which a free society democratically translates political speech into concrete governmental action," *Shrink Missouri,* 528 U.S. at 401 (Breyer, J., concurring), contribution limits, like other measures aimed at protecting the integrity of the process, tangibly benefit public participation in political debate. . . . The less rigorous standard of review we have applied to contribution limits (*Buckley*'s "closely drawn" scrutiny) shows proper deference to Congress' ability to weigh competing constitutional interests in an area in which it enjoys particular expertise. It also provides Congress with sufficient room to anticipate and respond to concerns about circumvention of regulations designed to protect the integrity of the political process.

. . . Complex as its provisions may be, § 323, in the main, does little more than regulate the ability of wealthy individuals, corporations, and unions to contribute large sums of money to influence federal elections, federal candidates, and federal officeholders.

Plaintiffs contend that we must apply strict scrutiny to § 323 because many of its provisions restrict not only contributions but also the spending and solicitation of funds raised outside of FECA's contribution limits. But for purposes of determining the level of scrutiny, it is irrelevant that Congress chose in § 323 to regulate contributions on the demand rather than the supply side. *See, e.g.,* National Right to Work, *supra,* at 206-21 (upholding a provision restricting PACs' ability to solicit funds). The relevant inquiry is whether the mechanism adopted to implement the contribution limit, or to prevent circumvention of that limit, burdens speech in a way that a direct restriction on the contribution itself would not. That is not the case here.

. . . The fact that party committees and federal candidates and officeholders must now ask only for limited dollar amounts or request that a corporation or union contribute money through its PAC in no way alters or impairs the political message "intertwined" with the solicitation. . . . And rather than chill such solicitations . . . the restriction here tends to increase the dissemination of information by forcing parties, candidates, and officeholders to solicit from a wider array of potential donors. As with direct limits on contributions, therefore, § 323's spending and solicitation restrictions have only a marginal impact on political speech.

Finally, plaintiffs contend that the type of associational burdens that § 323 imposes are fundamentally different from the burdens that accompanied Buckley's contribution limits, and merit the type of strict scrutiny we have applied to attempts to regulate the internal processes of political parties. *E.g., California Democratic Party v. Jones,* 530 U.S. 567, 573-574 (2000). In making this argument, plaintiffs greatly exaggerate the effect of § 323, contending that it precludes any collaboration among national, state, and local committees of the same party in fundraising and electioneering activities. We do not read the provisions in that way. Section 323 merely subjects a greater percentage of contributions to parties and candidates to FECA's source and amount limitations. . . .[9]

New FECA § 323(a)'s Restrictions on National Party Committees

The core of Title I is new FECA § 323(a). . . .

The main goal of § 323(a) is modest. In large part, it simply effects a return to the scheme that was approved in *Buckley* and that was subverted by the creation of the FEC's allocation regime, which permitted the political parties to fund federal electioneering efforts with a combination of hard and soft money. . . .

1. Governmental Interests Underlying New FECA § 323(a)

. . . Our cases have made clear that the prevention of corruption or its appearance constitutes a sufficiently important interest to justify political contribution limits. . . . Thus, "[i]n speaking of 'improper influence' and 'opportunities for abuse' in addition to '*quid pro quo* arrangements,' we [have] recognized a concern not confined to bribery of public officials, but extending to the broader threat from politicians too compliant with the wishes of large contributors." *Shrink Missouri,* 528 U.S. at 389. . . .

Of "almost equal" importance has been the Government's interest in combating the appearance or perception of corruption engendered by large campaign contributions. *Buckley, supra,* at 27. Take away Congress' authority to regulate the appearance of undue influence and "the cynical assumption that large donors call the tune could jeopardize the willingness of voters to take part in democratic governance." *Shrink Missouri,* 528 U.S. at 390. . . .

"The quantum of empirical evidence needed to satisfy heightened judicial scrutiny of legislative judgments will vary up or down with the novelty or the plausibility of the justification raised." *Shrink Missouri, supra,* at 391. The idea that large contributions to a national party can corrupt or, at the very least, create the appearance of corruption of federal candidates and officeholders is neither novel nor implausible. . . .

. . . Parties kept tallies of the amounts of soft money raised by each officeholder, and "the amount of money a Member of Congress raise[d] for

---

[9] [Court's footnote 43] Justice Kennedy is no doubt correct that the associational burdens imposed by a particular piece of campaign-finance regulation may at times be so severe as to warrant strict scrutiny. Ibid. In light of our interpretation of § 323(a), however, § 323 does not present such a case. . . .

the national political committees often affect[ed] the amount the committees g[a]ve to assist the Member's campaign." 251 F. Supp. 2d at 474–475
(Kollar-Kotelly, J.). Donors often asked that their contributions be credited
to particular candidates, and the parties obliged, irrespective of whether
the funds were hard or soft. *Id.* at 477–478 (Kollar-Kotelly, J.); *id.* at 824,
847 (Leon, J.). National party committees often teamed with individual
candidates' campaign committees to create joint fundraising committees. . . .[10]

Plaintiffs argue that without concrete evidence of an instance in which
a federal officeholder has actually switched a vote (or, presumably, evidence
of a specific instance where the public believes a vote was switched),
Congress has not shown that there exists real or apparent corruption. But
the record is to the contrary. The evidence connects soft money to manipula-
tions of the legislative calendar, leading to Congress' failure to enact, among
other things, generic drug legislation, tort reform, and tobacco
legislation. . . .

More importantly, plaintiffs conceive of corruption too narrowly. . . . Many
of the "deeply disturbing examples" of corruption cited by this Court in
Buckley, 424 U.S. at 27, to justify FECA's contribution limits were not
episodes of vote buying, but evidence that various corporate interests had
given substantial donations to gain access to high-level government
officials. . . .

The record in the present case is replete with similar examples of national
party committees peddling access to federal candidates and officeholders
in exchange for large soft-money donations. . . .

. . . Justice Kennedy would limit Congress' regulatory interest only to
the prevention of the actual or apparent *quid pro quo* corruption "inherent
in" contributions made directly to, contributions made at the express behest
of, and expenditures made in coordination with, a federal officeholder or
candidate. . . .

Justice Kennedy's interpretation of the First Amendment would render
Congress powerless to address more subtle but equally dispiriting forms
of corruption. Just as troubling to a functioning democracy as classic quid
pro quo corruption is the danger that officeholders will decide issues not
on the merits or the desires of their constituencies, but according to the
wishes of those who have made large financial contributions valued by the
officeholder. Even if it occurs only occasionally, the potential for such undue
influence is manifest. . . .

---

[10] [Court's footnote 46] . . . Particularly telling is the fact that, in 1996 and 2000, more
than half of the top 50 soft-money donors gave substantial sums to both major national parties,
leaving room for no other conclusion but that these donors were seeking influence, or avoiding
retaliation, rather than promoting any particular ideology. . . .

2. New FECA § 323(a)'s Restriction on Spending and Receiving Soft Money

Plaintiffs and the Chief Justice contend that § 323(a) is impermissibly overbroad because it subjects all funds raised and spent by national parties to FECA's hard-money source and amount limits, including, for example, funds spent on purely state and local elections in which no federal office is at stake. . . .

. . . The national committees of the two major parties are both run by, and largely composed of, federal officeholders and candidates. . . .

Given this close connection and alignment of interests, large soft-money contributions to national parties are likely to create actual or apparent indebtedness on the part of federal officeholders, regardless of how those funds are ultimately used.

This close affiliation has also placed national parties in a position to sell access to federal officeholders in exchange for soft-money contributions that the party can then use for its own purposes. Access to federal officeholders is the most valuable favor the national party committees are able to give in exchange for large donations. The fact that officeholders comply by donating their valuable time indicates either that officeholders place substantial value on the soft-money contribution themselves, without regard to their end use, or that national committees are able to exert considerable control over federal officeholders. . . . The Government's strong interests in preventing corruption, and in particular the appearance of corruption, are thus sufficient to justify subjecting all donations to national parties to the source, amount, and disclosure limitations of FECA.

3. New FECA § 323(a)'s Restriction on Soliciting or Directing Soft Money

Plaintiffs also contend that § 323(a)'s prohibition on national parties' soliciting or directing soft-money contributions is substantially overbroad. The reach of the solicitation prohibition, however, is limited. It bars only solicitations of soft money by national party committees and by party officers in their official capacities. The committees remain free to solicit hard money on their own behalf, as well as to solicit hard money on behalf of state committees and state and local candidates.[11] They also can contribute hard money to state committees and to candidates. In accordance with FEC regulations, furthermore, officers of national parties are free to solicit soft money in their individual capacities, or, if they are also officials of state parties, in that capacity. . . .

---

[11] [Court's footnote 52] Plaintiffs claim that the option of soliciting hard money for state and local candidates is an illusory one, since several States prohibit state and local candidates from establishing multiple campaign accounts, which would preclude them from establishing separate accounts for federal funds. . . . But the challenge we are considering is a facial one, and on its face § 323(a) permits solicitations. The fact that a handful of States might interfere with the mechanism Congress has chosen for such solicitations is an argument that may be addressed in an as-applied challenge.

4. New FECA § 323(a)'s Application to Minor Parties

The McConnell and political party plaintiffs contend that § 323(a) is substantially overbroad and must be stricken on its face because it impermissibly infringes the speech and associational rights of minor parties such as the Libertarian National Committee, which, owing to their slim prospects for electoral success and the fact that they receive few large soft-money contributions from corporate sources, pose no threat of corruption comparable to that posed by the RNC and DNC. In *Buckley,* we rejected a similar argument concerning limits on contributions to minor-party candidates. . . . We have thus recognized that the relevance of the interest in avoiding actual or apparent corruption is not a function of the number of legislators a given party manages to elect. . . . It is therefore reasonable to require that all parties and all candidates follow the same set of rules designed to protect the integrity of the electoral process.

We add that nothing in § 323(a) prevents individuals from pooling resources to start a new national party. Only when an organization has gained official status, which carries with it significant benefits for its members, will the proscriptions of § 323(a) apply. Even then, a nascent or struggling minor party can bring an as-applied challenge if § 323(a) prevents it from "amassing the resources necessary for effective advocacy." *Buckley, supra,* at 21.

5. New FECA § 323(a)'s Associational Burdens

Finally, plaintiffs assert that § 323(a) is unconstitutional because it impermissibly interferes with the ability of national committees to associate with state and local committees. By way of example, plaintiffs point to the Republican Victory Plans, whereby the RNC acts in concert with the state and local committees of a given State to plan and implement joint, full-ticket fundraising and electioneering programs. . . .

. . .Nothing on the face of § 323(a) prohibits national party officers, whether acting in their official or individual capacities, from sitting down with state and local party committees or candidates to plan and advise how to raise and spend soft money. As long as the national party officer does not personally spend, receive, direct, or solicit soft money, § 323(a) permits a wide range of joint planning and electioneering activity. Intervenor-defendants, the principal drafters and proponents of the legislation, concede as much. . . .

. . . Moreover, § 323(a) leaves national party committee officers entirely free to participate, in their official capacities, with state and local parties and candidates in soliciting and spending hard money; party officials may also solicit soft money in their unofficial capacities. . . .

Accordingly, we reject the plaintiffs' First Amendment challenge to new FECA § 323(a).

New FECA § 323(b)'s Restrictions on State and Local Party Committees

In constructing a coherent scheme of campaign finance regulation, Congress recognized that, given the close ties between federal candidates and state party committees, BCRA's restrictions on national committee activity would rapidly become ineffective if state and local committees remained available as a conduit for soft-money donations. Section 323(b) is designed to foreclose wholesale evasion of § 323(a)'s anticorruption measures by sharply curbing state committees' ability to use large soft-money contributions to influence federal elections. . . .

Section 323(b)(2), the so-called Levin Amendment. . . allows state and local party committees to pay for certain types of federal election activity with an allocated ratio of hard money and "Levin funds" — that is, funds raised within an annual limit of $10,000 per person. . . .

. . . [S]tate and local parties can use Levin money to fund only activities that fall within categories (1) and (2) of the statute's definition of federal election activity — namely, voter registration activity, voter identification drives, [Get Out the Vote] drives, and generic campaign activities [promoting a party rather than a particular candidate]. . . .

1. Governmental Interests Underlying New FECA § 323(b)

. . .We "must accord substantial deference to the predictive judgments of Congress," *Turner Broadcasting System, Inc. v. FCC,* 512 U.S. 622, 665 (1994), particularly when, as here, those predictions are so firmly rooted in relevant history and common sense. Preventing corrupting activity from shifting wholesale to state committees and thereby eviscerating FECA clearly qualifies as an important governmental interest.

2. New FECA § 323(b)'s Tailoring

Plaintiffs argue that even if some legitimate interest might be served by § 323(b) . . . the provision is substantially overbroad because it federalizes activities that pose no conceivable risk of corrupting or appearing to corrupt federal officeholders. . .

a. *§ 323(b)'s Application to Federal Election Activity* . . .

. . . § 323(b) is narrowly focused on regulating contributions that pose the greatest risk of . . . corruption: those contributions to state and local parties that can be used to benefit federal candidates directly. . . . We conclude that § 323(b) is a closely-drawn means of countering both corruption and the appearance of corruption. . . .[12]

---

[12] [Court's footnote 64] We likewise reject the argument that § 301(20)(A)(iii) is unconstitutionally vague. The words "promote," "oppose," "attack," and "support" clearly set forth the confines within which potential party speakers must act in order to avoid triggering the provision. These words "provide explicit standards for those who apply them" and "give the person of ordinary intelligence a reasonable opportunity to know what is prohibited." *Grayned v. City of Rockford,* 408 U.S. 104, 108–109 (1972). . . .

b. *Associational Burdens Imposed by the Levin Amendment*

Plaintiffs also contend that § 323(b) is unconstitutional because the Levin Amendment unjustifiably burdens association among party committees by forbidding transfers of Levin funds among state parties, transfers of hard money to fund the allocable federal portion of Levin expenditures, and joint fundraising of Levin funds by state parties. . . .

. . . Without the ban on transfers of Levin funds among state committees, donors could readily circumvent the $10,000 limit on contributions to a committee's Levin account by making multiple $10,000 donations to various committees that could then transfer the donations to the committee of choice. . . . Given the delicate and interconnected regulatory scheme at issue here, any associational burdens imposed by the Levin Amendment restrictions are far outweighed by the need to prevent circumvention of the entire scheme.

c. *New FECA § 323(b)'s Impact on Parties' Ability to Engage in Effective Advocacy*

Finally, plaintiffs contend that § 323(b) is unconstitutional because its restrictions on soft-money contributions to state and local party committees will prevent them from engaging in effective advocacy. . . . If the history of campaign finance regulation discussed above proves anything, it is that political parties are extraordinarily flexible in adapting to new restrictions on their fundraising abilities. . . . The question is not whether § 323(b) reduces the amount of funds available over previous election cycles, but whether it is "so radical in effect as to . . . drive the sound of [the recipient's] voice below the level of notice." *Shrink Missouri,* 528 U.S. at 397. If indeed state or local parties can make such a showing, as-applied challenges remain available.

We accordingly conclude that § 323(b), on its face, is closely drawn to match the important governmental interests of preventing corruption and the appearance of corruption.

New FECA § 323(d)'s Restrictions on Parties' Solicitations for, and Donations to, Tax-Exempt Organizations

Section 323(d) prohibits national, state, and local party committees, and their agents or subsidiaries, from "solicit[ing] any funds for, or mak[ing] or direct[ing] any donations" to, any organization established under § 501(c) of the Internal Revenue Code[13] that makes expenditures in connection with an election for federal office, and any political organizations established under § 527 "other than a political committee, a State, district, or local committee of a political party, or the authorized campaign committee of a candidate for State or local office." 2 U.S.C.A. § 441i(d). . . .

---

[13] [Court's footnote 66] Section 501(c) organizations are groups generally exempted from taxation under the Internal Revenue Code. 26 U.S.C. § 501(a). These include § 501(c)(3) charitable and educational organizations, as well as § 501(c)(4) social welfare groups.

1. New FECA § 323(d)'s Regulation of Solicitations

The Government defends § 323(d)'s ban on solicitations to tax-exempt organizations engaged in political activity as preventing circumvention of Title I's limits on contributions of soft money to national, state, and local party committees. That justification is entirely reasonable. . . . Absent the solicitation provision, national, state, and local party committees would have significant incentives to mobilize their formidable fundraising apparatuses, including the peddling of access to federal officeholders, into the service of like-minded tax-exempt organizations that conduct activities benefiting their candidates. . . .

Section 323(d)'s solicitation restriction is closely drawn to prevent political parties from using tax-exempt organizations as soft-money surrogates. . . .

2. New FECA § 323(d)'s Regulation of Donations

Section 323(d) also prohibits national, state, and local party committees from making or directing "any donatio[n]" to qualifying § 501(c) or § 527 organizations. 2 U.S.C.A. § 441i(d) (Supp. 2003). The Government again defends the restriction as an anticircumvention measure. We agree insofar as it prohibits the donation of soft money. . . . We will not disturb Congress' reasonable decision to close that loophole, particularly given a record demonstrating an already robust practice of parties' making such donations.

The prohibition does raise overbreadth concerns if read to restrict donations from a party's federal account — i.e., funds that have already been raised in compliance with FECA's source, amount, and disclosure limitations. Parties have many valid reasons for giving to tax-exempt organizations, not the least of which is to associate themselves with certain causes and, in so doing, to demonstrate the values espoused by the party. . . .

New FECA § 323(e)'s Restrictions on Federal Candidates and Officeholders

New FECA § 323(e) . . . prohibits federal candidates and officeholders from "solicit[ing], receiv[ing], direct[ing], transfer[ing], or spend[ing]" any soft money in connection with federal elections. § 441i(e)(1)(A). It also limits the ability of federal candidates and officeholders to solicit, receive, direct, transfer, or spend soft money in connection with state and local elections. . . .

No party seriously questions the constitutionality of § 323(e)'s general ban on donations of soft money made directly to federal candidates and officeholders, their agents, or entities established or controlled by them. Even on the narrowest reading of *Buckley,* a regulation restricting donations to a federal candidate, regardless of the ends to which those funds are ultimately put, qualifies as a contribution limit subject to less rigorous scrutiny. . . .

. . . Rather than place an outright ban on solicitations to tax-exempt organizations, § 323(e)(4) permits limited solicitations of soft money. . . . Similarly, §§ 323(e)(1)(B) and 323(e)(3) preserve the traditional fundraising role of federal officeholders by providing limited opportunities for federal candidates and officeholders to associate with their state and local colleagues through joint fundraising activities. . . .

New FECA § 323(f)'s Restrictions on State Candidates and Officeholders

. . . Section 323(f) generally prohibits candidates for state or local office, or state or local officeholders, from spending soft money to fund "public communications" as defined in § 301(20)(A)(iii) — i.e., a communication that "refers to a clearly identified candidate for Federal office . . . and that promotes or supports a candidate for that office, or attacks or opposes a candidate for that office." 2 U.S.C.A. § 441i(f)(1); § 431(20)(A)(iii). . . .

Section 323(f) places no cap on the amount of money that state or local candidates can spend on any activity. Rather, like §§ 323(a) and 323(b), it limits only the source and amount of contributions that state and local candidates can draw on to fund expenditures that directly impact federal elections. And, by regulating only contributions used to fund "public communications," § 323(f) focuses narrowly on those soft-money donations with the greatest potential to corrupt or give rise to the appearance of corruption of federal candidates and officeholders. . . .

B

[The Court rejected federalism challenges against the Act, noting that it only regulates private individuals whom Congress could regulate under its Election Clause power.]

C

Finally, plaintiffs argue that Title I violates the equal protection component of the Due Process Clause of the Fifth Amendment because it discriminates against political parties in favor of special interest groups such as the National Rifle Association (NRA), American Civil Liberties Union (ACLU), and Sierra Club. . . .

. . . Congress is fully entitled to consider the real-world differences between political parties and interest groups when crafting a system of campaign finance regulation. Interest groups do not select slates of candidates for elections. Interest groups do not determine who will serve on legislative committees, elect congressional leadership, or organize legislative caucuses. Political parties have influence and power in the legislature that vastly exceeds that of any interest group. . . .

IV. . .

BCRA § 201's Definition of "Electioneering Communication"

The first section of Title II, § 201 . . . coins a new term, "electioneering communication," to replace the narrowing construction of FECA's disclosure provisions adopted by this Court in "*Buckley*. As discussed further below, that construction limited the coverage of FECA's disclosure requirement to communications expressly advocating the election or defeat of particular candidates. By contrast, the term "electioneering communication" is not so limited, but is defined to encompass any "broadcast, cable, or satellite communication" that "(I) refers to a clearly identified candidate for Federal office. . . ."

. . . BCRA's use of this new term is not, however, limited to the disclosure context: A later section of the Act (BCRA § 203 . . .) restricts corporations' and labor unions' funding of electioneering communications. Plaintiffs challenge the constitutionality of the new term as it applies in both the disclosure and the expenditure contexts.

The major premise of plaintiffs' challenge to BCRA's use of the term "electioneering communication" is that *Buckley* drew a constitutionally mandated line between express advocacy and so-called issue advocacy, and that speakers possess an inviolable First Amendment right to engage in the latter category of speech. Thus, plaintiffs maintain, Congress cannot constitutionally require disclosure of, or regulate expenditures for, "electioneering communications" without making an exception for those "communications" that do not meet *Buckley* 's definition of express advocacy.

That position misapprehends our prior decisions, for the express advocacy restriction was an endpoint of statutory interpretation, not a first principle of constitutional law. In *Buckley* we. . . . provided examples of words of express advocacy, such as " 'vote for,' 'elect,' 'support,' . . . 'defeat,' [and] 'reject,' " *id.* at 44, n.52, and those examples eventually gave rise to what is now known as the "magic words" requirement. . . .

. . . In narrowly reading the FECA provisions in Buckley to avoid problems of vagueness and overbreadth, we nowhere suggested that a statute that was neither vague nor overbroad would be required to toe the same express advocacy line. . . .

BCRA § 201's Disclosure Requirements

. . . [W]e turn to . . . § 304's disclosure provisions. . . .

We agree with the District Court that the important state interests that prompted the *Buckley* Court to uphold FECA's disclosure requirements — providing the electorate with information, deterring actual corruption and avoiding any appearance thereof, and gathering the data necessary to enforce more substantive electioneering restrictions — apply in full to BCRA. Accordingly, *Buckley* amply supports application of FECA § 304's disclosure requirements to the entire range of "electioneering communications." . . .

The District Court was also correct that *Buckley* forecloses a facial attack on the new provision in § 304 that requires disclosure of the names of persons contributing $1,000 or more to segregated funds or individuals that spend more than $10,000 in a calendar year on electioneering communications. . . .

". . . Minor parties must be allowed sufficient flexibility in the proof of injury to assure a fair consideration of their claim. The evidence offered need show only a reasonable probability that the compelled disclosure of a party's contributors' names will subject them to threats, harassment, or reprisals from either Government officials or private parties." *Id.* at 74.

A few years later we . . . held that the First Amendment prohibits States from compelling disclosures that would subject identified persons to "threats, harassment, and reprisals," and that the District Court's findings had established a "reasonable probability" of such a result. *Brown v. Socialist Workers '74 Campaign Comm. (Ohio),* 459 U.S. 87, 100 (1982).

In this litigation the District Court applied *Buckley* 's evidentiary standard and found — consistent with our conclusion in *Buckley,* and in contrast to that in *Brown* — that the evidence did not establish the requisite "reasonable probability" of harm to any plaintiff group or its members. . . .

We also are unpersuaded by plaintiffs' challenge to new FECA § 304(f)(5), which requires disclosure of executory contracts for electioneering communications. . . .

As the District Court observed . . . the required disclosures " 'would not have to reveal the specific content of the advertisements, yet they would perform an important function in informing the public about various candidates' supporters *before* election day.' " 251 F. Supp. 2d at 241. . . .

BCRA § 202's Treatment of "Coordinated Communications" as Contributions

Section 202 . . . provide[s] that disbursements for "electioneering communication[s]" that are coordinated with a candidate or party will be treated as contributions to, and expenditures by, that candidate or party. . . . [T]here is no reason why Congress may not treat coordinated disbursements for electioneering communications in the same way it treats all other coordinated expenditures. . . .

BCRA § 203's Prohibition of Corporate and Labor Disbursements for Electioneering Communications

Since our decision in *Buckley,* Congress' power to prohibit corporations and unions from using funds in their treasuries to finance advertisements expressly advocating the election or defeat of candidates in federal elections has been firmly embedded in our law. . . .

Section 203 of BCRA . . . extend[s] this rule . . . to all "electioneering communications". . . . Thus, under BCRA, corporations and unions may not use their general treasury funds to finance electioneering communications, but they remain free to organize and administer segregated funds, or PACs, for that purpose. . . .

. . . [P]laintiffs . . . challenge the expanded regulation on the grounds that it is both overbroad and underinclusive. . . .

. . . [P]laintiffs do not . . . contend that the speech involved in so-called issue advocacy is any more core political speech than are words of express advocacy. . . . Rather, plaintiffs argue that the justifications that adequately support the regulation of express advocacy do not apply to significant quantities of speech encompassed by the definition of electioneering communications.

This argument fails to the extent that the issue ads broadcast during the 30-and 60-day periods preceding federal primary and general elections are the functional equivalent of express advocacy. The justifications for the regulation of express advocacy apply equally to ads aired during those periods if the ads are intended to influence the voters' decisions and have that effect. . . .

We are therefore not persuaded that plaintiffs have carried their heavy burden of proving that amended FECA § 316(b)(2) is overbroad. . . . Even if we assumed that BCRA will inhibit some constitutionally protected corporate and union speech, that assumption would not "justify prohibiting all enforcement" of the law unless its application to protected speech is substantial, "not only in an absolute sense, but also relative to the scope of the law's plainly legitimate applications." *Virginia v. Hicks,* 539 U.S. 113 (2003). Far from establishing that BCRA's application to pure issue ads is substantial, either in an absolute sense or relative to its application to election-related advertising, the record strongly supports the contrary conclusion.

Plaintiffs also argue that FECA § 316(b)(2)'s segregated-fund requirement for electioneering communications is underinclusive because it does not apply to advertising in the print media or on the Internet. The records developed in this litigation and by the Senate Committee adequately explain the reasons for this legislative choice. . . . As we held in *Buckley,* "reform may take one step at a time, addressing itself to the phase of the problem which seems most acute to the legislative mind." 424 U.S. at 105. . . .

In addition to arguing that [the] segregated-fund requirement is underinclusive, some plaintiffs contend that it unconstitutionally discriminates in favor of media companies. . . . Plaintiffs argue this provision gives free rein to media companies to engage in speech without resort to PAC money. . . . "A valid distinction . . . exists between corporations that are part of the media industry and other corporations that are not involved in the regular business of imparting news to the public." *Austin,* 494 U.S. at 668. . . .

BCRA § 204's Application to Nonprofit Corporations

Section 204 of BCRA . . . applies the prohibition on the use of general treasury funds to pay for electioneering communications to not-for-profit corporations. . . .

Because our decision in the [*Federal Election Commission v. Massachusetts Citizens For Life,* 479 U.S. 146 (2003)] case was on the books for many years before BCRA was enacted, we presume that the legislators who drafted § 316(c)(6) were fully aware that the provision could not validly apply to MCFL-type entities. . . .

BCRA § 213's Requirement that Political Parties Choose Between Coordinated and Independent Expenditures After Nominating a Candidate

Section 213 of BCRA amends FECA § 315(d)(4) to impose certain limits on party spending during the postnomination, preelection period. At first blush, the text of § 315(d)(4)(A) appears to require political parties to make a straightforward choice between using limited coordinated expenditures or unlimited independent expenditures to support their nominees. . . .

. . . [However, t]he consequence of the larger coordinated expenditure is not a complete prohibition of any independent expenditure, but the forfeiture of the right to make independent expenditures *for express advocacy.* . . .

In sum, the coverage of new FECA § 315(d)(4) is much more limited than it initially appears. A party that wishes to spend more than $5,000 in coordination with its nominee is forced to forgo only the narrow category of independent expenditures that make use of magic words. But while the category of burdened speech is relatively small, it plainly is entitled to First Amendment protection. *See Buckley*, 424 U.S. at 44–45, 48. . . . To survive constitutional scrutiny, a provision that has such consequences must be supported by a meaningful governmental interest.

The interest in requiring political parties to avoid the use of magic words is not such an interest. We held in *Buckley* that a $1,000 cap on expenditures that applied only to express advocacy could not be justified as a means of avoiding circumvention of contribution limits or preventing corruption and the appearance of corruption because its restrictions could easily be evaded: "So long as persons and groups eschew expenditures that in express terms advocate the election or defeat of a clearly identified candidate, they are free to spend as much as they want to promote the candidate and his views." *Id.* at 45. The same is true in this litigation. Any claim that a restriction on independent express advocacy serves a strong Government interest is belied by the overwhelming evidence that the line between express advocacy and other types of election-influencing expression is, for Congress' purposes, functionally meaningless. Indeed, Congress enacted the new "electioneering communication[s]" provisions precisely because it recognized that the express advocacy test was woefully inadequate at capturing communications designed to influence candidate elections. In light of that recognition, we are hard pressed to conclude that any meaningful purpose is served by § 315(d)(4)'s burden on a party's right to engage independently in express advocacy. . . .

BCRA § 214's Changes in FECA's Provisions Covering Coordinated Expenditures

Ever since our decision in *Buckley,* it has been settled that expenditures by a noncandidate that are "controlled by or coordinated with the candidate and his campaign" may be treated as indirect contributions subject to FECA's source and amount limitations. 424 U.S. at 46. . . . Section 214(a) of BCRA . . . applies the same rule to expenditures coordinated with "a national, State, or local committee of a political party." 2 U.S.C.A. § 441a(a)(7)(B)(ii). . . . Subsection (c) provides that the new "regulations shall not require agreement or formal collaboration to establish coordination." 2 U.S.C.A. § 441a(a) note.

Plaintiffs do not dispute that Congress may apply the same coordination rules to parties as to candidates. They argue instead that new FECA § 315(a)(7)(B)(ii) and its implementing regulations are overbroad and unconstitutionally vague because they permit a finding of coordination even in the absence of an agreement. Plaintiffs point out that political supporters may be subjected to criminal liability if they exceed the contribution limits with expenditures that ultimately are deemed coordinated. . . .

We are not persuaded that the presence of an agreement marks the dividing line between expenditures that are coordinated — and therefore may be regulated as indirect contributions — and expenditures that truly are independent. We repeatedly have struck down limitations on expenditures "made totally independently of the candidate and his campaign," *Buckley,* 424 U.S. at 47, on the ground that such limitations "impose far greater restraints on the freedom of speech and association" than do limits on contributions and coordinated expenditures, *id.* at 44, while "fail[ing] to serve any substantial governmental interest in stemming the reality or appearance of corruption in the electoral process," *id.* at 47–48. . . .

. . . By contrast, expenditures made after a "wink or nod" often will be "as useful to the candidate as cash." *Id.* at 442, 446. . . . Therefore, we cannot agree with the submission that new FECA § 315(a)(7)(B)(ii) is overbroad. . . .

V

Many years ago we observed that "[t]o say that Congress is without power to pass appropriate legislation to safeguard . . . an election from the improper use of money to influence the result is to deny to the nation in a vital particular the power of self protection." *Burroughs v. United States,* 290 U.S. at 545. We abide by that conviction in considering Congress' most recent effort to confine the ill effects of aggregated wealth on our political system. . . . In the main we uphold BCRA's two principal, complementary features: the control of soft money and the regulation of electioneering communications. . . .

CHIEF JUSTICE REHNQUIST delivered the opinion of the Court with respect to BCRA Titles III and IV. . . .[14]

BCRA § 305

[The Court dismissed for lack of standing challenges to §§ 304, 305, 307, 316, and 319 of the Act.] . . .

BCRA § 311

FECA § 318 requires that certain communications "authorized" by a candidate or his political committee clearly identify the candidate or committee or, if not so authorized, identify the payor and announce the lack of authorization. 2 U.S.C.A. § 441d. . . .

. . . We think BCRA § 311's inclusion of electioneering communications in the FECA § 318 disclosure regime bears a sufficient relationship to the important governmental interest of "shed[ding] the light of publicity" on campaign financing. *Buckley,* 424 U.S. at 81. . . .

BCRA § 318

BCRA § 318. . . prohibits individuals "17 years old or younger" from making contributions to candidates and contributions or donations to political parties. 2 U.S.C.A. § 441k. . . .

Minors enjoy the protection of the First Amendment. *See, e.g., Tinker v. Des Moines Independent Community School Dist.,* 393 U.S. 503, 511-513 (1969). Limitations on the amount that an individual may contribute to a candidate or political committee impinge on the protected freedoms of expression and association. *See Buckley supra*, at 20–22. When the Government burdens the right to contribute, we apply heightened scrutiny. . . . We ask whether there is a "sufficiently important interest" and whether the statute is "closely drawn" to avoid unnecessary abridgment of First Amendment freedoms. The Government asserts that the provision protects against corruption by conduit; that is, donations by parents through their minor children to circumvent contribution limits applicable to the parents. But the Government offers scant evidence of this form of evasion. . . . Absent a more convincing case of the claimed evil, this interest is simply too attenuated for § 318 to withstand heightened scrutiny. . . .

Even assuming, *arguendo,* the Government advances an important interest, the provision is overinclusive. The States have adopted a variety

---

14 [Court's footnote *] Justice O'CONNOR, Justice SCALIA, Justice KENNEDY, and Justice SOUTER join this opinion in its entirety. Justice STEVENS, Justice GINSBURG, and Justice BREYER join this opinion, except with respect to BCRA § 305. Justice THOMAS joins this opinion with respect to BCRA §§ 304, 305, 307, 316, and 319. . . .

of more tailored approaches — e.g., counting contributions by minors against the total permitted for a parent or family unit, imposing a lower cap on contributions by minors, and prohibiting contributions by very young children. Without deciding whether any of these alternatives is sufficiently tailored, we hold that the provision here sweeps too broadly. . . .

Justice BREYER delivered the opinion of the Court with respect to BCRA Title V.[15]

We consider here the constitutionality of § 504 [which] requires broadcasters to keep publicly available records of politically related broadcasting requests. . . .

II

BCRA § 504's "candidate request" requirements are virtually identical to those contained in a regulation that the Federal Communications Commission (FCC) promulgated as early as 1938. . . .

In its current form the FCC regulation requires broadcast licensees to "keep" a publicly available file "of all requests for broadcast time made by or on behalf of a candidate for public office," along with a notation showing whether the request was granted, and (if granted) a history that includes "classes of time," "rates charged," and when the "spots actually aired." 47 CFR § 73.1943(a) (2002); § 76.1701(a) (same for cable systems). These regulation-imposed requirements mirror the statutory requirements imposed by BCRA § 504 with minor differences which no one here challenges.

The McConnell plaintiffs argue that these requirements are "intolerabl-[y]" "burdensome and invasive." But we do not see how that could be so. The FCC has consistently estimated that its "candidate request" regulation imposes upon each licensee an additional administrative burden of six to seven hours of work per year. . . . That burden means annual costs of a few hundred dollars at most, a microscopic amount compared to the many millions of dollars of revenue broadcasters receive from candidates who wish to advertise. . . .

In any event, as the FCC wrote in an analogous context, broadcaster recordkeeping requirements " 'simply run with the territory.' " 40 Fed. Reg. 18398 (1975). . . .

. . . The FCC has pointed out that "[t]hese records are necessary to permit political candidates and others to verify that licensees have complied with their obligations relating to use of their facilities by candidates for political office" pursuant to the "equal time" provision of 47 U.S.C. § 315(a). 63 Fed.Reg. 49493 (1998). . . . They will help make the public aware of how much money candidates may be prepared to spend on broadcast messages. And they will provide an independently compiled set of data for purposes of verifying candidates' compliance with the disclosure

---

[15] [Court's footnote *] Justice STEVENS, Justice O'CONNOR, Justice SOUTER, and Justice GINSBURG join this opinion in its entirety.

requirements and source limitations of BCRA and the Federal Election Campaign Act of 1971. . . .

III

BCRA § 504's "election message request" requirements call for broadcasters to keep records of requests (made by any member of the public) to broadcast a "message" about "a legally qualified candidate" or "any election to Federal office." 47 U.S.C.A. §§ 315(e)(1)(B)(i), (ii) (Supp. 2003). Although these requirements are somewhat broader than the "candidate request" requirement, they serve much the same purposes. . . .

Given the nature of many of the messages, recordkeeping can help both the regulatory agencies and the public evaluate broadcasting fairness, and determine the amount of money that individuals or groups, supporters or opponents, intend to spend to help elect a particular candidate. . . .

IV

The "issue request" requirements call for broadcasters to keep records of requests (made by any member of the public) to broadcast "message[s]" about "a national legislative issue of public importance" or "any political matter of national importance." 47 U.S.C.A. §§ 315(e)(1)(B), (e)(1)(B)(iii) (Supp. 2003). These recordkeeping requirements seem likely to help the FCC determine whether broadcasters are carrying out their "obligations to afford reasonable opportunity for the discussion of conflicting views on issues of public importance," 47 CFR § 73.1910 (2002), and whether broadcasters are too heavily favoring entertainment, and discriminating against broadcasts devoted to public affairs, *see ibid.*; 47 U.S.C. § 315(a); *Red Lion*, 395 U.S. at 380.

The McConnell plaintiffs claim that the statutory language — "political matter of national importance" or "national legislative issue of public importance" — is unconstitutionally vague or overbroad. But that language is no more general than the language that Congress has used to impose other obligations upon broadcasters. . . .

Whether these requirements impose disproportionate administrative burdens is more difficult to say. . . .

The regulatory burden, in practice, will depend on how the FCC interprets and applies this provision. The FCC has adequate legal authority to write regulations that may limit, and make more specific, the provision's potential linguistic reach. . . .

The McConnell plaintiffs and The Chief Justice make one final claim. They say that the "issue request" requirement will force them to disclose information that will reveal their political strategies to opponents, perhaps prior to a broadcast. . . . [T]he "strategy disclosure" argument does not show that BCRA § 504 is unconstitutional on its face, but the plaintiffs remain free to raise this argument when § 504 is applied. . . .

JUSTICE SCALIA, concurring with respect to BCRA Titles III and IV, dissenting with respect to BCRA Titles I and V, and concurring in the judgment in part and dissenting in part with respect to BCRA Title II.

With respect to Titles I, II, and V: I join in full the dissent of The Chief Justice; I join the opinion of Justice Kennedy, except to the extent it upholds new § 323(e) of the Federal Election Campaign Act of 1971 (FECA) and § 202 of the Bipartisan Campaign Reform Act of 2002 (BCRA) in part; and because I continue to believe that *Buckley v. Valeo,* 424 U.S. 1 (1976) (*per curiam*), was wrongly decided, I also join Parts I, II-A, and II-B of the opinion of Justice Thomas. With respect to Titles III and IV, I join The Chief Justice's opinion for the Court. . . .

This is a sad day for the freedom of speech. . . . We are governed by Congress, and this legislation prohibits the criticism of Members of Congress by those entities most capable of giving such criticism loud voice: national political parties and corporations, both of the commercial and the not-for-profit sort. It forbids pre-election criticism of incumbents by corporations, even not-for-profit corporations, by use of their general funds; and forbids national-party use of "soft" money to fund "issue ads" that incumbents find so offensive.

To be sure, the legislation is evenhanded: . . . But . . . if incumbents and challengers are limited to the same quantity of electioneering, incumbents are favored. . . .

Beyond that, however, the present legislation *targets* for prohibition certain categories of campaign speech that are particularly harmful to incumbents. Is it accidental, do you think, that incumbents raise about three times as much "hard money" — the sort of funding generally *not* restricted by this legislation — as do their challengers? . . . And is it mere happenstance, do you estimate, that national-party funding, which is severely limited by the Act, is more likely to assist cash-strapped challengers than flush-with-hard-money incumbents? . . . Was it unintended, by any chance, that incumbents are free personally to receive some soft money and even to solicit it for other organizations, while national parties are not? . . .

(a) Money is Not Speech

It was said by congressional proponents of this legislation . . . that since this legislation regulates nothing but the expenditure of money for speech, as opposed to speech itself, the burden it imposes is not subject to full First Amendment scrutiny . . . Until today, however, that view has been categorically rejected by our jurisprudence. . . .

Our traditional view was correct, and today's cavalier attitude toward regulating the financing of speech (the "exacting scrutiny" test of *Buckley, see ibid.*, is not uttered in any majority opinion, and is not observed in the ones from which I dissent) frustrates the fundamental purpose of the First Amendment. . . .

. . . The right to speak would be largely ineffective if it did not include the right to engage in financial transactions that are the incidents of its exercise.

This is not to say that *any* regulation of money is a regulation of speech. The government may apply general commercial regulations to those who use money for speech if it applies them evenhandedly to those who use money for other purposes. But where the government singles out money used to fund speech as its legislative object, it is acting against speech as such, no less than if it had targeted the paper on which a book was printed or the trucks that deliver it to the bookstore. . . .

[A] law limiting the amount a person can spend to broadcast his political views is a direct restriction on speech. That is no different from a law limiting the amount a newspaper can pay its editorial staff or the amount a charity can pay its leafletters. It is equally clear that a limit on the amount a candidate can raise from any one individual for the purpose of speaking is also a direct limitation on speech. . . .

(b) Pooling Money is Not Speech

Another proposition which could explain at least some of the results of today's opinion is that the First Amendment right to spend money for speech does not include the right to combine with others in spending money for speech. . . . The freedom to associate with others for the dissemination of ideas — not just by singing or speaking in unison, but by pooling financial resources for expressive purposes — is part of the freedom of speech. . . .

(c) Speech by Corporations Can Be Abridged

But what about the danger to the political system posed by "amassed wealth"? The most direct threat from that source comes in the form of undisclosed favors and payoffs to elected officials — which have already been criminalized, and will be rendered no more discoverable by the legislation at issue here. The use of corporate wealth (like individual wealth) to speak to the electorate is unlikely to "distort" elections — *especially* if disclosure requirements *tell* the people where the speech is coming from. . . . Given the premises of democracy, there is no such thing as *too much* speech. . . .

. . . It cannot be denied, however, that corporate (like noncorporate) allies will have greater access to the officeholder, and that he will tend to favor the same causes as those who support him (which is usually *why* they supported him). That is the nature of politics — if not indeed human nature. . . .

But let us not be deceived. While the Government's briefs and arguments before this Court focused on the horrible "appearance of corruption," the most passionate floor statements during the debates on this legislation pertained to so-called attack ads, which the Constitution surely protects, but which Members of Congress analogized to "crack cocaine," 144 Cong. Rec. S868 (Feb. 24, 1998) (remarks of Sen. Daschle). . . .

Another theme prominent in the legislative debates was the notion that there is too much money spent on elections. . . .

And what exactly are these outrageous sums frittered away in determining who will govern us? A report prepared for Congress concluded that the total amount, in hard and soft money, spent on the 2000 federal elections was between $2.4 and $2.5 billion. . . . *All* campaign spending in the United States, including state elections, ballot initiatives, and judicial elections, has been estimated at $3.9 billion for 2000, Nelson, Spending in the 2000 Elections, in Financing the 2000 Election 24, Tbl. 2-1 (D. Magleby ed. 2002), which was a year that "shattered spending and contribution records," *id.* at 22. Even taking this last, larger figure as the benchmark, it means that Americans spent about half as much electing all their Nation's officials, state and federal, as they spent on movie tickets ($7.8 billion); about a fifth as much as they spent on cosmetics and perfume ($18.8 billion). . . .

Justice THOMAS, concurring with respect to BCRA Titles III and IV, except for BCRA 311 and 318, concurring in the result with respect to BCRA 318, concurring in the judgment in part and dissenting in part with respect to BCRA Title II, and dissenting with respect to BCRA Titles I, V, and 311.[16]

. . . [T]he Court today upholds what can only be described as the most significant abridgment of the freedoms of speech and association since the Civil War. With breathtaking scope, the Bipartisan Campaign Reform Act of 2002 (BCRA), directly targets and constricts core political speech, the "primary object of First Amendment protection." *Nixon v. Shrink Missouri Government PAC,* 528 U.S. 377, 410-411 (2000) (Thomas, J., dissenting). . . .

. . . Apparently, the marketplace of ideas is to be fully open only to defamers, nude dancers, pornographers, flag burners, and cross burners.

Because I cannot agree with the treatment given by Justice Stevens' and Justice O'Connor's opinion (hereinafter joint opinion) to speech that is "indispensable to the effective and intelligent use of the processes of popular government to shape the destiny of modern industrial society," *Thornhill v. Alabama,* 310 U.S. 88, 103 (1940), I respectfully dissent. I also dissent from Justice Breyer's opinion upholding BCRA § 504. I join The Chief Justice's opinion in regards to BCRA §§ 304, 305, 307, 316, 319, and 403(b); concur in the result as to § 318; and dissent from the opinion as to § 311. I also fully agree with Justice Kennedy's discussion of § 213 and join that portion of his opinion.

---

[16] [Court's footnote *] Justice SCALIA joins Parts I, II-A, and II-B of this opinion.

I

A

. . . [A]s I have previously noted, it is unclear why "[b]ribery laws [that] bar precisely the quid pro quo arrangements that are targeted here" and "disclosure laws" are not "less restrictive means of addressing [the Government's] interest in curtailing corruption." *Shrink Missouri, supra,* at 428.

The joint opinion not only continues the errors of *Buckley v. Valeo,* by applying a low level of scrutiny to contribution ceilings, but also builds upon these errors by expanding the anticircumvention rationale beyond reason. . . . [A] broadly drawn bribery law[17] would cover even subtle and general attempts to influence government officials corruptly . . . And, an effective bribery law would deter actual *quid pro quos* and would, in all likelihood, eliminate any appearance of corruption in the system. . . .

II

The Court is not content with "balanc[ing] away First Amendment freedoms," *Shrink Missouri,* 528 U.S. at 410,(Thomas, J., dissenting), in the context of the restrictions imposed by Title I, which could arguably (if wrongly) be thought to be mere contribution limits. The Court also, in upholding virtually all of Title II, proceeds to do the same for limitations on expenditures, which constitute "political expression 'at the core of our electoral process and of the First Amendment freedoms,'" *Buckley,* 424 U.S. at 39. Today's holding continues a disturbing trend: the steady decrease in the level of scrutiny applied to restrictions on core political speech. . . . Although this trend is most obvious in the review of contribution limits, it has now reached what even this Court today would presumably recognize as a direct restriction on core political speech: limitations on independent expenditures.

A

. . . The particular language used, "expenditures made by any person . . . in cooperation, consultation, or concert with, or at the request or suggestion of, a national, State, or local committee of a political party," BCRA § 214(a)(2), captures expenditures with "no constitutional difference" from "a purely independent one." *Id.* at 468 (Thomas, J., dissenting).[18]

---

17 [Court's footnote 2] Arguably, the current antibribery statute, 18 U.S.C. § 201, is broad enough to cover the unspecified other "attempts . . . to influence governmental action" that the *Buckley* Court seemed worried about. 424 U.S. at 28.

18 [Court's footnote 7] This is doubly so now that the Court has decided that there is no constitutional need for the showing even of an "agreement" in order to transform an expenditure into a "coordinated expenditur[e]" and hence into a contribution for FECA purposes.

C

I must now address an issue on which I differ from all of my colleagues: the disclosure provisions in BCRA § 201, now contained in new FECA § 304(f). The "historical evidence indicates that Founding-era Americans opposed attempts to require that anonymous authors reveal their identities on the ground that forced disclosure violated the 'freedom of the press.'" *McIntyre v. Ohio Elections Comm'n*, 514 U.S. 334, 361 (1995) (Thomas, J., concurring). Indeed, this Court has explicitly recognized. . .that "an author's decision to remain anonymous . . . is an aspect of the freedom of speech protected by the First Amendment." *Id.* at 342. The Court now backs away from this principle, allowing the established right to anonymous speech to be stripped away based on the flimsiest of justifications.

The right to anonymous speech cannot be abridged based on the interests asserted by the defendants. I would thus hold that the disclosure requirements of BCRA § 201 are unconstitutional. Because of this conclusion, the so-called advance disclosure requirement of § 201 necessarily falls as well.[19]

D

I have long maintained that *Buckley* was incorrectly decided and should be overturned. But, most of Title II should still be held unconstitutional even under the *Buckley* framework. Under *Buckley* and *Federal Election Comm'n v. Massachusetts Citizens for Life, Inc.*, 479 U.S. 238 (1986) (MCFL), it is, or at least was, clear that any regulation of political speech beyond communications using words of express advocacy is unconstitutional. Hence, even under the joint opinion's framework, most of Title II is unconstitutional, as both the "primary definition" and "backup definition" of "electioneering communications" cover a significant number of communications that do not use words of express advocacy. . . .

Justice KENNEDY, concurring in the judgment in part and dissenting in part with respect to BCRA Titles I and II.[20]

The First Amendment guarantees our citizens the right to judge for themselves the most effective means for the expression of political views and

---

[19] [Court's footnote 10] BCRA § 212(a) is also unconstitutional. Although the plaintiffs only challenge the advance disclosure requirement of § 212(a), by requiring disclosure of communications using express advocacy, the entire reporting requirement is unconstitutional for the same reasons that § 201 is unconstitutional. Consequently, it follows that the advance disclosure provision is unconstitutional.

BCRA §§ 311 and 504 also violate the First Amendment. By requiring any television or radio advertisement that satisfies the definition of "electioneering communication" to include the identity of the sponsor, and even a "full-screen view of a representative of the political committee or other person making the statement" in the case of a television advertisement, new FECA § 318, § 311 is a virtual carbon copy of the law at issue in McIntyre v. Ohio Elections Comm'n, 514 U.S. 334 (1995). . . .

[20] [Court's footnote *] THE CHIEF JUSTICE joins this opinion in its entirety. Justice SCALIA joins this opinion except to the extent it upholds new FECA § 323(e) and BCRA § 202. Justice THOMAS joins this opinion with respect to BCRA § 213.

to decide for themselves which entities to trust as reliable speakers. Significant portions of Titles I and II of the Bipartisan Campaign Reform Act of 2002 (BCRA or Act) constrain that freedom. These new laws force speakers to abandon their own preference for speaking through parties and organizations. . . .

. . . To reach today's decision, the Court surpasses *Buckley*'s limits and expands Congress' regulatory power. . . .

A few examples show how BCRA reorders speech rights and codifies the Government's own preferences for certain speakers. BCRA would have imposed felony punishment on Ross Perot's 1996 efforts to build the Reform Party. Compare Federal Election Campaign Act of 1971 (FECA) §§ 309(d)(1)(A), 315(a)(1)(B), and 323(a)(1) (prohibiting, by up to five years' imprisonment, any individual from giving over $25,000 annually to a national party), with Spending By Perot, The Houston Chronicle, Dec. 13, 1996, p. 43 (reporting Perot's $8 million founding contribution to the Reform Party). BCRA makes it a felony for an environmental group to broadcast an ad, within 60 days of an election, exhorting the public to protest a Congressman's impending vote to permit logging in national forests. *See* BCRA § 203. BCRA escalates Congress' discrimination in favor of the speech rights of giant media corporations and against the speech rights of other corporations, both profit and nonprofit. . . .

Our precedents teach, above all, that Government cannot be trusted to moderate its own rules for suppression of speech. . . .

With respect, I dissent from the majority opinion upholding BCRA Titles I and II. I concur in the judgment as to BCRA § 213 and new FECA § 323(e) and concur in the judgment in part and dissent in part as to BCRA §§ 201, 202, and 214.

I. TITLE I AND COORDINATION PROVISIONS

Title I principally bans the solicitation, receipt, transfer and spending of soft money by the national parties (new FECA § 323(a), 2 U.S.C.A. § 441i(a) (Supp. 2003)). It also bans certain uses of soft money by state parties (new FECA § 323(b)); the transfer of soft money from national parties to nonprofit groups (new FECA § 323(d)); the solicitation, receipt, transfer, and spending of soft money by federal candidates and officeholders (new FECA § 323(e)); and certain uses of soft money by state candidates (new FECA § 323(f)). . . . Even a cursory review of the speech and association burdens these laws create makes their First Amendment infirmities obvious:

> Title I bars individuals with shared beliefs from pooling their money above limits set by Congress to form a new third party. *See* new FECA § 323(a). Title I bars national party officials from soliciting or directing soft money to state parties for use on a state ballot initiative. This is true even if no federal office appears on the same ballot as the state initiative. *See* new FECA § 323(a).

A national party's mere involvement in the strategic planning of fundraising for a state ballot initiative risks a determination that the national party is exercising "indirect control" of the state party. If that determination is made, the state party must abide by federal regulations. . . . *See* new FECA § 323(a).

Title I compels speech. Party officials who want to engage in activity such as fundraising must now speak magic words to ensure the solicitation cannot be interpreted as anything other than a solicitation for hard, not soft, money. *See ibid.*

Title I prohibits the national parties from giving any sort of funds to nonprofit entities, even federally regulated hard money, and even if the party hoped to sponsor the interest group's exploration of a particular issue in advance of the party's addition of it to their platform. *See* new FECA § 323(d).

By express terms, Title I imposes multiple different forms of spending caps on parties, candidates, and their agents. *See* new FECA §§ 323(a), (e), and (f). Title I allows state parties to raise quasi-soft money Levin funds for use in activities that might affect a federal election; but the Act prohibits national parties from assisting state parties in developing and executing these fundraising plans, even when the parties seek only to advance state election interests. *See* new FECA § 323(b).

Until today's consolidated cases, the Court has accepted but two principles to use in determining the validity of campaign finance restrictions. First is the anticorruption rationale. . . . Second, the Court . . .has said that the willing adoption of the entity form by corporations and unions justifies regulating them differently: Their ability to give candidates quids may be subject not only to limits but also to outright bans; their electoral speech may likewise be curtailed.

A. Constitutionally Sufficient Interest

In *Buckley,* the Court held that one, and only one, interest justified the significant burden on the right of association involved there: eliminating, or preventing, actual corruption or the appearance of corruption stemming from contributions to candidates. . . .

[T]he Court in fact upheld limits on conduct possessing *quid pro quo* dangers, and nothing more.

The Court ignores these constitutional bounds and in effect interprets the anticorruption rationale to allow regulation not just of "actual or apparent *quid pro quo* arrangements," *ibid.,* but of any conduct that wins goodwill from or influences a Member of Congress. . . . The Court . . . concludes that access, without more, proves influence is undue. . . .

The generic favoritism or influence theory articulated by the Court is at odds with standard First Amendment analyses because it is unbounded and susceptible to no limiting principle. . . .

. . . Democracy is premised on responsiveness. *Quid pro quo* corruption has been, until now, the only agreed upon conduct that represents the bad form of responsiveness and presents a justiciable standard with a relatively clear limiting principle. . . .

. . . Under *Buckley* 's holding . . . the Court asked whether the Government had proved that the regulated conduct, the expenditures, posed inherent *quid pro quo* corruption potential. . . .

1. New FECA §§ 323(a), (b), (d), and (f)

Sections 323(a), (b), (d), and (f), 2 U.S.C.A. §§ 441i(a), (b), (d), and (f) (Supp. 2003), cannot stand because they do not add regulation to conduct that poses a demonstrable *quid pro quo* danger. . . .

Section 323(a) . . . only adds regulation to soft money party donations not solicited by, or spent in coordination with, a candidate or officeholder.

These donations (noncandidate or officeholder solicited soft money party donations that are independently spent) do not pose the *quid pro quo* dangers that provide the basis for restricting protected speech. . . .

Even § 323(b)'s narrowest regulation, which bans state party soft money funded ads that (1) refer to a clearly identified federal candidate, and (2) either support or attack any candidate for the office of the clearly mentioned federal candidate fails the constitutional test. . . .

Section 323(d), which governs relationships between the national parties and nonprofit groups, fails for similar reasons. . . . Congress is determining what future course the creation of ideas and the expression of views must follow. Its attempt to foreclose new and creative partnerships for speech, as illustrated here, is consistent with neither the traditions nor principles of our Free Speech guarantee. . . .

When one recognizes that §§ 323(a), (b), (d), and (f) do not serve the interest the anticorruption rationale contemplates, Title I's entirety begins to look very much like an incumbency protection plan. . . That impression is worsened by the fact that Congress exempted its officeholders from the more stringent prohibitions imposed on party officials. . . .

The law in some respects even weakens the regulation of federal candidates and officeholders. Under former law, officeholders were understood to be limited to receipt of hard money by their campaign committees. BCRA, however, now allows them and their campaign committees to receive soft money that fits the hard money source and amount restrictions, so long as the officeholders direct that money on to other nonfederal candidates. . . .

2. New FECA § 323(e)

Ultimately, only one of the challenged Title I provisions satisfies *Buckley*'s anticorruption rationale and the First Amendment's guarantee. It is § 323(e). . . . These provisions . . . limit candidates' and their agents' solicitation of soft money. . . .

I agree with the Court that the broader solicitation regulation does further a sufficient interest. The making of a solicited gift is a *quid* both to the recipient of the money and to the one who solicits the payment (by granting his request). . . .

B. Standard of Review

. . . In *Buckley,* we applied "closely drawn" scrutiny to contribution limitations and strict scrutiny to expenditure limitations. Against that backdrop, the majority assumes that because *Buckley* applied the rationale in the context of contribution and expenditure limits, its application gives Congress and the Court the capacity to classify any challenged campaign finance regulation as either a contribution or an expenditure limit. Thus, it first concludes Title I's regulations are contributions limits and then proceeds to apply the lesser scrutiny. . . .

Title I's provisions prohibit the receipt of funds; and in most instances, but not all, this can be defined as a contribution limit. They prohibit the spending of funds; and in most instances this can be defined as an expenditure limit. They prohibit the giving of funds to nonprofit groups; and this falls within neither definition as we have ever defined it. Finally, they prohibit fundraising activity. . . .

Despite the parties' and the majority's best efforts on both sides of the question, it ignores reality to force these regulations into one of the two legal categories as either contribution or expenditure limitations. Instead, these characteristics seem to indicate Congress has enacted regulations that are neither contribution nor expenditure limits, or are perhaps both at once.

Even if the laws could be classified in broad terms as only contribution limits, as the majority is inclined to do, that still leaves the question what "contribution limits" can include if they are to be upheld under *Buckley*. *Buckley*'s application of a less exacting review to contribution limits must be confined to the narrow category of money gifts that are directed, in some manner, to a candidate or officeholder. Any broader definition of the category contradicts *Buckley*'s *quid pro quo* rationale and overlooks *Buckley*'s language . . . .

The majority makes *Buckley*'s already awkward and imprecise test all but meaningless in its application. If one is viewing BCRA through *Buckley*'s lens, as the majority purports to do, one must conclude the Act creates markedly greater associational burdens than the significant burden created by contribution limitations and, unlike contribution limitations, also creates significant burdens on speech itself. While BCRA contains federal contribution limitations, which significantly burden association, it goes even further. The Act entirely reorders the nature of relations between national political parties and their candidates, between national political parties and state and local parties, and between national political parties and nonprofit organizations. . . .

II. TITLE II PROVISIONS

A. Disclosure Provisions

. . . Section 201's advance disclosure requirement. . . .imposes real burdens on political speech that *post hoc* disclosure does not. It forces disclosure of political strategy by revealing where ads are to be run and what their content is likely to be (based on who is running the ad). It also provides an opportunity for the ad buyer's opponents to dissuade broadcasters from running ads. . . .

B. BCRA § 203

The majority permits a new and serious intrusion on speech when it upholds § 203, the key provision in Title II that prohibits corporations and labor unions from using money from their general treasury to fund electioneering communications. . . .

1.

The majority's holding cannot be reconciled with *First Nat. Bank of Boston v. Bellotti,* 435 U.S. 765 (1978), which invalidated a Massachusetts law prohibiting banks and business corporations from making expenditures "for the purpose of" influencing referendum votes on issues that do not "materially affect" their business interests. *Id.* at 767. . . .

Austin [*v. Michigan Chamber of Commerce,* 494 U.S. 652 (1990),] was the first and, until now, the only time our Court had allowed the Government to exercise the power to censor political speech based on the speaker's corporate identity. . . .

To be sure, *Bellotti* concerns issue advocacy, whereas *Austin* is about express advocacy. . . .

Austin was based on a faulty assumption. Contrary to Justice Stevens' proposal that there is "vast difference between lobbying and debating public issues on the one hand, and political campaigns for election to public office on the other," *ibid.,* there is a general recognition now that discussions of candidates and issues are quite often intertwined in practical terms. . . .

2.

Even under *Austin,* BCRA § 203 could not stand. . . .

The Government is unwilling to characterize § 203 as a ban, citing the possibility of funding electioneering communications out of a separate segregated fund. This option, though, does not alter the categorical nature of the prohibition on the corporation. . . .

Our cases recognize the practical difficulties corporations face when they are limited to communicating through PACs. . . .

The majority can articulate no compelling justification for imposing this scheme of compulsory ventriloquism. . . .

The prohibition, with its crude temporal and geographic proxies, is a severe and unprecedented ban on protected speech. . . . [S]uppose a few Senators want to show their constituents in the logging industry how much they care about working families and propose a law, 60 days before the election, that would harm the environment by allowing logging in national forests. Under § 203, a nonprofit environmental group would be unable to run an ad referring to these Senators in their districts. The suggestion that the group could form and fund a PAC in the short time required for effective participation in the political debate is fanciful. . . . [M]oreover, an ad hoc PAC would not be as effective as the environmental group itself in gaining credibility with the public. Never before in our history has the Court upheld a law that suppresses speech to this extent. . . .

CONCLUSION

. . . The First Amendment . . . cannot be read to allow Congress to provide for the imprisonment of those who attempt to establish new political parties and alter the civic discourse. . . .

Chief Justice REHNQUIST, dissenting with respect to BCRA Titles I and V.[21]

Although I join Justice Kennedy's opinion in full, I write separately to highlight my disagreement with the Court on Title I of the Bipartisan Campaign Reform Act of 2002 (BCRA), 116 Stat. 81, and to dissent from the Court's opinion upholding § 504 of Title V.

I

The issue presented by Title I is . . . whether Congress can permissibly regulate much speech that has no plausible connection to candidate contributions or corruption to achieve those goals. . . .

The lynchpin of Title I, new FECA § 323(a) . . . does not regulate only donations given to influence a particular federal election; it regulates *all donations* to national political committees, no matter the use to which the funds are put.

The Court attempts to sidestep the unprecedented breadth of this regulation by stating that the "close relationship between federal officeholders and the national parties" makes all donations to the national parties "suspect." . . . The Court's willingness to impute corruption on the basis of a relationship greatly infringes associational rights and expands Congress' ability to regulate political speech. And there is nothing in the Court's analysis that limits congressional regulation to national political parties. In fact, the Court relies in part on this closeness rationale to regulate *nonprofit organizations*. . . .

. . . For sure, national political party committees exist in large part to elect federal candidates, but as a majority of the District Court found, they

---

[21] [Court's footnote *] Justice SCALIA and Justice KENNEDY join this opinion in its entirety.

also promote coordinated political messages and participate in public policy debates unrelated to federal elections, promote, even in off-year elections, state and local candidates and seek to influence policy at those levels, and increase public participation in the electoral process. . . .

As these activities illustrate, political parties often foster speech crucial to a healthy democracy, and fulfill the need for like-minded individuals to ban together and promote a political philosophy. . . . [T]he means chosen by Congress, restricting all donations to national parties no matter the purpose for which they are given or are used, are not "closely drawn to avoid unnecessary abridgment of associational freedoms," *Buckley,* at 25.

BCRA's overinclusiveness is not limited to national political parties. . . . For example, new FECA § 323(b) . . . prohibits state parties from using nonfederal funds for general partybuilding activities such as voter registration, voter identification, and get out the vote for state candidates even if federal candidates are not mentioned. New FECA § 323(d) prohibits state and local political party committees, like their national counterparts, from soliciting and donating "any funds" to nonprofit organizations such as the National Rifle Association or the National Association for the Advancement of Colored People (NAACP). . . .[22]

II

BCRA § 504 . . . differs from other BCRA disclosure sections because it requires broadcast licensees to disclose *requests* to purchase broadcast time rather than requiring *purchasers* to disclose their *disbursements* for broadcast time.

This section is deficient because of the absence of a sufficient governmental interest to justify disclosure of mere requests to purchase broadcast time, as well as purchases themselves. The Court approaches § 504 almost exclusively from the perspective of the broadcast licensees, ignoring the interests of candidates and other purchasers, whose speech and association rights are affected by § 504. . . .

Justice STEVENS, dissenting with respect to § 305.[23]

. . . I would entertain plaintiffs' challenge to § 305 on the merits and uphold the section. Like BCRA §§ 201, 212, and 311, § 305 serves an important — and constitutionally sufficient — informational purpose. . . .

Finally, I do not regard § 305 as a constitutionally suspect "viewpoint-based regulation." . . . Although the section reaches only ads that mention opposing candidates, it applies equally to all such ads. . . .

---

[22] [Court's footnote 4] BCRA does not even close all of the "loopholes" that currently exist. Nonprofit organizations are currently able to accept, without disclosing, unlimited donations for voter registration, voter identification, and get-out-the-vote activities, and the record indicates that such organizations already receive large donations, sometimes in the millions of dollars, for these activities. . . .

[23] [Court's footnote *] Justice GINSBURG and Justice BREYER join this opinion in its entirety.

§ 15.03 Government Funding of Speech-Related Activities

Page 1371: [Insert the following after *Nat'l Endowment for Arts v. Finley*]

Library Pornography. In *United States v. Am. Library Ass'n*, 539 U.S. 194 (2003), Chief Justice Rehnquist upheld (6-3) a statute that withholds funding from public libraries unless they install computer software that prevents viewing pornography. Previously enacted statutes offer a discounted rate for libraries to purchase Internet access, and provide grants to "state library administrative agencies" to public libraries in connecting to the Internet. Due to the abundance of pornography that is available on the Internet, Congress worried that the programs that they passed that assisted libraries in obtaining Internet access "were facilitating access to illegal and harmful pornography." The Children's Internet Protection Act (CIPA) provides that a public library will not be eligible for federal funding to provide Internet access without first having installed "software to block images that constitute obscenity or child pornography, and to prevent minors from obtaining access to material that is harmful to them."

The Court applied principles in *Arkansas Ed. Television Comm'n v. Forbes*, casebook p. 1247, and *Nat'l Endowment for Arts v. Finley*, casebook p. 1369. Both forum analysis and heightened judicial scrutiny are "incompatible with the discretion that public libraries must have to fulfill their traditional missions. Public library staffs necessarily consider content in making collection decisions and enjoy broad discretion in making them." Internet access does not qualify as a public forum, either traditional or designated. Libraries have always been charged with deciding what material is suitable for their collections. This liberty extends to deciding on Internet material. When filtering, software sometimes blocks access to constitutionally protected speech that does not fall into the categories that adult users may simply ask the librarian to disable the filter or unblock a specific site.

The Appellees alternatively argue "that CIPA imposes an unconstitutional condition on the receipt of federal assistance." *Rust v. Sullivan*, casebook p. 1346, affords the government broad discretion to limit the use of public funds. Congress' programs that provided federal assistance to libraries were meant to allow libraries to continue "their traditional role of obtaining material of requisite and appropriate quality for educational and informational purposes." Traditionally, libraries have not included pornographic material in their collections. CIPA only restricts libraries from allowing unfiltered access with federal funding. Libraries are able to offer this without the federal assistance.

Concurring in the judgment, Justice Kennedy argues that if a library is unable to unblock a particular site, or if an adult patron's right to view protected material is substantially burdened, these can be dealt with by as-applied challenges. Concurring in the judgment, Justice Breyer would neither apply a rational basis test nor strict scrutiny level of review. "Given the comparatively small burden that the Act imposes upon the library patron seeking legitimate Internet materials, I cannot say that any speech-related harm that the Act may cause is disproportionate when considered in relation to the Act's legitimate objectives."

Dissenting, Justice Stevens argues that the filtering software underblocks because they limit access to sites based on text, not images. At the same time, these programs will restrict access to a large number of sites that, while harmless, contain a word that triggers the filter.

Justice Souter dissents, and Justice Ginsburg joins. Libraries have evolved away from the "conception of a public library's mission" upon which the plurality relied. There has been an "evolution" toward a rule allowing any adult "access to any of its holdings."

§ 15.04   Commercial Speech

[1]—Protection for Commercial Speech: General Principles

Page 1397: [Insert the following after Note (1)(b)]

(c) *Generic advertising and government speech.* In *Johanns v. Livestock Marketing Association*, 125 S. Ct. 2055 (2005), the Court rejected a facial challenge to a generic Beef advertising campaign, funded by a $1 assessment per head of cattle ("checkoff") imposed by the Secretary of Agriculture, as it funded the government's own speech. Plaintiffs, who were subject to the checkoff, sued because they disagreed with the messages of the advertisements they were funding. Plaintiffs relied on *United States v. United Foods, Inc.*, casebook p. 1397, which invalidated a mandatory checkoff for generic mushroom advertising because it violated the First Amendment.

Writing for the majority, Justice Scalia noted that compelled speech challenges fell into two categories. First, the Court has invalidated cases of "true 'compelled speech'" in which government compels an individual to express a message he disagrees with. *See West Virginia Board of Education v. Barnette*, 319 U.S. 624 (1943), (invalidating a law compelling school children to recite the pledge of allegiance). Second, in "compelled subsidy" cases, such as *United Foods*, the Court has stopped government from imposing fees on an individual to subsidize a message with which he disagrees. *See United Foods*. However, the Court has allowed such mandatory fees if they are part of a "broader regulatory scheme." Moreover, a compelled subsidy of government's own speech does not necessarily violate the First Amendment, as compelled support of the government is constitutional and it is inevitable that some funds raised by the government will be spent on speech to advocate its own positions.

Despite the prominent role of the Beef Board, which is not a government entity, in the advertising campaign, "when, as here, the government sets the overall message to be communicated and approves every word that is disseminated, it is not precluded from relying on the government-speech doctrine merely because is solicits assistance from nongovernmental sources in developing specific messages." The advertisements were government speech despite their being funded by a targeted assessment rather than general tax revenues. There is "no *First Amendment* right not to fund government speech." Finally, the Court rejected a facial challenge on the basis that crediting the advertisements to "America's Beef Producers" impermissibly implies that plaintiffs endorse a message with which they do not agree. This theory may support an as-applied challenge if the producers establish that beef advertisements were actually attributed to them.

Justices Thomas and Breyer each wrote concurring opinions. Justice Thomas stated that an as-applied challenge would exist if the advertisements "associated" their generic message with the plaintiffs. Justice Ginsburg, concurring in judgment, would uphold the assessments "as permissible economic regulation."

Justice Souter dissented, joined by Justices Stevens and Kennedy. He argued that this case was indistinguishable from *United Foods*, as the speech regulation was not "incidental" to a "comprehensive regulatory scheme." Moreover, the advertisements are not government speech because government is not required to signal that it is providing the advertisements.

Page 1402: [Insert the following after *Lorillard Tobacco Co. v. Reilly*]

Compounded drugs. In *Thompson v. Western States Medical Center*, 535 U.S. 357 (2002), the Court invalidated an advertising restriction on "compounded drugs." The restriction exempted compounded drugs from the normal testing required to approve new drugs if pharmacists did not promote or advertise them. Writing for the majority of the Court, Justice O'Connor applied the *Central Hudson*, casebook, p. 1384, test. The Government has important interests both in wanting to subject new drugs to FDA approval, and in permitting compounded drugs that can tailor medications to meet particular needs of particular patients. Such specific mixtures should not have to undergo the testing process for new drugs. Consequently, "the Government needs to be able to draw a line between small-scale compounding and large-scale drug manufacturing." Nonetheless, the Government failed to demonstrate that its advertising restrictions are "not more extensive than is necessary to serve" the interests it advances. In this case, the Government could differentiate between compounding and manufacturing with lines unrelated to speech. For example, the Government could "ban the use of 'commercial scale manufacturing or testing equipment for compounding drug products.'" It could limit compounding to "prescriptions already received." It could prohibit selling compounded drugs at wholesale prices for resale. It could cap "the amount of any particular compounded drug, either by drug volume, number of prescriptions, gross revenue, or profit that a pharmacist or pharmacy may make or sell in a given period of time."

While the dissent described another governmental interest, that of "prohibiting the sale of compounded drugs to 'patients who may not clearly need them,'" the Government did not advance this interest. Finally, the Government's ban could prevent useful advertising. For example, pharmacists could post information about compounds that make it easier for children to swallow pills or that change the flavor of a particular medication.

Justice Thomas concurred, but reaffirmed his position that the *Central Hudson* test should not apply to commercial speech restrictions, "at least when, as here, the asserted interest is one that is to be achieved through keeping would-be recipients of the speech in the dark."

Justice Breyer dissented joined by Chief Justice Rehnquist and Justices Stevens and Ginsburg. Justice Breyer maintained that "an overly rigid 'commercial speech' doctrine will transform what ought to be a legislative or regulatory decision about the best way to protect the health and safety of the American public into a constitutional decision." In light of the history of the Due Process Clause, this would be a "tragic constitutional misunderstanding."

§ 15.05 Obscenity

[1]—The Constitutional Standard

Page 1421: [Insert the following to Note (7)]

(a) **ASHCROFT v. THE FREE SPEECH COALITION**, 535 U.S. 234 (2002). In *The Free Speech Coalition*, the Court invalidated parts of the Child Pornography Prevention Act of 1996 (CPPA) that prohibited "sexually explicit images that appear to depict minors but were produced without using any real children."

Before 1996, Congress defined child pornography as "images made using actual minors." In addition, § 2256(8)(B) of the 1996 Act prohibits "'any visual depiction, including any photograph, film, video, picture, or computer or computer-generated image or picture' that 'is, or appears to be, of a minor engaging in sexually explicit conduct.'" Its prohibition encompasses "'virtual child pornography,' which include computer-generated images."[24] Also

---

[24] "The statute also prohibits Hollywood movies, filmed without any child actors, if a jury believes an actor 'appears to be' a minor engaging in 'actual or simulated . . . sexual intercourse.'"

Section 2256(8)(C), which is not at issue, "prohibits a more common and lower tech means of creating virtual images, known as computer morphing. Rather than creating original images, pornographers can alter innocent pictures of real children so that the children appear to be engaged in sexual activity." Such images "implicate the interests of real children, and are in that sense closer to the images in" *New York v. Ferber*, casebook, p. 1422.

at issue, § 2256(8)(D) bans "any sexually explicit image that was 'advertised, promoted, presented, described, or distributed in such a manner that conveys the impression' it depicts 'a minor engaging in sexually explicit conduct.'" Under the CPPA, "[a] first offender may be imprisoned for 15 years," while a "repeat offender" may be imprisoned for 5–30 years.

Writing for the majority, Justice Kennedy found both §§ 2256(8)(B) and 2256(8)(D) "substantially overbroad." While the First Amendment does not protect "certain categories of speech, including defamation, incitement, obscenity, and pornography produced with real children," the regulations at issue involved none of these. The CPPA proscribed materials that did not meet the three-part test for obscenity set forth in *Miller v. California*. [25] First, the materials "need not appeal to the prurient interest," as the CPPA banned all depictions "of sexually explicit activity, no matter how it is presented." Second, the images need not be patently offensive. For example, "[p]ictures of what appear to be 17-year-olds engaging in sexually explicit activity do not in every case contravene community standards." Additionally, the "CPPA prohibits speech despite its serious literary, artistic, political, or scientific value." Teenage sexuality "is a fact of modern society and has been a theme in art and literature throughout the ages." Moreover, age eighteen is "higher than the legal age for marriage in many States, as well as the age at which persons may consent to sexual relations." Finally, under the First Amendment, "a single explicit scene" does not determine a work's "artistic merit." Instead, the work must be considered "as a whole." In contrast, the CPPA punishes the possessor of a film containing "a single graphic depiction of sexual activity within the statutory definition" regardless of "the work's redeeming value."

In contrast to child pornography, "the CPPA prohibits speech that records no crime and creates no victims by its production. Virtual child pornography is not 'intrinsically related' to the sexual abuse of children." In contrast to *New York v. Ferber*, casebook, pp. 1422–1424, "harm does not necessarily follow from the speech, but depends upon some unqualified potential for subsequent criminal acts."

Importantly, "*Ferber's* judgment about child pornography was based upon how it was made, not on what it communicated." Moreover, *Ferber* recognized that some child pornography "might have significant value." *Ferber* itself said, "[i]f it were necessary for literary or artistic value," a film could use "a person over the statutory age who perhaps looked younger" or a "[s]imulation." As such, § 2256(8)(B) "is inconsistent with *Miller,* and finds no support in *Ferber*."

The Government, however, sought to justify Section 2256(8)(B) in other ways. Rejecting the argument that "the CPPA is necessary because pedophiles may use virtual child pornography to seduce children," Justice Kennedy noted that "[t]here are many things innocent in themselves, such as cartoons, video games, and candy, that might be used for immoral

---

[25] 413 U.S. 15 (1973), casebook, p.1409.

purposes, yet we would not expect those to be prohibited because they can be misused." Second, the Government submits that "virtual child pornography whets the appetites of pedophiles and encourages them to engage in illegal conduct." However, "[t]he mere tendency of speech to encourage unlawful acts is not a sufficient reason for banning it." Third, Justice Kennedy rejected the argument that virtual images are indistinguishable from real ones; "[i]f virtual images were identical to illegal child pornography, the illegal images would be driven from the market by the indistinguishable substitutes. Few pornographers would risk prosecution by abusing real children if fictional, computerized images would suffice."

Fourth, Justice Kennedy rejected the Government's argument that "producing images by using computer imaging makes it very difficult for it to prosecute those who produce pornography by using real children." This argument "turns the First Amendment upside down," as "Government may not suppress lawful speech as the means to suppress unlawful speech." Section 2256(8)(B) is overbroad because the First Amendment "prohibits the Government from banning unprotected speech if a substantial amount of protected speech is prohibited or chilled in the process."

Justice Kennedy also struck down § 2256(8)(D) of the CPPA. "[P]andering may be relevant, as an evidentiary matter, to the question whether particular materials are obscene." However, § 2256(8)(D) is "substantially overbroad" because it punishes "possession of material described, or pandered, as child pornography by someone earlier in the distribution chain."

Justice Thomas concurred in the judgment. He noted that "technology may evolve to the point where it becomes impossible to enforce actual child pornography laws because the Government cannot prove that certain pornographic images are of real children." At that time, "the Government may well have a compelling interest in barring or otherwise regulating some narrow category of 'lawful speech' in order to enforce effectively laws against pornography made through the abuse of real children."

Chief Justice Rehnquist, with whom Justice Scalia joins in part, dissenting, agreed with Justice O'Connor that "Congress has a compelling interest in ensuring the ability to enforce prohibitions of actual child pornography, and we should defer to its findings that rapidly advancing technology soon will make it all but impossible to do so."[26] Chief Justice Rehnquist also argued that "the CPPA can be limited so as not to reach any material that was not already unprotected before."[27] The Chief Justice would also uphold the pandering prohibition, but limit its reach to the panderer. He concluded

---

[26] Chief Justice Rehnquist also agrees with Justice O'Connor that "serious First Amendment concerns would arise were the Government ever to prosecute someone for simple distribution or possession of a film with literary or artistic value, such as 'Traffic' or 'American Beauty.'"

[27] "The CPPA's definition of 'sexually explicit conduct' is quite explicit in this regard. It makes clear that the statute only reaches 'visual depictions' of: 'actual or simulated . . . sexual intercourse, including genital-genital, oral-genital, anal-genital, or oral-anal, whether between persons of the same or opposite sex; . . . bestiality; . . . masturbation; . . . sadistic or masochistic abuse; . . . or lascivious exhibition of the genitals or pubic area of any person.'"

that "while potentially impermissible applications of the CPPA may exist, I doubt that they would be 'substantial . . . in relation to the statute's plainly legitimate sweep.'" The CPPA focuses on "computer-generated images that are virtually indistinguishable from real children engaged in sexually explicit conduct. The statute need not be read to do any more than precisely this."

Justice O'Connor filed an opinion, in which she concurred in part, and dissented in part. In Part I of her opinion, Justice O'Connor agreed with the majority that the pandering ban of § 2256(8)(D) "fails strict scrutiny." In Part I, Justice O'Connor also agreed with the Court that the CPPA's ban on "pornographic images of adults that look like children" is overbroad. However, Justice O'Connor would invalidate § 2256(8)(B) "only insofar as it is applied to the class of youthful-adult pornography."

In Part II of her opinion, Justice O'Connor, joined by Chief Justice Rehnquist and Justice Scalia, disagreed that "the CPPA's prohibition of virtual-child pornography is overbroad." This ban is supported by the long-recognized "compelling interest in protecting our Nation's children," which is "supported by the CPPA's ban on virtual-child pornography." Specifically, "[s]uch images whet the appetites of child molesters . . . who may use the images to seduce young children." Justice O'Connor also believed "that defendants indicted for the production, distribution, or possession of actual-child pornography may evade liability by claiming that the images attributed to them are in fact computer-generated." Because of "rapid" advances in "computer-graphics technology, the Government's concern is reasonable."

Justice O'Connor read the statute "only to bar images that are virtually indistinguishable from actual children," which would render its ban "narrowly tailored, but would also assuage any fears that the 'appears to be . . . of a minor' language is vague." Litigants challenging as overbroad a regulation, which is narrowly tailored to a compelling state interest, "bear the heavy burden of demonstrating that the regulation forbids a substantial amount of valuable or harmless speech." The challengers here "provide no examples of films or other materials that are wholly computer-generated and contain images that 'appear to be . . . of minors' engaging in indecent conduct, but that have serious value or do not facilitate child abuse. Their overbreadth challenge therefore fails."

Page 1425: [Insert the following after Note (2)]

Community Standards for Internet? In *Ashcroft v. American Civil Liberties Union*, 535 U.S. 564 (2002), the Court rejected a facial challenge against the Child Online Protection Act's (COPA) reliance on "community standards" to identify "material that is harmful to minors." Congress initially "attempted to protect children from exposure to pornographic material on the Internet" through the Communications Decency Act of 1996 (CDA). However, *Reno v. American Civil Liberties Union*, casebook, p. 1115, held the Act overbroad. Writing for a majority of the Court, Justice Thomas noted that following the *Reno* decision, Congress passed the more limited

Child Online Protection Act (COPA). First, unlike the CDA which applied to all Internet communications including e-mails, COPA applies only to displays on the World Wide Web. Second, "unlike the CDA, COPA covers only communications made for 'commercial purposes.'" Finally, unlike the CDA's prohibition of "indecent" and "patently offensive" communications, COPA restricts only the narrower category of "material that is harmful to minors," as defined in *Miller v. California,* casebook, p. 1409. COPA also allows affirmative defenses, if an individual "in good faith, has restricted access by minors to material that is harmful to minors — (A) by requiring the use of a credit card, debit account, adult access code, or adult personal identification number; (B) by accepting a digital certificate that verifies age; or (C) by any other reasonable measures that are feasible under available technology." Violating COPA is a crime punishable by a maximum prison sentence of 6 months or maximum fine of $50,000.

Writing for a plurality of four, Justice Thomas noted that unlike CDA, COPA only bans works that "'depict, describe, or represent, in a manner patently offensive with respect to minors,' particular sexual acts or parts of the anatomy, they must also be designed to appeal to the prurient interests of minors, and 'taken as a whole, lack serious literary, artistic, political, or scientific value for minors.'" Moreover, adopting *Miller's* approach, COPA adopts a national standard to assess serious value.

Writing for a plurality of three, Justice Thomas concluded that when a statute is sufficiently narrowed by "'serious value'" and "'prurient interest'" inquiries, both *Hamling v. United States*, casebook p. 1419, and *Sable Communications of Cal., Inc. v. FCC*, casebook pp. 1195–1196, hold that "requiring a speaker disseminating material to a national audience to observe varying community standards does not violate the First Amendment." The fact that Internet publishers cannot control where their materials go does not change this result. Publication over the Internet is necessarily national. When a publisher sends material to a community, it must "abide by that community's standards," even if the publisher "decides to distribute its material to every community in the Nation." If the application of community standards to the Web rendered COPA unconstitutional, *Miller* also could not apply to the Web; however, *Reno* held that "the application of the CDA to obscene speech was constitutional."

Writing for a majority, Justice Thomas held that "COPA's reliance on community standards to identify 'material that is harmful to minors' does not *by itself* render the statute substantially overbroad." The Court did not express "any view as to whether COPA suffers from substantial overbreadth for other reasons, including whether the statute is unconstitutionally vague, or whether the District Court correctly concluded that the statute likely will not survive strict scrutiny."

Concurring in part and concurring in the judgment, Justice O'Connor would adopt "a national standard for defining obscenity on the Internet." Concurring in part and concurring in the judgment, Justice Breyer also would adopt a "nationally uniform adult-based standard." Application of this standard by different local juries does not violate the First Amendment.

Justice Kennedy concurred in the judgment, joined by Justices Souter and Ginsburg. "In order to discern whether the variation creates substantial overbreadth," it was "necessary to know what speech COPA regulates and what community standards it invokes." Justice Stevens dissented.

[2]—Procedural Issues in Obscenity Cases — "Prior Restraints" and Seizure of Materials

Page 1429: [Insert to Note (1)]

(b) *Prompt Judicial Review.* **LITTLETON v. Z.J. GIFTS**, 541 U.S. 774 (2004). In *Littleton v. Z.J. Gifts*, the Court upheld a city ordinance requiring a license for adult businesses. The ordinance set forth "eight specific circumstances" which require "the city to deny a license." License denials may be appealed to the state district court. Rather than apply for a license, Z.J. Gifts, D-4 mounted a facial challenge, claiming that the ordinance failed to provide for prompt judicial review. In response to the city's defenses of the law, the Court said that *Freedman v. Maryland* and *FW/PBS, Inc. v. City of Dallas* (*see* casebook p. 1428) requires not only prompt access to judicial review, but also " 'prompt judicial *determination*' " of the validity of denying a license to an adult business. Nevertheless, the Court held that state law did provide for a "prompt judicial determination."

Writing for the majority, Justice Breyer explained that "ordinary court procedural rules and practices, in Colorado as elsewhere," allow courts to accelerate the review process to sufficiently "avoid delay-related First Amendment harm." Unlike *Freedman* , the instant ordinance is not designed to censor, but instead "applies reasonable objective, nondiscriminatory criteria."

Z.J. Gifts did not suffer any judicial delay, but merely challenged the law on its face. "Where (as here and as in *FW/PBS*) the regulation simply conditions the operation of an adult business on compliance with neutral and nondiscretionary content, an adult business is not entitled to an unusually speedy judicial decision of the *Freedman* type. Colorado's rules provide for a flexible system of review in which judges can reach a decision promptly in the ordinary case, while using their judicial power to prevent significant harm to First Amendment interests where circumstances require." Justice Breyer left open the possibility of an as applied challenge to address "special problems of undue delay." Justices Stevens and Souter each filed opinions concurring in part and concurring in the judgment. Justice Kennedy joined Justice Souter's opinion. Justice Scalia filed a separate opinion concurring in the judgment.

Chapter XVI

RELIGIOUS FREEDOM

§ 16.02 The Establishment Clause and Aid to Religious Institutions

[1]—Aid to Religious Schools

Page 1466: [Insert the following to the end of Note (2)]

But cf. Locke v. Davey, 540 U.S. 712 (2004) (denying a free exercise right to funding for degrees in devotional theology even though the state provides such funding for non-devotional theology degree programs).

Page 1486: [Insert the following after *Guy Mitchell v. Mary L. Helms*]

ZELMAN v. SIMMONS–HARRIS

536 U.S. 639, 122 S. Ct. 2460, 153 L. Ed. 2d 604 (2002)

CHIEF JUSTICE REHNQUIST delivered the opinion of the Court.

The State of Ohio has established a pilot program designed to provide educational choices to families with children who reside in the Cleveland City School District. The question presented is whether this program offends the Establishment Clause of the United States Constitution. We hold that it does not.

There are more than 75,000 children enrolled in the Cleveland City School District. The majority of these children are from low-income and minority families. Few of these families enjoy the means to send their children to any school other than an inner-city public school. For more than a generation, however, Cleveland's public schools have been among the worst performing public schools in the Nation. In 1995, a Federal District Court declared a "crisis of magnitude" and placed the entire Cleveland school district under state control. *See Reed v. Rhodes*, 1 F. Supp. 2d 705. Shortly thereafter, the state auditor found that Cleveland's public schools were in the midst of a "crisis that is perhaps unprecedented in the history of American education." Cleveland City School District Performance Audit 2–1 (Mar. 1996). The district had failed to meet any of the 18 state standards for minimal acceptable performance. Only 1 in 10 ninth graders could pass a basic proficiency examination, and students at all levels performed at a dismal rate compared with students in other Ohio public schools. More than two-thirds of high school students either dropped or failed out before graduation. Of those students who managed to reach their senior year, one of every four still failed to graduate. Of those students who did graduate, few could read, write, or compute at levels comparable to their counterparts in other cities.

It is against this backdrop that Ohio enacted, among other initiatives, its Pilot Project Scholarship Program, Ohio Rev. Code Ann. §§ 3313.974–3313.979 (Anderson 1999 and Supp. 2000) (program). The program provides financial assistance to families in any Ohio school district that is or has been "under federal court order requiring supervision and operational management of the district by the state superintendent." Cleveland is the only Ohio school district to fall within that category.

The program provides two basic kinds of assistance to parents of children in a covered district. First, the program provides tuition aid for students in kindergarten through third grade, expanding each year through eighth grade, to attend a participating public or private school of their parent's choosing. Second, the program provides tutorial aid for students who choose to remain enrolled in public school.

The tuition aid portion of the program is designed to provide educational choices to parents who reside in a covered district. Any private school, whether religious or nonreligious, may participate in the program and accept program students so long as the school is located within the boundaries of a covered district and meets statewide educational standards. Participating private schools must agree not to discriminate on the basis of race, religion, or ethnic background, or to "advocate or foster unlawful behavior or teach hatred of any person or group on the basis of race, ethnicity, national origin, or religion." Any public school located in a school district adjacent to the covered district may also participate in the program. Adjacent public schools are eligible to receive a $2,250 tuition grant for each program student accepted in addition to the full amount of per-pupil state funding attributable to each additional student. All participating schools, whether public or private, are required to accept students in accordance with rules and procedures established by the state superintendent.

Tuition aid is distributed to parents according to financial need. Families with incomes below 200% of the poverty line are given priority and are eligible to receive 90% of private school tuition up to $2,250. For these lowest-income families, participating private schools may not charge a parental co-payment greater than $250. For all other families, the program pays 75% of tuition costs, up to $1,875, with no co-payment cap. These families receive tuition aid only if the number of available scholarships exceeds the number of low-income children who choose to participate.[1] . . . If parents choose a private school, checks are made payable to the parents who then endorse the checks over to the chosen school.

The tutorial aid portion of the program provides tutorial assistance through grants to any student in a covered district who chooses to remain

---

[1] [Court's footnote 2] The number of available scholarships per covered district is determined annually by the Ohio Superintendent for Public Instruction.

in public school. Parents arrange for registered tutors to provide assistance to their children and then submit bills for those services to the State for payment. Students from low-income families receive 90% of the amount charged for such assistance up to $360. All other students receive 75% of that amount. The number of tutorial assistance grants offered to students in a covered district must equal the number of tuition aid scholarships provided to students enrolled at participating private or adjacent public schools.

The program has been in operation within the Cleveland City School District since the 1996–1997 school year. In the 1999–2000 school year, 56 private schools participated in the program, 46 (or 82%) of which had a religious affiliation. None of the public schools in districts adjacent to Cleveland have elected to participate. More than 3,700 students participated in the scholarship program, most of whom (96%) enrolled in religiously affiliated schools. Sixty percent of these students were from families at or below the poverty line. In the 1998–1999 school year, approximately 1,400 Cleveland public school students received tutorial aid. This number was expected to double during the 1999–2000 school year.

The program is part of a broader undertaking by the State to enhance the educational options of Cleveland's schoolchildren in response to the 1995 takeover. That undertaking includes programs governing community and magnet schools. Community schools are funded under state law but are run by their own school boards, not by local school districts. These schools enjoy academic independence to hire their own teachers and to determine their own curriculum. They can have no religious affiliation and are required to accept students by lottery. During the 1999–2000 school year, there were 10 start-up community schools in the Cleveland City School District with more than 1,900 students enrolled. For each child enrolled in a community school, the school receives state funding of $4,518, twice the funding a participating program school may receive.

Magnet schools are public schools operated by a local school board that emphasize a particular subject area, teaching method, or service to students. For each student enrolled in a magnet school, the school district receives $7,746, including state funding of $4,167, the same amount received per student enrolled at a traditional public school. As of 1999, parents in Cleveland were able to choose from among 23 magnet schools, which together enrolled more than 13,000 students in kindergarten through eighth grade. . . .

. . . In December 1999, the District Court granted summary judgment for respondents. 72 F. Supp. 2d 834. In December 2000, a divided panel of the Court of Appeals affirmed the judgment of the District Court, finding that the program had the "primary effect" of advancing religion. . . . 234 F.3d 945 (CA6). . . .

The Establishment Clause of the First Amendment, applied to the States through the Fourteenth Amendment, prevents a State from enacting laws that have the "purpose" or "effect" of advancing or inhibiting religion.

Agostini v. Felton, 521 U.S. 203 (1997). . . . There is no dispute that the program challenged here was enacted for the valid secular purpose of providing educational assistance to poor children in a demonstrably failing public school system. Thus, the question presented is whether the Ohio program nonetheless has the forbidden "effect" of advancing or inhibiting religion.

To answer that question, our decisions have drawn a consistent distinction between government programs that provide aid directly to religious schools, *Mitchell v. Helms,* 530 U.S. 793, 810 (2000) (plurality opinion); *id.* at 841–844 (O'Connor, J., concurring in judgment); *Agostini, supra,* at 225–227; and programs of true private choice, in which government aid reaches religious schools only as a result of the genuine and independent choices of private individuals, *Mueller v. Allen,* 463 U.S. 388 (1983); *Witters v. Washington Dept. of Servs. for Blind*, 474 U.S. 481 (1986); *Zobrest v. Catalina Foothills School Dist.,* 509 U.S. 1 (1993). While our jurisprudence with respect to the constitutionality of direct aid programs has "changed significantly" over the past two decades, *Agostini, supra,* at 236, our jurisprudence with respect to true private choice programs has remained consistent and unbroken. Three times we have confronted Establishment Clause challenges to neutral government programs that provide aid directly to a broad class of individuals, who, in turn, direct the aid to religious schools or institutions of their own choosing. Three times we have rejected such challenges.

In *Mueller*, we rejected an Establishment Clause challenge to a Minnesota program authorizing tax deductions for various educational expenses, including private school tuition costs, even though the great majority of the program's beneficiaries (96%) were parents of children in religious schools. . . .

In *Witters*, we used identical reasoning to reject an Establishment Clause challenge to a vocational scholarship program that provided tuition aid to a student studying at a religious institution to become a pastor. . . .

Five Members of the Court, in separate opinions, emphasized the general rule from *Mueller* that the amount of government aid channeled to religious institutions by individual aid recipients was not relevant to the constitutional inquiry. . . .

Finally, in *Zobrest*, we applied *Mueller* and *Witters* to reject an Establishment Clause challenge to a federal program that permitted sign-language interpreters to assist deaf children enrolled in religious schools. . . .

. . . Our focus again was on neutrality and the principle of private choice, not on the number of program beneficiaries attending religious schools. . . .

Mueller, Witters, and *Zobrest* thus make clear that where a government aid program is neutral with respect to religion, and provides assistance directly to a broad class of citizens who, in turn, direct government aid to religious schools wholly as a result of their own genuine and independent private choice, the program is not readily subject to challenge under the

Establishment Clause. A program that shares these features permits government aid to reach religious institutions only by way of the deliberate choices of numerous individual recipients. The incidental advancement of a religious mission, or the perceived endorsement of a religious message, is reasonably attributable to the individual recipient, not to the government, whose role ends with the disbursement of benefits. . . .

We believe that the program challenged here is a program of true private choice, consistent with *Mueller*, *Witters*, and *Zobrest*, and thus constitutional. As was true in those cases, the Ohio program is neutral in all respects toward religion. It is part of a general and multifaceted undertaking by the State of Ohio to provide educational opportunities to the children of a failed school district. It confers educational assistance directly to a broad class of individuals defined without reference to religion. . . . The program permits the participation of *all* schools within the district, religious or nonreligious. Adjacent public schools also may participate and have a financial incentive to do so. . . .

There are no "financial incentives" that "skew" the program toward religious schools. *Witters*, *supra*, at 487–488. Such incentives "[are] not present . . . where the aid is allocated on the basis of neutral, secular criteria that neither favor nor disfavor religion, and is made available to both religious and secular beneficiaries on a nondiscriminatory basis." *Agostini*, *supra*, at 231. The program here in fact creates financial *dis*incentives for religious schools, with private schools receiving only half the government assistance given to community schools and one-third the assistance given to magnet schools. Adjacent public schools, should any choose to accept program students, are also eligible to receive two to three times the state funding of a private religious school. Families too have a financial disincentive to choose a private religious school over other schools. Parents that choose to participate in the scholarship program and then to enroll their children in a private school (religious or nonreligious) must copay a portion of the school's tuition. Families that choose a community school, magnet school, or traditional public school pay nothing. Although such features of the program are not necessary to its constitutionality, they clearly dispel the claim that the program "creates . . . financial incentives for parents to choose a sectarian school." *Zobrest,* 509 U.S. at 10.

Respondents suggest that even without a financial incentive for parents to choose a religious school, the program creates a "public perception that the State is endorsing religious practices and beliefs." But we have repeatedly recognized that no reasonable observer would think a neutral program of private choice, where state aid reaches religious schools solely as a result of the numerous independent decisions of private individuals, carries with it the *imprimatur* of government endorsement. . . . Any objective observer familiar with the full history and context of the Ohio program would reasonably view it as one aspect of a broader undertaking to assist poor children in failed schools, not as an endorsement of religious schooling in general.

. . . The Establishment Clause question is whether Ohio is coercing parents into sending their children to religious schools, and that question must be answered by evaluating *all* options Ohio provides Cleveland schoolchildren, only one of which is to obtain a program scholarship and then choose a religious school.

Justice Souter speculates that because more private religious schools currently participate in the program, the program itself must somehow discourage the participation of private nonreligious schools.[2] But Cleveland's preponderance of religiously affiliated private schools certainly did not arise as a result of the program; it is a phenomenon common to many American cities. . . . It is true that 82% of Cleveland's participating private schools are religious schools, but it is also true that 81% of private schools in Ohio are religious schools. To attribute constitutional significance to this figure, moreover, would lead to the absurd result that a neutral school-choice program might be permissible in some parts of Ohio, such as Columbus, where a lower percentage of private schools are religious schools, but not in inner-city Cleveland, where Ohio has deemed such programs most sorely needed, but where the preponderance of religious schools happens to be greater. . . .

Respondents and Justice Souter claim that even if we do not focus on the number of participating schools that are religious schools, we should attach constitutional significance to the fact that 96% of scholarship recipients have enrolled in religious schools. . . . We need not consider this argument in detail, since it was flatly rejected in *Mueller*, where we found it irrelevant that 96% of parents taking deductions for tuition expenses paid tuition at religious schools. Indeed, we have recently found it irrelevant even to the constitutionality of a direct aid program that a vast majority of program benefits went to religious schools. *See Agostini.* . . . The constitutionality of a neutral educational aid program simply does not turn on whether and why, in a particular area, at a particular time, most private schools are run by religious organizations, or most recipients choose to use the aid at a religious school. . . .

This point is aptly illustrated here. The 96% figure upon which respondents and Justice Souter rely discounts entirely (1) the more than 1,900 Cleveland children enrolled in alternative community schools, (2) the more than 13,000 children enrolled in alternative magnet schools, and (3) the more than 1,400 children enrolled in traditional public schools with tutorial assistance. Including some or all of these children in the denominator of children enrolled in nontraditional schools during the 1999–2000 school

---

[2] [Court's footnote 4] Justice Souter appears to base this claim on the unfounded assumption that capping the amount of tuition charged to low-income students (at $2,500) favors participation by religious schools. But elsewhere he claims that the program spends *too much* money on private schools. . . . Indeed, the actual operation of the program refutes Justice Souter's argument that few but religious schools can afford to participate: Ten secular private schools operated within the Cleveland City School District when the program was adopted. . . . And while no religious schools have been created in response to the program, several *nonreligious* schools have been created. . . .

year drops the percentage enrolled in religious schools from 96% to under 20%. *See also* J. Greene, The Racial, Economic, and Religious Context of Parental Choice in Cleveland 11, Table 4 (Oct. 8, 1999), App. 217a (reporting that only 16.5% of nontraditional schoolchildren in Cleveland choose religious schools). The 96% figure also represents but a snapshot of one particular school year. In the 1997–1998 school year, by contrast, only 78% of scholarship recipients attended religious schools. The difference was attributable to two private nonreligious schools that had accepted 15% of all scholarship students electing instead to register as community schools, in light of larger per-pupil funding for community schools and the uncertain future of the scholarship program generated by this litigation. . . .[3]

Respondents finally claim that we should look to *Committee for Public Ed. & Religious Liberty v. Nyquist,* 413 U.S. 756 (1973), to decide these cases. We disagree for two reasons. First, the program in *Nyquist* was quite different from the program challenged here. *Nyquist* involved a New York program that gave a package of benefits exclusively to private schools and the parents of private school enrollees. Although the program was enacted for ostensibly secular purposes, we found that its "function" was "*unmistakably* to provide desired financial support for nonpublic, sectarian institutions." Its genesis, we said, was that private religious schools faced "increasingly grave fiscal problems." The program thus provided direct money grants to religious schools. It provided tax benefits "unrelated to the amount of money actually expended by any parent on tuition," ensuring a windfall to parents of children in religious schools. It similarly provided tuition reimbursements designed explicitly to "offer . . . an incentive to parents to send their children to sectarian schools." Indeed, the program flatly prohibited the participation of any public school, or parent of any public school enrollee.

Second, . . . we expressly reserved judgment with respect to "a case involving some form of public assistance (*e.g.*, scholarships) made available generally without regard to the sectarian-nonsectarian, or public-nonpublic nature of the institution benefitted." . . . To the extent the scope of *Nyquist* has remained an open question in light of these later decisions, we now hold that *Nyquist* does not govern neutral educational assistance programs that, like the program here, offer aid directly to a broad class of individual recipients defined without regard to religion.[4]

---

[3] [Court's footnote 5] . . . Experience in Milwaukee, which since 1991 has operated an educational choice program similar to the Ohio program, demonstrates that the mix of participating schools fluctuates significantly from year to year. . . . Since the Wisconsin Supreme Court declared the Milwaukee program constitutional in 1998, *Jackson v. Benson,* 218 Wis. 2d 835 (1998), several nonreligious private schools have entered the Milwaukee market, and now represent 32% of all participating schools. . . .

[4] [Court's footnote 7] Justice Breyer would raise the invisible specters of "divisiveness" and "religious strife" to find the program unconstitutional. It is unclear exactly what sort of principle Justice Breyer has in mind, considering that the program has ignited no "divisiveness" or "strife" other than this litigation. . . . We quite rightly have rejected the claim that some speculative potential for divisiveness bears on the constitutionality of educational aid programs. . . .

In sum, the Ohio program is entirely neutral with respect to religion. It provides benefits directly to a wide spectrum of individuals, defined only by financial need and residence in a particular school district. It permits such individuals to exercise genuine choice among options public and private, secular and religious. . . .

JUSTICE O'CONNOR, concurring. . . .

II

. . . The Court's opinion . . . clarifies the basic inquiry when trying to determine whether a program that distributes aid to beneficiaries, rather than directly to service providers, has the primary effect of advancing or inhibiting religion, *Lemon v. Kurtzman*, or, as I have put it, of "endorsing or disapproving . . . religion," *Lynch v. Donnelly* (concurring opinion) . . . .

III

. . . Justice Souter rejects the Court's notion of neutrality, proposing that the neutrality of a program should be gauged not by the opportunities it presents but rather by its effects. . . . But Justice Souter's notion of neutrality is inconsistent with that in our case law. As we put it in *Agostini*, government aid must be "made available to both religious and secular beneficiaries on a nondiscriminatory basis." 521 U.S. at 231 . . . .

To support his hunch about the effect of the cap on tuition under the voucher program, Justice Souter cites national data to suggest that, on average, Catholic schools have a cost advantage over other types of schools. Even if national statistics were relevant for evaluating the Cleveland program, Justice Souter ignores evidence which suggests that, at a national level, nonreligious private schools may target a market for different, if not higher, quality of education. . . .

Ultimately, Justice Souter relies on very narrow data to draw rather broad conclusions. One year of poor test scores at four community schools targeted at the most challenged students from the inner city says little about the value of those schools, let alone the quality of the 6 other community schools and 24 magnet schools in Cleveland. Justice Souter's use of statistics confirms the Court's wisdom in refusing to consider them when assessing the Cleveland program's constitutionality. What appears to motivate Justice Souter's analysis is a desire for a limiting principle to rule out certain nonreligious schools as alternatives to religious schools in the voucher program. But the goal of the Court's Establishment Clause jurisprudence is to determine whether, after the Cleveland voucher program was enacted, parents were free to direct state educational aid in either a nonreligious or religious direction. That inquiry requires an evaluation of all reasonable educational options. . . .

JUSTICE THOMAS, concurring.

Frederick Douglass once said that "education . . . means emancipation. It means light and liberty. It means the uplifting of the soul of man into

the glorious light of truth, the light by which men can only be made free."
Today many of our inner-city public schools deny emancipation to urban
minority students. Despite this Court's observation nearly 50 years ago in
Brown v. Board of Education, that "it is doubtful that any child may
reasonably be expected to succeed in life if he is denied the opportunity of
an education," 347 U.S. 483, 493 (1954), urban children have been forced
into a system that continually fails them. . . . Besieged by escalating
financial problems and declining academic achievement, the Cleveland City
School District was in the midst of an academic emergency when Ohio
enacted its scholarship program.

I

. . . The Establishment Clause originally protected States, and by
extension their citizens, from the imposition of an established religion by
the Federal Government. Whether and how this Clause should constrain
state action under the Fourteenth Amendment is a more difficult question.

The Fourteenth Amendment fundamentally restructured the relationship
between individuals and the States. . . .

Consequently, in the context of the Establishment Clause, it may well
be that state action should be evaluated on different terms than similar
action by the Federal Government. "States, while bound to observe strict
neutrality, should be freer to experiment with involvement [in religion] —
on a neutral basis — than the Federal Government." *Walz v. Tax Comm'n
of City of New York,* 397 U.S. 664, 699 (1970) (Harlan, J., concurring). Thus,
while the Federal Government may "make no law respecting an establishment of religion," the States may pass laws that include or touch on
religious matters so long as these laws do not impede free exercise rights
or any other individual religious liberty interest.

II

. . . [T]he students at Cleveland's Catholic schools score significantly
higher on Ohio proficiency tests than students at Cleveland public schools.
Of Cleveland eighth graders taking the 1999 Ohio proficiency test, 95
percent in Catholic schools passed the reading test, whereas only 57 percent
in public schools passed. And 75 percent of Catholic school students passed
the math proficiency test, compared to only 22 percent of public school
students. But the success of religious and private schools is in the end
beside the point, because the State has a constitutional right to experiment
with a variety of different programs to promote educational opportunity. . . .

[T]he promise of public school education has failed poor inner-city blacks.
While in theory providing education to everyone, the quality of public
schools varies significantly across districts. Just as blacks supported public
education during Reconstruction, many blacks and other minorities now
support school choice programs because they provide the greatest

educational opportunities for their children in struggling communities. Opponents of the program raise formalistic concerns about the Establishment Clause but ignore the core purposes of the Fourteenth Amendment.

While the romanticized ideal of universal public education resonates with the cognoscenti who oppose vouchers, poor urban families just want the best education for their children, who will certainly need it to function in our high-tech and advanced society. . . . For instance, a black high school dropout earns just over $13,500, but with a high school degree the average income is almost $21,000. Blacks with a bachelor's degree have an average annual income of about $37,500, and $75,500 with a professional degree. . . .[5] The failure to provide education to poor urban children perpetuates a vicious cycle of poverty, dependence, criminality, and alienation that continues for the remainder of their lives. If society cannot end racial discrimination, at least it can arm minorities with the education to defend themselves from some of discrimination's effects.

Ten States have enacted some form of publicly funded private school choice as one means of raising the quality of education provided to underprivileged urban children. . . . Society's other solution to these educational failures is often to provide racial preferences in higher education. Such preferences, however, run afoul of the Fourteenth Amendment's prohibition against distinctions based on race. *See Plessy,* 163 U.S. at 555 (Harlan, J., dissenting). By contrast, school choice programs that involve religious schools appear unconstitutional only to those who would twist the Fourteenth Amendment against itself by expansively incorporating the Establishment Clause. . . .

JUSTICE STEVENS, dissenting.

Is a law that authorizes the use of public funds to pay for the indoctrination of thousands of grammar school children in particular religious faiths a "law respecting an establishment of religion" within the meaning of the First Amendment? In answering that question, I think we should ignore three factual matters that are discussed at length by my colleagues.

First, the severe educational crisis that confronted the Cleveland City School District when Ohio enacted its voucher program is not a matter that should affect our appraisal of its constitutionality. In the 1999–2000 school year, that program provided relief to less than five percent of the students enrolled in the district's schools. The solution to the disastrous conditions that prevented over 90 percent of the student body from meeting basic proficiency standards obviously required massive improvements unrelated to the voucher program. . . .

Second, the wide range of choices that have been made available to students *within the public school system* has no bearing on the question whether the State may pay the tuition for students who wish to reject public

---

[5] [Court's footnote 8] In 1997, approximately 68 percent of prisoners in state correctional institutions did not have a high school degree.

education entirely and attend private schools that will provide them with a sectarian education. . . .

Third, the voluntary character of the private choice to prefer a parochial education over an education in the public school system seems to me quite irrelevant to the question whether the government's choice to pay for religious indoctrination is constitutionally permissible. . ..

[T]he Court's decision is profoundly misguided. Admittedly, in reaching that conclusion I have been influenced by my understanding of the impact of religious strife on the decisions of our forbears to migrate to this continent, and on the decisions of neighbors in the Balkans, Northern Ireland, and the Middle East to mistrust one another. Whenever we remove a brick from the wall that was designed to separate religion and government, we increase the risk of religious strife and weaken the foundation of our democracy. . . .

JUSTICE SOUTER, with whom JUSTICE STEVENS, JUSTICE GINSBURG, and JUSTICE BREYER join, dissenting. . . .

Today . . . the majority holds that the Establishment Clause is not offended by Ohio's Pilot Project Scholarship Program, under which students may be eligible to receive as much as $2,250 in the form of tuition vouchers transferable to religious schools. . . . The money will thus pay for eligible students' instruction not only in secular subjects but in religion as well, in schools that can fairly be characterized as founded to teach religious doctrine and to imbue teaching in all subjects with a religious dimension. . . .

I

The majority's statements of Establishment Clause doctrine cannot be appreciated without some historical perspective on the Court's announced limitations on government aid to religious education, and its repeated repudiation of limits previously set. . . .

Viewed with the necessary generality, the cases can be categorized in three groups. In the period from 1947 to 1968, the basic principle of no aid to religion through school benefits was unquestioned. Thereafter for some 15 years, the Court termed its efforts as attempts to draw a line against aid that would be divertible to support the religious, as distinct from the secular, activity of an institutional beneficiary. Then, starting in 1983, concern with divertibility was gradually lost in favor of approving aid in amounts unlikely to afford substantial benefits to religious schools, when offered evenhandedly without regard to a recipient's religious character, and when channeled to a religious institution only by the genuinely free choice of some private individual. Now, the three stages are succeeded by a fourth, in which the substantial character of government aid is held to have no constitutional significance, and the espoused criteria of neutrality in offering aid, and private choice in directing it, are shown to be nothing but examples of verbal formalism.

A

Everson v. *Board of Ed. of Ewing,* [330 U.S. 1 (1947)], inaugurated the modern development of Establishment Clause doctrine. . . . [N]o Justice disagreed with the basic doctrinal principle already quoted, that "no tax in any amount . . . can be levied to support any religious activities or institutions, . . . whatever form they may adopt to teach . . . religion." *Id.* at 16 . . . .

B

. . . To avoid the entanglement, the Court's focus in the post[*Bd. of Educ. v. Allen,* 392 U.S. 236 (1968)] cases was on the principle of divertibility, on discerning when ostensibly secular government aid to religious schools was susceptible to religious uses. The greater the risk of diversion to religion (and the monitoring necessary to avoid it), the less legitimate the aid scheme was under the no-aid principle. On the one hand, the Court tried to be practical, and when the aid recipients were not so "pervasively sectarian" that their secular and religious functions were inextricably intertwined, the Court generally upheld aid earmarked for secular use. *See, e.g., Roemer v. Board of Public Works of Md.,* 426 U.S. 736 (1976); *Hunt v. McNair,* 413 U.S. 734 (1973); *Tilton v. Richardson,* 403 U.S. 672 (1971). But otherwise the principle of nondivertibility was enforced strictly. . . .

The fact that the Court's suspicion of divertibility reflected a concern with the substance of the no-aid principle is apparent in its rejection of stratagems invented to dodge it. In *Committee for Public Ed. & Religious Liberty v. Nyquist,* 413 U.S. 756 (1973), for example, the Court struck down a New York program of tuition grants for poor parents and tax deductions for more affluent ones who sent their children to private schools. The *Nyquist* Court dismissed warranties of a "statistical guarantee," that the scheme provided at most 15% of the total cost of an education at a religious school, *id.* at 787–788, which could presumably be matched to a secular 15% of a child's education at the school. . . .

C

Like all criteria requiring judicial assessment of risk, divertibility is an invitation to argument, but the object of the arguments provoked has always been a realistic assessment of facts aimed at respecting the principle of no aid. . . . *Mueller v. Allen,* 463 U.S. 388 (1983), however, . . . started down the road from realism to formalism.

The aid in *Mueller* was in substance indistinguishable from that in *Nyquist, see* 463 U.S. at 396–397, n.6, and both were substantively difficult to distinguish from aid directly to religious schools. . . .

To be sure, the aid in *Agostini* was systemic and arguably substantial, but . . . the majority there chose to view it as a bare "supplement." 521 U.S. at 229. And this was how the controlling opinion described the systemic aid in our most recent case, *Mitchell v. Helms,* 530 U.S. 793 (2000), as aid going merely to a "portion" of the religious schools' budgets, *id.* at 860 (O'Connor, J., concurring in judgment) . . . .

. . . [N]ot until today that substantiality of aid has clearly been rejected as irrelevant by a majority of this Court, just as it has not been until today that a majority, not a plurality, has held purely formal criteria to suffice for scrutinizing aid that ends up in the coffers of religious schools. . . .

II

Although it has taken half a century since *Everson* to reach the majority's twin standards of neutrality and free choice, the facts show that, in the majority's hands, even these criteria cannot convincingly legitimize the Ohio scheme.

A

Consider first the criterion of neutrality. As recently as two Terms ago, a majority of the Court recognized that neutrality conceived of as even-handedness toward aid recipients had never been treated as alone sufficient to satisfy the Establishment Clause, *Mitchell,* 530 U.S. at 838–839 (O'Connor, J., concurring in judgment); *id.* at 884 (Souter, J., dissenting) . . . . Today, however, the majority employs the neutrality criterion in a way that renders it impossible to understand. . . .

In order to apply the neutrality test, . . . [t]he majority looks not to the provisions for tuition vouchers, but to every provision for educational opportunity. . . .

The illogic is patent. If regular, public schools (which can get no voucher payments) "participate" in a voucher scheme with schools that can, and public expenditure is still predominantly on public schools, then the majority's reasoning would find neutrality in a scheme of vouchers available for private tuition in districts with no secular private schools at all. "Neutrality" as the majority employs the term is, literally, verbal and nothing more. . . .

B

The majority addresses the issue of choice the same way it addresses neutrality, by asking whether recipients or potential recipients of voucher aid have a choice of public schools among secular alternatives to religious schools. . . . The majority now has transformed this question about private choice in channeling aid into a question about selecting from examples of state spending (on education) including direct spending on magnet and community public schools that goes through no private hands and could never reach a religious school under any circumstance. . . .

. . . If "choice" is present whenever there is any educational alternative to the religious school to which vouchers can be endorsed, then there will always be a choice and the voucher can always be constitutional. . . . And because it is unlikely that any participating private religious school will enroll more pupils than the generally available public system, it will be easy to generate numbers suggesting that aid to religion is not the significant intent or effect of the voucher scheme. . . .

If, contrary to the majority, we ask the right question about genuine choice to use the vouchers, the answer shows that something is influencing choices in a way that aims the money in a religious direction: of 56 private schools in the district participating in the voucher program (only 53 of which accepted voucher students in 1999–2000), 46 of them are religious; 96.6% of all voucher recipients go to religious schools, only 3.4% to nonreligious ones. . . . Evidence shows . . . that almost two out of three families using vouchers to send their children to religious schools did not embrace the religion of those schools. The families made it clear they had not chosen the schools because they wished their children to be proselytized in a religion not their own, or in any religion, but because of educational opportunity.[6]

Even so, the fact that some 2,270 students chose to apply their vouchers to schools of other religions, might be consistent with true choice if the students "chose" their religious schools over a wide array of private nonreligious options, or if it could be shown generally that Ohio's program had no effect on educational choices and thus no impermissible effect of advancing religious education. But both possibilities are contrary to fact. First, even if all existing nonreligious private schools in Cleveland were willing to accept large numbers of voucher students, only a few more than the 129 currently enrolled in such schools would be able to attend, as the total enrollment at all nonreligious private schools in Cleveland for kindergarten through eighth grade is only 510 children, and there is no indication that these schools have many open seats. Second, the $2,500 cap that the program places on tuition for participating low-income pupils has the effect of curtailing the participation of nonreligious schools: "nonreligious schools with higher tuition (about $4,000) stated that they could afford to accommodate just a few voucher students." By comparison, the average tuition at participating Catholic schools in Cleveland in 1999–2000 was $1,592, almost $1,000 below the cap.

Of course, the obvious fix would be to increase the value of vouchers so that existing nonreligious private and non-Catholic religious schools would be able to enroll more voucher students, and to provide incentives for educators to create new such schools given that few presently exist. . . . And to get to that hypothetical point would require that such massive

---

6 [Court's footnote 12] When parents were surveyed as to their motives for enrolling their children in the voucher program, 96.4% cited a better education than available in the public schools, and 95% said their children's safety. When asked specifically in one study to identify the most important factor in selecting among participating private schools, 60% of parents mentioned academic quality, teacher quality, or the substance of what is taught (presumably secular); only 15% mentioned the religious affiliation of the school as even a consideration.

financial support be made available to religion as to disserve every objective of the Establishment Clause even more than the present scheme does.[7]

And contrary to the majority's assertion, public schools in adjacent districts hardly have a financial incentive to participate in the Ohio voucher program, and none has.[8]

III

A

. . . The scale of the aid to religious schools approved today is unprecedented. . . . Each measure has received attention in previous cases. . . . [T]he sheer quantity of aid, when delivered to a class of religious primary and secondary schools, was suspect on the theory that the greater the aid, the greater its proportion to a religious school's existing expenditures, and the greater the likelihood that public money was supporting religious as well as secular instruction. . . .

B

. . . [E]very objective underlying the prohibition of religious establishment is betrayed by this scheme, . . . the first being respect for freedom of conscience. Jefferson described it as the idea that no one "shall be compelled to . . . support any religious worship, place, or ministry whatsoever," A Bill for Establishing Religious Freedom, in 5 The Founders' Constitution 84 (P. Kurland & R. Lerner eds. 1987), even a "teacher of his own religious persuasion," *ibid.* . . .

As for the second objective, to save religion from its own corruption. . . .

. . . [A] condition of receiving government money under the program is that participating religious schools may not "discriminate on the basis of . . . religion," Ohio Rev. Code Ann. § 3313.976(A)(4) (West Supp. 2002), which means the school may not give admission preferences to children who are members of the patron faith; children of a parish are generally consigned to the same admission lotteries as non-believers. . . .

. . . [I]s there reason to wonder when dependence will become great enough to give the State of Ohio an effective veto over basic decisions on

---

[7] [Court's footnote 16] The majority notes that I argue both that the Ohio program is unconstitutional because the voucher amount is too low to create real private choice and that any greater expenditure would be unconstitutional as well. The majority is dead right about this, and there is no inconsistency here: any voucher program that satisfied the majority's requirement of "true private choice" would be even more egregiously unconstitutional than the current scheme due to the substantial amount of aid to religious teaching that would be required.

[8] [Court's footnote 17] As the Court points out, an out-of-district public school that participates will receive a $2,250 voucher for each Cleveland student on top of its normal state funding. The basic state funding, though, is a drop in the bucket as compared to the cost of educating that student, as much of the cost (at least in relatively affluent areas with presumptively better academic standards) is paid by local income and property taxes. . . .

the content of curriculums? A day will come when religious schools will learn what political leverage can do, just as Ohio's politicians are now getting a lesson in the leverage exercised by religion.

Increased voucher spending is not, however, the sole portent of growing regulation of religious practice in the school, for state mandates to moderate religious teaching may well be the most obvious response to the third concern behind the ban on establishment, its inextricable link with social conflict. As appropriations for religious subsidy rise, competition for the money will tap sectarian religion's capacity for discord. . . .

. . . Religious teaching at taxpayer expense simply cannot be cordoned from taxpayer politics, and every major religion currently espouses social positions that provoke intense opposition. Not all taxpaying Protestant citizens, for example, will be content to underwrite the teaching of the Roman Catholic Church condemning the death penalty. Nor will all of America's Muslims acquiesce in paying for the endorsement of the religious Zionism taught in many religious Jewish schools, which combines "a nationalistic sentiment" in support of Israel with a "deeply religious" element. Nor will every secular taxpayer be content to support Muslim views on differential treatment of the sexes, or, for that matter, to fund the espousal of a wife's obligation of obedience to her husband, presumably taught in any schools adopting the articles of faith of the Southern Baptist Convention. Views like these, and innumerable others, have been safe in the sectarian pulpits and classrooms of this Nation not only because the Free Exercise Clause protects them directly, but because the ban on supporting religious establishment has protected free exercise, by keeping it relatively private. . . .

If the divisiveness permitted by today's majority is to be avoided in the short term, it will be avoided only by action of the political branches at the state and national levels. Legislatures not driven to desperation by the problems of public education may be able to see the threat in vouchers negotiable in sectarian schools. . . .

. . . I hope that a future Court will reconsider today's dramatic departure from basic Establishment Clause principle.

JUSTICE BREYER, with whom JUSTICE STEVENS and JUSTICE SOUTER join, dissenting.

I write separately to emphasize the risk that publicly financed voucher programs pose in terms of religiously based social conflict. I do so because I believe that the Establishment Clause concern for protecting the Nation's social fabric from religious conflict poses an overriding obstacle to the implementation of this well-intentioned school voucher program. . . .

I

"The history of governmentally established religion, both in England and in this country, showed that whenever government had allied itself with one particular form of religion, the inevitable result had been that it had incurred the hatred, disrespect and even contempt of those who held contrary beliefs." [*Engel v. Vitale,* 370 U.S. 421 (1962)] . . . .

When it decided . . . 20th century Establishment Clause cases, the Court did not deny that an earlier American society might have found a less clear-cut church/state separation compatible with social tranquility. Indeed, historians point out that during the early years of the Republic, American schools — including the first public schools — were Protestant in character. Their students recited Protestant prayers, read the King James version of the Bible, and learned Protestant religious ideals. . . .

The 20th century Court was fully aware, however, that immigration and growth had changed American society dramatically since its early years. . . .

. . . Catholics sought equal government support for the education of their children in the form of aid for private Catholic schools. But the "Protestant position" on this matter, scholars report, "was that public schools must be 'nonsectarian' (which was usually understood to allow Bible reading and other Protestant observances) and public money must not support 'sectarian' schools (which in practical terms meant Catholic)." *Id.* at 301 . . . .

The upshot is the development of constitutional doctrine that reads the Establishment Clause as avoiding religious strife, *not* by providing every religion with an *equal opportunity* (say, to secure state funding or to pray in the public schools), but by drawing fairly clear lines of *separation* between church and state — at least where the heartland of religious belief, such as primary religious education, is at issue.

II

The principle underlying these cases — avoiding religiously based social conflict — remains of great concern. As religiously diverse as America had become when the Court decided its major 20th century Establishment Clause cases, we are exponentially more diverse today. . . .

. . . Why will different religions not become concerned about, and seek to influence, the criteria used to channel this money to religious schools? Why will they not want to examine the implementation of the programs that provide this money — to determine, for example, whether implementation has biased a program toward or against particular sects, or whether recipient religious schools are adequately fulfilling a program's criteria? . . .

In a society as religiously diverse as ours, the Court has recognized that we must rely on the Religion Clauses of the First Amendment to protect against religious strife, particularly when what is at issue is an area as central to religious belief as the shaping, through primary education, of the next generation's minds and spirits. . . .

III

. . . School voucher programs differ . . . in both *kind* and *degree* from aid programs upheld in the past. They differ in kind because they direct financing to a core function of the church: the teaching of religious truths to young children. . . .

Private schools that participate in Ohio's program, for example, recognize the importance of primary religious education, for they pronounce that their goals are to "communicate the gospel," "provide opportunities to . . . experience a faith community," "provide . . . for growth in prayer," and "provide instruction in religious truths and values." . . .

Vouchers also differ in *degree*. The aid programs recently upheld by the Court involved limited amounts of aid to religion. But the majority's analysis here appears to permit a considerable shift of taxpayer dollars from public secular schools to private religious schools. . . .

IV

. . . Parental choice cannot help the taxpayer who does not want to finance the religious education of children. It will not always help the parent who may see little real choice between inadequate nonsectarian public education and adequate education at a school whose religious teachings are contrary to his own. . . .

V

. . . In a society composed of many different religious creeds, I fear that this present departure from the Court's earlier understanding risks creating a form of religiously based conflict potentially harmful to the Nation's social fabric. . . .

§ 16.03   Government Support for Religious Practices

[2]—Religious Displays

Page 1530: [Insert the following after Note (2)]

VAN ORDEN v. PERRY

125 S. Ct. 2854 (2005)

CHIEF JUSTICE REHNQUIST delivered the opinion of the Court.

The question here is whether the Establishment Clause of the First Amendment allows the display of a monument inscribed with the Ten Commandments on the Texas State Capitol grounds. We hold that it does.

The 22 acres surrounding the Texas State Capitol contain 17 monuments and 21 historical markers commemorating the "people, ideals, and events

that compose Texan identity." Tex. H. Con. Res. 38, 77th Leg. (2001).[9] The
monolith challenged here stands 6-feet high and 3-feet wide. It is located
to the north of the Capitol building, between the Capitol and the Supreme
Court building. Its primary content is the text of the Ten Commandments.
An eagle grasping the American flag, an eye inside of a pyramid, and two
small tablets with what appears to be an ancient script are carved above
the text of the Ten Commandments. Below the text are two Stars of David
and the superimposed Greek letters Chi and Rho, which represent Christ.
The bottom of the monument bears the inscription "PRESENTED TO THE
PEOPLE AND YOUTH OF TEXAS BY THE FRATERNAL ORDER OF
EAGLES OF TEXAS 1961."

The legislative record surrounding the State's acceptance of the monument from the Eagles — a national social, civic, and patriotic organization
— is limited to legislative journal entries. After the monument was
accepted, the State selected a site for the monument based on the recommendation of the state organization responsible for maintaining the Capitol
grounds. The Eagles paid the cost of erecting the monument, the dedication
of which was presided over by two state legislators.

Petitioner Thomas Van Orden is a native Texan and a resident of
Austin. . . .

Forty years after the monument's erection and six years after Van Orden
began to encounter the monument frequently, he sued numerous state officials in their official capacities under Rev. Stat. § 1979, 42 U.S.C. § 1983,
seeking both a declaration that the monument's placement violates the
Establishment Clause and an injunction requiring its removal. After a bench
trial, the District Court held that the monument did not contravene the
Establishment Clause. It found that the State had a valid secular purpose
in recognizing and commending the Eagles for their efforts to reduce
juvenile delinquency. The District Court also determined that a reasonable
observer, mindful of the history, purpose, and context, would not conclude
that this passive monument conveyed the message that the State was seeking to endorse religion. The Court of Appeals affirmed the District Court's
holdings with respect to the monument's purpose and effect. 351 F.3d 173
(CA5 2003). We granted certiorari, 543 U.S. _____ (2004), and now affirm.

Our cases, Januslike, point in two directions in applying the Establishment Clause. One face looks toward the strong role played by religion and
religious traditions throughout our Nation's history. . . .

The other face looks toward the principle that governmental intervention
in religious matters can itself endanger religious freedom.

This case, like all Establishment Clause challenges, presents us with the
difficulty of respecting both faces. Our institutions presuppose a Supreme

---

9 [Court's footnote 1] The monuments are: Heroes of the Alamo, Hood's Brigade, Confederate
Soldiers, Volunteer Fireman, Terry's Texas Rangers, Texas Cowboy, Spanish-American War,
Texas National Guard, Ten Commandments, Tribute to Texas School Children, Texas Pioneer
Woman, The Boy Scouts' Statue of Liberty Replica, Pearl Harbor Veterans, Korean War
Veterans, Soldiers of World War I, Disabled Veterans, and Texas Peace Officers.

Being, yet these institutions must not press religious observances upon their citizens. One face looks to the past in acknowledgment of our Nation's heritage, while the other looks to the present in demanding a separation between church and state. Reconciling these two faces requires that we neither abdicate our responsibility to maintain a division between church and state nor evince a hostility to religion by disabling the government from in some ways recognizing our religious heritage[.] . . .

These two faces are evident in representative cases both upholding and invalidating laws under the Establishment Clause. Over the last 25 years, we have sometimes pointed to *Lemon v. Kurtzman*, 403 U.S. 602 (1971), as providing the governing test in Establishment Clause challenges. . . . Yet, just two years after *Lemon* was decided, we noted that the factors identified in *Lemon* serve as "no more than helpful signposts." *Hunt v. McNair*, 413 U.S. 734, 741 (1973). Many of our recent cases simply have not applied the *Lemon* test. *See, e.g., Zelman v. Simmons-Harris*, 536 U.S. 639 (2002); *Good News Club v. Milford Central School*, 533 U.S. 98 (2001). Others have applied it only after concluding that the challenged practice was invalid under a different Establishment Clause test.

Whatever may be the fate of the *Lemon* test in the larger scheme of Establishment Clause jurisprudence, we think it not useful in dealing with the sort of passive monument that Texas has erected on its Capitol grounds. Instead, our analysis is driven both by the nature of the monument and by our Nation's history.

As we explained in *Lynch v. Donnelly,* 465 U.S. 668 (1984): "There is an unbroken history of official acknowledgment by all three branches of government of the role of religion in American life from at least 1789." *Id.,* at 674. For example, both Houses passed resolutions in 1789 asking President George Washington to issue a Thanksgiving Day Proclamation to "recommend to the people of the United States a day of public thanksgiving and prayer, to be observed by acknowledging, with grateful hearts, the many and signal favors of Almighty God." 1 Annals of Cong. 90, 914. President Washington's proclamation directly attributed to the Supreme Being the foundations and successes of our young Nation[.] . . .

In this case we are faced with a display of the Ten Commandments on government property outside the Texas State Capitol. Such acknowledgments of the role played by the Ten Commandments in our Nation's heritage are common throughout America. We need only look within our own Courtroom. Since 1935, Moses has stood, holding two tablets that reveal portions of the Ten Commandments written in Hebrew, among other lawgivers in the south frieze. Representations of the Ten Commandments adorn the metal gates lining the north and south sides of the Courtroom as well as the doors leading into the Courtroom. Moses also sits on the exterior east facade of the building holding the Ten Commandments tablets.

Similar acknowledgments can be seen throughout a visitor's tour of our Nation's Capital. For example, a large statue of Moses holding the Ten Commandments, alongside a statue of the Apostle Paul, has overlooked the rotunda of the Library of Congress' Jefferson Building since 1897. And the Jefferson Building's Great Reading Room contains a sculpture of a woman beside the Ten Commandments with a quote above her from the Old Testament (Micah 6:8). A medallion with two tablets depicting the Ten Commandments decorates the floor of the National Archives. Inside the Department of Justice, a statue entitled "The Spirit of Law" has two tablets representing the Ten Commandments lying at its feet. In front of the Ronald Reagan Building is another sculpture that includes a depiction of the Ten Commandments. So too a 24-foot-tall sculpture, depicting, among other things, the Ten Commandments and a cross, stands outside the federal courthouse that houses both the Court of Appeals and the District Court for the District of Columbia. Moses is also prominently featured in the Chamber of the United States House of Representatives.[10]

. . . The Executive and Legislative Branches have also acknowledged the historical role of the Ten Commandments. . . .

Of course, the Ten Commandments are religious — they were so viewed at their inception and so remain. The monument, therefore, has religious significance. According to Judeo-Christian belief, the Ten Commandments were given to Moses by God on Mt. Sinai. But Moses was a lawgiver as well as a religious leader. And the Ten Commandments have an undeniable historical meaning, as the foregoing examples demonstrate. Simply having religious content or promoting a message consistent with a religious doctrine does not run afoul of the Establishment Clause. *See Lynch v. Donnelly*, 465 U.S., at 680, 687; *Marsh v. Chambers*, 463 U.S., at 792; *McGowan v. Maryland, supra*, at 437–440; *Walz v. Tax Comm'n of City of New York*, 397 U.S. 664, 676–678 (1970).

There are, of course, limits to the display of religious messages or symbols. For example, we held unconstitutional a Kentucky statute requiring the posting of the Ten Commandments in every public schoolroom. *Stone v. Graham*, 449 U.S. 39 (1980) *(per curiam)*. In the classroom context, we found that the Kentucky statute had an improper and plainly religious purpose. As evidenced by *Stone*'s almost exclusive reliance upon two of our school prayer cases, *id.*, at 41–42 (citing *School Dist. of Abington Township v. Schempp*, 374 U.S. 203 (1963), and *Engel v. Vitale*, 370 U.S. 421 (1962)), it stands as an example of the fact that we have "been particularly vigilant in monitoring compliance with the Establishment Clause in elementary and secondary schools," *Edwards v. Aguillard*, 482 U.S. 578, 583–584 (1987). . . .[11]

---

[10] [Court's footnote 9] Other examples of monuments and buildings reflecting the prominent role of religion abound. For example, the Washington, Jefferson, and Lincoln Memorials all contain explicit invocations of God's importance. . . .

[11] [Court's footnote 11] Nor does anything suggest that *Stone* would extend to displays of the Ten Commandments that lack a "plainly religious," "pre-eminent purpose," [*Stone v. Graham*, 449 U.S. 39 (1980).] . . . Indeed, we need not decide in this case the extent to which a primarily religious purpose would affect our analysis because it is clear from the record that there is no evidence of such a purpose in this case.

. . .Texas has treated her Capitol grounds monuments as representing the several strands in the State's political and legal history. The inclusion of the Ten Commandments monument in this group has a dual significance, partaking of both religion and government. . . .

The judgment of the Court of Appeals is affirmed.

JUSTICE SCALIA, concurring.

I join the opinion of The Chief Justice because I think it accurately reflects our current Establishment Clause jurisprudence — or at least the Establishment Clause jurisprudence we currently apply some of the time. I would prefer to reach the same result by adopting an Establishment Clause jurisprudence that is in accord with our Nation's past and present practices, and that can be consistently applied — the central relevant feature of which is that there is nothing unconstitutional in a State's favoring religion generally, honoring God through public prayer and acknowledgment, or, in a nonproselytizing manner, venerating the Ten Commandments.

JUSTICE THOMAS, concurring. . . .

This case would be easy if the Court were willing to abandon the inconsistent guideposts it has adopted for addressing Establishment Clause challenges, and return to the original meaning of the Clause. I have previously suggested that the Clause's text and history "resist incorporation" against the States. If the Establishment Clause does not restrain the States, then it has no application here, where only state action is at issue.

Even if the Clause is incorporated. . . our task would be far simpler if we returned to the original meaning of the word "establishment" than it is under the various approaches this Court now uses. The Framers understood an establishment "necessarily [to] involve actual legal coercion." *Newdow, supra,* at 52 (Thomas, J., concurring in judgment); *Lee v. Weisman,* 505 U.S. 577, 640 (1992) (Scalia, J., dissenting). . . "In other words, establishment at the founding involved, for example, mandatory observance or mandatory payment of taxes supporting ministers." *Cutter,* [544 U.S. _____ (2005)] (Thomas, J., concurring). . . .

There is no question that, based on the original meaning of the Establishment Clause, the Ten Commandments display at issue here is constitutional. In no sense does Texas compel petitioner Van Orden to do anything. . . .

. . . All told, this Court's jurisprudence leaves courts, governments, and believers and nonbelievers alike confused — an observation that is hardly new.

First, this Court's precedent permits even the slightest public recognition of religion to constitute an establishment of religion. For example, . . . a park ranger has claimed that a cross erected to honor World War I veterans on a rock in the Mojave Desert Preserve violated the Establishment Clause, and won. *See Buono v. Norton,* 212 F. Supp. 2d 1202 (CD Cal. 2002). If a cross in the middle of a desert establishes a religion, then no religious observance is safe from challenge. . . .

Second, in a seeming attempt to balance out its willingness to consider almost any acknowledgment of religion an establishment, in other cases Members of this Court have concluded that the term or symbol at issue has no religious meaning by virtue of its ubiquity or rote ceremonial invocation. *See, e.g., id.*, at 630–631 (O'Connor, J., concurring); *Lynch v. Donnelly*, 465 U.S. 668, 716–717 (1984) (Brennan, J., dissenting). But words such as "God" have religious significance. For example, just last Term this Court had before it a challenge to the recitation of the Pledge of Allegiance, which includes the phrase "one Nation under God.". . .

Finally, the very "flexibility" of this Court's Establishment Clause precedent leaves it incapable of consistent application. . . . The inconsistency between the decisions the Court reaches today in this case and in *McCreary County v. American Civil Liberties Union of Ky.*, [545 U.S. _____ (2005)], only compounds the confusion.

The unintelligibility of this Court's precedent raises the further concern that, either in appearance or in fact, adjudication of Establishment Clause challenges turns on judicial predilections. . . .

Much, if not all, of this would be avoided if the Court would return to the views of the Framers and adopt coercion as the touchstone for our Establishment Clause inquiry. . . .

JUSTICE BREYER, concurring in the judgment. . . .

If the relation between government and religion is one of separation, but not of mutual hostility and suspicion, one will inevitably find difficult borderline cases. And in such cases, I see no test-related substitute for the exercise of legal judgment. . . .

The case before us is a borderline case. It concerns a large granite monument bearing the text of the Ten Commandments located on the grounds of the Texas State Capitol. On the one hand, the Commandments' text undeniably has a religious message, invoking, indeed emphasizing, the Diety. On the other hand, focusing on the text of the Commandments alone cannot conclusively resolve this case. Rather, to determine the message that the text here conveys, we must examine how the text is *used*. And that inquiry requires us to consider the context of the display.

In certain contexts, a display of the tablets of the Ten Commandments can convey not simply a religious message but also a secular moral message (about proper standards of social conduct). And in certain contexts, a display of the tablets can also convey a historical message (about a historic relation between those standards and the law) — a fact that helps to explain the display of those tablets in dozens of courthouses throughout the Nation, including the Supreme Court of the United States.

Here the tablets have been used as part of a display that communicates not simply a religious message, but a secular message as well. The circumstances surrounding the display's placement on the capitol grounds and its physical setting suggest that the State itself intended the latter, nonreligious aspects of the tablets' message to predominate. And the monument's 40-year history on the Texas state grounds indicates that that has been its effect.

The group that donated the monument, the Fraternal Order of Eagles, a private civic (and primarily secular) organization, while interested in the religious aspect of the Ten Commandments, sought to highlight the Commandments' role in shaping civic morality as part of that organization's efforts to combat juvenile delinquency. The Eagles' consultation with a committee composed of members of several faiths in order to find a nonsectarian text underscores the group's ethics-based motives. The tablets, as displayed on the monument, prominently acknowledge that the Eagles donated the display, a factor which, though not sufficient, thereby further distances the State itself from the religious aspect of the Commandments' message.

The physical setting of the monument, moreover, suggests little or nothing of the sacred. The monument sits in a large park containing 17 monuments and 21 historical markers, all designed to illustrate the "ideals" of those who settled in Texas and of those who have lived there since that time. The setting does not readily lend itself to meditation or any other religious activity. But it does provide a context of history and moral ideals. . . . [T]he context suggests that the State intended the display's moral message — an illustrative message reflecting the historical "ideals" of Texans — to predominate.

. . . [A] further factor is determinative here. As far as I can tell, 40 years passed in which the presence of this monument, legally speaking, went unchallenged (until the single legal objection raised by petitioner). . . . Those 40 years suggest that the public visiting the capitol grounds has considered the religious aspect of the tablets' message as part of what is a broader moral and historical message reflective of a cultural heritage.

. . . The display is not on the grounds of a public school, where, given the impressionability of the young, government must exercise particular care in separating church and state. *See, e.g., Weisman*, 505 U.S., at 592; *Stone v. Graham*, 449 U.S. 39 (1980) *(per curiam)*. This case also differs from *McCreary County*, where the short (and stormy) history of the courthouse Commandments' displays demonstrates the substantially religious objectives of those who mounted them, and the effect of this readily apparent objective upon those who view them. . . . And, in today's world, in a Nation of so many different religious and comparable nonreligious fundamental beliefs, a more contemporary state effort to focus attention upon a religious text is certainly likely to prove divisive in a way that this longstanding, pre-existing monument has not.

For these reasons, I believe that the Texas display — serving a mixed but primarily nonreligious purpose, not primarily "advancing" or "inhibiting religion," and not creating an "excessive government entanglement with religion," — might satisfy this Court's more formal Establishment Clause tests. *Lemon*, 403 U.S., at 612–613; *see also Capitol Square*, 515 U.S., at 773–783 (O'Connor, J., concurring in part and concurring in judgment). But, . . . I rely less upon a literal application of any particular test than upon consideration of the basic purposes of the First Amendment's Religion Clauses themselves. This display has stood apparently uncontested for nearly two generations. That experience helps us understand that as a practical matter of *degree* this display is unlikely to prove divisive. And this matter of degree is, I believe, critical in a borderline case such as this one.

At the same time, to reach a contrary conclusion here, based primarily upon on the religious nature of the tablets' text would, I fear, lead the law to exhibit a hostility toward religion that has no place in our Establishment Clause traditions. Such a holding might well encourage disputes concerning the removal of longstanding depictions of the Ten Commandments from public buildings across the Nation. And it could thereby create the very kind of religiously based divisiveness that the Establishment Clause seeks to avoid. . . .

In light of these considerations, I cannot agree with today's plurality's analysis. Nor can I agree with Justice Scalia's dissent in *McCreary County*. I do agree with Justice O'Connor's statement of principles in *McCreary County*, though I disagree with her evaluation of the evidence as it bears on the application of those principles to this case.

I concur in the judgment of the Court.

JUSTICE STEVENS, with whom JUSTICE GINSBURG joins, dissenting.

. . . The message transmitted by Texas' chosen display is quite plain: This State endorses the divine code of the "Judeo-Christian" God. . . .

I

In my judgment, at the very least, the Establishment Clause has created a strong presumption against the display of religious symbols on public property. . . .

. . . [T]he Establishment Clause demands religious neutrality. . . .

. . . The wall that separates the church from the State does not prohibit the government from acknowledging the religious beliefs and practices of the American people, nor does it require governments to hide works of art or historic memorabilia from public view just because they also have religious significance.

This case, however, is not about historic preservation or the mere recognition of religion. . . .[12]

---

12 [Court's footnote 9] Though this Court has subscribed to the view that the Ten Commandments influenced the development of Western legal thought, . . . the District Court categorically rejected respondent's suggestion that the State's actual purpose in displaying the Decalogue was to signify its influence on secular law and Texas institutions.

. . . This Nation's resolute commitment to neutrality with respect to religion is flatly inconsistent with the plurality's wholehearted validation of an official state endorsement of the message that there is one, and only one, God. . . .

II

Though the State of Texas may genuinely wish to combat juvenile delinquency, and may rightly want to honor the Eagles for their efforts, it cannot effectuate these admirable purposes through an explicitly religious medium. . . .

. . . For many followers, the Commandments represent the literal word of God as spoken to Moses and repeated to his followers after descending from Mount Sinai. The message conveyed by the Ten Commandments thus cannot be analogized to an appendage to a common article of commerce ("In God we Trust") or an incidental part of a familiar recital ("God save the United States and this honorable Court"). . . .

Even if . . . the message of the monument . . . fairly could be said to represent the belief system of all Judeo-Christians, it would still run afoul of the Establishment Clause by prescribing a compelled code of conduct from one God, namely a Judeo-Christian God, that is rejected by prominent polytheistic sects. . . .

Recognizing the diversity of religious and secular beliefs held by Texans and by all Americans, it seems beyond peradventure that allowing the seat of government to serve as a stage for the propagation of an unmistakably Judeo-Christian message of piety would have the tendency to make nonmonotheists and nonbelievers "feel like [outsiders] in matters of faith, and [strangers] in the political community." [*Capitol Square Review & Advisory Board v.*] *Pinette*, 515 U.S., at 799 (Stevens, J., dissenting). . . .

III

. . . The permanent placement of a textual religious display on state property . . . amalgamates otherwise discordant individual views into a collective statement of government approval. Moreover, the message never ceases to transmit itself to objecting viewers whose only choices are to accept the message or to ignore the offense by averting their gaze. In this sense, although Thanksgiving Day proclamations and inaugural speeches undoubtedly seem official, in most circumstances they will not constitute the sort of governmental endorsement of religion at which the separation of church and state is aimed.

The plurality's reliance on early religious statements and proclamations made by the Founders is also problematic because those views were not espoused at the Constitutional Convention in 1787 nor enshrined in the Constitution's text. . . .

. . . Not insignificant numbers of colonists came to this country with memories of religious persecution by monarchs on the other side of the Atlantic. . . .

. . . [T]here is another critical nuance lost in the plurality's portrayal of history. . . .

. . . [F]or nearly a century after the Founding, many accepted the idea that America was not just a *religious* nation, but "a Christian nation." *Church of Holy Trinity v. United States*, 143 U.S. 457, 471 (1892).

The original understanding of the type of "religion" that qualified for constitutional protection under the Establishment Clause likely did not include those followers of Judaism and Islam who are among the preferred "monotheistic" religions Justice Scalia has embraced in his *McCreary County* opinion. . . .

It is our duty . . . to interpret the First Amendment's command that "Congress shall make no law respecting an establishment of religion" not by merely asking what those words meant to observers at the time of the founding, but instead by deriving from the Clause's text and history the broad principles that remain valid today. . . . [W]e have construed the Equal Protection Clause of the Fourteenth Amendment to prohibit segregated schools even though those who drafted that Amendment evidently thought that separate was not unequal. . . .

. . . We serve our constitutional mandate by expounding the meaning of constitutional provisions with one eye towards our Nation's history and the other fixed on its democratic aspirations. . . .

. . . Fortunately, we are not bound by the Framers' expectations — we are bound by the legal principles they enshrined in our Constitution. . . .

IV

The judgment of the Court in this case stands for the proposition that the Constitution permits governmental displays of sacred religious texts. This makes a mockery of the constitutional ideal that government must remain neutral between religion and irreligion. If a State may endorse a particular deity's command to "have no other gods before me," it is difficult to conceive of any textual display that would run afoul of the Establishment Clause. . . .

JUSTICE O'CONNOR, dissenting.

For essentially the reasons given by Justice Souter, as well as the reasons given in my concurrence in *McCreary County v. American Civil Liberties Union of Ky.,* I respectfully dissent.

JUSTICE SOUTER, with whom JUSTICE STEVENS and JUSTICE GINSBURG join, dissenting.

Although the First Amendment's Religion Clauses have not been read to mandate absolute governmental neutrality toward religion, the Establishment Clause requires neutrality as a general rule. . . .

. . . [A] pedestrian happening upon the monument at issue here needs no training in religious doctrine to realize that the statement of the Commandments, quoting God himself, proclaims that the will of the divine being is the source of obligation to obey the rules, including the facially secular ones. . . . [T]he most eye-catching segment of the quotation is the declaration "I AM the LORD thy God." What follows, of course, are the rules against other gods, graven images, vain swearing, and Sabbath breaking. And the full text of the fifth Commandment puts forward filial respect as a condition of long life in the land "which the Lord they God giveth thee. . . ."

To drive the religious point home, and identify the message as religious to any viewer who failed to read the text, the engraved quotation is framed by religious symbols: two tablets with what appears to be ancient script on them, two Stars of David, and the superimposed Greek letters Chi and Rho as the familiar monogram of Christ. Nothing on the monument, in fact, detracts from its religious nature,[13] see [*County of Allegheny v. American Civil Liberties Union, Greater Pittsburgh Chapter*, 492 U.S. 573, 598 (1989)] ("Here, unlike in *Lynch* [*v. Donnelly*, 465 U.S. 668 (1984)], nothing in the context of the display detracts from the creche's religious message"), and the plurality does not suggest otherwise. It would therefore be difficult to miss the point that the government of Texas is telling everyone who sees the monument to live up to a moral code because God requires it, with both code and conception of God being rightly understood as the inheritances specifically of Jews and Christians. And it is likewise unsurprising that the District Court expressly rejected Texas's argument that the State's purpose in placing the monument on the capitol grounds was related to the Commandments' role as "part of the foundation of modern secular law in Texas and elsewhere."

The monument's presentation of the Commandments with religious text emphasized and enhanced stands in contrast to any number of perfectly constitutional depictions of them, the frieze of our own Courtroom providing a good example, where the figure of Moses stands among history's great lawgivers. While Moses holds the tablets of the Commandments showing some Hebrew text, no one looking at the lines of figures in marble relief is likely to see a religious purpose behind the assemblage or take away a religious message from it. Only one other depiction represents a religious leader, and the historical personages are mixed with symbols of moral and intellectual abstractions like Equity and Authority. Since Moses enjoys no especial prominence on the frieze, viewers can readily take him to be there as a lawgiver in the company of other lawgivers; and the viewers may just as naturally see the tablets of the Commandments (showing the later ones, forbidding things like killing and theft, but without the divine preface) as background from which the concept of law emerged, ultimately having a secular influence in the history of the Nation. Government may, of course, constitutionally call attention to this influence, and may post displays or

---

[13] [Court's footnote 2] That the monument also surrounds the text of the Commandments with various American symbols (notably the U.S. flag and a bald eagle) only underscores the impermissibility of Texas's actions: by juxtaposing these patriotic symbols with the Commandments and other religious signs, the monument sends the message that being American means being religious (and not just being religious but also subscribing to the Commandments, *i.e.*, practicing a monotheistic religion).

erect monuments recounting this aspect of our history no less than any other, so long as there is a context and that context is historical. Hence, a display of the Commandments accompanied by an exposition of how they have influenced modern law would most likely be constitutionally unobjectionable. [14] And the Decalogue could, as *Stone* [*v.Graham*, 449 U.S. 39 (1980)] suggested, be integrated constitutionally into a course of study in public schools. *Stone,* 449 U.S., at 42.

Texas seeks to take advantage of the recognition that visual symbol and written text can manifest a secular purpose in secular company, when it argues that its monument (like Moses in the frieze) is not alone and ought to be viewed as only 1 among 17 placed on the 22 acres surrounding the state capitol. Texas, indeed, says that the Capitol grounds are like a museum for a collection of exhibits, the kind of setting that several Members of the Court have said can render the exhibition of religious artifacts permissible, even though in other circumstances their display would be seen as meant to convey a religious message forbidden to the State. . . .

But 17 monuments with no common appearance, history, or esthetic role scattered over 22 acres is not a museum, and anyone strolling around the lawn would surely take each memorial on its own terms without any dawning sense that some purpose held the miscellany together more coherently than fortuity and the edge of the grass. One monument expresses admiration for pioneer women. One pays respect to the fighters of World War II. And one quotes the God of Abraham whose command is the sanction for moral law. . . . In like circumstances, we rejected an argument similar to the State's, noting in *County of Allegheny* that "the presence of Santas or other Christmas decorations elsewhere in the . . . courthouse, and of the nearby gallery forum, fail to negate the [creche's] endorsement effect. . . ."

---

14 [Court's footnote 4] For similar reasons, the other displays of the Commandments that the plurality mentions do not run afoul of the Establishment Clause. The statues of Moses and St. Paul in the Main Reading Room of the Library of Congress are 2 of 16 set in close proximity, statues that "represent men illustrious in the various forms of thought and activity . . . ." Moses and St. Paul represent religion, while the other 14 (a group that includes Beethoven, Shakespeare, Michelangelo, Columbus, and Plato) represent the nonreligious categories of philosophy, art, history, commerce, science, law, and poetry. Similarly, the sculpture of the woman beside the Decalogue in the Main Reading Room is one of 8 such figures "representing eight characteristic features of civilized life and thought," the same 8 features (7 of them nonreligious) that Moses, St. Paul, and the rest of the 16 statues represent. The inlay on the floor of the National Archives Building is one of four such discs, the collective theme of which is not religious. Rather, the discs "symbolize the various types of Government records that were to come into the National Archive." (. . . Each disc is paired with a winged figure; the disc containing the depiction of the Commandments, a depiction that, notably, omits the Commandments' text, is paired with a figure representing legislation.) As for Moses's "prominent featuring in the Chamber of the United States House of Representatives," Moses is actually 1 of 23 portraits encircling the House Chamber, each approximately the same size, having no religious theme. The portraits depict "men noted in history for the part they played in the evolution of what has become American law." More importantly for purposes of this case, each portrait consists only of the subject's face; the Ten Commandments appear nowhere in Moses's portrait.

. . . [I]t is not until the end of its opinion that the plurality turns to the relevant precedent of *Stone*, a case actually dealing with a display of the Decalogue.

When the plurality finally does confront *Stone,* it tries to avoid the case's obvious applicability by limiting its holding to the classroom setting. . . . [O]ur numerous prior discussions of *Stone* have never treated its holding as restricted to the classroom.

. . . The monument in this case sits on the grounds of the Texas State Capitol. There is something significant in the common term "statehouse" to refer to a state capitol building: it is the civic home of every one of the State's citizens. If neutrality in religion means something, any citizen should be able to visit that civic home without having to confront religious expressions clearly meant to convey an official religious position that may be at odds with his own religion, or with rejection of religion. *See County of Allegheny*, 492 U.S., at 626 (O'Connor, J., concurring in part and concurring in judgment) ("I agree that the creche displayed on the Grand Staircase of the Allegheny County Courthouse, the seat of county government, conveys a message to nonadherents of Christianity that they are not full members of the political community . . . .").

Finally, though this too is a point on which judgment will vary, I do not see a persuasive argument for constitutionality in the plurality's observation that Van Orden's lawsuit comes "forty years after the monument's erection . . . [.]" It is not that I think the passage of time is necessarily irrelevant in Establishment Clause analysis. We have approved framing-era practices because they must originally have been understood as constitutionally permissible, *e.g., Marsh v. Chambers*, 463 U.S. 783 (1983) (legislative prayer), and we have recognized that Sunday laws have grown recognizably secular over time, *McGowan v. Maryland*, 366 U.S. 420 (1961). There is also an analogous argument, not yet evaluated, that ritualistic religious expression can become so numbing over time that its initial Establishment Clause violation becomes at some point too diminished for notice. But I do not understand any of these to be the State's argument, which rather seems to be that 40 years without a challenge shows that as a factual matter the religious expression is too tepid to provoke a serious reaction and constitute a violation. . . . I doubt that a slow walk to the courthouse, even one that took 40 years, is much evidentiary help in applying the Establishment Clause. . . .

McCREARY COUNTY v. AMERICAN CIVIL LIBERTIES UNION OF KENTUCKY, 125 S. Ct. 2722 (2005). In *McCreary County v. American Civil Liberties Union of Kentucky*, the Court declared unconstitutional a display of the Ten Commandments in certain courthouses. The Court held "that the counties' manifest objective may be dispositive of the constitutional enquiry, and that the development of the presentation should be considered when determining its purpose." Two counties had first hung in their courthouses "large, gold-framed copies of an abridged text of the King James version of the Ten Commandments, including a citation to the Book of Exodus." Shortly after the American Civil Liberties Union of Kentucky sued, the counties authorized "a second, expanded display" stating that "the Ten Commandments are 'the precedent legal code upon which the civil and criminal codes of . . . Kentucky are founded.'"[15] The second version of the displays added "copies of the resolution" authorizing the displays and "eight other documents in smaller frames, each either having a religious theme or excerpted to highlight a religious element."[16] The final display, "the third within a year," contained "nine framed documents of equal size" with the Ten Commandments being "quoted at greater length than before."[17] This third display included the words: " 'The Ten Commandments provide the moral background of the Declaration of Independence and the foundation of our legal tradition.' "

Writing for a 5-4 majority, Justice Souter began by discussing the Court's decision 25 years ago in *Stone v. Graham*, casebook, p. 1498. *Stone* stated that "that the Commandments 'are undeniably a sacred text in the Jewish and Christian faiths' and held that their display in public classrooms violated" the Establishment Clause. "The touchstone" for the majority's analysis was "governmental neutrality between religion and religion, and between religion and nonreligion." Relying on Justice O'Connor's concurrence in *Santa Fe Independent School Dist. v. Doe*, casebook, p. 1502, Justice Souter stated: "The eyes that look to purpose belong to an 'objective observer,' one who takes account of the traditional external signs that show up in the 'text, legislative history, and implementation of the statute,' or comparable official act."

Lemon v. Kurtzman, casebook, p. 1452, "said that government action must have 'a secular . . . purpose'" and cases since then have shown "that although a legislature's stated reasons will generally get deference, the secular purpose required has to be genuine, not a sham, and not merely secondary to a religious objective." When "in those unusual cases where the

---

[15] In support of this assertion, the counties referred to the fact that in 1993, the state House of Representatives "voted unanimously. . . to adjourn. . . 'in remembrance and honor of Jesus Christ, the Prince of Ethics,'" and also claimed "that the 'Founding Fathers [had an] explicit understanding of the duty of elected officials to publicly acknowledge God as the source of America's strength and direction.'"

[16] The other documents on display included "the 'endowed by their Creator' passage from the Declaration of Independence; the Preamble to the Constitution of Kentucky; the national motto, 'In God We Trust'; a page from the Congressional Record of February 2, 1983, proclaiming the Year of the Bible and including a statement of the Ten Commandments; a proclamation by President Abraham Lincoln designating April 30, 1863, a National Day of Prayer and Humiliation; an excerpt from President Lincoln's 'Reply to Loyal Colored People of Baltimore upon Presentation of a Bible,' reading that 'the Bible is the best gift God has ever given to man'; a proclamation by President Reagan marking 1983 the Year of the Bible; and the *Mayflower Compact.*"

[17] The documents in the third display, "entitled 'The Foundations of American Law and Government Display'" included "copies of the Magna Carta, the Declaration of Independence, the Bill of Rights, the lyrics of the Star Spangled Banner, the Mayflower Compact, the National Motto, the Preamble to the Kentucky Constitution, and a picture of Lady Justice" in addition to the Ten Commandments. Each document was accompanied by "a statement about its historical and legal significance."

claim was an apparent sham, or the secular purpose secondary the unsurprising results have been findings of no adequate secular object, as against a predominantly religious one."[18] The determination takes "historical context" into consideration: "reasonable observers have reasonable memories, and our precedents sensibly forbid an observer 'to turn a blind eye to the context in which [the] policy arose.'" Consequently, "the same government action may be constitutional if taken in the first instance and unconstitutional if it has a sectarian heritage."

Because this case came "on appeal from a preliminary injunction," the Court reviewed "the District Court's legal rulings de novo, and its ultimate conclusion for abuse of discretion." While *Stone* is "the initial legal benchmark," that case did not determine "the constitutionality of every possible way the Commandments might be set out," and with "the Establishment Clause detail is key." Therefore, "we look to the record of evidence showing the progression leading up to the third display of the Commandments."[19] At the county "ceremony for posting the framed Commandments" a pastor proclaimed "the certainty of the existence of God." After being sued, the counties "modified the exhibits and invited additional insight into their purpose in a display that hung for about six months." The second display included "the statement of the government's purpose expressly set out in the county resolutions, and underscored it by juxtaposing the Commandments to other documents with highlighted references to God as their sole common element." Understandably, "the Counties make no attempt to defend their undeniable objective" in the second display "but the reasonable observer could not forget it." The third exhibit, entitled "Foundations of American Law and Government," displayed "the Commandments in the company of other documents the Counties thought especially significant in the historical foundation of American government." However, neither the District Court of Appeals "found legitimizing secular purpose in this third version of the display." "'When both courts [that have already passed on this case] are unable to discern an arguably valid secular purpose, this Court normally should hesitate to find one.'" But even though "repeal of the earlier county authorizations would not have erased them from the record of evidence bearing on current purpose, the extraordinary resolutions for the second display passed just months earlier were not repealed." In fact, the third exhibit, "which quoted more of the purely religious language of the Commandments than the first two displays had done," enhanced "the sectarian spirit" of the resolution common to the second and third displays.

The Court did "not decide that the Counties' past actions forever taint any effort on their part to deal with the subject matter. We hold only that purpose needs to be taken seriously under the Establishment Clause and

---

[18] The dissent maintains "that the purpose test is satisfied" by "any secular purpose for the government action," however this "would leave the purpose test with no real bite."

[19] Displaying the text of the Commandments is "different from a symbolic depiction, like tablets with 10 roman numerals, which could be seen as alluding to a general notion of law, not a sectarian conception of faith."

needs to be understood in light of context." If conditions changed in a "constitutionally significant" manner, the "district courts are fully capable of adjusting preliminary relief." The Court did not "hold that a sacred text can never be integrated constitutionally into a governmental display on the subject of law, or American history." Indeed, the courtroom in which the Supreme Court hears oral argument itself displays "the figure of Moses holding tablets exhibiting a portion of the Hebrew text of the later, secularly phrased Commandments," alongside "17 other lawgivers, most of them secular."

In responding to the dissent, Justice Souter admitted that the "two clauses tied to 'religion'" sometimes "compete: spending government money on the clergy looks like establishing religion, but if the government cannot pay for military chaplains a good many soldiers and sailors would be kept from the opportunity to exercise their chosen religions. At other times, limits on governmental action that might make sense as a way to avoid establishment could arguably limit freedom of speech when the speaking is done under government auspices." Because of these difficulties, "the principle of neutrality has provided a good sense of direction: the government may not favor one religion over another, or religion over irreligion." This allows "not only to protect the integrity of individual conscience in religious matters, but to guard against the civic divisiveness that follows when the Government weighs in on one side of the religious debate."

Reviewing the drafts of the Establishment Clause, "the final language" specifically "extended [the] prohibition to state support for "religion" in general." Indeed, Thomas Jefferson "refused to issue Thanksgiving Proclamations because he believed that they violated the Constitution." In light of this information, "the dissent fails to show a consistent original understanding from which to argue that the neutrality principle should be rejected," but "does manage to deliver a surprise" by proposing "that the deity the Framers had in mind was the God of monotheism." This "apparently means that government should be free to approve the core beliefs of a favored religion over the tenets of others."[20] Because "[h]istorical evidence" does not provide a "solid argument for changing course" the Court found no reason to abandon its "interpretive approach invoked for 60 years now."

Justice O'Connor concurred. "Free people are entitled to free and diverse thoughts, which government ought neither to constrain nor to direct." Current world events evidence "the violent consequences of the assumption of religious authority by government," but our "constitutional boundaries"

---

[20] Quoting Justice Story as probably reflecting "the thinking of the framing generation," Justice Souter noted, "that the purpose of the Clause was 'not to countenance, much less to advance, Mahometanism, or Judaism, or infidelity, by prostrating Christianity; but to exclude all rivalry among Christian sects.'" The majority argued that "the Framers would, therefore, almost certainly object to the dissent's unstated reasoning that because Christianity was a monotheistic "religion," monotheism with Mosaic antecedents should be a touchstone of establishment interpretation."

have enabled "private religious exercise to flourish."[21] Justice O'Connor continued: "Those who would renegotiate the boundaries between church and state must therefore answer a difficult question: Why would we trade a system that has served us so well for one that has served others so poorly?" Permitting "government to be a potential mouthpiece for competing religious ideas risks the sort of division that might easily spill over into suppression of rival beliefs." To join "secular and religious authority together poses risks to both." Considering "the history of this particular display of the Ten Commandments" it violates the Establishment Clause as "it conveys an unmistakable message of endorsement to the reasonable observer."

Justice Scalia dissented, joined by the Chief Justice and Justices Kennedy and Thomas. France exemplifies "one model of the relationship between church and state," whose Constitution begins " 'France is [a] . . . secular . . . Republic.' " America did not follow this example.[22] Today "the views of our people on" religion have not "significantly changed."[23] Considering the evidence, "how can the Court *possibly* assert that 'the First Amendment mandates governmental neutrality between . . . religion and nonreligion?' " This proposition is unsupported except by "the Court's own say-so, citing as support only the unsubstantiated say-so of earlier Courts going back no farther than the mid-20th century." Notably, "a majority of the Justices on the current Court (including at least one Member of today's majority) have, in separate opinions, repudiated the brain-spun '*Lemon* test' that embodies the supposed principle of neutrality between religion and irreligion." Furthermore, the test "is discredited because the Court has not had the courage (or the foolhardiness) to apply the neutrality principle consistently." For example, "when the government relieves churches from the obligation to pay property taxes, when it allows students to absent themselves from public school to take religious classes, and when it exempts religious organizations from generally applicable prohibitions of religious discrimination, it surely means to bestow a benefit on religious practice" and the Court has approved all of this.

"Our Nation's historical practices" make clear "that the Establishment Clause permits this disregard of polytheists and believers in unconcerned

---

[21] The statement made in *Zorach v. Clauson,* " 'we are a religious people,' has proved true. Americans attend their places of worship more often than do citizens of other developed nations."

[22] For instance, "George Washington added to the form of Presidential oath" the "words 'so help me God,' " the Marshall Court "opened its sessions with the prayer, 'God save the United States and this Honorable Court,' " and "the First Congress" opened "its legislative sessions with a prayer." Additionally, the very "week that Congress submitted the Establishment Clause as part of the Bill of Rights for ratification" they also provided for "paid chaplains in the House and Senate" and "the day after the First Amendment was proposed, the same Congress" asked "the President to proclaim 'a day of public thanksgiving and prayer, to be observed.' " The First Congress also included in the Northwest Territory Ordinance language about " 'religion, morality, and knowledge, being necessary to good government.' "

[23] "Presidents continue to conclude the Presidential oath with the words 'so help me God,' " and "this Court" continues "to open with. . . prayer." Likewise, "our coinage bears the motto 'IN GOD WE TRUST,' " and the "Pledge of Allegiance contains" the words "under God."

deities, just as it permits the disregard of devout atheists. The Thanksgiving Proclamation issued by George Washington at the instance of the First Congress was scrupulously nondenominational — but it was monotheistic." Significantly, "Christianity, Judaism, and Islam — which combined account for 97.7% of all believers — are monotheistic" and each believes "that the Ten Commandments were given by God to Moses." Unlike the majority, who relied on "mere 'proclamations and statements' of the Founders," Justice Scalia maintains that he "relied primarily upon official acts and official proclamations of the United States or of the component branches of its Government." Justice Scalia also rejected the criticism that this position violates the rights of nonmonotheists. "Invocation of God despite their beliefs is permitted not because nonmonotheistic religions cease to be religions recognized by the religion clauses of the First Amendment, but because governmental invocation of God is not an establishment."

The Court's decision "modifies *Lemon* to ratchet up the Court's hostility to religion." In relying on the "objective observer," the "inquiry focuses not on the *actual purpose* of government action, but the 'purpose apparent from government action.'" The decision also "replaces *Lemon's* requirement that the government have '*a* secular . . . purpose' with the heightened requirement that the secular purpose 'predominate.'" Even so, "the displays at issue here were constitutional." Styled "The Foundations of American Law and Government Display," the Ten Commandments were "the same size and had the same appearance" as the eight accompanying government documents in the display.[24]

"The frequency of these displays testifies to the popular understanding that the Ten Commandments are a foundation of the rule of law, and a symbol of the role that religion played, and continues to play, in our system of government."[25] The problem for the majority lay in "the Counties' *purpose* in erecting the Foundations Displays, not the displays themselves." The result is that "[d]isplays erected in silence (and under the direction of good legal advice) are permissible, while those hung after discussion and debate are deemed unconstitutional." The majority advances "a revisionist agenda of secularization." Moreover, "it is unlikely that a reasonable observer *would even have been aware* of the resolutions, so there would be nothing to 'cast off.'"

"In sum: The first displays did not necessarily evidence an intent to further religious practice; nor did the second displays, or the resolutions authorizing them; and there is in any event no basis for attributing whatever intent motivated the first and second displays to the third." The majority "may well be correct in identifying the third displays as the fruit

---

[24] The exhibit also included "a document that informs passersby that it 'contains documents that played a significant role in the foundation of our system of law and government.'"

[25] The dissent emphasized: "The Supreme Court building itself includes depictions of Moses with the Ten Commandments in the Courtroom and on the east pediment of the building, and symbols of the Ten Commandments 'adorn the metal gates lining the north and south sides of the Courtroom, as well as the doors leading into the Courtroom.' Similar depictions of the Decalogue appear on public buildings and monuments throughout our Nation's Capital."

of a desire to display the Ten Commandments, but neither our cases nor our history support its assertion that such a desire renders the fruit poisonous."

§ 16.05   Free Exercise of Religion

Page 1578: [Insert the following after Note (3)]

(4) In *Locke v. Davey,* 540 U.S. 712 (2004), the Court held that a state college scholarship program that denied funds to students majoring in devotional theology did not violate the Free Exercise Clause. The Promise Scholarship Program sought to aid the state's qualified high school graduates with college expenses through grants from the state's general fund. The grant was $1,125 and $1,542 for the academic years of 1999 and 2000, respectively. Eligibility depended on certain academic and economic criteria. However, consistent with the Washington Constitution, the funds could be used for any degree program except devotional theology. While Davey received a Promise Scholarship, Washington would not let him use it to "pursue a double major in pastoral ministries and business management / administration" at Northwest College, "a private, Christian college affiliated with the Assemblies of God denomination."

Writing for a 7-2 majority, Chief Justice Rehnquist noted that "the *Establishment Clause and the Free Exercise Clause* are frequently in tension." To alleviate this tension, the Court has "long said that 'there is room for play in the joints' between them. . . . In other words, there are some state actions permitted by the *Establishment Clause* but not required by the *Free Exercise Clause*." Citing *Witters v. Washington Dept. Of Services for Blind,* casebook p. 1466, the Court noted that funding a study in devotional theology did not violate the Establishment Clause if students voluntarily chose to pursue this degree. However, the Free Exercise Clause does not require the state to fund this degree program. The program "imposes neither criminal nor civil sanctions on any type of religious service or rite. It does not deny to ministers the right to participate in the political affairs of the community. . . . And it does not require students to choose between their religious beliefs and receiving a government benefit. . . . The State has merely chosen not to fund a distinct category of instruction."

The Washington Constitution can scrutinize the establishment of religion more stringently than the United States Constitution. Washington evidences no hostility toward religion as students can use the funds to "attend pervasively religious schools," or to attend a school that requires several courses in devotional theology. "Since the founding of our country, there have been popular uprisings against procuring taxpayer funds to support church leaders." Neither the text nor the history of the Washington Constitution nor the operation of the scholarship program indicates any "animus towards religion." Such "denial of funding for vocational religious instruction alone is [not] inherently constitutionally suspect." Washington's "interest in not funding the pursuit of devotional degrees is substantial and the exclusion of such funding places a relatively minor burden on Promise Scholars."

In a dissent joined by Justice Thomas, Justice Scalia argued that the statute was unconstitutional on its face as it withheld a generally available benefit on the basis of religion. In a separate dissent, Justice Thomas noted that the program denied funding to pursue any degree in theology although he acknowledged that the parties agreed that the term " 'theology' " was limited to degrees in " 'devotional theology.' "

CUTTER v. WILKINSON, 125 S. Ct. 2113 (2005). In *Cutter v. Wilkinson*, a unanimous Court rejected a facial challenge asserting that the Religious Land Use and Institutionalized Persons Act of 2000 (RLUIPA) violates the Establishment Clause. The plaintiffs were current and former prisoners who practiced " 'nonmainstream' religions" such as "Satanist, Wicca, and Asatru" and "the Church of Jesus Christ Christian." They brought suit alleging violation of their right to practice their religion as protected by the RLUIPA.

Writing for the Court, Justice Ginsburg said, "This Court has long recognized that the government may. . .accommodate religious practices. . .without violating the Establishment Clause, *Hobbie v. Unemployment Appeals Comm'n of Fla.*," casebook, p. 1554. In *Locke v. Davey*, p. 294 of this supplement, the Court reiterated that " 'there is room for play in the joints between' the *Free Exercise* and *Establishment Clauses*, allowing the government to accommodate religion beyond free exercise requirements, without offense to the *Establishment Clause*."

After *City of Boerne v. Flores* struck down the Religious Freedom Restoration Act, on the grounds that it exceeded Congress' remedial power under § 5 of the Fourteenth Amendment, Congress responded with the more limited RLUIPA, under their Spending and Commerce powers. The Act applies to substantial burdens on religious exercise which affect institutions receiving federal funds, or interstate or international commerce. One section of the Act deals with "land-use regulation"; and the other, with "religious exercise by institutionalized persons." The section at issue prohibits government from imposing " 'a substantial burden on the religious exercise of a person residing in or confined to an institution,' unless the government shows that the burden furthers 'a compelling governmental interest' and does so by 'the least restrictive means.' "

The Court of Appeals for the Sixth Circuit had invalidated RLUIPA as violating the Establishment Clause using the analysis in *Lemon v. Kurtzman*. In reversing the Sixth Circuit, the Court declined to apply the *Lemon* test. "We resolve this case on other grounds."[26] Instead, focusing in on the Establishment Clause, the Court emphasized that " 'there is room for play in the joints' between the Clauses, some space for legislative action neither compelled by the *Free Exercise Clause* nor prohibited by the *Establishment*

---

[26] Moreover, Justice Ginsburg did not consider Ohio's arguments concerning the Spending and Commerce Clauses because those arguments were not heard below.

Clause." This Act falls within that space. Consequently, the Act is a "permissible legislative accommodation of religion that is not barred by the *Establishment Clause.*"

At bottom, "RLUIPA's institutionalized-persons provision" is "compatible with the *Establishment Clause* because it alleviates exceptional government-created burdens on private religious exercise." *Bd. of Ed. of Kiryas Joel Village School Dist. v. Grumet*, casebook, p. 1544. Importantly, the Act "covers state-run institutions — mental hospitals, prisons, and the like — in which the government exerts a degree of control unparalleled in civilian society and severely disabling to private religious exercise." Proper application of the RLUIPA conforms to precedent, for "courts must take adequate account of the burdens a requested accommodation may impose on nonbeneficiaries," *Estate of Thornton v. Caldor, Inc.*, casebook, p. 1554, "and they must be satisfied that the Act's prescriptions are and will be administered neutrally among different faiths." *Kiryas Joel.* The Court also rejected Ohio's Establishment argument that RLUIPA encourages the adoption of religious beliefs in order to gain accommodation because "Ohio already facilitates religious services for mainstream faiths."

RLUIPA does not "elevate accommodation of religious observances over an institution's need to maintain order and safety." Moreover, Justice Ginsburg had "no cause to believe that RLUIPA would not be applied in an appropriately balanced way, with particular sensitivity to security concerns." In this connection, "the federal Bureau of Prisons has managed the largest correctional system in the Nation under the same heightened scrutiny standard as RLUIPA without compromising prison security, public safety, or the constitutional rights of other prisoners."

Justice Thomas wrote a concurring opinion in which he evaluated the Establishment Clause as a "federalism provision." He acknowledged the argument advanced by Ohio that "some of the Framers may have believed that the National Government had no authority to legislate concerning religion, because no enumerated power gave it that authority." In a future case, "Ohio's Spending Clause and Commerce Clause challenges, therefore, may well have merit." However, Ohio's Establishment Clause challenge is with history, as the RLUIPA is "a law respecting religion, but not one respecting an establishment of religion."